COMPUTING SCIENCE

SECOND EDITION

Peter Bishop

Nelson

Thomas Nelson and Sons Ltd
Nelson House Mayfield Road
Walton-on-Thames Surrey
KT12 5PL UK

51 York Place
Edinburgh
EH1 3JD UK

Thomas Nelson (Hong Kong) Ltd
Toppan Building 10/F
22A Westlands Road
Quarry Bay Hong Kong

Distributed in Australia by

Thomas Nelson Australia
480 La Trobe Street
Melbourne Victoria 3000
and in Sydney, Brisbane, Adelaide and Perth

© Peter Bishop 1987

First published by Thomas Nelson and Sons Ltd 1987

ISBN 0-17-431272-5

NCN 21-KCS-3821-01

Printed in Hong Kong

Preface

The aim of this book is to give a broad and thorough introduction to Computing Science. The book is tailored to meet the requirements of all the examination boards in the United Kingdom which are offering courses in Computer Studies or Computing Science at Advanced level. Almost all the material in the syllabuses for these courses is covered in this book, which contains a number of questions from past examination papers. Also covered are syllabuses in other Commonwealth countries which are equivalent to the UK courses.

In addition, this book has been written with the requirements of the computing industry in mind. A few topics, notably software engineering, artificial intelligence, expert systems and fifth generation computers are covered because of their significance in the world of computing. It is assumed that in due course these topics will be assimilated into Computing Science syllabuses.

It is realised that a book of this nature is useful for a number of other purposes. These include a reference book for teachers preparing to teach computing at Ordinary or Advanced level, a textbook for students of Advanced Level and equivalent courses at colleges of further education, and a foundation book for students embarking on computing courses at universities or polytechnics.

This book covers five major subject areas: the principles of computing, the design of computer hardware, the various layers of computer software, the theory and practice of computer applications, and a brief look at the social implications and likely future of computing. Microprocessors are given due, but not undue, attention.

A model computer, the AMC, has been designed to introduce the topics of processor architecture and operation, and low level language. The AMC is tailored specifically to the requirements of the book. In the same series as this book there is a software package which enables the AMC to be simulated on a microcomputer.

Many of the topics introduced in general terms are reinforced by case studies, drawn from various aspects of the world of computing. Case studies include processor architecture, high level languages, compilers, operating systems, data communication networks and computer applications.

Some sections and exercise questions in the book are marked ●. This indicates that they are considerably above the average level of difficulty of the material, and may be omitted without loss of continuity.

The Second Edition

The Second Edition retains the aims and objectives of the First Edition. All the material has been revised to bring it up to date with developments in the computing industry, and changes in syllabuses. There are six new chapters:

- Artificial Intelligence
- Processor Fabrication
- Software Development Tools
- Software Engineering
- Expert Systems
- Fifth Generation Computers

Other changes include more detailed coverage of floating point numbers, compilers and the control of peripheral devices; a reorganisation of the material on file structures and backing store devices; case studies of the programming languages C, Lisp and Prolog; more about the simplification of Boolean expressions (including Karnaugh maps); and closer links between the theory of data structures and the programming of these structures in high and low level languages. These changes ensure that the book gives a comprehensive, balanced coverage of the whole field of computing, and should cover any new material introduced into syllabuses in the next few years.

Acknowledgements

I am grateful to a number of people who have given their time, expertise and enthusiasm to help me with various aspects of this book.

From Imperial College, London: Valerie Downes gave advice on the overall structure of the book, and reviewed all the material in detail; Derek Brough helped with the design of the AMC, and with the material on compilers and interpreters; James Jacobsen advised me on databases and Cobol; Martin Cripps gave a second opinion on the AMC design; Meir Lehman provided advice and source material on software engineering; John Darlington advised on functional programming and fifth generation computer architecture and Richard Ennals provided material on logic programming and fifth generation developments.

Help with the case studies has come from a number of sources. The following people have provided source material, reviewed drafts of sections and given other helpful advice: William White of Cray Research (UK) Limited for the Cray-2 case study; Judy Robertson and Paul Hoggett of Research Machines Limited for the RM Nimbus case study; Mr E. Wilson of ICL for the ICL 2900 Series case study and its operating system, VME/B; Tony Hetherington of Prospero Software for the ProPascal case study; Richard Mulholland of Cognos Limited for the Powerhouse software development system; David Brantigan for the London traffic control system; Christopher Long at ITN for the VT80 case study; Keith Simmonds and John Clarke of CBS Records for the case study on the CBS European manufacturing system; Dr Alan Gadd from the Meteorological Office for the weather forecasting system.

Thanks are due to the following examination boards, who gave permission to reproduce questions from past examination papers: the Associated Examining Board, the Joint Matriculation Board, the University of London School Examinations Council, the Oxford Delegacy of Local Examinations, the Welsh Joint Education Committee, the Northern Ireland Examinations Board, the Scottish Examinations Board and the University of Cambridge Local Examinations Syndicate.

A number of people have given useful comments on the First Edition of the book, most of which have been taken into account in the Second Edition. In particular the advice of members of staff of the Curriculum Development Institute of Singapore has been most valuable. My thanks go to Sarah Bishop and Stephen Allum who typed the entire First Edition of the book onto a word processor, prior to revision for the Second Edition. The Second Edition was typed and edited on Research Machines 380Z and Nimbus computers, using the Wordstar word processing system.

Peter Bishop
23rd December 1985

Past Examination Papers

The following abbreviations are used to identify questions from past examination papers:

AEB	Associated Examining Board
OLE	Oxford Delegacy of Local Examinations
UL	University of London School Examinations Council
JMB	Joint Matriculation Board
UCLES	University of Cambridge Local Examination Syndicate
WJEC	Welsh Joint Education Committee.
NIEB	Northern Ireland Examinations Board
SEB	Scottish Examinations Board

Contents
overview

Contents

Computing in Context

1

Introduction

A study of computing at Advanced level is no mean undertaking. At the commencement of such a study, it is essential to give some thought to the objectives to be borne in mind, the skills which will be developed along the way, and the ground which will be covered. This chapter covers these three areas. It discusses the objectives of a study of computing at this level, lists the skills which are taught, and concludes with an overview of computing.

This chapter makes no assumptions of previous knowledge of the subject. For those who do have previous knowledge of computing, it acts as a concise review of what is already known. In either case, it paves the way for the following chapter, which discusses the fundamental concepts of computing in some detail.

1.1 Objectives of the Book

The overall objective of this book is to provide a grounding in all the major aspects of computing, which is both sufficiently broad and sufficiently thorough for the courses for which the book is intended. Thus the book covers a wide range of material, each aspect being treated in a fair amount of detail.

More specifically, the objectives of the book are as follows:

1 To introduce and develop some fundamental concepts which form the basis of computing and the design of computers.
2 To introduce the essential features of the design of computers, and of associated devices which make up a computer system.
3 To introduce the types of instructions which govern the way in which computers work, and discuss in some detail the functions performed by sets of these instructions at various levels.
4 To introduce the techniques used in the application of computers to specific tasks, and discuss the range of tasks currently performed by computers.
5 To provide an introduction to the computing industry.
6 To place computing in its proper perspective, both in terms of the wider implications of the use of computers, and from the point of view of the likely future of computing.

These objectives indicate a mixture of theory and practice, of abstract and concrete. Broadly speaking, the overall structure of the book is based on these objectives, in the order stated above.

1.2 Skills Taught

It is unrealistic to assert that all the skills listed in this section will definitely be acquired; nevertheless they do represent directions in which efforts should be directed. It must be emphasised that these skills can only be developed through practice. Working through the exercises at the end of each chapter of the book is a vital first step.

The skills acquired during a Computing Science course are listed below, not in any particular order of importance. Some are related specifically to computers, others are more general.

1 The ability to perceive structures in collections of information, and manipulate these information structures.
2 A familiarity with the theory of logic which underlies much of the theory of computing.
3 An appreciation of the principles of computer design.
4 An ability to reproduce manually some of the processes commonly done on computers.
5 An ability to write simple programs in a low level programming language.
6 A thorough grounding in the principles of information processing.
7 An appreciation of the concept of a system, and an ability to use this concept in practical situations.
8 An ability to apply concepts of computing to practical situations.

9 Clear thinking.

10 Clear, concise use of language, particularly in communicating technical information.

This might seem a rather daunting list, but the benefits of posssessing some or all of these skills are considerable. The last skill mentioned, the clear, concise use of language, cannot be overemphasised. A poor performance here can obscure capabilities in all the other areas.

1.3 An Overview of Computing

The word 'computing' is used very frequently in this book. It is an old word which has begun to acquire a new meaning. Computing is the theory, design, manufacture and use of computers. It encompasses all activities relating to computers in any way. Other terms, such as 'informatics' and 'information technology' are used in a similar context, but the word 'computing' is adequate for the purposes of this book.

Computing, as it is now understood, is a young, optimistic and sometimes aggressive activity. Like nuclear energy, radar and jet propulsion, it had its origins in the Second World War. Although the beginnings of computing were much less spectacular than those of the other technologies, the computing industry has grown to become one of the world's largest single industries. Its growth is not always steady, and a number of computer companies have prospered for a while, and then gone out of business. However, in spite of these short-term setbacks, and uncertain economic conditions, computing continues to grow and prosper.

Computing is an activity which provides employment for millions of people, directly and indirectly. It affects hundreds of millions of others. Although its effects are generally beneficial, this is by no means always the case.

1.4 What is a Computer?

In general terms, a computer may be described as a digital electronic information processing machine:

Digital means that computers work by storing information in digital form, in codes which represent letters or the digits of numbers. Sounds and pictures are also represented in digital form.

Electronic implies that a computer is built up around a number of solid-state electronic components, known as integrated circuits or, more commonly, as chips.

Information processing is a general term which desribes the range of work which computers can do. Almost everything we do, from writing a letter to landing spacecraft on the moon, involves information processing in some way. Computers can be of assistance in any information processing activity.

Machine is a reminder that computers are in the same broad line of descent as windmills, printing presses, steam locomotives and sewing machines. Machines can work well or badly, and no machine is infallible.

1.5 Capabilities and Limitations of Computers

Computers can carry out seven types of operations, all involving information. These are **input, output, storage, retrieval, sending, receiving** and **processing** of information.

Input is the action of getting information into a computer from its environment. The commonest method of input is via a keyboard like a typewriter keyboard.

Output is the action of getting information out of a computer. The commonest methods of output are to display information on a screen or to print it.

Storage is making a permanent copy of information which the computer can use again later. The commonest methods of storage are magnetic tapes and magnetic disks.

Retrieval is the action of reading the information back from a magentic disk or tape.

Sending is transferring information to another computer, via a data communications network. The network may be local, connecting computers in the same building, or long-distance, via telephone lines and satellite links.

Receiving is accepting information sent by another computer.

Processing includes sorting, selecting, combining and rearranging information, as well as performing calculations. Computers are also able to draw conclusions from information.

Information processing includes tasks which require some measure of intelligence when carried out by a person, but the extent to which computers may be regarded as intelligent is limited at present. For example, computers cannot take initiatives, respond to unforeseen circumstances or make moral judgements. Artificial intelligence is an area of very rapid development.

1.6 Conclusion

This chapter has outlined the objectives of the book, given an indication of some of the skills which may be acquired during its study, and taken a general look at the field of computing, and at the nature, capabilities and limitations of computers.

The next chapter takes some of the ideas introduced here, and restates them in a much more precise way. Towards the end of the book is a further examination of the broader implications of computing.

2
Concepts of Computing

This chapter builds on the general ideas introduced in the previous chapter. It introduces a small number of key concepts of computing. Each concept is discussed, and, without being too formal, a working definition of the concept is given. This working definition is adequate for the purposes of this book.

2.1 Information and Data

Information is a general term covering facts and figures, which may or may not be related. The word is used in this book in its generally accepted sense. Information may be vital or trivial, true or false. That is of no concern here.

Data, on the other hand, has a much more precise meaning. Data is information in a coded form, acceptable for input to, and processing by, a computer system. In other words, data is a representation of information. Data may be used as individual items, but is much more commonly processed in large, structured collections. Items of data are significant both in themselves and in relation to the structure in which they occur.

An important point to realise is that data, on its own, has no meaning. Only when some interpretation is placed on the data does it acquire meaning. In other words:

data + interpretation = meaningful information.

Furthermore, computers cannot place interpretations on data. Only people are capable of interpreting data. This is an important point to bear in mind when considering the general concept of a computer, and the extent to which computers may be regarded as intelligent.

2.2 System

The idea of a **system** is very important in the world of computers. A computer is often referred to as a computer system. Essentially, a system is a collection of parts working together towards some common goal. For example, a well-trained sports team is a system, a poorly trained team is not.

Just as goals have sub-goals, so do systems have **subsystems**. A subsystem is a part of a system which accomplishes a part of the goals of the system. For example, a motor car is a system, and its braking system is a subsystem. The braking system accomplishes one aspect of the goals of the car.

A computer is a system, containing a number of subsystems. Computers in use are always part of larger systems: business systems, research systems, administrative systems, etc.

2.3 Computer and Program

In Section 1.4, a computer is described as a digital electronic information processing machine, capable of seven types of operation: input, output, storage, retrieval, sending, receiving and processing. In this section, a fuller definition is discussed.

Making use of the concept of data, a concise definition of a computer is as follows:

A computer is a machine which, under the control of a stored program, automatically accepts and processes data, and supplies the results of that processing.

Although a slightly broader definition of a computer will be considered in a moment, several points in this definition deserve closer study.

A computer is controlled by a stored **program**. A program is a set of instructions which control the operation of a computer. The instructions which a computer is using at a particular time are stored inside the computer. The computer works through the instructions automatically. Furthermore, instructions and data are stored together, and no distinction is made between them. Under some circumstances, instructions are manipulated like data.

A computer is a data processing machine. In Section 2.1 it was pointed out that data is a representation of information, without any inherent meaning. Processing is manipulating this data in a number of ways: a computer is essentially a symbol manipulation machine. It follows that processing does not have any inherent meaning - a computer does not understand what it is doing. For example, computers can manipulate text (word processing) but at present they cannot interpret extended passages in a natural language, nor can they translate such passages from one language to another.

Computers are called intelligent machines. The word 'intelligent' in this context must be treated with caution. What it means is that computers can be instructed to manipulate data in a way which people interpret as intelligent. Recent developments in computing are leading to increased intelligence built into computers.

The above definition implies that a computer is a **general-purpose** machine. The phrase 'data processing' encompasses a very wide range of activities. Processing includes sorting and selecting data, performing calculations and making decisions based on the data. These functions can be put to use in a great number of applications. Furthermore, any particular computer is usually capable of a wide variety of tasks. In contrast to general-purpose computers there are **dedicated** computers; these are discussed in Section 2.8.

The above definition of a computer, as a single processing device controlled by a single program, although adequate for many purposes, is somewhat limited. An extended definition, more in line with contemporary computer design, is now developed.

Most computers contain more than one processing element, and require several programs for their operation. Computers draw on large stores of structured data as they work. The functional units, programs and sets of data, are referred to as the **resources** of the computer. The management of its own resources is one of the tasks performed by a computer. Accordingly, the working definition of a computer used in this book is as follows:

> **A computer is a collection of resources, including digital electronic processing devices, stored programs and sets of data, which, under the control of the stored programs, automatically inputs, outputs, stores, retrieves and processes the data, and may also transmit data to and receive it from other computers. A computer is capable of drawing reasoned conclusions from the processing it carries out.**

2.4 Hardware and Software

In theory, the distinction between the terms hardware and software is quite clear:

> **Hardware is the physical components, solid-state and otherwise, which make up a computer;**

and

> **Software is the programs which direct the operation of a computer.**

In practice, the distinction becomes rather blurred. For example, in some computers multiplication is done directly by hardware, while in others it is done by repeated addition, controlled by software. As long as the hardware of a computer can do a small number of essential operations, more sophisticated operations can be done either by special hardware elements, or by software, or by any combination of these.

Furthermore, computers have some software permanently stored in read-only memory (ROM). This is known as **firmware**, being somewhere between hardware and software.

2.5 Algorithm

In order that a task can be carried out on a computer, a method for the task must be described very precisely, in terms of all its different steps. An **algorithm** is a description of the steps of a task, using a particular method. Writing an algorithm is the first step taken in preparing a task to be done by a computer.

For it to be of any use to a computer, an algorithm must express a task as a finite number of steps. No matter how fast a computer works, there comes a point at which it must be told to stop, even if it means giving up.

A number of different ways of writing algorithms have been developed, including a series of programming languages called Algol. One of the commonest methods is also the simplest: it is to use clear, concise English, and simple algebra where necessary. This method is adopted in this book. Below is an example of a very simple algorithm, for adding up a set of numbers:

> **Set total to zero.**
> **While there are more numbers, repeat**
> > **Add next number to total.**

Note that the third line is **indented** to show that it is controlled by the line above it.

2.6 Module and Interface

Computers are probably the most complex artefacts ever produced. The concepts of **module** and **interface** are essential in reducing this complexity, and making it possible to design and program computers, and to understand how they work.

A **module** is an interchangeable unit. It performs a specific function, and has specific connections with its environment. For example, in many hi-fi sets, the amplifier, turntable, cassette deck and speakers are separate modules.

An **interface** is a point of contact between one module and another, or between a module and its environment.

The benefits of the concepts of module and interface are as follows: if the function and interfaces of a module are known, it is seldom necessary to understand how the module performs its function. It will make no difference if a module is replaced by another one which works differently, but performs the same task using the same interfaces.

Modules and interfaces are used in the design and construction of the hardware and software of computers. In both cases, the task to be performed is split up into a number of sub-tasks. A module is specified for each sub-task, together with its interfaces to other modules. The task can be understood in terms of these sub-tasks and interfaces, without knowing the details of how each sub-task is performed. This makes the designing of hardware and software of computers, and the understanding of them, much easier.

One of the most important interfaces of a computer system is its point of contact with its human users. This is known as the **user interface, human interface,** or (unfortunately) **man-machine interface**. In the past, user interfaces have been designed around the capabilities of the computer, without much regard for the needs and way of thinking of the user. The current trend is to reverse this situation, and make the computer conform to a much greater extent to the requirements of the users.

2.7 Design and Implementation

In computing, as in most activities, there is a certain gap between theory and practice. In theory, ideas are efficient, clean and neat, and programs always work. In practice, things are seldom so simple. Nevertheless, it is important to formulate ideas in theory before being concerned about how they can be put into practice.

For these reasons, a distinction is made between the **design** of a computer, a program or a programming language, and its **implementation**. The design is theoretical, free of awkward constraints so often found in practice. The implementation of a design is the way it is put into practice under a certain set of circumstances. Most designs have several implementations. For example, many computer languages are implemented on a number of different types of computers. In general, no two implementations are exactly alike.

Several key chapters of this book make use of a model computer, the AMC. This computer has been designed to illustrate concepts of computer design, free of the restrictions imposed by implementations.

2.8 General-Purpose and Dedicated Computers

Historically, computers evolved as calculating machines. Once the general principles of computer design had been established, it became evident that they could do far more than just calculate. The phrase 'information processing' was chosen to describe the capabilities of computers. A **general-purpose** computer conforms to this description. It can do a very wide range of information processing tasks, from scientific 'number crunching' to commercial file processing.

A **dedicated** computer is designed for a specific task, or narrow range of tasks. A common example is a computer dedicated to controlling a machine. The introduction of very cheap, small, microprocessor-based computers has led to a resurgence of dedicated computers.

In practice, dedicated and general-purpose computers must be regarded as two extremes. Most computers are somewhere between the two extremes, though the emphasis is strongly on general-purpose machines.

2.9 The Theory of Computing

The fundamental principles behind the design and construction of digital electronic computers have been developed over a period of nearly a century. Although a large number of people have contributed in various ways to the development and understanding of these principles, the work of four people is of particular significance. These people are **Charles Babbage, George Boole, Alan Turing** and **John von Neumann.**

Although Babbage's ideas were conceived in relation to mechanical computers, many of them apply to electronic machines. Babbage (1791-1871) identified the stages of a computing task as input, processing and output, and designed the units of his machines accordingly. He originated the idea of a program as a set of instructions to control the operation of a computing machine.

George Boole (1815-1864) is the founder of the theory of the mathematical logic. He devised an algebra for representing logical quantities, and investigated the operations which can be performed on these quantities. Boolean logic is the theoretical basis both for the design of the circuits in digital computers, and for many techniques in programming.

Alan Turing (1912-1954) originated the general concept of a computing machine. He formulated his ideas in terms of an abstract computer, called a Turing Machine. Although a Turing Machine can only carry out one simple operation at a time, he identified a very wide class of problems which it could solve in a finite number of steps. Turing's work has been particularly valuable in understanding the capabilities and limitations of computers, in the design of programming languages, and in the study of artificial intelligence.

John Von Neumann (1903-1957) assisted in the design and development of several early electronic computers at end of the Second World War. In 1946 he published a paper outlining the general design principles of an electronic digital computer. He envisaged a machine controlled by a set of instructions, with a small number of central processing elements. The instructions are processed in sequence in a repeated cycle of operations. The two main points in the paper relate to the concept of a stored program:

1 All data and instructions are represented in a binary code, and are stored together in the computer memory.

2 The computer makes no distinction between data and instructions.

Although the principles set out in this paper have been enhanced in modern computer designs, they remain to this day the theoretical basis of the design of all digital electronic computers.

2.10 Conclusion

The main points of this chapter may be summarised as follows:

- Data is information in a coded form, acceptable for input to, and processing by, a computer system:
  data + interpretation = meaningful information.
- A system is a collection of parts working together towards some common objectives. A computer is a system, part of a larger system in any particular application.
- A program is a set of instructions which control the operation of a computer.
- A computer is a collection of resources, including digital electronic processing devices, stored programs and sets of data, which, under the control of the stored programs, automatically inputs, outputs, stores, retrieves and processes the data, and may also transmit data to and receive it from other computers. A computer is capable of drawing reasoned conclusions from the processing it carries out.
- Hardware is the physical components, solid-state and otherwise, which make up a computer.
- Software is the programs which direct the operation of a computer.
- An algorithm is a description of the steps of a task, using a particular method.
- A module is an interchangeable unit which performs a specific function, and has specific connections with its environment.
- An interface is the point of contact between one module and another, or between a module and its environment.
- The implementation of a design is the way it is put into practice under a particular set of circumstances.
- A general-purpose computer is capable of a wide range of applications.
- A dedicated computer is designed for a specific task, or narrow range of tasks.

Exercise 2

1 The discussion of each concept in this chapter includes a working definition of the concept. Identify these working definitions.

2 List some examples of systems, and some things which are not systems. In each case, justify your choice.

3 State, with reasons, which of the following devices satisfy the definition of a computer introduced in this chapter, and which devices do not: slide rule; automatic washing machine; programmable pocket calculator; television game; motor car electronic ignition system.

4 Make a list of devices which are programmable. In each case state what distinguishes the device from a computer, as defined in this chapter.

5 Make a collection of statements from the press or the media about computers, which contradict the definition of a computer contained in this chapter. Discuss your findings.

6 A hi-fi set is quoted in the chapter as an example of modular construction. For each module of a hi-fi set state:
   a) its function;
   b) its interface(s) with other modules;
   c) its external interface(s), i.e. those to its environment.

7 Write down at least three examples of modular systems, other than computers and hi-fi sets. For each example, work through parts a) to c) of Question 6.

8 Discuss the significance of the modular construction of systems.

9 Briefly state and discuss the similarities and differences between the user interface of a microcomputer system and a motor car.

10 Find out more about the work of Babbage, Turing, Boole and von Neumann. Write a report on the contributions of one or more of them to the theory of computing, expanding the ideas presented in the text.

●11 Other people who have made contributions to the theory of computing include:
   Noam Chomsky   (a classification of languages, applicable to programming languages)
   Marshall McLuhan (originator of the phrase 'information processing')
   Claude Shannon   (the relationship between electrical circuits and Boolean algebra)
   Ada Byron   (the first computer programmer)
   Find out about, and write reports on, the work of one or more of these people.

3
Data

This chapter covers ways in which data is represented in computer systems, both in the internal storage of a computer, and on external media accessed by a computer. Data storage is discussed in general terms: the techniques introduced here are implemented in a variety of ways on different computers.

A certain amount of computer arithmetic is considered in this chapter. This is because the method of coding the numbers determines the way in which some arithmetic operations are performed. However, most of the discussion of computer arithmetic is in Chapter 5.

3.1 Binary Coding of Data

All data used by computers is in code. Different computers use different codes, and different codes are used in various parts of the same computer. But all these codes have one thing in common — they are based on two characters, the digits 0 and 1 only.

The reason for the use of two digits only is that all the devices used in computer systems, and all the data storage media they access, have two **states** only. For example, switches are on or off, transistors are conducting or non-conducting, magnetic tape is magnetised in one or the other direction, a signal is a pulse or no pulse, etc. This has several advantages, notably simplicity, and wide tolerances. As long as it is clear whether a device is in a 0 or a 1 state, a high level of precision does not matter. For this reason, the electronic components of a computer are much more crudely (and cheaply) constructed than those in, for example, a hi-fi set.

Most of the numeric codes used in computers are based on the **binary** (base two) number system, which also uses the digits 0 and 1 only. A binary digit is called a **bit**.

3.2 Place Value

Much of what is to follow in this chapter depends on the concept of **place value**. A reminder of this concept is in order at this point.

In all modern number systems, the value of any digit depends on its position in the number. The place values for decimal integers are (from the right) units, tens, hundreds, etc. For binary integers they are units, twos, fours, eights, etc. Similarly, 'decimal' fractions have place values (from the left) tenths, hundredths, etc., and binary fractions halves, quarters, eighths, etc.

The digit with the highest place value in a number is called the **most significant digit**, or, in binary, the **most significant bit**. If the digits of a number are grouped, then the phrase **high order** describes the group with higher place values than others.

3.3 Character Code

Input, output, backing store and data communications media and devices transfer, store and manipulate data in a character code. Characters include letters, digits and characters such as punctuation marks. These are called **alphabetic, numeric** (together known as **alphanumeric**) and **special** characters respectively. In addition there are **control characters** such as the Delete character. These have no printed or displayed representation, but cause various actions to be carried out when they are encountered. The set of characters which can be coded is called the **character set** of the computer, or programming language.

Character code is one in which each character is coded separately as a set of binary digits. Six, seven or eight bits per character are most commonly used. Figure 3.1 shows a common character code, the seven bit **American Standard**

Character	Bit pattern	Decimal equivalent	Hexadecimal equivalent	Character	Bit pattern	Decimal equivalent	Hexadecimal equivalent
space	0100000	32	20	P	1010000	80	50
!	0100001	33	21	Q	1010001	81	51
"	0100010	34	22	R	1010010	82	52
#	0100011	35	23	S	1010011	83	53
$	0100100	36	24	T	1010100	84	54
%	0100101	37	25	U	1010101	85	55
&	0100110	38	26	V	1010110	86	56
'	0100111	39	27	W	1010111	87	57
(	0101000	40	28	X	1011000	88	58
)	0101001	41	29	Y	1011001	89	59
*	0101010	42	2A	Z	1011010	90	5A
+	0101011	43	2B	[	1011011	91	5B
,	0101100	44	2C	\	1011100	92	5C
-	0101101	45	2D	]	1011101	93	5D
.	0101110	46	2E	↑	1011110	94	5E
/	0101111	47	2F	←	1011111	95	5F
0	0110000	48	30	`	1100000	96	60
1	0110001	49	31	a	1100001	97	61
2	0110010	50	32	b	1100010	98	62
3	0110011	51	33	c	1100011	99	63
4	0110100	52	34	d	1100100	100	64
5	0110101	53	35	e	1100101	101	65
6	0110110	54	36	f	1100110	102	66
7	0110111	55	37	g	1100111	103	67
8	0111000	56	38	h	1101000	104	68
9	0111001	57	39	i	1101001	105	69
:	0111010	58	3A	j	1101010	106	6A
;	0111011	59	3B	k	1101011	107	6B
<	0111100	60	3C	l	1101100	108	6C
=	0111101	61	3D	m	1101101	109	6D
>	0111110	62	3E	n	1101110	110	6E
?	0111111	63	3F	o	1101111	111	6F
@	1000000	64	40	p	1110000	112	70
A	1000001	65	41	q	1110001	113	71
B	1000010	66	42	r	1110010	114	72
C	1000011	67	43	s	1110011	115	73
D	1000100	68	44	t	1110100	116	74
E	1000101	69	45	u	1110101	117	75
F	1000110	70	46	v	1110110	118	76
G	1000111	71	47	w	1110111	119	77
H	1001000	72	48	x	1111000	120	78
I	1001001	73	49	y	1111001	121	79
J	1001010	74	4A	z	1111010	122	7A
K	1001011	75	4B	{	1111011	123	7B
L	1001100	76	4C	|	1111100	124	7C
M	1001101	77	4D	}	1111101	125	7D
N	1001110	78	4E	~	1111110	126	7E
O	1001111	79	4F				

Figure 3.1
ASCII code

Code for Information Interchange (ASCII) code. Not shown in Figure 3.1 is the set of control characters which forms part of the ASCII code.

Alphabetic data remains in character code during processing by a computer, but numeric data is converted to one of the numeric codes described below. All conversion from one code to another is carried out by hardware, firmware or software within the computer system.

3.4 Binary Coded Decimal

Binary Coded Decimal (BCD) is a simple and increasingly popular way of representing numbers within a computer. In this system, each decimal digit is coded separately in binary. For example:

379 = 0011 0111 1001

Four bits are the minimum needed to code one decimal digit, since 9 = 1001. BCD numbers using four bits per decimal digit are known as **packed decimal** numbers. In some implementations more than four bits are used per decimal digit, with the remaining bit positions filled with zeros.

3.5 Sign-and-Magnitude Code

This section, and the two which follow it, introduce the three commonest ways of dealing with negative numbers. The first method involves representing the sign of a number, and its magnitude (or modulus), separately. This is called **sign-and-magnitude** (or sign-and-modulus) code.

If one bit is used for the sign, the convention is 0 for positive and 1 for negative. For example:

```
+13 = 0 1 1 0 1
−13 = 1 1 1 0 1
```

The most significant bit is the sign bit.

3.6 Twos Complement Numbers

Twos complement coding is the commonest way of representing integers during processing on a computer. In this code, the normal binary place values are used, except that the most significant bit represents a negative quantity. For example, using six bits:

−32	16	8	4	2	1		
0	1	1	1	1	1 =		31
0	0	0	0	0	1 =		1
0	0	0	0	0	0 =		0
1	1	1	1	1	1 =	−32 + 31 =	−1
1	0	0	0	0	0 =		−32

This example shows the range of numbers which can be stored: −32 to 31.

One reason for using twos complement form is that it is easy to change from a positive to the corresponding negative number (and vice versa). Consequently, subtraction can be performed by negating the second number and then adding it to the first number. For example, $7 - 5$ is the same as $7 + (-5)$.

The method of changing from a positive to the corresponding negative number is as follows: Change all the 0s to 1s and all the 1s to 0s, and then add 1. For example:

		−32	16	8	4	2	1	
19 =		0	1	0	0	1	1	
Interchange bits		1	0	1	1	0	0	
Add 1	+						1	
		1	0	1	1	0	1	= −19

This method will also change a negative number to the corresponding positive number. For example:

		−32	16	8	4	2	1	
−23 =		1	0	1	0	0	1	
Interchange bits		0	1	0	1	1	0	
Add 1	+						1	
		0	1	0	1	1	1	= 23

Two examples of subtraction using this technique follow.

Example 1
29 − 7 = 29 + (−7)

	−32	16	8	4	2	1
Code 7	0	0	0	1	1	1
Interchange bits	1	1	1	0	0	0
Add 1, gives − 7	1	1	1	0	0	1
Code 29	0	1	1	1	0	1 +
Add −7 and 29	0	1	0	1	1	0 = 22.

1 carry

Note that there is a 1 carried from the most significant bit. Most computers have a **carry bit** which is set to 1 if this occurs. The significance of this is discussed in Section 5.2.

Example 2
5 − 18 = 5 + (−18)

	−32	16	8	4	2	1
Code 18	0	1	0	0	1	0
Interchange bits	1	0	1	1	0	1
Add 1, gives −18	1	0	1	1	1	0
Code 5	0	0	0	1	0	1 +
Add −18 and 5	1	1	0	0	1	1 = −13.

Problems arise when the result of a calculation is outside the range of numbers which can be represented. For example:

14 + 19

	−32	16	8	4	2	1
14 =	0	0	1	1	1	0
19 =	0	1	0	0	1	1 +
	1	0	0	0	0	1 = −31

The result, -31, is not correct. This problem is examined in Section 5.2.

3.7 Ones Complement Numbers

Similar to twos complements, but less popular, is the method of storing integers called **ones complements**. In this system, the most significant place value is one less (in magnitude) than the corresponding twos complement place value. For example, using six bits:

−31	16	8	4	2	1		
0	1	1	1	1	1 =		31
0	0	0	0	0	1 =		1
0	0	0	0	0	0 =		0
1	1	1	1	1	1 =	−31 + 31 =	0
1	1	1	1	1	0 =	−31 + 30 =	−1
1	0	0	0	0	0 =		−31

Notice the range of numbers (31 to -31) and the two different codes for 0.

The advantage of using ones complements is that the negative of a number is produced simply by reversing the bits. For example:

	-31	16	8	4	2	1	
$20 =$	0	1	0	1	0	0	
Interchange bits	1	0	1	0	1	1	$= -31 + 11 = -20$

This technique is used in subtraction. However, any carry produced by the most significant bit of the result must be added at the least significant end to produce a correct answer. The examples of the previous section are repeated using ones complement coding.

Example 1
$29 - 7 = 29 + (-7)$

	-31	16	8	4	2	1	
Code 7	0	0	0	1	1	1	
Reverse bits, gives -7	1	1	1	0	0	0	
Code 29	0	1	1	1	0	1+	
Add -7 and 29	0	1	0	1	0	1	
Add carry						1+	
	0	1	0	1	1	0	$= 22$

This technique is called **wrap-around carry**.

Example 2
$5 - 18 = 5 + (-18)$

	-31	16	8	4	2	1	
Code 18	0	1	0	0	1	0	
Reverse bits, gives -18	1	0	1	1	0	1	
Code 5	0	0	0	1	0	1+	
Add -18 and 5	1	1	0	0	1	0	$= -13$

In this example, no wrap-around carry is generated.

3.8 Fractions

Fractions may be coded in ways very similar to those introduced above for coding integers. For example, using sign-and-magnitude coding:

sign	$\frac{1}{2}$	$\frac{1}{4}$	$\frac{1}{8}$	$\frac{1}{16}$	$\frac{1}{32}$
1	0	1	1	0	1

$-\frac{13}{32} =$

Twos complement coding may also be used. For example:

-1	$\frac{1}{2}$	$\frac{1}{4}$	$\frac{1}{8}$	$\frac{1}{16}$	$\frac{1}{32}$
1	1	0	0	1	1

$-\frac{13}{32} = -1 + \frac{19}{32} =$

These methods of coding fractions, and the methods of coding integers introduced above, are called **fixed point** codes. In these codes, the binary point is at a fixed position, though it is not coded explicitly.

The problem with fixed point codes is that the range of values that can be represented is limited. For example, some computers allocate 16 bits to store integers. Using twos complement notation, this gives a range of -32768 to 32767, which is not sufficient for many applications.

3.9 Floating Point Numbers

The technique of **floating point numbers** is used to extend the range of numbers that can be represented by a given number of bits. Floating point numbers are similar to the scientific method of representing base ten numbers, called **standard form**. A standard form number is the product of two parts. The first is a number between 1 and 10, and the second is a power of ten. For example:

$$5.75 \times 10^4 = 57\ 500$$
$$6.7 \times 10^{-5} = 0.000\ 067$$

Note that the size of the number is determined by the power of ten, and the number of significant figures, or precision of the number, is determined by the number of decimal places in the first part.

Floating point numbers apply the same principles in base two. A number is expressed as the product of two parts. The first part is a fraction between $\frac{1}{2}$ and 1 (the **mantissa**), and the second is a power of two (the **exponent**). The following examples use four bits for each, in sign-and-magnitude coding:

	mantissa				exponent				
sign	$\frac{1}{2}$	$\frac{1}{4}$	$\frac{1}{8}$	sign	4	2	1		
0	1	0	0	0	0	0	1	$= \frac{1}{2} \times 2^1 = 1$
0	1	0	1	0	1	0	0	$= \frac{5}{8} \times 2^4 = 10$
0	1	1	0	1	0	1	0	$= \frac{3}{4} \times 2^{-2} = \frac{3}{16}$
1	1	1	1	0	1	1	0	$= -\frac{7}{8} \times 2^6 = -56$

The bit in the $\frac{1}{2}$ column is a 1, unless the whole number is zero. This is to ensure that the fraction part lies between $\frac{1}{2}$ and 1, and is callled **normalisation**. Normalisation ensures that the maximum number of bit positions are available to store the fraction part of the number. It provides maximum precision of a number within the available number of bits.

Ways of implementing floating point numbers differ considerably between different types of computer. The mantissa is coded in sign-and-magnitude or twos complement form. The exponent is sometimes coded in one of these forms, but the **biased exponent** method of coding is also used. With this method, a fixed value is subtracted from the stored representation of the exponent in order to determine its actual value. For example, if eight bits are allocated to the exponent, the stored values can be between 0 and 255. The fixed value 128 (the bias) is, however, subtracted from the stored value, giving an actual range of exponents of -128 to 127. In some computers, the exponent does not represent a power of two, but some larger base, such as sixteen.

The number of bits allocated to each part of a floating point number also differs widely between computers. The general principle is that between two and three times as many bits are allocated to the mantissa as to the exponent. Below is an example using sixteen bits for a floating point number, with eleven bits for the mantissa and five bits for the exponent. Sign-and-magnitude coding is used for both parts of the number.

sign				mantissa							sign		exponent		
	$\frac{1}{2}$	$\frac{1}{4}$	$\frac{1}{8}$	$\frac{1}{16}$	$\frac{1}{32}$	$\frac{1}{64}$	$\frac{1}{128}$	$\frac{1}{256}$	$\frac{1}{512}$	$\frac{1}{1024}$		8	4	2	1
0	1	0	1	1	0	0	0	0	0	0	0	1	1	0	0

$$= \tfrac{11}{16} \times 2^{12} = \tfrac{11}{16} \times 4096 = 2816$$

The same number with a biased exponent (offset 16) is:

sign				mantissa								exponent		
	$\frac{1}{2}$	$\frac{1}{4}$	$\frac{1}{8}$	$\frac{1}{16}$	$\frac{1}{32}$	$\frac{1}{64}$	$\frac{1}{128}$	$\frac{1}{256}$	$\frac{1}{512}$	$\frac{1}{1024}$	16	8	4	2	1
0	1	0	1	1	0	0	0	0	0	0	1	1	1	0	0

The stored exponent is $11100 = 28$, which gives 12 when the bias of 16 is subtracted.

Arithmetic using floating point numbers, and errors which can arise in this arithmetic are discussed in Chapter 5.

The method of representing floating point numbers in the IBM 370 range of computers illustrates many of the techniques described above. Either one or two 32-bit words are used. In both cases, the most significant bit is the sign bit. The next seven bits are for the exponent, and the remaining 24 or 56 bits are used for the mantissa, which is stored as a binary fraction. The exponent is biased by 64, and represents a power, not of 2, but of 16. For example, in a 32-bit word:

	sign	exponent							mantissa						
Bit position	1	2	3	4	5	6	7	8	9	10	11	12	13	...	32
	0	1	0	0	0	0	1	0	1	1	1	0	0	...	0

$$= \tfrac{7}{8} \times 16^{66-64} = \tfrac{7}{8} \times 256 = 224$$

	sign	exponent							mantissa						
Bit position	1	2	3	4	5	6	7	8	9	10	11	12	13	...	32
	1	0	1	1	1	1	1	0	1	0	1	0	0	...	0

$$= -\tfrac{5}{8} \times 16^{62-64} = -\tfrac{5}{8} \times \tfrac{1}{256} = -\tfrac{5}{2048}$$

3.10 Bits, Bytes and Words

For most purposes, a bit (a 0 or a 1) is too small a unit of data to be manipulated separately. Hence bits are generally handled in groups. **Bytes** and **words** are the two commonest groupings.

A **byte** is a set of bits containing the code for one character. A byte is now generally accepted as comprising eight bits. The data on most input, output and backing store media is grouped in bytes. Early microcomputers - the 8-bit micros - did all their processing in units of bytes.

A **word** is a larger grouping of bits, from 16 to 512 bits depending on the size of the computer. A word is a set of bits which can be manipulated by a particular computer in one operation. The **wordlength** is the number of bits in one word. The registers in processors, which store one data item during processing, contain one word.

However, in many modern computers, the number of bits which are manipulated in one operation can vary. The phrase **variable wordlength** describes this situation. Whether a word is of fixed or variable length, it almost always contains an integral number of bytes: 16, 24, 32, or 64 bits.

3.11 Octal and Hexadecimal Numbers

Binary numbers and codes suffer from the disadvantage of being very long for the amount of information they represent. Decimal numbers are much more concise, but are difficult to convert to binary. As a compromise, **octal** (base eight) and **hexadecimal** (base sixteen) numbers are often used to represent binary quantities. These numbers have the advantages of conciseness and ease of conversion to binary.

Octal

To convert from base eight to base two, convert each octal digit to its binary equivalent, using three bits. For example:

$$725_8 = 111\,010\,101_2$$

Converting from binary to octal is done by grouping the bits in threes from the least significant end, and converting each group to an octal digit. For example:

$$1\ 1/1\ 1\ 0/0\ 0\ 0_2 = 360_8$$

Hexadecimal

Conversion between binary and hexadecimal numbers is similar, except that groups of four bits are used. The hexadecimal digits A to F are used for the decimal quantities 10 to 15. For example:

$$3A7_{16} = 0\ 0\ 1\ 1/1\ 0\ 1\ 0/0\ 1\ 1\ 1_2$$

and

$$1\ 1\ 1\ 1/1\ 0\ 0\ 1\ 0_2 = 1F2_{16}$$

It must be remembered that octal and hexadecimal digits are a shorthand way of representing binary codes, which themselves may represent non-numeric data. For example, the ASCII code for the symbol ? is 0 1 1 1 1 1 1. This may be represented by the octal digits 077, or the hexadecimal digits 3F.

Octal and hexadecimal numbers are used for writing certain types of computer programs, for representing data stored in a computer during processing, and for recovering from errors. They are very seldom used for input and output data. Hexadecimal numbers have the advantage that two hexadecimal digits represent eight bits, or one byte. For this reason they are more commonly used than octal numbers.

3.12 Self-checking Codes: Parity

Much attention is devoted, in the design of computer systems, to the detection and correction of errors. One valuable technique, of great assistance in achieving this objective, is the concept of a **self-checking code**. A self-checking code is one which contains enough information within the coded form of a data item, to determine whether that data item has been coded (or transmitted) correctly.

The simplest and commonest self-checking code requires the inclusion of a **parity bit** in the code of a data item. The parity is set to a 0 or a 1 so that the total number of 1s in the data item is even, for **even parity**, or odd, for **odd parity**. For example, using even parity and the most significant bit the parity bit:

0 1 1 0 1 0 1

is correct, with four 1s, but

1 0 0 1 1 0 0

is incorrect, with three 1s.

Parity checks are used to determine whether the parity of a data item is correct. These are most commonly carried out after a data item has been transmitted to or from an input, output or backing store device or on a data communications network, as this is where errors are most likely. Odd parity is slightly more useful than even parity, as it will detect the failure of a transmission line, which will result in all the bits of a data item being zero. Other self-checking codes are discussed in Section 14.7.

3.13 Data Encryption

In many computer applications, it is essential that the data stored on disk or transmitted on a communications network is completely secure. One technique which provides a high level of security is **data encryption** - 'scrambling' the bits representing the data items so that they do not follow any standard data code, and require decoding in a secret way before they can be interpreted. In all cases where data is encrypted in this fashion, the encoding and decoding is done automatically by hardware or software within the secure computer system.

A variety of encryption techniques are used. Some are based on an algorithm which encodes and decodes the data using random numbers. Others are based on remainders when the data values are divided by a very large prime number. The **key** to codes of this nature is an even larger integer (more than 100 decimal digits) which is the product of two large prime numbers, one of which is used for the division. If the key integer is known to an outsider, the process of factorising it is very difficult, and takes a long time on even the largest computers. By the time the information is decoded, it is generally out of date.

The making and breaking of secret codes for data is one of the oldest applications of digital electronic computers. It remains a topic of intense interest and extreme secrecy to this day.

3.14 Analogue Data

Digital computers store and process data in one of the digital codes described in the previous sections of this chapter. However, in many applications, a digital computer has inputs and/or outputs in **analogue** form. These are almost always in the form of electrical voltages which are proportional to some physical quantity. For example, a computer which has voice input receives an analogue signal which varies according to the sound waves reaching it. If it produces synthesised speech output, the final form of the output signal is an analogue voltage which follows the pattern of the speech.

The conversion from analogue to digital form is done by an interfacing device known as an **analogue-to-digital converter (ADC)**. These devices **sample** the analogue signal at fixed intervals, and convert the values they obtain to digital form, using one of the numeric codes described above, or the Gray code below. The **sampling frequency** measures the rate at which samples are taken. Some form of **scaling** is carried out so that the results are in appropriate units. No matter how many bits are allocated to the digital representation of the signal, there is always a loss of precision when changing from analogue to digital form.

When converting in the other direction, an ADC converts a stream of digital values to their analogue equivalents, and produces a smoothed analogue waveform from them. The reconstructed analogue waveform is again an approximation to the original, the closeness being determined by the precision of the digital numbers, and the sampling frequency. See Figure 3.2.

A common problem in analogue-to-digital converters is the errors which arise if the analogue signal is sampled just as its value is changing from one digital value to another. In many cases the digital bit positions are determined by separate circuits, which do not all switch at exactly the same time. For example, if a signal were changing from (digital) 0 1 1 1 to 1 0 0 0, and the most significant bit changed from 0 to 1 before the others changed from 1 to 0, it could be read as 1 1 1 1 if it were sampled during the transition. One way of minimising the errors which can arise in this situation is to use a **Gray** code for the digital representation, where there is never more than one change in a bit value between two successive numbers. The four bit Gray code is shown below.

Decimal	Gray Code	Decimal	Gray Code
0	0 0 0 0	8	1 1 0 0
1	0 0 0 1	9	1 1 0 1
2	0 0 1 1	10	1 1 1 1
3	0 0 1 0	11	1 1 1 0
4	0 1 1 0	12	1 0 1 0
5	0 1 1 1	13	1 0 1 1
6	0 1 0 1	14	1 0 0 1
7	0 1 0 0	15	1 0 0 0

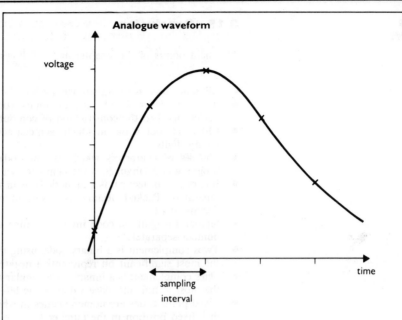

Digital samples

Time	Voltage
0.0	1.3
0.2	8.0
0.4	9.8
0.6	7.4
0.8	4.0

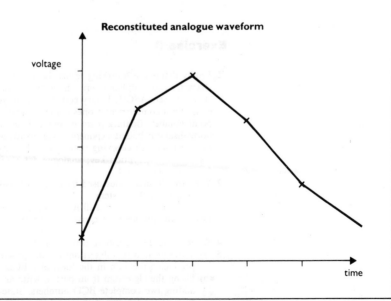

Figure 3.2
Analogue to digital conversion

3.15 Conclusion

The main points of this chapter are as follows:

- All codes used for data storage are based on the binary digits 0 and 1 only.
- A major reason for the use of binary codes in computers is that all the devices used in the construction of computers have two states only.
- Character code is one in which each character is coded separately as a set of binary digits.
- The set of characters which can be coded by a particular computer or programming language is the character set of that computer or language.
- Binary coded decimal is a numeric code in which each decimal digit is coded separately. Packed decimal is a variant of this code, with four bits per decimal digit.
- Sign-and-magnitude code involves coding the sign and the magnitude of a number separately.
- Twos complement is a binary code, using the usual place values, except that the most significant bit represents a negative quantity.
- Ones complement is a binary code, similar to twos complements, except that the most significant place value is one less in magnitude.
- Fixed point codes are numeric codes in which the (assumed) binary point is in a fixed position in the number.
- Floating point codes are numeric codes in which a number is expressed as a product of a fraction between $\frac{1}{2}$ and 1 (the mantissa) and an integral power of two (the exponent).
- A byte is a set of bits containing the code for one character. A byte is generally eight bits.
- A word is a set of bits which can be manipulated by a particular computer in one operation.
- Octal (base eight) and hexadecimal (base sixteen) numbers are often used as 'shorthand' representations of binary numbers.
- A common self-checking code includes a parity bit which adjusts the total number of 1s in the data item to an even (for even parity) or odd (for odd parity) number.
- Analogue input and output data is converted to digital form for processing by analogue-to-digital converters.

Exercise 3

1 Briefly define the following terms: binary; bit; place value; most significant digit; character code; alphanumeric character; special character; control character; character set; ASCII; binary coded decimal; packed decimal; sign-and-magnitude code; twos complements; ones complements; carry bit; wrap-around carry; fixed point number; floating point number; standard form; mantissa; exponent; normalisation; biased exponent; byte; word; wordlength; variable wordlength; octal; hexadecimal; self-checking code; parity bit; even parity; parity check; data encryption; encryption key; analogue data; analogue-to-digital converter; sampling frequency; Gray code.

2 Why are all data codes used by computers based on two digits only? List the advantages of this system.

3 Name a number system still in use which does not use the concept of place value. Discuss the problems of converting between this number system and a computer code.

4 What is the distinguishing feature of character code?

5 a) Write an informal algorithm for the process of adding two BCD digits, and producing the sum in the form of a BCD digit together with a carry bit.
  ●b) Using the algorithm from part a, write an informal algorithm for the process of adding two complete BCD numbers. State any additional assumptions you make, such as the lengths of the numbers.

6 Write the decimal numbers 1, −1, 3 and −3 in twos complement form, using (a) four bits, (b) six bits, (c) eight bits. In the light of your answers, state how a twos complement number can be extended to a larger number of bits without altering its value.

7 Repeat Question 6 using ones complement numbers.

8 In twos complement notation, what is the range of integers which can be represented by (a) four bits, (b) six bits, (c) eight bits, (d) sixteen bits, (e) n bits? What are the corresponding ranges using ones complements?

9 Change the following (decimal) fractions into six bit, twos complement notation: $\frac{3}{8}$, $-\frac{5}{16}$, $-\frac{17}{32}$, $\frac{1}{3}$. Hint: in the last case, change the numerator and denominator to binary, and divide the denominator into the numerator. The result is a recurring fraction.

10 The following numbers are in floating point form:

sign	mantissa										sign	exponent			
	$\frac{1}{2}$	$\frac{1}{4}$	$\frac{1}{8}$	$\frac{1}{16}$	$\frac{1}{32}$	$\frac{1}{64}$	$\frac{1}{128}$	$\frac{1}{256}$	$\frac{1}{512}$	$\frac{1}{1024}$		8	4	2	1
0	1	0	1	0	0	0	0	0	0	0	0	0	1	0	0
0	1	1	1	1	0	0	0	0	0	0	0	1	1	1	0
1	1	0	0	0	0	0	0	0	0	0	0	0	0	0	1
0	1	1	1	0	0	0	0	0	0	0	1	0	1	0	0
1	1	0	1	0	0	0	0	0	0	0	1	0	1	1	1
1	1	1	1	1	0	0	0	0	0	0	0	1	0	0	0

a) Convert the numbers to base ten.

b) Express the decimal numbers 80, −3072, $-\frac{1}{2}$, 1.5 in this form.

c) Bearing in mind that floating point numbers must be normalised, what is the range of positive numbers which can be expressed in this form?

d) Convert the decimal numbers from part b) into the biased exponent floating point form used in the second example in Section 3.9.

•e) Convert the decimal numbers from part b) into the IBM 370 floating point format illustrated at the end of Section 3.9.

11 If the floating point numbers in Question 10 are stored with twos complements mantissas, the most significant bit represents the value −1.

a) Convert the decimal numbers obtained in part a) of Question 10 back to floating point form, using twos complement mantissas.

b) Examine the results from part a) and derive a rule for the normalisation of mantissas of floating point numbers stored in twos complements form.

12 A computer has a 64 bit wordlength.

a) How many bytes are contained in one word?

b) How many packed decimal digits can be stored in one word?

c) Suggest a way in which a word may be used to contain a floating point number. Justify your allocation of bits.

13 Convert the following decimal numbers (a) to binary, (b) to octal, (c) to hexadecimal: 45, 21, 32, 4097.

14 The main store of a particular computer has an extra parity bit for every byte stored. Furthermore, after every eight bytes, there is an additional parity byte, where each bit adjusts the parity of the corresponding 'column' in the eight bytes. Odd parity is used throughout. Below is the contents of a portion of the main store of this computer:

	bytes							parity bits
1	0	0	1	0	0	1	0	0
0	0	0	0	0	0	0	0	1
1	1	1	1	1	1	1	1	1
1	0	1	1	0	1	0	1	0
1	1	0	1	1	0	1	1	0
0	1	1	0	1	1	0	1	0
0	0	0	0	0	0	0	0	1
1	0	1	1	1	1	0	1	1

parity byte: 0 0 1 0 1 1 1 0 1

a) Check the parity of each byte.

b) Check the parity of each column against the parity byte.

c) Assuming that only one bit has been stored incorrectly, identify this bit.

15 a) A data item and its parity bit are copied from one part of a computer to another. A subsequent parity check fails. Is it certain that the data item is now incorrect? Explain your answer.

b) If, in the above case, the parity check does not fail, is it certain that the data item is now correct? Explain your answer.

c) In the light of your answers to parts a) and b), comment on the usefulness of parity checks.

16 a) List some examples of digital computer systems with analogue inputs and/or outputs.

b) One application of Gray code is measuring the rotation of a shaft. A disk attached to the shaft has concentric segments coloured in dark and light zones in order to provide the Gray code of the shaft position. The shades are read by a set of photo-electric cells, one for each bit position. List other similar applications of Gray code.

4
Data
Structures

The previous chapter showed how items of data may be represented on computer systems. This chapter shows how individual items of data may be associated in various ways to form **data structures**. These structures enable large and potentially unwieldy collections of data to be managed by relatively simple operations. Concepts associated with data structures have led to advances in computer architecture, and in the design of computer programs.

Six data structures are introduced in this chapter: **strings, arrays, stacks, queues, lists** and **trees**. They are the most important data structures used in the main stores of computers. In Chapter 26, the backing store data structures **files, records, fields** and **hash tables** are discussed.

4.1 The Concept of Structured Data

The structure of a set of data is created by **relationships** between individual data items. These relationships can be formally expressed as a set of rules, or, more simply, by specifying how to insert and delete items of data, while preserving the structure. Together with a description of an empty data structure, this is sufficient for a structure to be created and used.

Structured Information in Everyday Life
Most of the information we encounter in everyday life is structured in some way. The commonest example is the words of our language, which are linked together in phrases, sentences and other more complex structures. The rules for constructing these structures are extremely complicated, yet we apply them by intuition.

Other examples of structured information include dictionaries, telephone directories and encyclopaedias. These are all large stores of information which would be useless if the information were not strictly arranged according to a few simple rules. The structure of a collection of information makes it easy to locate individual items of information, and to insert new items, or delete items. The same reasoning applies to structured information stored in computers.

4.2 Pointers

A **pointer** is a data item which indicates the location of another data item. It may be thought of as an arrow, as shown in Figure 4.1.

Pointers are used to build data structures. They provide the links which join elements of the structure. Of particular significance are pointers to the front and back of a data structure. Occasionally it is required that a pointer does not point to anything; in this situation, the pointer is said to have a null value. See Figure 4.2.

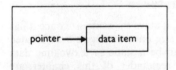

Figure 4.1
A pointer

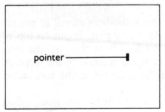

Figure 4.2
A null pointer

4.3 Strings

A **string** is a sequence of characters regarded as a single data item. Strings may be of fixed or variable length. The length of a string is indicated either by the number of characters in the string placed at the front of the string, or by a special character called an **end-of-string** marker at the end. The following example shows these two methods of representing the same string:

    10CAPITAL194   CAPITAL194#

Operations on strings are of two types: operations which join two or more strings to produce a single string, and operations which divide a string to produce two or more sub-strings.

4.4 Arrays

An **array** is a set of data items of identical types, stored together. The number of elements in the array is fixed when the array is created. Each element is accessed by an **index**, which indicates the position of the element in the array.

For example, if the array BEATLES has elements as follows:

```
BEATLES:  JOHN
          PAUL
          GEORGE
          RINGO
```

then the element with index value 3, BEATLES(3) is the name GEORGE. Sometimes it is more useful to use the index value 0 for the first array element. Under this arrangement, BEATLES(3) is the name RINGO. In some ways, the entire main store of a computer may be regarded as an array. The index of each memory cell is known as the **address** of the cell. The address is a number which locates a cell within the main store.

Arrays can have more than one **dimension**. A two-dimensional array may be thought of as having rows and columns like a matrix. Two indices are required to locate an item in the array, corresponding to row and column indices in a matrix. For example, the state of a game of noughts and crosses may be represented by a two-dimensional array, GAME, with three rows and three columns:

```
GAME:  O X O
       X X O
       O X
```

If the top left element is GAME(1,1), then the O in the third column of the second row is GAME(2,3) and the blank element is GAME(3,1).

When the word 'array' is used on its own, it is generally understood to mean a one-dimensional array. Arrays with more than two dimensions are occasionally used.

4.5 Static and Dynamic Data Structures

An array is a **static data structure**, that is to say, it stays the same size once it has been created. Data structures which change in size once they have been created are called **dynamic data structures**. A string can be a static or a dynamic data structure. The structures introduced in the remainder of this chapter are dynamic data structures. They generally require pointers for their implementation.

4.6 Stacks

You have probably seen the way in which plates are sometimes stored in restaurants. A pile of plates is supported on a spring. As a new plate is put on top of the pile, it pushes the rest down. When a plate is taken from the pile, the next plate pops up. Such a structure is a **stack** in the computing sense of the word. A stack is a collection of data items which may only be accessed at one end, called the **top** of the stack.

Only two operations may be carried out on a stack. Adding a new item, called **pushing** or **stacking** the item, involves placing it on top of the stack. Removing an item involves **popping** it from the stack.

If a number of items are pushed onto a stack, and then popped from the stack, the last item added will be the first one removed. For this reason a stack is called a **last-in-first-out (LIFO) stack**. Other names for a stack are **push-down stack** and **push-down list**.

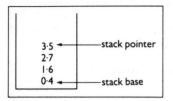

Figure 4.3
A stack

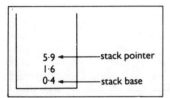

Figure 4.4

When a stack is stored in a computer memory, the elements do not move up and down as the stack is pushed and popped. Instead, the position of the top of the stack changes. A pointer called a **stack pointer** indicates the position of the top of the stack (or, in some applications, the first free space above the top of the stack). Another pointer is used to indicate the base of the stack. This pointer, called the **stack base**, keeps the same value as long as the stack is in existence. Figure 4.3 shows a stack pointer and stack base in use. If the sequence of operations **pop, pop, push 5.9**, is carried out on this stack, the result is shown in Figure 4.4. Representing an empty stack is important. If the stack pointer indicates the first available space above the top of the stack, then this is shown in Figure 4.5. When the stack is empty, the stack pointer has the same value as the stack base.

The stack is one of the most important data structures in computing. Stacks are used in calculations, for translating from one computer language to another, and for transferring control from one part of a program to another. Most modern processors include a stack pointer as an architectural feature, and some regard their entire memory as a set of stacks.

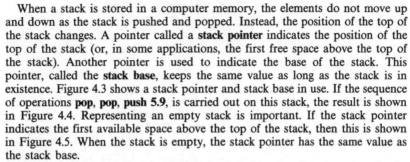

Figure 4.5

4.7 Queues

In spite of the American origins of many ideas associated with computers, that great British institution, the **queue**, has found its way into the theory of computing. Everyone knows how a queue works: newcomers join at the rear, service is provided at the front, and no pushing-in is allowed. Exactly the same rules apply to queues of data stored in a computer memory: data items are added at the back and removed from the front. A queue is a **first-in-first-out (FIFO)** data structure.

There are several ways of implementing the storage of a queue in a computer memory. A particularly simple way involves storing the queue elements in adjacent memory locations, and providing pointers to the front and rear of the queue. See Figure 4.6. When an element is added to the queue, the rear pointer is adjusted to point to the new element. Similarly, when an element is removed from the queue, the front pointer is adjusted to point to the new front element.

The problem with this method of storage of a queue is that the queue moves down the store as the elements are added and removed. The usual solution is to allocate a fixed area of store for the queue, and then let the rear of the queue 'wrap around' to the start of the area. See Figure 4.7. An area of store used in this way is called a **circular buffer**.

Although queues are used slightly less frequently than stacks, they do have a variety of applications. These include queuing data items in transit between a processor and a peripheral device, or at intermediate points in a data communications network.

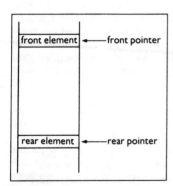

Figure 4.6
A queue

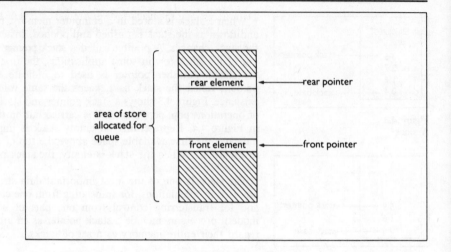

Figure 4.7
A queue wrapped around in a
fixed area of store

4.8 Lists

A **list** is a set of data items stored in some order. Data items may be inserted or
deleted at any point in the list. In this respect, a list is less restrictive than a
stack or queue. The simplest way of implementing a list makes use of a pointer
from each item to the one following it in the list. There is also a pointer to the
start of the list, while the last item in the list has a null pointer. See Figure 4.8.

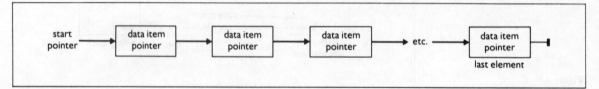

Figure 4.8
A list

A data structure of this type is also known as a **linked list**. A **list element**
consists of a data item and its pointer. In many applications a list element
contains a number of data items. Since elements can easily be added to the rear
or removed from the front of the linked list, this structure may also be used to
implement a queue. Inserting an element into a list is achieved by adjusting the
pointers to include the new element. See Figure 4.9. Removing an element is
achieved in a similar way, as shown in Figure 4.10.

A variation on the idea of a list is the case where the pointer from the end of
the list is linked to the front of the list. This creates a **circular list**, as shown in
Figure 4.11.

Data items in a list are in order, in the sense that one data item is behind
another in the list. Lists are, however, frequently used in cases where the data
items are in numerical or alphabetical order. Such lists are called **ordered lists**.
Lists are very useful for storing ordered sets of data, if insertions and deletions
of data items are frequent.

An alternative form of a list is a structure which contains an identified data
item as the **head**, and the remaining items forming the **tail** of the list. The usual
notation is as follows:

(A | B)   is the list with element **A** at the head
and list **B** as the tail.

(A | (B | (C D))) is the list with element **A** at the
head, and a tail comprising a list
with element **B** at the head, and the
list containing elements **C** and **D** as
the tail.

Data items may themselves be entire lists. Lists of this nature are widely used in artificial intelligence research, and form the basis of the programming language Lisp (Section 19.7).

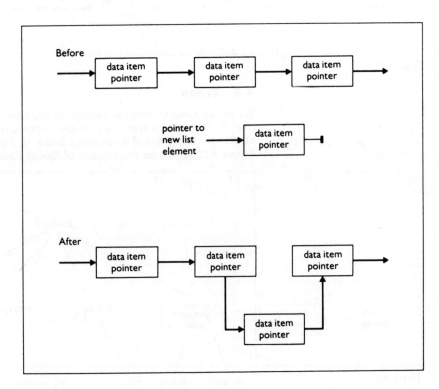

Figure 4.9
Inserting an element into a list

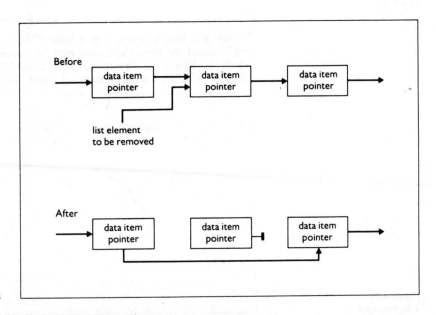

Figure 4.10
Removing an element from a list

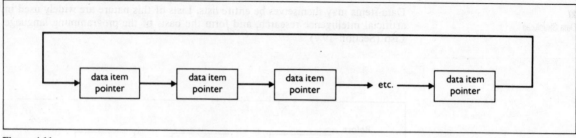

Figure 4.11
A circular list

4.9 Trees

We are all familiar with the phrases 'family tree' and 'getting to the top of the tree'. In this sense, a **tree** is a structure implying a hierarchy, with each element of the tree being linked to elements below it. For example, the family tree in Figure 4.12 shows the descendants of Queen Elizabeth II.

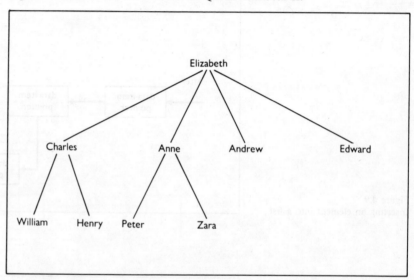

Figure 4.12
A family tree

Each data item in a tree is at a **node** of the tree. The node at the top of the tree is called the **root**. Each node may be connected to one or more **subtrees**, which also have a tree structure. A node at the bottom of the tree, which has no subtrees, is called a **terminal node**, or a **leaf**. See Figure 4.13.

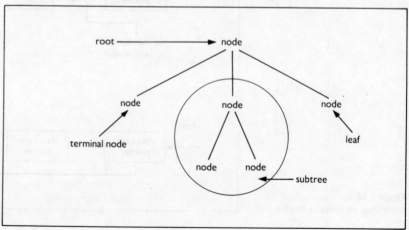

Figure 4.13
Tree concepts

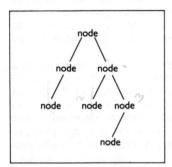

Figure 4.14
A binary tree

A special type of tree is commonly used in computing. This is a **binary tree**, in which each node may have at most two subtrees. These are called the **left** and **right subtrees** and are binary trees in their own right. Figure 4.14 shows a binary tree. Notice how each node has zero, one or two subtrees.

The usual way of representing a tree involves the use of pointers. For a binary tree, each node consists of a data item plus two pointers. One or both of the pointers may have null values if they have no subtrees to point to. Figure 4.15 shows how pointers may be used to construct the same tree as illustrated in Figure 4.14. Notice how terminal nodes have null values of both pointers.

A number of operations may be carried out on trees. Two binary trees may be **joined** to an additional node, which becomes the root of a larger binary tree, with the original trees as subtrees. A tree may be **traversed** in several ways. Traversing a tree is accessing its elements in a systematic way. Tree traversal is dealt with in the exercise at the end of this chapter.

Trees have a number of applications in computing. The modules of many programs are linked together in a tree structure. Trees are also used to represent arithmetic expressions, and for sorting and searching. Some computers regard their entire memory as if it were partitioned into a tree structure.

The essential feature of a tree is that each node is connected to subtrees, which themselves have the structure of trees. In other words, wherever you are in a tree, the structure 'below' you is a tree. In this sense a tree is a **recursive** data structure, and can be manipulated by recursive programs (Section 18.5). This is the property of trees which makes them so useful from a computing point of view.

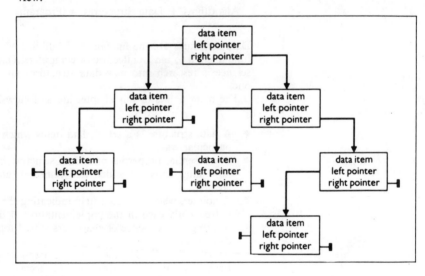

Figure 4.15
Pointers used to construct a binary tree

4.10 Data Types

A concept which links this chapter with the previous chapter is that of a **data type**. Data types include both individual data items and data structures. For many purposes it is covenient to treat entire data structures as single objects. Many program languages allow complete structures to be manipulated as if they were single data items. Data structures and individual items are often identified in the same way.

A number of program languages require that the type of each data item be **declared** before the data item is used in a program. A data item may be an integer, an array, or a list, to name just a few examples. The concept of data types is discussed further in the chapters on high level languages, Chapters 18 and 19.

4.11 Implementation of Data Structures

The data structures introduced in this chapter are described in general terms. In these terms they are sometimes known as **abstract data types**, with essential properties defined completely independently of computers. This is necessary to preserve the simplicity of these structures, and to investigate what further properties they possess.

A number of problems arise when representing any of these structures on a computer. In almost all cases the method of representation interferes with the properties of the structure. Some of the cleanness and simplicity of the abstract structure is lost. The commonest problem is that computers do not have an unlimited memory capacity. All the dynamic data structures introduced in this chapter have no theoretical limits on the size to which they can grow. In practice, a limit has to be placed on their size, and checks carried out whenever a new data item is added.

4.12 Conclusion

The significance of data structures cannot be stressed too much. The title of an important book on computer programming states the case very succinctly:

Algorithms + Data Structures = Programs.

Data structures are the fundamental building blocks of programs, and are also fundamental to the architecture of computers. One of the frontiers of computing science is research into new data structures and further properties of existing ones.

The main points of this chapter are as follows:

- A data structure is a set of data items which are related to each other in a particular way.
- The essential properties of a data structure can be described by specifying how data items are added and removed, and how an empty structure is created.
- A pointer, which is a data item indicating the location of another data item, is frequently used in the implementation of data structures.
- A string is a sequence of characters stored together and regarded as a single data item.
- An array is a fixed number of data items of identical type, stored together. Each element in an array may be accessed by one or more indices, the number of indices indicating the dimension of the array.
- Static data structures are ones which stay the same size once they have been created, whereas dynamic data structures can vary in size.
- A stack, or last-in-first-out (LIFO) structure, is a collection of data items which can only be accessed at one end, the top of the stack.
- A queue, or first-in-first-out (FIFO) structure, has items added at the rear and removed from the front.
- A list is a set of data where items may be inserted or deleted at any point.
- A tree is a data structure in which each element may be linked to one or more elements below it.
- The concept of data types includes individual data items, which may, for example, be literal or numeric, and data structures, which may be stacks, queues, lists or trees.
- In most cases when data structures are implemented, some restrictions on their properties have to be imposed. This has given rise to the concept of abstract data types, which retain their 'pure' features.

Exercise 4

1 Briefly define the following terms: data structure; pointer; null pointer; string; array; index; dimension; static and dynamic data structures; stack; top of stack; push; pop; LIFO; stack pointer; stack base; queue; FIFO; circular buffer; list; circular list; ordered list; tree; node; root; subtree; leaf; binary tree; tree traversal; data type; declaration, and abstract data type.

2 Give at least three reasons for the use of data structures in computing.

3 a) Name some examples of structured data encountered in everyday life, in addition to those mentioned in the text.
  b) Describe a collection of data occurring in everyday life which could not be called structured. Give reasons for your choice of the particular collection.

4 Briefly state the requirements that a set of data must satisfy in order to be called structured.

● 5 Three different data structures have been mentioned in this chapter as models for a computer memory.
  a) Name the structures
  b) In the light of your knowledge of data structures, suggest why each of them might have been chosen.

6 Mention three examples of the use of null pointers.

7 A text editing program allows strings of characters to be inserted into the middle of other strings. For example, the string THE CAT SAT ON MAT can be edited to become THE CAT SAT ON THE MAT.
  Give an informal algorithm, using separating and joining operations only, for this insertion operation.

8 An algorithm for setting all the elements of an array X to zero is as follows:

    Let index I = 1
    While I < = 10, repeat
      Let X(I) = 0
      Increase I by 1

  Write similar algorithms for each of the following processes:
  a) Adding each element of array X to the corresponding element of array Y, which also has ten elements, to produce array Z.
  b) Adding up all the elements of array X to produce a single total.
  ●c) Producing the 'product' of array X and array Y, defined as folows:

  $$P = X(1).Y(1) + X(2).Y(2) + ... + X(10).Y(10)$$

  (the dot means multiplication in this case).

9 The elements of the two-dimensional array A, with three rows and three columns, are to be copied into the one-dimensional array B, with nine elements, one row at a time. The first few elements are transferred as follows:

  A(1,1) into B(1)
  A(1,2) into B(2)
  A(1,3) into B(3), etc.

  a) Continue the above list, showing how all the elements of A are transferred.
  ●b) Derive a formula for the index of array B in terms of the indices of array A.
  ●c) Repeat the question with all the indices starting from 0 instead of 1. Comment on your results.

10 A stack is often used to do calculations on a computer in the manner introduced in the following examples:

Example 1
6 + 7 × 4:   Stack 6 | 6 |

                    Stack 7 | 7 |
                                         | 6 |

                    Stack 4 | 4 |
                                         | 7 |
                                         | 6 |

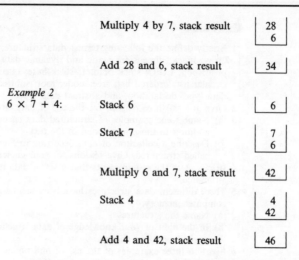

Multiply 4 by 7, stack result	28 / 6
Add 28 and 6, stack result	34

Example 2
$6 \times 7 + 4$:

Stack 6	6
Stack 7	7 / 6
Multiply 6 and 7, stack result	42
Stack 4	4 / 42
Add 4 and 42, stack result	46

In other words load the numbers onto the stack until an operation can be performed on the top two numbers. These two numbers are replaced by the result of the operation. The process continues until the final answer is left on the stack. Using this method, show the steps of the following calculations. Make sure that you know the order in which the calculations must be performed before you start.

a) $21 - 10 / 5$
b) $39 / 13 - 2$
c) $6 \times 4 + 5 \times 3$
d) $6 \times (4 + 5) \times 3$
e) $7 + 9 + 15 - 2$

Another way of writing calculations, called **reverse Polish notation**, is introduced later in the book. It is intended for use when calculations are to be carried out using a stack.

11 One method of representing a queue is to store the elements next to each other, with a pointer to the front of the queue, and a pointer to the space behind the rear of the queue. Figure 4.16 shows an example. The data items are names of programs waiting to be run on a computer.

a) Draw a diagram of the queue after the programs **CHESS1** and **OX053** have been run, and the program **STRM5** has joined the queue.
b) If no further programs are added, draw diagrams of the queue when there is one program left to run, and when the queue is empty.
c) Mention a disadvantage of storing a queue in this way in a computer memory.

12 An alternative method of implementing a list is to have two pointers associated with each element. One pointer points to the list element in front, the other to the element behind.

a) Draw a diagram of a list implemented in this way.
b) Draw diagrams to show the process of inserting a new data item into a list, using pointers in both directions.
c) Labelling the relevant pointers, specify precisely what operations are performed to accommodate the new item.

13 Draw a diagram of a circular list using pointers in both directions.

14 A set of names is stored, in alphabetical order, in an array. The last few elements of the array contain free spaces. Write informal algorithms showing the principal steps of inserting and deleting elements of this array, while preserving its alphabetical ordering and keeping the free spaces at the back. (Write the algorithms as brief English sentences. Do not specify index values in detail.)

From your results, comment on the suitability of arrays for storing ordered data.

15 Trees can be used to describe the structure of arithmetic or algebraic expressions, as shown in the following examples:

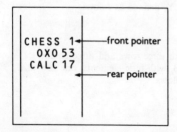

Figure 4.16

Example 1

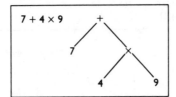

Figure 4.17

Example 2

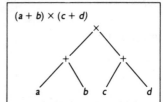

Figure 4.18

The parts of the calculations which are to be performed first form the lowest branches of the tree.

Represent the following expressions in a similar manner to the above examples:

a) 8 − 5/7
b) (x − y) − (p × q)
c) ((x + y) × 2) / (a − 7)
d) a + b + c
e) (s + t) × (u − v) / (p + q)

16 Two arrays are used to represent a tree, in the following manner. One array stores the data items in the tree. The other array contains blocks of pointers , one for each node. The first pointer in a node is the index of the data item at that node. Subsequent pointers point to blocks for nodes branching from the node. The block ends with a zero.

For example, the tree showing the component subjects of computing science is shown in Figure 4.19. The arrays corresponding to this tree are shown below.

pointers array		data array	
index	item	index	item
1	2	1	applications
2	7	2	computing
3	9	3	data
4	11	4	hardware
5	13	5	software
6	0		
7	3		
8	0		
9	4		
10	0		
11	5		
12	0		
13	1		
14	0		

Arrows have been drawn to show the effects of the first few pointers.

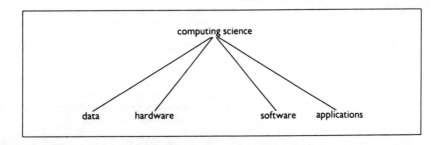

Figure 4.19

Figure 4.20

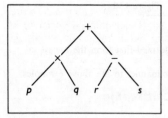

Figure 4.21

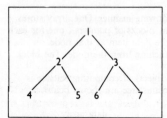

Figure 4.22

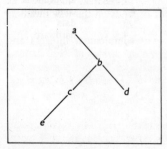

Figure 4.23

Construct similar arrays to represent the following trees:

a) Figure 4.20
b) Figure 4.21

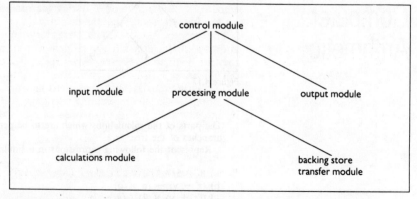

17 An array can be used to store the elements in a binary tree in a fairly simple manner. The correspondence of array indices and nodes in the tree is shown in Figure 4.22

a) Store the tree in part (b) of Question 16 in this manner.
b) The array: $\begin{bmatrix} a \\ - \\ b \end{bmatrix}$ stores the binary tree: a b.

   Represent the binary tree in Figure 4.23 in an array in this way.
c) Compare this method of representing trees by arrays with one introduced in Question 16. Comment on the suitability of this method of storing binary trees.

●18 Traversing a tree is accessing its elements in a systematic way. The commonest order is 'from left to right', i.e. left subtree, node, right subtree. This way might be described by the following algorithm:

   traverse tree

   if tree not null

   then **traverse** left subtree
   output node
   traverse right subtree

This algorithm is recursive, in the sense that it 'calls' itself. Applied to the tree in Figure 4.15, it produces the elements in the order $7 + 4 \times 9$.

a) Apply this algorithm to the trees in Figures 4.22 and 4.23, and list the elements in the order in which they are output.
b) Change the algorithm so that it traverses both subtrees before the node is output.
c) Write down the output produced by applying the revised algorithm to the trees in Figures 4.17, 4.22 and 4.23.

19 The rules for sorting a list of integers using a binary tree are as follows:
   i) take the first integer as the data element at the root,
   ii) compare the next integer with the element at the root; if it is greater it is placed on the right at the next level, otherwise on the left,
   iii) for each subsequent integer in the list the process described in (ii) is repeated, with comparisons continuing through the tree until a vacant position is found.

a) Using these rules, construct a sort tree for the list 36, 75, 26, 92, 36 23, 20, 46, 33.
b) Describe an algorithm which will retrieve the sorted list of data from the tree.
c) If it is known that the data contains many repeated items, suggest an improvement to the rules above.
d) What characteristics of the initial data list would cause this sorting method to become particularly inefficient?

UCLES 81 I (Specimen)

5
Computer
Arithmetic

This chapter concerns one aspect of the processing carried out by computers: **computer arithmetic**. Arithmetic is only one of the many ways in which a computer can process data - the days of computers being used for 'number crunching' only have long passed. On the other hand, computers do a certain amount of simple arithmetic during the running of all programs, whether they are for numerical applications or not.

This chapter introduces the elementary theory of computer arithmetic. Pencil and paper calculations are done here in a manner similar to the way in which they are done on computers. Some of the electronic circuits which actually carry out the various arithmetic operations are introduced in Chapter 8.

This chapter builds on foundations laid in Chapter 3, concerning data representation. Ways of representing numbers, and some elementary operations of computer arithmetic, are introduced in that chapter. From time to time it will be necessary to refer to material in Chapter 3 during the study of this chapter.

5.1 Characteristics of Computer Arithmetic

The arithmetic carried out by computers differs from our customary way of doing arithmetic in a number of ways. Although arithmetic operations are implemented differently on different computers, they all have a few common characteristics. These are a binary representation of numbers, a finite range of numbers, a finite precision of numbers, and some operations done in terms of other operations. Each of these characteristics is now briefly discussed.

Binary Representation of Numbers
Various binary representations of numbers are discussed in Chapter 3. The most important point to remember at this stage is that numbers can be represented in several ways, such as in binary coded decimal form, as integers or fractions, or as floating point numbers. Furthermore, integers and fractions can be in sign-and-magnitude form, or as twos complement or ones complement numbers. The way in which arithmetic operations are carried out depends on the way numbers are represented.

This chapter is confined to a discussion of twos complement integers and floating point numbers, as these are the commonest ways of representing numbers on computers. In many programming languages the programmer can choose which of these two forms is to be used for each numeric data item.

Finite Range of Numbers
Whichever way numbers are represented on a computer, there is always an upper and a lower limit on their size. These limits depend on the number representation used, and on the number of bits allocated to the number. The term **overflow** is used if an operation results in a number which is outside these limits (the term **underflow** is used in relation to the lower limit).

Finite Precision of Numbers
When a base ten number is written as a decimal fraction, the number of decimal places reflects the **precision** of the number. Most fractions cannot be represented exactly in a finite number of decimal places. The precision of a decimal fraction is a measure of how closely it comes to representing the number exactly.

In computers, fractions and floating point numbers are stored in a finite number of binary places. As in the case of decimal fractions, this limits the precision of these numbers. This means that a calculation using floating point numbers seldom gives exactly the right answer.

Some Operations Done in Terms of Other Operations
Most computers do not have separate processing circuits for all arithmetic operations. One of the reasons for using complementary numbers is that subtraction can be done by complementation and addition. On many computers

multiplication is done by a process of shifting and addition. Division is done by shifting and subtraction. An algorithm for doing multiplication in this way is given in Section 5.2.

The roles of hardware and software in computer arithmetic are important. Operations such as integer addition, which are carried out directly, are done by hardware. Operations done in terms of other operations are supervised by software. Each type of computer has its own mixture of hardware and software implementation of arithmetic operations. In general, the larger the computer, the more operations which are done directly by hardware.

5.2 Integer Arithmetic

In this section, integers are assumed to be represented in twos complement form. This form is introduced in Chapter 3, where it is explained how subtraction can be carried out by complementation and addition. Three further aspects of integer arithmetic are now discussed: overflow, multiplication and division.

Overflow

Overflow occurs when the result of a calculation is outside the range of numbers which can be represented. There is no way of preventing overflow; all that a computer can do is detect it when it occurs.

In twos complement arithmetic, overflow is related to the numbers carried into and out of the most significant place value during addition. Four examples are introduced below to illustrate this point, after which some general conclusions are drawn. Six bit, twos complement numbers are used throughout.

Note carefully the numbers carried into and out of the most significant bit of the calculations below, and whether or not the result is correct.

	−32	16	8	4	2	1	
Example 1: 14 + 9							
14 =	0	0	1	1	1	0	
9 =	0	0	1	0	0	1	+
	0	1	0	1	1	1	= 23
	0	0					
	carry out	carry in					

Carry in = 0, carry out = 0, answer correct.

	−32	16	8	4	2	1	
Example 2: 25 + 18							
25 =	0	1	1	0	0	1	
18 =	0	1	0	0	1	0	+
	1	0	1	0	1	1	= −21
	0	1					
	carry out	carry in					

Carry in = 1, carry out = 0, answer incorrect.

	−32	16	8	4	2	1	
Example 3: 17 − 13 = 17 + (−13)							
17 =	0	1	0	0	0	1	
−13 =	1	1	0	0	1	1	+
	0	0	0	1	0	0	= 4
	1	1					
	carry out	carry in					

Carry in = 1, carry out = 1, answer correct.

Example 4: $-8 - 31 = -8 + (-31)$

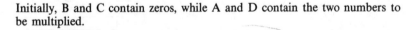

$$
\begin{array}{r}
-8 = \\
-31 =
\end{array}
\qquad
\begin{array}{ccccccl}
1 & 1 & 1 & 0 & 0 & 0 & \\
1 & 0 & 0 & 0 & 0 & 1 & + \\
\hline
0 & 1 & 1 & 0 & 0 & 1 & = 25 \\
\hline
1 & 0 & & & & &
\end{array}
$$

carry out   carry in

Carry in = 0, carry out = 1, answer incorrect.

From the four results it can be seen that the answer is correct when the number carried in to the most significant place is the same as the number carried out. This is true in general. In other words, overflow occurs when, at the most significant bit, carry in is not equal to carry out. Most computers have a special **overflow bit** which is set to 1 when overflow is detected in this manner. The above examples use six bit arithmetic, but the situation is the same, in twos complement arithmetic, however many bits are used.

Integer Multiplication

If multiplication is not performed directly by computer hardware, the commonest technique is to use a process of **shifting** and **addition**. It is very similar to the method of doing binary multiplication by hand.

You will recall that there are rules for determining the sign of a product from the signs of the numbers which are multiplied. These rules are generally applied separately from the actual multiplication process. Accordingly, this section considers the multiplication of positive integers only.

An algorithm is presented below for the multiplication of two positive binary integers, by a process of shifting and addition. It is not the only one used by computers, but is representative of them. The algorithm requires a **working area**, which might be imagined as shown in Figure 5.1. There are three storage spaces for binary integers, labelled A, C and D. The storage space labelled B is for the carry bit resulting from an addition.

The algorithm is as follows:

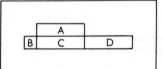

Figure 5.1

Initially, B and C contain zeros, while A and D contain the two numbers to be multiplied.

Repeat, for each bit of the numbers:

If the least significant bit of D is 1, then add A to C, placing the sum in C and the carry in B.

Shift the bits in B, C and D together one place to the right. Thus B passes into C, a bit passes from C to D and the least significant bit of D is lost.

When this process is complete, the product of the two numbers is in C and D.

An example of this process is shown in Figure 5.2. For simplicity, four bit integers 1 1 0 1 and 1 0 0 1 are used. Thus the shifting and addition is repeated four times. Afterwards the product of the two numbers, 0 1 1 1 0 1 0 1, is in C and D. The result can be checked by converting the numbers and the product to decimal.

You will notice that the product is twice as long as the original numbers. Overflow can occur if this number must be stored in the space for a single integer. Four bit numbers are used in the above example for simplicity. The steps of the algorithm are the same if longer numbers are used.

Integer Division

Integer division is done by a process of shifting and subtraction, very similar to the process of integer multiplication. The result is obtained as a quotient and a remainder. In most computers the result of the division is taken to be the

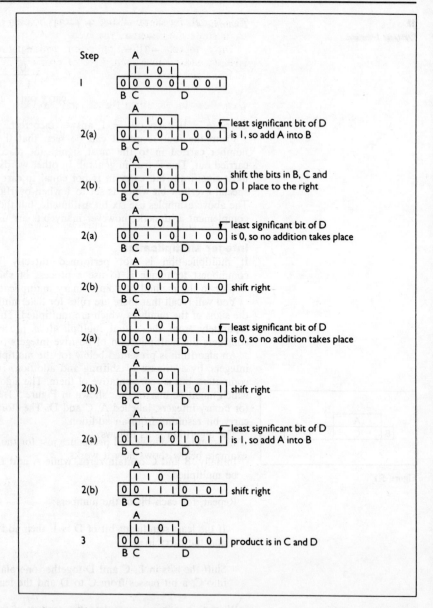

Figure 5.2
1101×1001

quotient, without any rounding up being done. In other words, the result of dividing 20 by 7, using integer arithmetic is 2.

5.3 Floating Point Arithmetic

Methods of representing floating point numbers are discussed in Chapter 3. You will recall that a floating point number consists of a fraction part, or mantissa, multiplied by a power of two, or exponent. For simplicity, all floating point numbers used in this chapter are of the following form:

	mantissa					exponent		
sign	$\frac{1}{2}$	$\frac{1}{4}$	$\frac{1}{8}$	$\frac{1}{16}$		sign	2	1

For example

0	1	1	0	1		0	1	0

$$= \tfrac{13}{16} \times 2^2 = \tfrac{13}{16} \times 4 = 3\tfrac{1}{4}.$$

This form is far shorter than any actual floating point representation, but serves to illustrate the principles involved.

Three aspects of floating point arithmetic are now discussed: **overflow**, **addition** and **multiplication**. Loss of precision is investigated in the context of addition and multiplication.

Overflow in Floating Point Arithmetic

As in the case of integers, there is an upper and a lower limit to the size of floating point numbers which can be represented by a particular number of bits. These limits are determined by the number of bits allocated to the exponent. For the above allocation of bits, the limits to the exponent are -3 and 3. This gives an approximate range of the size of the numbers of 2^{-3} to 2^3, i.e. $\frac{1}{8}$ to 8. In practice, this range is of course much wider.

If a number exceeds the upper limits of the range, **overflow** is said to occur. If a number exceeds the lower limit, some computers will set the number to zero. The term **underflow** is used when this occurs.

Floating Point Addition

An algorithm for the addition of two floating point numbers is as follows:

> If the exponents of the two numbers are not equal
>   then For the number with the smaller exponent, repeat:
>   Shift the mantissa one place to the right
>   Increase the exponent by 1
>   Until the exponent equals that of the other number.
> Add the mantissas of the two numbers.
> If the addition results in a carry from the most significant place
>   then Shift this carry bit into the mantissa and the
>   rest of the mantissa one place to the right
>   Increase the exponent by 1.

This is quite a complicated procedure just for the addition of two numbers. The example below shows how it works.

		mantissa					exponent		
	sign	$\frac{1}{2}$	$\frac{1}{4}$	$\frac{1}{8}$	$\frac{1}{16}$	sign	2	1	
	0	1	1	0	1	0	1	0	$(= 3\frac{1}{4})$
+	0	1	0	0	1	0	0	1	$(= 1\frac{1}{8})$

The second number has the smaller exponent, so the mantissa is shifted one place to the right and the exponent is increased by 1. One bit of the mantissa is lost. The result is as follows:

$$0 \quad 0 \quad 1 \quad 0 \quad 0 \quad 0 \quad 1 \quad 0$$

As the exponents are now equal, the mantissas can be added:

	0	1	1	0	1
+	0	0	1	0	0
	0	0	0	0	1

carry: 1

The carry bit is shifted into the mantissa, and the exponent is increased by 1. Again one bit of the mantissa is lost. The result is as follows:

	mantissa					exponent		
sign	$\frac{1}{2}$	$\frac{1}{4}$	$\frac{1}{8}$	$\frac{1}{16}$	sign	2	1
0	1	0	0	0	0	1	1

$$= \tfrac{1}{2} \times 2^3 = \tfrac{1}{2} \times 8 = 4$$

Adding the decimal values of the original numbers gives the result as 4 ⅜. An error has been introduced, due to the limited number of bits allocated to the mantissa. This type of error is called a **truncation error**. A remedy for this kind of error is to allocate more bits to the mantissa. This increases the precision of the numbers. Although it reduces this kind of error, it will never eliminate it. The error can be reduced by **rounding**, discussed in the exercise at the end of this chapter.

Subtraction of floating point numbers is carried out by a very similar process, and can result in the same kind of errors.

Floating Point Multiplication

An algorithm for the multiplication of two floating point numbers is as follows:

Multiply the mantissas of the numbers, and add their exponents.

Shift the bits of the product to the left until there is a 1 in the most significant place. Reduce the exponent by 1 for each place shifted.

Truncate the product to the number of bits allocated to the mantissa of a floating point number.

The following example, using the same floating point numbers as before, shows how this algorithm works.

	mantissa				exponent			
sign	½	¼	⅛	1/16	sign	2	1	
0	1	1	0	1	0	1	0	(= 3 ¼)
× 0	1	0	0	1	0	0	1	(= 1 ⅛)

Multiplying the mantissas and adding the exponents gives the following results:

product of mantissas: 0 1 1 1 0 1 0 1
sum of exponents: 1 1

The product is shifted one place to the left, and the exponent is reduced by 1. This gives:

product of mantissas: 1 1 1 0 1 0 1
sum of exponents: 1 0

Truncating the product into the mantissa gives the following floating point result:

	mantissa				exponent		
sign	½	¼	⅛	1/16	sign	2	1
0	1	1	1	0	0	1	0

$$= \tfrac{7}{8} \times 2^2 = \tfrac{7}{8} \times 4 = 3\tfrac{1}{2}$$

Multiplying the decimal values of the original numbers gives the result 3 21/32. Once again a truncation error has been introduced. As before, this error can be reduced, but not eliminated, by increasing the number of bits allocated to the mantissa or by rounding. Floating point division suffers similar limitations.

5.4 Conclusion

This chapter has introduced some of the techniques of computer arithmetic, and demonstrated, by means of a few simple examples, some of the errors which can arise. Although the number representations used in this chapter are much shorter than those used by any actual computer, the principles and the problems are the same.

The main points raised in this chapter are as follows:

- The characteristics of computer arithmetic are a binary representation of numbers, generally in more than one code, a finite range and a finite precision of numbers, and some arithmetic operations done in terms of other operations.
- In integer arithmetic, overflow is related to the numbers carried into and out of the most significant place value during addition.
- Integer multiplication can be carried out by a process of shifting and addition. Integer division results in a quotient and a remainder.
- In floating point arithmetic, the range of numbers which can be represented depends on the number of bits allocated to the exponent. Overflow or underflow occurs if this range is exceeded.
- Truncation errors occur in floating point arithmetic when the mantissa of the result is cut off to fit the number of bits allocated to it. Truncation errors are reduced by normalisation (shifting the mantissa so that there is always a 1 in the most significant place), and rounding the result (see Question 9 below). If rounding is carried out, the error is known as a **rounding error**.

Exercise 5

1 Briefly define the following terms: overflow; precision; normalisation; overflow bit; truncation error, rounding error.

2 For a number of different computers, find out what arithmetic operations are carried out by hardware and what operations are supervised by software.

3 Verify the rule established in the chapter relating carry to overflow, by carrying out the following calculations, using four bit, twos complement numbers: $2+5$; $6+3$; $4-5$; $-2-7$.

4 Do the four calculations in the examples from the section on carry and overflow, using ones complement representation. From your results, state under what conditions overflow occurs in this representation.

5 Use the algorithm for integer multiplication to multiply 1 1 0 1 by 1 1 1 0.

- **6** Design an algorithm for integer division by a process of shifting and subtraction. A similar layout of working areas can be used to that for integer multiplication. Test your algorithm with some suitable numbers

7

	sign	mantissa $\frac{1}{2}$	$\frac{1}{4}$	$\frac{1}{8}$	$\frac{1}{16}$	sign	exponent 2	1
Let A =	0	1	1	0	0	0	1	0
Let B =	0	1	1	0	1	0	0	1
Let C =	0	1	0	1	0	0	0	0
Let D =	0	1	1	1	1	0	1	1

Perform the following calculations on these numbers, using floating point arithmetic: $A+B$; $B+C$; $A\times B$; $A\times C$; $A\times D$; $B\times D$; $C\times D$; $A+D$. In each case, comment on any errors which arise.

8 A particular computer allocates 24 bits to a floating point number. Six of these bits are for the exponent, the first of which is a sign bit. What is the approximate range of numbers which can be represented in this way?

9 Errors can be reduced in computer arithmetic by the technique of **rounding**. Rounding is carried out when bits of a number, generally the mantissa of a floating point number, are discarded. The retained bits are rounded by adding 1 to the least significant retained bit if the most significant discarded bit is 1.

For example, if the eight bit mantissa 1 1 0 1 1 0 1 1 is rounded to four bits, the result is 1 1 1 0.

a) Round each of the following numbers, discarding the rightmost bits:
  0 1 1 0 1 1 0 1   to four bits
  0 1 1 1 1 0 1 1   to four bits
  1 0 0 1 1 0 0 1   to six bits

b) Round the results of the floating point addition and multiplication examples in this chapter, and repeat Question 7, rounding the results. Convert the numbers obtained to decimal, and comment on your results.

●10 Write an algorithm to convert an eight-bit integer, stored in sign-and-magnitude form, into a floating point number using the format of Question 7. Test your algorithm by converting the following integers:

```
0 1 1 0 0 0 0 0
0 1 0 1 1 1 0 1
1 0 0 0 1 0 1 0
1 1 0 1 0 1 0 1
```

6

Boolean Logic

This chapter introduces the theory behind the way in which computers manipulate data. This theory has been given the name **Boolean logic** after the English mathematician George Boole (1810 - 1864). In 1847, Boole published the first thorough investigation of the principles of mathematical logic.

This chapter builds on ideas introduced in earlier chapters, particularly Chapter 3, on data representation and storage. Concepts introduced in this chapter form the basis of the material in Chapter 8, on logic circuits, and the part of the book devoted to computer architecture, Chapters 9 to 15. The set of logic symbols used in this chapter is becoming the most widely accepted in the computing industry. If another set is preferred, Figure 6.7 compares the common sets of logic symbols.

6.1   Two-state Representation of Data

Boolean logic comprises a set of operations which manipulate logical, or Boolean variables. A **Boolean variable** is a quantity which can have either of two values, or states only. Depending on the context, these states may be called **true** and **false**, **set** and **clear**, **high** and **low**, or **0** and **1**.

As discussed in Chapter 3, all data inside a computer is represented in terms of two states only. In other words, all data is made up of Boolean variables. Furthermore, all processing of this data by the computer is carried out in terms of Boolean operations. The elementary operations of Boolean logic are introduced in this chapter. Chapter 8 shows how these operations are combined in various functional circuits of a computer.

6.2   The Elementary Logic Operations

Boolean operations transform one or more Boolean variables, producing a further Boolean variable. The value of the resulting variable depends on the values of the original variables.

Each logic operation is characterised by an **operation table**, also called a **truth table**. This table shows values of the resulting variable for all combinations of input variables. Two symbols associated with each logic operation are also introduced. The first symbol is the **logic circuit** symbol. This symbol indicates the logic operation in a logic circuit, which is rather like an electrical circuit. The other symbol is the **Boolean algebra** symbol for the operation. Boolean algebra is a way of representing logic operations, similar to the way ordinary algebra represents arithmetic operations.

Later in the chapter, combinations of logic operations are introduced. Like individual operations, these combinations can be described by truth tables, logic circuits or expressions in Boolean algebra.

The six commonest operations of Boolean logic are discussed below. In the context of logic circuits, these operations are sometimes referred to as **gates**.

NOT

The NOT operation has one input variable and one output variable. The value of the output variable is the opposite of that of the input variable. See Figure 6.1.

Operation table

Input	Output
P	$Q = NOT\ P$
0	1
1	0

Boolean expression: $Q = \overline{P}$

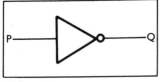

Figure 6.1
A NOT gate

AND

The AND operation has two or more input variables and one output variable. The output variable is 1 if **all** input variables are 1, otherwise it is 0. See Figure 6.2.

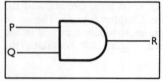

Figure 6.2
An AND gate

Operation table (for two inputs)

Input		Output
P	Q	R = P AND Q
0	0	0
0	1	0
1	0	0
1	1	1

Boolean expression: $R = P \cdot Q$

The operation table for an AND operation may be extended to three or more input variables using the rule for the AND operation quoted above.

OR

The OR operation has two or more input variables and one output variable. The output variable is 1 if **any** of the input variables are 1, otherwise it is 0. See Figure 6.3.

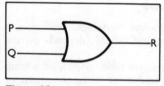

Figure 6.3
An OR gate

Operation table (for two inputs)

Input		Output
P	Q	R = P OR Q
0	0	0
0	1	1
1	0	1
1	1	1

Boolean expression: $R = P + Q$

It turns out that combinations of the NOT gate and either the AND or the OR gate are sufficient to carry out any logical operation on any number of inputs. However, three other logic gates are in common use, as introduced below.

Exclusive OR

The **exclusive OR** or **non-equivalence** operation has two input variables and one output variable. Considered as an exclusive OR, the rule for its operation is as follows: the output variable is 1 if either, but not both, inputs are 1. (An alternative rule is that the output is 1 if the inputs are different.) See Figure 6.4.

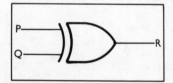

Figure 6.4
An Exclusive OR gate

Operation table

Input		Output
P	Q	R = P EOR Q
0	0	0
0	1	1
1	0	1
1	1	0

Boolean expression: $R = P \oplus Q$

NAND

The NAND operation may be considered as an AND operation followed by a NOT operation. It has two or more input variables and one output variable. The output variable is 0 if **all** the input variables are 1, otherwise it is 1. See Figure 6.5.

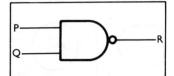

Figure 6.5
A NAND gate

Operation table (for two inputs)

Input		Output
P	Q	R = P NAND Q
0	0	1
0	1	1
1	0	1
1	1	0

Boolean expression: $R = \overline{P \cdot Q}$

NOR

The NOR operation may be considered as an OR operation followed by a NOT operation. It has two or more input variables and one output variable. The output variable is 0 if any of the input variables are 1, otherwise it is a 1. See Figure 6.6.

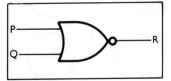

Figure 6.6
A NOR gate

Operation table (for two inputs)

Input		Output
P	Q	R = P NOR Q
0	0	1
0	1	0
1	0	0
1	1	0

Boolean expression: $R = \overline{P + Q}$

6.3 Logic Operation Symbols

There are several sets of symbols for logic operations in current use. Figure 6.7 shows the relationship between them.

6.4 Combinations of Logic Operations

The logic operations introduced in the previous section are seldom used on their own. Combinations of these operations may be imagined as connecting the output of one gate to the input of another gate. Some of the logic circuits of even the simplest computers are extremely complex. Such complexity is deliberately avoided here. The objective of this section is to show how logic elements can be combined, and how the operation table for a combination can be determined from the operation tables of the individual gates. Boolean expressions for the combinations of operations are also given.

Example 1

The logic circuit shown in Figure 6.8 combines an AND, an OR and a NOT gate. The Boolean expressions for this combination is

$$D = (A \cdot \overline{B}) + C$$

There are two ways of obtaining the operation table for a circuit such as this.

Operation	Boolean algebra symbols		Logic circuit symbols	
NOT	$\bar{P}$	$\sim P$		NOT
AND	$P \cdot Q$	$P \wedge Q$		AND
OR	$P + Q$	$P \vee Q$		OR
Exclusive OR	$P \oplus Q$	$P \not\equiv Q$		EOR
NAND	$\overline{P \cdot Q}$	$\sim (P \wedge Q)$		NAND
NOR	$\overline{P + Q}$	$\sim (P \vee Q)$		NOR

Figure 6.7
Different sets of logic symbols

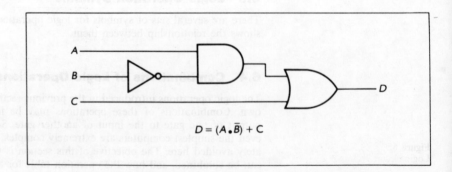

$$D = (A \cdot \bar{B}) + C$$

Figure 6.8
Logic circuit Example 1

One is to follow all possible combinations of inputs through the circuit, and obtain the value of the output for each input. The other is to build up the operation table through a series of intermediate columns. There is a column for each part of the Boolean expression. The columns are combined according to the rules for Boolean operations, until a column for the whole expression is obtained. This process is shown in the following table.

Input			$\bar{B}$	$A\cdot\bar{B}$	Output $D = (A\cdot\bar{B}) + C$
A	B	C			
0	0	0	1	0	0
0	0	1	1	0	1
0	1	0	0	0	0
0	1	1	0	0	1
1	0	0	1	1	1
1	0	1	1	1	1
1	1	0	0	0	0
1	1	1	0	0	1

Example 2

The logic circuit shown in Figure 6.9 combines a NAND and a NOR gate. The Boolean expression for this combination is:

$$S = \overline{(\overline{P + Q})\cdot R}$$

As before, the operation table for the circuit is obtained by using intermediate columns for parts of the Boolean expression.

Input			Output	
P	Q	R	$\overline{P + Q}$	$S = \overline{(\overline{P + Q})\cdot R}$
0	0	0	1	1
0	0	1	1	0
0	1	0	0	1
0	1	1	0	1
1	0	0	0	1
1	0	1	0	1
1	1	0	0	1
1	1	1	0	1

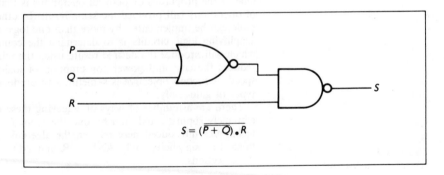

Figure 6.9
Logic circuit Example 2

Example 3

The logic circuit shown in Figure 6.10 combines two 3-input AND gates, two NOT gates and an exclusive OR gate. The Boolean expression for this combination is:

$$D = (\overline{A}\cdot B\cdot C) \oplus (A\cdot\overline{B}\cdot C)$$

The operation table for the circuit is obtained by the same method as before.

Input							Output
A	B	C	$\overline{A}$	$\overline{B}$	$\overline{A}\cdot B\cdot C$	$A\cdot\overline{B}\cdot C$	$D = (\overline{A}\cdot B\cdot C) \oplus (A\cdot\overline{B}\cdot C)$
0	0	0	1	1	0	0	0
0	0	1	1	1	0	0	0
0	1	0	1	0	0	0	0
0	1	1	1	0	1	0	1
1	0	0	0	1	0	0	0
1	0	1	0	1	0	1	1
1	1	0	0	0	0	0	0
1	1	1	0	0	0	0	0

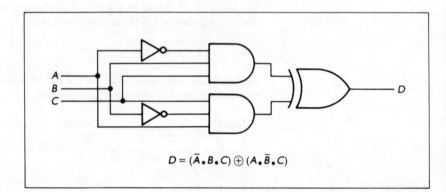

$$D = (\overline{A}\bullet B\bullet C) \oplus (A\bullet\overline{B}\bullet C)$$

Figure 6.10
Logic circuit Example 3

These examples show how the operation table for a logic circuit can be obtained from the expression for the circuit. In practice, in designing the logic circuits of a computer, one starts with a required operation table, and derives the Boolean expression and logic circuit to produce this table. This process is discussed in Section 6.7.

●6.5 Simplification of Combinations of Logic Operations

One of the properties of Boolean operations is that more than one combination of operations will produce the same result. In other words, the same operation table can be implemented by more than one logic circuit. The main objective of **simplifying** logic circuits is to determine the combinations of logic operations which will produce the desired result, using the minimum number of gates. This reduces the cost and power consumption of logic circuits, and increases their speed. A second objective is sometimes to produce a logic circuit using certain types of gates only.

There are a number of ways of achieving these objectives, some of which are extremely sophisticated, and beyond the scope of this book. The simplification techniques introduced here rely on the algebraic properties of Boolean operations. For simplicity, only AND, OR and NOT operations are considered in these sections.

●6.6 Algebraic Properties of Boolean Operations

The elementary algebraic properties of Boolean operations are listed below. You will notice how several of these resemble the algebraic properties of ordinary arithmetic operations.

Double negative: $\overline{\overline{A}} = A$

Associative: $(A + B) + C = A + (B + C)$

                       $(A\cdot B)\cdot C = A\cdot(B\cdot C)$

Distributive: $A + (B \cdot C) = (A + B) \cdot (A + C)$
$$A \cdot (B + C) = (A \cdot B) + (A \cdot C)$$

Absorption: $A \cdot A = A$
$$A + A = A$$

De Morgan's Laws: $\overline{A + B} = \overline{A} \cdot \overline{B}$
$$\overline{A \cdot B} = \overline{A} + \overline{B}$$

These properties may be proved by writing out the operation table for each side of the equation. This is done below, as an example, for the first of the distributive rules.

				Left hand side				Right hand side
A	B	C	$B \cdot C$	$A + (B \cdot C)$	$A + B$	$A + C$	$(A + B) \cdot (A + C)$
0	0	0	0	0	0	0	0
0	0	1	0	0	0	1	0
0	1	0	0	0	1	0	0
0	1	1	1	1	1	1	1
1	0	0	0	1	1	1	1
1	0	1	0	1	1	1	1
1	1	0	0	1	1	1	1
1	1	1	1	1	1	1	1

The column for the left hand side of the equation, and that for the right hand side, can be seen to be the same.

6.7 Examples of Simplifying Logic Circuits

Three examples of simplifying logic circuits are introduced below. In each case, a logic circuit and its Boolean expression are given. The Boolean expression is then simplified by means of the rules introduced above. The logic circuit of the resulting expression is drawn. In each case the objective is to reduce the number of gates in the circuit.

Example 1
Figure 6.11 shows a logic circuit containing three NOT gates and an AND gate. Its Boolean expression is as follows:

$$Z = \overline{\overline{X} \cdot \overline{Y}}$$

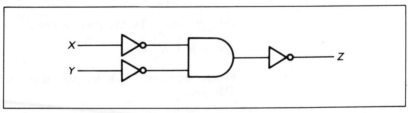

Figure 6.11
Simplification Example 1 (before)

Examining the rules, you will notice that the right hand side of the first of De Morgan's laws matches part of the above expression. Substituting the left hand side of this law gives the following expression:

$$Z = \overline{\overline{X + Y}}$$

Now the double negative rule may be used to give

$$Z = X + Y$$

This is the simplest possible form of the expression. Four gates in the original expression have been reduced to a single gate. The resulting logic circuit is shown in Figure 6.12.

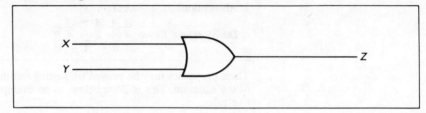

Figure 6.12
Simplification Example 1 (after)

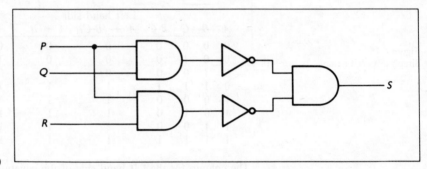

Figure 6.13
Simplification Example 2 (before)

Example 2

Figure 6.13 shows a logic circuit containing three AND gates and two NOT gates:

$$S = \overline{(P \cdot Q)} \cdot \overline{(P \cdot R)}$$

Applying the second of De Morgan's laws to the terms in brackets gives the following:

$$S = (\overline{P} + \overline{Q}) \cdot (\overline{P} + \overline{R})$$

The first of the distributive rules may now be used, giving:

$$S = \overline{P} + (\overline{Q} \cdot \overline{R})$$

Using the first of De Morgan's laws on the second part of the expression gives:

$$S = \overline{P} + \overline{(Q + R)}$$

Finally, the second of De Morgan's laws can be used on the whole expression. This gives:

$$S = \overline{P \cdot (Q + R)}$$

The circuit for this expression is shown in Figure 6.14. It contains three gates, as opposed to five in the original circuit.

Figure 6.14
Simplification Example 2 (after)

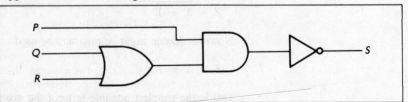

Example 3

Figure 6.15 shows a logic circuit containing two AND gates and three NOT gates. Its Boolean expression is:

$$D = \overline{(A \cdot \overline{B}) \cdot \overline{C}}$$

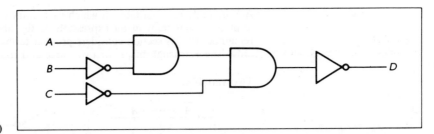

Figure 6.15
Simplification Example 3 (before)

The associative rule is first used to collect the two negated inputs together. This gives:

$$D = \overline{A \cdot (\overline{B} \cdot \overline{C})}$$

The first of De Morgan's rules can be used on the term in brackets. This results in the following expression:

$$D = \overline{A \cdot \overline{(B + C)}}$$

Remembering that $\overline{\overline{A}}$ is the same as A, the first of De Morgan's rules can be used on the whole expression. This gives:

$$D = \overline{\overline{A}} + \overline{\overline{(B + C)}}$$

The double negative rule simplifies this to:

$$D = \overline{A} + (B + C)$$

The circuit for this expression is shown in Figure 6.16. Once again, five gates in the original circuit have been reduced to three gates in the simplified circuit.

In practice far more sophisticated techniques, some involving the use of computers, are used to simplify logic circuits. Nevertheless, the principles of simplifying logic circuits are the ones introduced here.

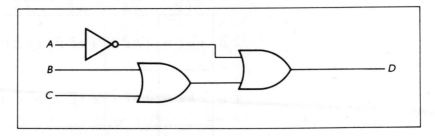

Figure 6.16
Simplification Example 3 (after)

•6.8 Karnaugh Maps

A simple but powerful method of determining the Boolean expression of a given operation table, and of simplifying the expression in order to use the minimum number of gates, is the **Karnaugh map**. In this context, the OR operation is referred to as the **sum**, and the AND operation as the **product**. Karnaugh maps use Boolean expressions which are either the sum of products, such as

$$D = \overline{A}\cdot B\cdot C + A\cdot\overline{B}\cdot C + A\cdot B\cdot\overline{C}$$

or products of sums, such as

$$D = (\overline{A} + B + C)\cdot(A + \overline{B} + C)\cdot(A + B + \overline{C})$$

A Karnaugh map is a table in which each entry corresponds either to a product term or a sum term in an expression of the above form. For simplicity, the remainder of this section considers product terms (the first of the above forms) only. The Karnaugh maps for two, three and four variables are shown below.

Two variables

	$\overline{A}$	A
$\overline{B}$	$\overline{A}\cdot\overline{B}$	$A\cdot\overline{B}$
B	$\overline{A}\cdot B$	$A\cdot B$

Three variables

	$\overline{A}\cdot\overline{B}$	$\overline{A}\cdot B$	$A\cdot B$	$A\cdot\overline{B}$
$\overline{C}$	$\overline{A}\cdot\overline{B}\cdot\overline{C}$	$\overline{A}\cdot B\cdot\overline{C}$	$A\cdot B\cdot\overline{C}$	$A\cdot\overline{B}\cdot\overline{C}$
C	$\overline{A}\cdot\overline{B}\cdot C$	$\overline{A}\cdot B\cdot C$	$A\cdot B\cdot C$	$A\cdot\overline{B}\cdot C$

Four variables

	$\overline{A}\cdot\overline{B}$	$\overline{A}\cdot B$	$A\cdot B$	$A\cdot\overline{B}$
$\overline{C}\cdot\overline{D}$	$\overline{A}\cdot\overline{B}\cdot\overline{C}\cdot\overline{D}$	$\overline{A}\cdot B\cdot\overline{C}\cdot\overline{D}$	$A\cdot B\cdot\overline{C}\cdot\overline{D}$	$A\cdot\overline{B}\cdot\overline{C}\cdot\overline{D}$
$\overline{C}\cdot D$	$\overline{A}\cdot\overline{B}\cdot\overline{C}\cdot D$	$\overline{A}\cdot B\cdot\overline{C}\cdot D$	$A\cdot B\cdot\overline{C}\cdot D$	$A\cdot\overline{B}\cdot\overline{C}\cdot D$
$C\cdot D$	$\overline{A}\cdot\overline{B}\cdot C\cdot D$	$\overline{A}\cdot B\cdot C\cdot D$	$A\cdot B\cdot C\cdot D$	$A\cdot\overline{B}\cdot C\cdot D$
$C\cdot\overline{D}$	$\overline{A}\cdot\overline{B}\cdot C\cdot\overline{D}$	$\overline{A}\cdot B\cdot C\cdot\overline{D}$	$A\cdot B\cdot C\cdot\overline{D}$	$A\cdot\overline{B}\cdot C\cdot\overline{D}$

Note that the cells are so arranged in each table that there is only one change between the values in any particular cell and its vertical or horizontal neighbours. This is also true if the rows of the three-variable table, and the rows and columns of the four-variable table are 'wrapped around' from left to right and top to bottom.

A Karnaugh map as shown above is used to obtain the Boolean expression for a given operation table as a sum of products, and to simplify the expression in order to minimise the number of gates needed. The method is best introduced by some examples.

Example 1

Obtain and simplify a Boolean expression for the operation table below:

\multicolumn{3}{c}{Inputs}	Output
A	B	C	D
0	0	0	0
0	0	1	1
0	1	0	0
0	1	1	1
1	0	0	1
1	0	1	1
1	1	0	0
1	1	1	0

The first step is to copy the outputs into the cells of a three-variable Karnaugh map, using the inputs to identify the cells as follows:

$$A = 0 \quad B = 0 \quad C = 0 \quad \text{is} \quad \overline{A} \cdot \overline{B} \cdot \overline{C}$$
$$A = 0 \quad B = 0 \quad C = 1 \quad \text{is} \quad \overline{A} \cdot \overline{B} \cdot C \quad \text{etc.}$$

This gives:

	$\overline{A} \cdot \overline{B}$	$\overline{A} \cdot B$	$A \cdot B$	$A \cdot \overline{B}$
$\overline{C}$	0	0	0	1
C	1	1	0	1

A Boolean expression for this operation as a sum of products is the terms which have a 1 in their map cells:

$$D = A \cdot \overline{B} \cdot \overline{C} + \overline{A} \cdot \overline{B} \cdot C + \overline{A} \cdot B \cdot C + A \cdot \overline{B} \cdot C$$

Simplifying the expression is done by grouping the adjacent cells containing 1s. A single term is written for each group, containing the variables which are constant within the group, and leaving out the variable(s) which change in value within the group. The left group in the above table contains a change in the value of B, with A and C constant. The right group has A and B constant, and a change in C. The simplified expression is:

$$D = \overline{A} \cdot C + A \cdot \overline{B}$$

Example 2

Obtain and simplify the Boolean expression for the following operation table:

Inputs				Output
A	B	C	D	E
0	0	0	0	0
0	0	0	1	0
0	0	1	0	0
0	0	1	1	0
0	1	0	0	0
0	1	0	1	1
0	1	1	0	0
0	1	1	1	1
1	0	0	0	1
1	0	0	1	0
1	0	1	0	1
1	0	1	1	0
1	1	0	0	0
1	1	0	1	1
1	1	1	0	0
1	1	1	1	1

Filling in a four-variable Karnaugh map gives the following:

	$\overline{A}\cdot\overline{B}$	$\overline{A}\cdot B$	$A\cdot B$	$A\cdot\overline{B}$
$\overline{C}\cdot\overline{D}$	0	0	0	1
$\overline{C}\cdot D$	0	1	1	0
$C\cdot D$	0	1	1	0
$C\cdot\overline{D}$	0	0	0	1

An expression for the operation table as a sum of products is:

$$E = A\cdot\overline{B}\cdot\overline{C}\cdot\overline{D} + \overline{A}\cdot B\cdot\overline{C}\cdot D + A\cdot B\cdot\overline{C}\cdot D + \overline{A}\cdot B\cdot C\cdot D + A\cdot B\cdot C\cdot D + A\cdot\overline{B}\cdot C\cdot\overline{D}$$

To simplify the expression, the cells containing 1s are grouped. The wraparound property of the table means that there are in fact only two groups, as shown above. In the first group of four cells, the variables A and C change value, while B and D remain constant. In the second group, the variable C changes, while A, B and D remain constant. Accordingly, the simplified expression is

$$E = B\cdot D + A\cdot\overline{B}\cdot\overline{D}$$

Karnaugh maps may be used for up to six input variables, after which more sohpisticated computer-based techniques are necessary.

6.9 Conclusion

This chapter has introduced the operations which form the basis of all processing done by computers. Ways of combining these operations have been demonstrated, together with some ways of simplifying these combinations. In the process, some of the properties of logic operations have been noted.

The concepts which have been introduced here form the basis of the next few chapters of this book. These chapters cover some of the more important logic circuits used in computers, and how the structure of a computer is built up from these circuits.

The most important points of this chapter are as follows:

- The theoretical basis for the operation of computers is Boolean logic. It consists of a number of operations which can be applied to Boolean or logical variables, having two states only.
- Boolean operations can be represented by symbols in Boolean algebra, logic circuits, in which they appear as gates, or operation tables.
- All logic operations can be expressed as a combination of the elementary operations AND, OR and NOT. However, three other operations, NAND, NOR and non-equivalence, are in common use.
- Logic expressions can be simplified, in order to reduce the number of operations, or use only certain operations, while still achieving the same results.

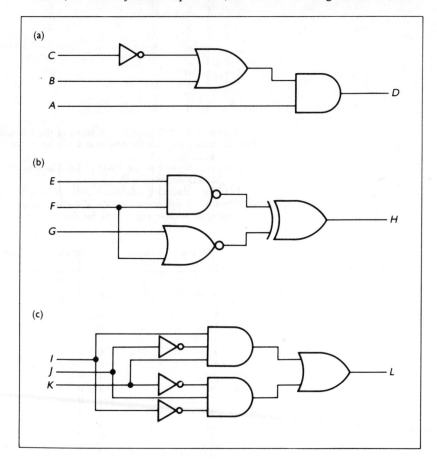

Figure 6.17
Logic circuit exercises

Exercise 6

1 Briefly define the following terms: Boolean logic; Boolean variable; operation table; logic circuit; Boolean algebra; Boolean operation; gate; sum of products; Karnaugh map.

2 Draw the truth tables for three-input AND, OR, NAND and NOR gates.

3 Summarise the connection between two-state representation of data and Boolean logic.

4 a) Write Boolean expressions for each of the logic circuits in Figure 6.17.
  b) Obtain the operation table for each of these logic circuits.

5 Draw logic circuits for each of the following Boolean expressions:

$$V = \overline{K \cdot L}, \qquad\qquad W = \overline{K} \cdot L, \qquad\qquad X = P \cdot Q + \overline{P} \cdot R$$

$$Y = A \cdot (B + C), \qquad\qquad\qquad Z = (D + E) \cdot (\overline{D} + F)$$

● **6** Express the exclusive OR operation in terms of AND, OR and NOT operations.

7 a) Draw logic circuits for each of the following Boolean expressions:

$$K = \overline{A} + \overline{B}, \qquad L = (C + \overline{D}) \cdot (C + \overline{E}), \qquad M = (P \cdot (\overline{Q \cdot R})) + (P \cdot (Q \cdot R))$$

  b) Simplify these expressions to reduce the number of operations they contain.
  c) Draw logic circuits for the simplified expressions.

● **8** Write a Boolean expression and draw a logic circuit for the following operation table:

Input			Output
A	B	C	D
0	0	0	0
0	0	1	0
0	1	0	0
0	1	1	1
1	0	0	1
1	0	1	0
1	1	0	0
1	1	1	0

9 Express the AND operation in terms of the OR and NOT operations.

●**10** a) Draw a diagram to show how a two-input NAND gate can be used as a NOT gate.
  b) Hence show how the AND and OR operations can be expressed in terms of the NAND operation only.
  c) What conclusion can you draw from these results?

●**11** Draw Karnaugh maps for each of the following operation tables, and obtain simplified Boolean expressions for them.

a)

Inputs			Output
A	B	C	D
0	0	0	1
0	0	1	0
0	1	0	1
0	1	1	0
1	0	0	0
1	0	1	1
1	1	0	0
1	1	1	1

b)

Inputs				Output
A	B	C	D	E
0	0	0	0	0
0	0	0	1	0
0	0	1	0	0
0	0	1	1	0
0	1	0	0	1
0	1	0	1	1
0	1	1	0	1
0	1	1	1	1
1	0	0	0	0
1	0	0	1	1
1	0	1	0	0
1	0	1	1	1
1	1	0	0	0
1	1	0	1	0
1	1	1	0	0
1	1	1	1	0

c)

Inputs				Output
A	B	C	D	E
0	0	0	0	1
0	0	0	1	0
0	0	1	0	1
0	0	1	1	0
0	1	0	0	0
0	1	0	1	1
0	1	1	0	0
0	1	1	1	0
1	0	0	0	1
1	0	0	1	0
1	0	1	0	1
1	0	1	1	0
1	1	0	0	0
1	1	0	1	0
1	1	1	0	0
1	1	1	1	1

7

Artificial
Intelligence

Ever since computers were first thought of, there has been research, discussion and speculation about the extent to which computers may be regarded as intelligent. In spite of all these efforts, there has been very little progress in resolving the problem. Nevertheless, fifth generation computers, which are planned for the 1990s, are being designed to incorporate a much higher level of intelligence than those in use at present. The question of machine intelligence has now become very important.

Underlying the question of artificial intelligence is a serious difficulty: our knowledge of human intelligence is not clear enough to provide a firm basis for ideas of artificial intelligence. For this reason, there is no generally accepted definition of the term 'artificial intelligence'.

7.1 Notions of Intelligence

It is quite possible to set out an approximate scale of intelligence: most people are more intelligent than most chimpanzees, a word processor is a more intelligent machine than a typewriter, etc. Nevertheless there is no scientific definition of intelligence. Intelligence is related to the ability to recognise patterns, draw reasoned conclusions, analyse complex systems into simple elements and resolve contradictions, yet it is more than all of these. Intelligence is at a higher level than information and knowledge, but below the level of wisdom. It contains an indefinable 'spark' which enables new insights to be gained, new theories to be formulated and new knowledge to be established.

Intelligence can also be examined from the point of view of language. Information can easily be represented as words, numbers or some other symbols. Knowledge is generally expressed in a language or as mathematics. Intelligence is at the upper limit of language: instances of patterns or deductive reasoning can be written down, and certain general principles can be stated. However, the creative 'spark' of intelligence is almost impossible to express in language.

7.2 Machine Intelligence

The only widely accepted definition of artificial intelligence is based on a test devised by Alan Turing in 1950:

> **Suppose there are two identical terminals in a room, one connected to a computer, and the other operated remotely by a person. If someone using the two terminals is unable to decide which is connected to the computer, and which is operated by the person, then the computer can be credited with intelligence.**

The definition of artificial intelligence which follows from this test is:

> **Artificial intelligence is the science of making machines do things that would require intelligence if done by people.**

No computer system has come anywhere near to passing the Turing test in general terms. Nevertheless, progress has been made in a number of specific fields. It would take a very good chess player in the 1980s to be able to tell whether he or she were playing against a computer or a human opponent. Most car drivers are unaware which parts of their cars have been assembled by robots, and which by manual workers.

7.3 Knowledge Representation

Conventional data processing is based on information; artificial intelligence is based on knowledge. A central problem for artificial intelligence is an adequate representation of knowledge on a computer. On the one hand, the representation must be 'rich' enough to be of practical use. On the other hand, it must be simple enough for processing by a computer.

The Three Levels of Knowledge Representation

The method of knowledge representation which has been most sucessful is to use three levels. At the lowest level are **associations** between objects. For example 'smoking is a cause of lung cancer', generally written as follows:

```
cause-of (smoking, lung-cancer).
```

Associations of this form are known as **propositions** in knowledge-based systems. The relations themselves (such as 'cause-of') are known as **predicates**.

The second level of representation of knowledge is sets of **rules** which connect propositions. For example:

```
If cause-of (x,y) and practices (z,x) then risk-of
    (z,y)
```

which means that if x is a cause of disease y, and person z practices x, then z is at risk of y.

Rules of this nature may be manipulated by a set of general **rules of inference**, such as:

```
If A is true and B is true then (A and B) is true.
```

The problem, in any particular situation, is to know in what sequence to apply the rules of inference to the given set of rules. This gives rise to the third level of representation of knowledge on a computer: a **strategy** to control the application of the rules of inference to the particular rules in any situation. Development of effective control strategies has been one of the most difficult problems facing researchers in artificial intelligence.

There have been two approaches to this problem. One has been to look for general methods, which apply to large numbers of situations. This has led, amongst other things, to the development of the Prolog programming language (Section 19.8). The other has been to develop strategies which are applicable in certain areas. This approach has been behind the development of expert systems (Chapter 31).

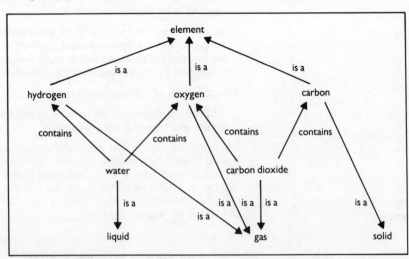

Figure 7.1
A semantic network

Semantic Networks

A technique of knowledge representation which is widely used is **semantic networks**. As shown in Figure 7.1, a semantic network shows a set of relationships between objects. It is a flexible method of representation, allowing new objects and new relationships to be added to a knowledge base. Accordingly, semantic networks are often used in computer systems which have some form of learning capacity.

Frames

More formal than semantic networks is the idea of a **frame** to represent a related set of information. A frame, shown in Figure 7.2, contains a set of related data itmes, together with certain properties of the items. For example, a frame may contain the range of possible values of a data item. In some cases a frame may include the formula for the calculation of the value of a data item. A frame may also contain pointers to other frames.

Production Rules

A popular method of expressing the rules which specify how new knowledge is derived from existing knowledge is the use of **production rules**. These are sequences of rules of the form:

```
if <condition> then <action>
```

An empty frame for chemical compounds

Name:	compound
Element-1:	element-name
Element-2:	element-name
Element-3:	element-name
Type:	range (solid, liquid, gas)

Figure 7.2
A frame

A frame for a particular compound

Name:	water
Element-1:	hydrogen
Element-2:	oxygen
Element-3:	-
Type:	liquid

Figure 7.2
continued

which are applied according to some strategy. For example, a set of rules to control a robot fitting car door handles could be as follows:

```
If <car in position> and <got handle> then <fit
  handle>.
If not <got handle> then <pick up handle>.
If not <handle fits> then <report and stop>.
If not <found handle> then <report and stop>.
```

The rules are repeatedly checked, and if the condition for any one is true, then the corresponding action takes place.

7.4 Game Playing Programs

Much of the progress in artificial intelligence has come through work on game playing programs. Games such as chess have the advantage of being simple enough to represent on a computer, while requiring a high level of intelligence on the part of the player. A number of successful strategies for playing games have been worked out. They are all based on searching a large number of possible moves and counter-moves, and selecting the best one to make. In some games, such as noughts and crosses, it is possible to search right through to the end of the game for each possible next move. In other games, notably chess, this is not possible, as the number of moves is too large even for the most powerful computer. The best chess programs achieve the right balance between the breadth of the search (the number of possible moves investigated), the depth of the search (the number of consequent moves investigated for each possibility) and the way of assessing the favourability of the moves.

Many of the methods used for game playing programs are being transferred to other fields of artificial intelligence.

7.5 Reasoning Programs

Reasoning programs have been used to solve the kind of pattern recognition problems found in intelligence tests, and to solve problems in formal logic. An example of programs of this sort is the use of a computer to assist in the proof of the **Four Colour Theorem**. It has been known for centuries that no more than four colours are needed to colour in any map, so that no two adjacent zones have the same colours. See Figure 7.3. This theorem was finally proved with the aid of a computer program in 1976.

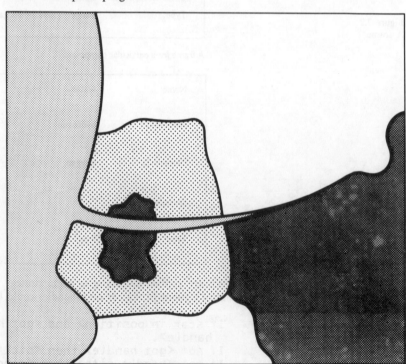

Figure 7.3
The Four Colour Theorem

7.6 Natural Language Recognition

One of the conclusions reached in Chapter 1 is that computers cannot interpret continuous passages in a natural language. Nevertheless, computers can cope with individual words and phrases, and longer passages of natural language in specific topics. A major topic of artificial intelligence research has been the recognition of natural language by computer. There are two aspects of this work: **syntax** and **semantics**.

Natural languages are composed of structures such as sentences, which are constructed according to rules of syntax. For example, the sentence:

`The boy stood on the burning deck`

can be analysed (or parsed) as:

`<subject> <verb> <object>`

where <subject> ('the boy') can be further parsed as

`<article> <noun> etc.`

The problem with syntax analysis is that the rules for sentence construction are very complex, there are many exceptions, and the rules are gradually modified as languages evolve.

In order to understand a passage in a natural language, the **semantics** or meaning of the piece must be studied. This depends on the context and what has been said before, as well as the meanings of individual words. Semantics is very difficult. In some cases an alternative interpretation of a single word can alter the meaning of a whole passage.

Computer programs have been devised which will cope with the syntax and semantics of complete sentences, but only within limited contexts. Even for these restricted situations, the programs are very complex. However, if current research into fifth generation computers is successful, systems with a much more powerful natural language capability will be available during the 1990s.

7.7 Image Recognition

Although computers can construct complex graphics displays, far less progress has been made with problem of interpreting visual information, supplied, for example, by a video camera. Image processing is an important computer application in its own right, and also as an interface for a number of other applications, notably robots.

The commenest approach to this problem has been to construct sets of general rules for the interpretation of visual patterns, and apply these to various situations. Most systems start by identifying the boundaries of the objects (a much more difficult task than it first appears), and then deducing their shape and other properties. Programs have been developed which will decide correctly, in most cases, whether the silhouette of a person is that of a man or a woman, and identify blocks of various shapes. Research is being directed towards a visual capability for robots which will enable them too 'see' where to position themselves, and to distinguish between the objects they are manipulating.

7.8 Expert Systems

The most successful aspect of artificial intelligence has been expert systems. An expert system is a computer program which matches the level of human expertise in a particular field. Expert systems are a product of the line of research which has concentrated on transferring specific aspects of human intelligence to computers. Expert systems are one of the main application areas of fifth generation computers, and are discussed further in Chapter 31.

7.9 Conclusion

In spite of many difficulties, progress has been made in certain aspects of artificial intelligence. In particular, it has proved possible to transfer a measure of intelligence from person to computer in specific fields. One of the biggest challenges to be overcome, before major breakthroughs are possible, is the automation of human common sense. The rate of progress in artificial intelligence is likely to accelerate in the next few years, in view of the importance of the work in the development of fifth generation computers.

The main points of this chapter are as follows:

- One of the most serious problems of artificial intelligence is the lack of a precise understanding of human intelligence.
- Intelligence can be placed in a scale: information, knowledge, intelligence and wisdom.
- Language and mathematics can cope with information and knowledge, but only to some extent with intelligence.
- A widely accepted test for artificial intelligence is the Turing test:

  Suppose there are two identical terminals in a room, one connected to a computer, and the other operated remotely by a person. If someone using the two terminals is unable to decide which is connected to the computer, and which is operated by the person, then the computer can be credited with intelligence.

- A definition of artificial intelligence is as follows:

  Artificial intelligence is the science of making machines do things that would require intelligence if done by people.

- The commonest way of representing knowledge on a computer is in terms of three levels:

  associations between objects (propositions)

  rules which relate propositions and higher level rules known as rules of inference

  strategies for applying rules.

- Advances in artificial intelligence have been made in game playing programs, reasoning programs, natural language recognition, image recognition and expert systems.

Exercise 7

1 Briefly define each of the following terms: artificial intelligence; proposition; predicate; rule of inference; syntax; semantics; parse; expert system.
2 a) Place the following tasks in ascending order of the intelligence (in your view) required to perform them:
   Calculating a weekly wage.
   Formulating the economic policy for a country.
   Reading road signs.
   Selecting the right size nut for a particular bolt.
   Choosing a meal from a menu.
   Deciding which car to buy for a particular purpose.
   Interpreting the instructions from an air traffic controller.
   b) Compare your ordering with those of others, and discuss the reasons for the differences.
   c) Which of the above tasks can be carried out entirely by computers at present?

    d) Which of the above tasks can be carried out with the assistance of computers at present?

    e) In your view, how will the answers to parts c) and d) change over the next ten years?

3 Given the following propositions:

likes (John, Fred)
likes (Susan, John)
likes (John, Helen)
likes (Helen, Jean)

and the rule

if likes (x, y) and likes (y, z) then likes (x, z)

what new propositions can be generated by applying the rule to the given propositions?

4 a) Comment on the different meanings of the word 'saw' in the following sentence:

    When he saw the red light, he saw that he had to stop.

    b) Collect as many other sentences or pairs of sentences as you can in which the same word is used with different meanings.

    c) Comment on the significance of your findings for natural language recognition by computer.

5 The instructions given by the person in charge of a ship are an example of the use of a small subset of natural language in a practical situation. All the statements have precisely defined meanings. List other such situations, and in each case state whether a computer could be usefully employed to generate or interpret some or all of the statements.

6 List some potential applications of robots with some form of visual perception.

8

Logic Circuits

This is the first chapter in the part of the book concerned with computer hardware. It examines some of the essential processing circuits inside a computer. The electronic components of these circuits are briefly considered, but the emphasis is on their logical structure and properties. The circuit designs presented here are independent of any actual computer, but form the basis of the circuits commonly used.

This chapter relates closely to a number of other chapters. It is an application of the theory of Boolean logic introduced in Chapter 6. The logic gates introduced in that chapter are used extensively here. This chapter also relates to earlier chapters on data representation and computer arithmetic. Many of the circuits introduced here show how ideas from these chapters are put into practice. Finally, this chapter paves the way for the rest of this part of the book, which is a study of various aspects of computer hardware.

8.1   Hardware Implementation of Logic Operations

A Boolean variable is one which can take on the values 0 and 1 only, and Boolean operations manipulate variables of this nature. It turns out that solid-state electronic components can be made to behave like Boolean operations. The 'variables' which they manipulate are voltages. In many, but not all, cases, a high voltage represents the value 1, and a low, or zero, voltage represents the value 0. The devices which carry out these operations are solid-state integrated circuits, commonly known as chips.

Transistors

You will recall from Chapter 6 that a logic operation can be regarded as a gate. The most general gate combines one or more inputs to produce a single output. Its behaviour is governed by a truth table.

A **transistor** is an electronic component with three connections. These can be arranged so that two are for input and one is for output. Furthermore, the behaviour of the transistor, or a simple combination of transistors, can be made to correspond to the truth table of the gate. This is the basis of the way in which logic circuits are constructed. Figure 8.1 shows a logic gate and a transistor.

Integrated Circuits

For about ten years, from 1955 to 1965, the logic circuits of computers were made from individual transistors for logic gates, as described above. Then it was realised that circuits could be constructed containing a number of transistors and other components as a single, solid-state unit. These **integrated circuits** perform the function of a large number of logic gates. The principle on which they work is, however, the same as that for an individual transistor.

The design of integrated circuits has evolved through several stages. The first integrated circuits were equivalent to approximately ten transistors. Then came **medium scale integration (MSI)**, with hundreds of components on one chip. Today we are moving from the era of **large scale integration (LSI)**, with thousands or tens of thousands of components on one chip, and entering the phase of **very large scale integration (VLSI)**, with hundreds of thousands or millions of individual elements on a chip. Single chips can contain large portions of computer memories, or all the processing circuits of a computer. The latter type of chip is called a **microprocessor**. The most recent type of chip, the **transputer**, combines processor, memory and input/output channels on a single very fast chip.

There are several reasons for the rapid acceptance of very large scale integrated circuits. These chips are small, consume very little electrical energy (and therefore do not produce much heat), and are very reliable. However, the overriding consideration is cost. As the capabilities of individual chips have increased, their costs have continued to decrease.

The logic circuits introduced in this chapter are explained in terms of Boolean

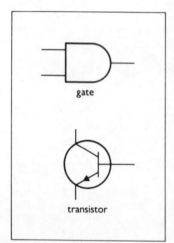

gate

transistor

Figure 8.1
A gate and a transistor

operations. Most of them are implemented as parts of processor or memory chips.

Gate Delay

One property of integrated circuits must be mentioned at this point. This is that, after the input voltages have been altered, there is a delay before the output voltage stabilises at its new value. This property is called **gate delay**. It is one of the factors which limits the speed of the computer, and it affects the design of logic circuits.

8.2 Control Switches

Data, addresses and control signals are sent from place to place inside a computer by means of data **channels**, also known as data **buses**. Data channels are parallel connections, with one path for each bit of the data item. **Control switches** regulate the flow of data in a channel. A control switch is opened to allow a data item to pass, or closed to block the passage of the data.

A control switch uses a set of AND gates, one for each bit of the data item, arranged in parallel. Figure 8.2 shows a four bit control switch. Each AND gate has one input from the data channel, and one from the common control input.

A control switch works in the following manner. If the control input is 0, then all outputs are 0, no matter what the data inputs are. The switch is open, and no data passes. However, if the control input is 1, then each output has the same value as the corresponding data input. This can be checked from the operation table of an AND gate. The switch is closed, and data passes along the channel.

All computers contain a large number of control switches of this type. They regulate the flow of data between the functional circuits, and into and out of the storage elements.

8.3 Masks

More general-purpose than a control switch, but still using parallel AND gates, is a **mask** circuit. It can be imagined as a set of control switches, with a separate switch for each bit of the data. Figure 8.3 shows a four bit mask circuit.

The purpose of a mask is to select certain bits of a data item, and 'mask out' the remaining bits. If a particular bit of the data item is required, then the corresponding control input is set to 1. If the bit is to be masked out, then the corresponding control input is set to 0. The operation table of an AND gate can be used to verify this. The control input is sometimes referred to as a mask. For example, if the three most significant bits of an eight bit data item are required, then a mask of 11100000 is used.

8.4 Decoders

A **decoder** is a circuit which selects one of a number of outputs according to the code of an input data item. Working in base ten for a moment, the principle is as follows: if there are 20 outputs, then an input number between 1 and 20 will cause the corresponding output to be selected. For example, the number 13 will cause the thirteenth output to be selected.

The decoder shown in Figure 8.4 has two inputs and four outputs. The outputs may be numbered (in binary) 00, 01, 10 and 11. The circuit works in such a way that any binary number input will cause the output with the corresponding number to be selected. Figure 8.5 shows the number 10 causing the output numbered 10 to be selected.

The decoders used in most computers contain more inputs and far more outputs than those illustrated here. They are used to locate memory cells (where

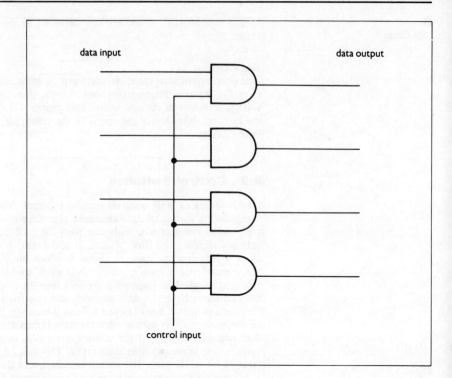

Figure 8.2
A four bit control switch

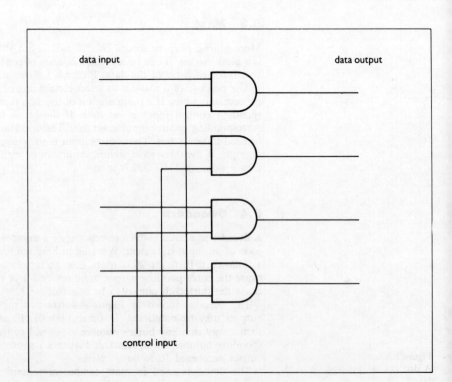

Figure 8.3
A four bit mask circuit

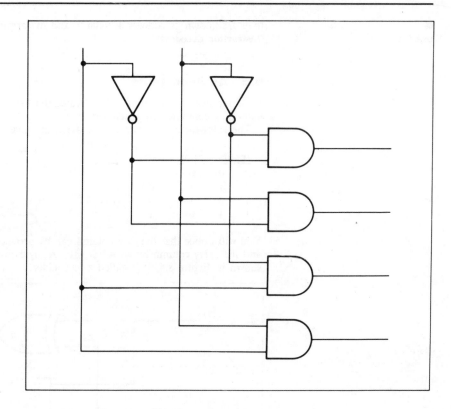

Figure 8.4
A decoder

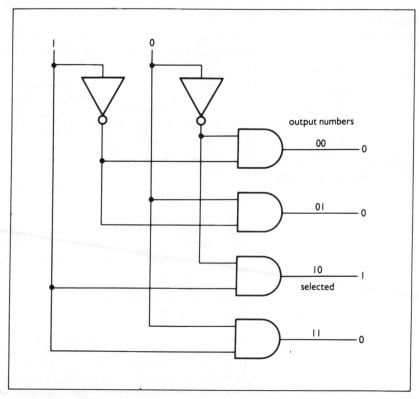

Figure 8.5
A decoder in operation

they are known as **address decoders**), and in carrying out program instructions (**instruction decoders**).

8.5 Addition Units

All computers do addition by hardware: the logic circuits forming the **addition units** of a computer are discussed in this section.

The rules for adding two binary digits are given in the following table:

Inputs		Sum	Carry
0	0	0	0
0	1	1	0
1	0	1	0
1	1	0	1

You will notice that the sum column can be produced by an exclusive OR gate, and the carry column by an AND gate. A logic circuit containing these gates is shown in Figure 8.6. It is called a **half adder**.

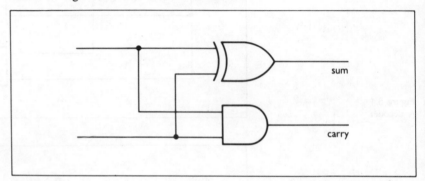

Figure 8.6
A half adder

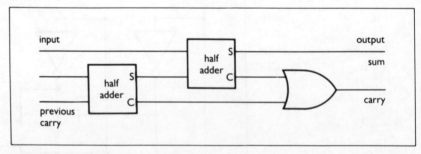

Figure 8.7
A full adder made from two half adders

If two complete binary numbers are added, the carry from the previous column must also be taken into account. A **full adder** is a circuit which adds two bits, together with a previous carry, to produce a sum and a carry. A full adder may be constructed from two half adders, as shown in Figure 8.7, or it may be implemented directly. This latter method is discussed in the exercise at the end of the chapter.

There are two approaches to adding complete binary numbers. One is to have a full adder to each pair of bits. All the additions take place at the same time. A circuit of this type is called a **parallel adder**, shown in Figure 8.8. The other (less common) method is to add one pair of bits at a time. This gives rise to a **serial adder**, which is discussed in the exercise at the end of the chapter.

Returning to the parallel adder for a moment, Figure 8.8 shows that a parallel adder has a **carry out** and a **carry in**. The carry out is the same as the carry bit discussed in Chapters 3 and 5. The carry in is very useful, as it enables a number to be increased by 1. One application of this which has already been discussed is the process of obtaining the twos complement of a number, by negating the bits and then adding 1. Figure 8.9 shows a combined addition/subtraction unit based on this principle.

As mentioned in Section 8.1, there is a delay associated with data passing through each logic gate in a circuit. Although the circuits in Figure 8.8 operate in parallel, a carry might have to be passed across all the full adders in the circuit. This involves a considerable delay, and addition is not quite 'in parallel'. To minimise this delay, some parallel adders include **carry prediction circuits**, which determine the value of each carry directly from the inputs.

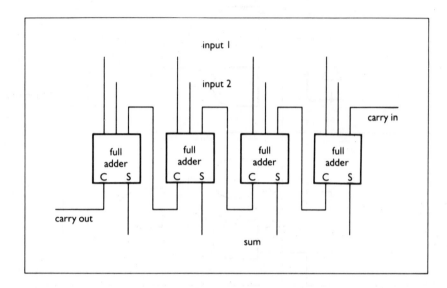

Figure 8.8
A four bit parallel adder

8.6 Flip-Flops

The logic circuits introduced up to now are all concerned with the processing of data. Attention is now focused on an important class of circuits used to **store** data. Storage circuits differ from processing circuits in one important respect. The output of a processing circuit is completely determined by the state of its inputs at the time (the name **combinational** logic is used to describe this property). However, the output of a storage circuit is determined by its inputs and also its previous output state. This is because storage circuits always contain connections which 'feed back' from output to input. Circuits whose output depends on past states are called **serial** logic circuits.

Several types of storage circuits are used in computers. Two of the commonest ones are discussed here; a further type is introduced in the exercise at the end of the chapter.

RS Flip-Flop

The simplest storage circuit is called an **RS flip-flop** or **bistable**. One way of constructing it is to use two NOR gates, connected as shown in Figure 8.10. Notice how the outputs are 'fed back' into the inputs.

This circuit has acquired its name because it can be made to 'flip' from one stable output to the other by a signal at the inputs. One input is called the **set** input, the other is called the **reset** input. The two outputs are always in opposite states, hence their labels Q and Q'.

The operation table for an RS flip-flop is given below. It shows the current output Q in terms of the inputs R and S, and the previous value of Q.

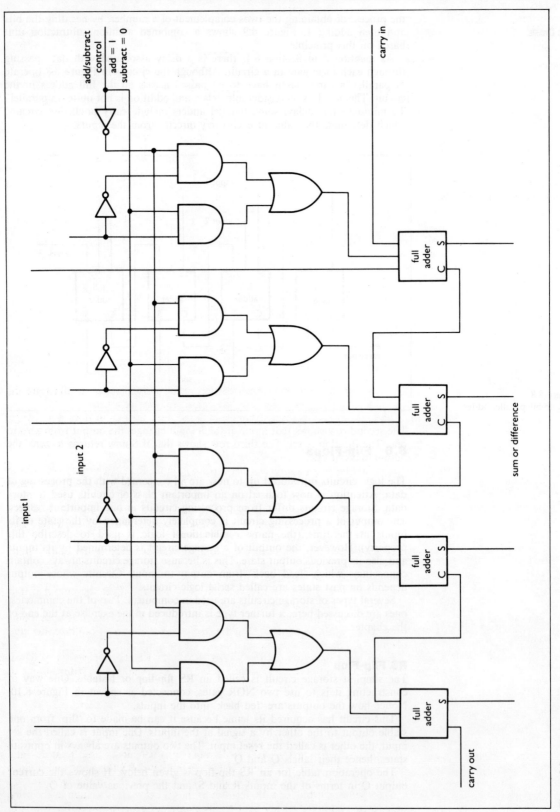

Figure 8.9
A four bit combined addition/subtraction unit

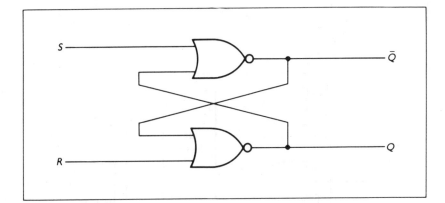

Figure 8.10
An RS flip-flop made from two
NOR gates

R	S	previous Q	current Q
0	0	0	0
0	1	0	1
0	0	1	1
1	0	1	0
0	0	0	0
1	0	0	0
0	1	1	1
1	1	0	0 or 1
1	1	1	0 or 1

The rows of the table have been written in an unusual order, to illustrate the way the circuit is used. The rows are considered one at a time.

The first row shows that if both inputs are zero, the output does not change. The second row shows that a one at the S input changes the output from zero to one. The flip-flop is set. The third row shows that if S now returns to zero, the output stays at one.

The first three rows indicate that a **pulse** at input S, i.e. a change from zero to one and back to zero, causes the output to flip from zero to one **and stay there**. In other words, the pulse at S is 'remembered'.

Rows 3, 4 and 5 of the table illustrate the reverse process. Row 3 shows the circuit in the set state. If input R becomes one, as shown in the fourth row, then the output changes from one to zero. The fifth row, which is a copy of the first row, shows that input R can return to zero without affecting the output state. These rows show that a pulse from R causes the output to flip from one to zero **and stay there**. The flip-flop is reset.

The next two rows show that a pulse at R will not affect the output if it is already zero, and a pulse at S will not change the output if it is already one.

The last two rows show the problem associated with this circuit. If both inputs become one at the same time, then the output is not known. It can be either zero or one.

From this description of the way in which an RS flip-flop works, you will realise that it can be used to store one bit of data. A pulse at S causes a one to be stored, and a pulse at R causes a zero to be stored.

JK Flip-Flop

There are a number of problems associated with RS flip-flops, in particular the undefined state when both inputs are one. Accordingly, a more sophisticated circuit, known as a **master-slave** or **JK flip-flop** is commonly used to store data. See Figure 8.11. You will notice that it contains two RS flip-flops and a **clock input**. The clock input is used to control the timing of the storage of data.

The operation table for a JK flip-flop is shown below. It is written in the same order as the table for an RS flip-flop. The only difference between the two is in

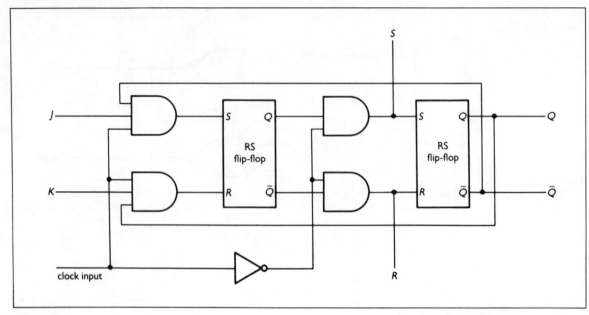

Figure 8.11
A JK flip-flop

the last two lines. For simplicity, the clock signal and the set (S) and reset (R) inputs are omitted.

K	J	previous Q	current Q
0	0	0	0
0	1	0	1
0	0	1	1
1	0	1	0
0	0	0	0
1	0	0	0
0	1	1	1
1	1	0	1
1	1	1	0

RS and JK flip-flops are not the only circuits used to store data on computers. However, all data storage circuits have the proerty that a pulse at one input causes the output to change from one state to the other and stay there. All computers use large numbers of data storage circuits.

8.7 Registers

Several data storage circuits may be combined to form a **register**, which stores a complete data item. Figure 8.12 shows one arrangement of a register. Notice how all the bits can be cleared from one input, and how the storage of input data is timed by a clock input.

Most computers contain a number of registers to store, among other things, data items which are currently being processed, and instructions which are currently being carried out.

Shift Registers

A type of register which desrves special mention is a **shift register**. Such a register enables bits of a data item to be shifted from one position to the next. Figure 8.13 shows how a number of JK flip-flops can be combined to form a shift register. Every time the clock line is pulsed, each bit of the data item moves one place to the right.

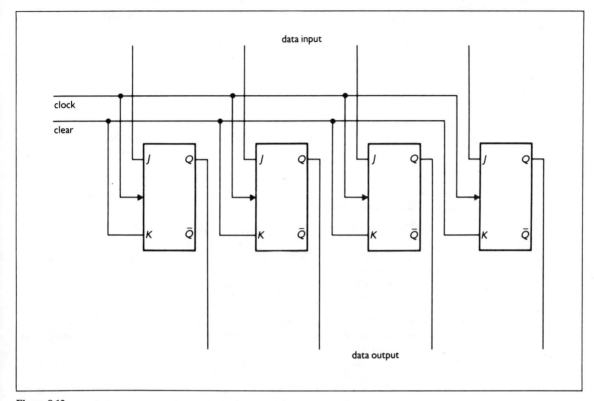

Figure 8.12
A four bit register made from JK
flip-flops

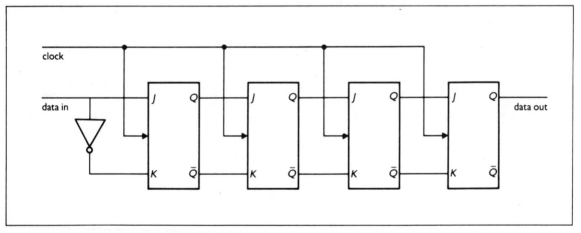

Figure 8.13
A four bit shift register made
from JK flip-flops

Shift registers have a number of uses. These include multiplication, division and serial addition, and accepting input from serial input devices. One significant application, known as a **USART**, is discussed in the exercise at the end of this chapter.

8.8 Uncommitted Logic Arrays

A type of chip which is becoming increasingly important is made up of a regular pattern of identical elements, such as NAND gates. (It can be proved that any logic operation can be carried out by a combination of NAND gates only, and similarly for NOR gates.) This arrangement of gates on a chip is known as an **uncommitted logic array (ULA)**. The connections between the gates are specified by the purchaser of the chip, and form a separate layer from those forming the processing elements. The chip is fabricated in two stages: first the array of processing elements, then the interconnections.

ULA chips enable small runs of special-purpose chips to be produced quickly and cheaply. They are used for particular processing operations, such as encoding and decoding signals for data communication. In many computers, the processing circuits for all the 'odd jobs' required are collected together and placed on a ULA chip. This reduces the size and price of the computer, and helps to improve reliability.

8.9 Conclusion

The most important points made in this chapter are as follows:

- The electronic components used to implement logic operations are integrated circuits or chips.
- Solid-state circuits have now reached the stage of very large-scale integration, including complete processors on a single chip, called microprocessors.
- Control switches regulate the flow of data on data channels.
- A mask is a logic circuit which selects certain bits in a data item.
- A decoder selects one of a number of outputs according to the code of an input data item.
- Addition is generally carried out by means of a parallel adder, containing a number of full adders which add pairs of bits.
- The basic storage element in a computer is a flip-flop, which has two stable output states. A signal at either of its inputs can cause it to flip from one state to another.
- A register is a storage element for a complete item of data.
- A shift register enables bits of a data item to be shifted from one position to the next.

Exercise 8

1 Briefly define the following terms: integrated circuit; microprocessor; gate delay; data channel; control switch; mask; decoder; full adder; parallel adder; bistable; register; shift register; uncommitted logic array; transputer.
2 The first, third and fifth bits (counting from the left) of an eight bit data item are to be examined. The remaining bits are not required.
  a) What arrangement of mask bits will enable this to be done?
  b) What is the result of masking the data item 11011010 in this way?
3 The decoder shown in Figure 8.4 has two inputs and four outputs.
  a) How many outputs does a three-input decoder have?
  b) How many outputs does an n-input decoder have?
  c) Design a three-input decoder similar to the one in Figure 8.4. Number the outputs from 000 to 111. Show how the input bit pattern 101 will cause the 101th output to be selected.
●4 a) Draw up the operation table for a full adder. Label the inputs A, B and C (for carry in), and the outputs S (sum) and T (carry out).
  b) Use this table to verify that the logic expressions for S and T are as follows:

$$S = A \cdot B \cdot C + A \cdot \overline{B} \cdot \overline{C} + \overline{A} \cdot B \cdot \overline{C} + \overline{A} \cdot \overline{B} \cdot C$$

$$T = A \cdot B + B \cdot C + A \cdot C$$

  c) Use the above expressions to design a logic circuit for S and one for T. The circuit for S requires three NOT gates, four three-input AND gates and one four-input OR gate. The circuit for T uses three two-input AND gates and one three-input OR gate.

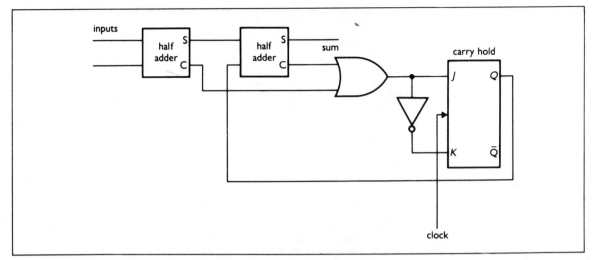

Figure 8.14
Part of a serial addition unit

● 5 Figure 8.14 shows the processing part of a serial addition unit. If two bits are supplied at the inputs, and the clock line at the carry hold flip-flop is pulsed, it will add the input bits and the previous carry, producing a sum bit and storing the carry bit in the carry hold. It is now ready to repeat the process for the next pair of bits.
  a) Connect three four-bit shift registers to this circuit, to supply the input numbers and store the sum. Draw a diagram showing the complete serial addition unit.
  b) Draw two extra connections onto your diagram, showing how a carry in and a carry out can be included.
● 6 At the beginning of this book, the concept of a **module** is introduced (Section 2.6). Although it has not been explicitly mentioned, this concept has been used a number of times in this chapter. Explain, with examples, how the concept of a module is used in the context of logic circuits.
  7 Combine two of the diagrams in this chapter to show how data can be passed from one register to another, using a control switch.
  8 A commonly used data storage element is the **D type flip-flop**. It has the following properties:
  i) Inputs are a single data line and a clock line.
  ii) A NOT gate and an RS flip-flop are used.
  iii) The flip-flop takes the value at its input when a clock pulse appears, and remains in the same state until the next clock pulse appears.
  iv) Outputs are the same as those for an RS flip-flop.
    From this information, draw a diagram of a D type flip-flop.
● 9 A circuit frequently used for serial input and output is a Universal Synchronous/ Asynchronous Receiver/Transmitter, or **USART**. It is a register which can be loaded with either serial or parallel data, and which will output either serial or parallel data.

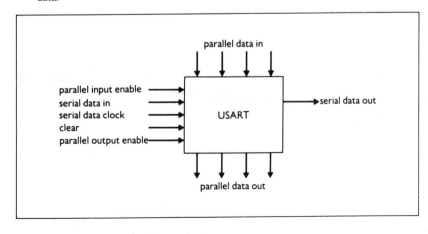

Figure 8.15
A USART

A 'black box' view of a four bit USART is shown in Figure 8.15. Notice that there are control signals for parallel data in and parallel data out, a clear signal and a clock signal for serial data in and out.

Using JK flip-flops, AND gates and a NOT gate, construct the internal circuits of this black box.

Hints: Use the S inputs of the flip-flop for parallel data in, and the R inputs for the clear signals. Also see Figures 8.12 and 8.13.

10 a) Explain what is meant by a truth table. Illustrate your answer by means of a truth table for the logical function NAND.

    b) Given a decimal integer in the range 0 to 127, construct either a logical function or a flow diagram to decide whether there are just three ones in the binary equivalent.

    c) Show why the logical function AND can be described as multiplication modulo two.

OLE 80 I

11 A **multiplexer** is a logic circuit with a number of data inputs, a number of control inputs and a single data output. Its purpose is to select a single data input which is copied to the data output.

Using the design of a four bit decoder (Figure 8.4) draw a logic circuit diagram of a four bit multiplexer. It has four data inputs, two control inputs and a data output. The binary number formed by the control inputs determines which data input is copied to the output. For example if the control inputs form the binary number 01 then the data item on the input labelled 01 is copied to the output.

9
Computer Structure

This chapter gives an overall view of the hardware of a computer system. The units making up typical computer configurations of various sizes are discussed. Brief descriptions of the functions of these units are given, and some problems arising from their different characteristics are mentioned.

It is worth remembering at this stage that a computer is a system, a collection of parts working towards some common objectives. This chapter considers a computer as a total system. It paves the way for later chapters which consider various parts of a computer, notably the processor, in more detail.

9.1 The Functional Units of a Computer

The definition of a computer given in Section 2.3 is as follows:

A computer is a collection of resources, including digital electronic processing devices, stored programs and sets of data, which, under the control of the stored programs, automatically inputs, outputs, stores, retrieves and processes the data, and may also transmit data to and receive it from other computers. A computer is capable of drawing reasoned conclusions from the processing it carries out.

From the hardware point of view, the essential features of this definition are 'a collection of . . . digital electronic processing devices'.

Computers vary enormously in size, processing power and cost. Nevertheless, all computers consist of one or more functional devices, each carrying out one or more of the tasks described above, and shown in Figure 9.1. Each device performs a precisely specified task, and connects to other modules via defined interfaces. Modules of the same type of computer may be exchanged, and new modules added, without modification to their internal workings. The phrase **plug-compatible** describes units which may be connected in this manner.

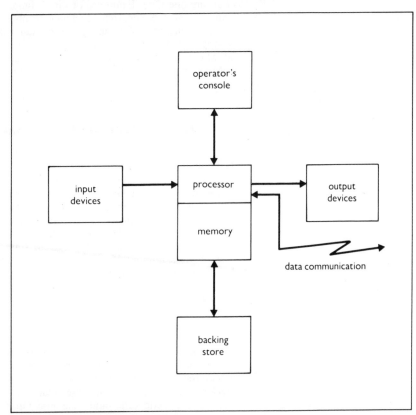

Figure 9.1
The general structure of a computer

The modules which make up typical computer configurations of various sizes are now discussed. It must be emphasised that these configurations are no more than convenient examples. In practice there is a continuous variation in size and complexity from very small to very large systems.

9.2 Mainframes, Minis and Micros

Very broadly speaking, there are three classes of computers, according to their size and complexity. These classes are known as **mainframes**, **minicomputers** (or **minis**) and **microcomputers** (or **micros**).

Mainframes are large computers, comprising a number of free-standing units. Mainframes are generally housed in specially designed, air-conditioned rooms. Connections between the units are made by wires running beneath the floor of the room. Mainframes are very powerful, and support a number of applications running concurrently. Examples of mainframes are the ICL 2900 series, the IBM 3000 series and the Burroughs B6700 series. Very large mainframes are known as **supercomputers**. These include the Cyber 205 and the Cray 2.

Minicomputers are smaller than mainframes, with several functional devices mounted in a rack in a single unit. Minicomputers do not generally require an air-conditioned environment. They are often to be found in laboratories, factories and offices. Minicomputers can support more than one application running concurrently, though not as many as mainframes. The Digital Equipment Vax series is the most popular minicomputer. Others are made by Prime, Data General and Hewlett Packard.

Microcomputers are the newest addition to the computer family. They are small and cheap, and are (generally) contained in a few small units. Their distinguishing feature is that processing is carried out on a single microprocessor chip. Although they are very versatile, microcomputers can only support one application at any one time. Examples of microcomputers are the IBM PC, the Apple Macintosh and the Research Machines Nimbus.

The classification of computers into mainframes, minis and micros is only very approximate. Computers are getting smaller and more powerful all the time. Micros are being introduced with the capability of minis only a few years old. Minicomputers are incorporating microprocessors to assume the capability of mainframes.

9.3 A Typical Medium Sized Computer

Figure 9.2 shows the units of a typical medium sized computer, and the flow of data between them. The computer could be a small mainframe or large mini. The function of each type of unit is now discussed.

Processing of data takes place in the **central processing unit**, or **CPU**, now becoming more commonly known as a **processor**. This consists entirely of solid-state electronic components, in circuits such as those introduced in Chapter 8. Some processors, particularly in mainframes, have a **front panel** which contains switches and lights to indicate the current state of the processor. Linked to the processor are a number of **peripheral** devices.

Input devices supply data to the processor. Data is entered at a keyboard or read from a variety of media such as magnetic ink characters, optically read characters and bar codes, and sent in a binary code to the processor. Voice input is used on a few systems. **Output devices** print or display data from the processor. These include various types of printers, plotters and devices which reproduce data on microfilm. Synthesised speech output is beginning to be used.

Terminals are general-purpose input/output devices. They consist of a keyboard for input, and a display screen for output. They sometimes incorporate bar code readers. Terminals may be linked to the processor from long distances.

Backing store is storage of large quantities of data for rapid access by the processor. Magnetic disks and magnetic tapes are the most common storage

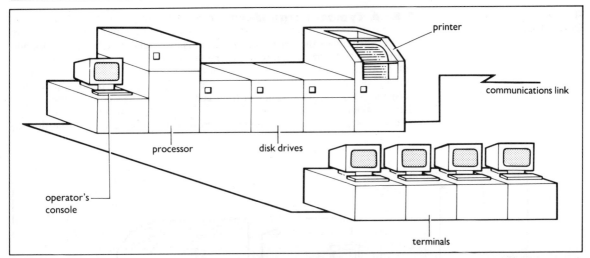

Figure 9.2
A medium sized computer

media. Optical disks are beginning to be used for backing store. **Data communications links** enable the computer to send data to, and receive data from other computers. The links may be local or long-distance via the telecommunications network. The **operator's console** allows the person operating the computer to interact with it. In appearance and structure it resembles a terminal.

Although it is made up of separate units, it must be remembered that a computer is a system. In other words, the individual units work together to achieve some common objectives. The step-by-step control of the system is in the hands of the processor. Overall control, however, rests with the person operating the computer.

9.4 A Microcomputer

Figure 9.3 shows the structure of a typical microcomputer. In some models, the units are separate, as shown in the diagram. In others, the processor and backing store or the processor and keyboard are combined in a single unit. Many micros are connected to a character printer.

Backing store media are small, flexible magnetic disks, called **floppy disks** or **diskettes**. In larger models, hard, high capacity Winchester disks are also used.

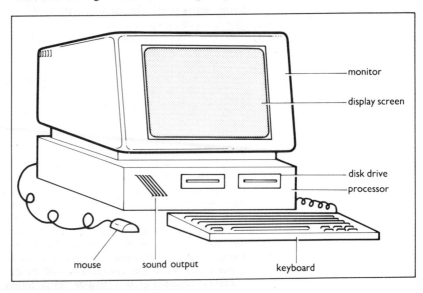

Figure 9.3
A microcomputer

9.5 A Typical Large Mainframe

At the other end of the scale, with processing power (and cost) tens of thousands of times that of a microcomputer, is the large mainframe system or supercomputer. As can be seen from Figure 9.4, supercomputers are characterised by multiple processing units, and a number of different types of peripheral devices.

At the centre of the system is a **front-end processor**. This controls the flow of data between the central processors and the various peripheral devices in the system. A separate **communications processor** is required to control the flow of

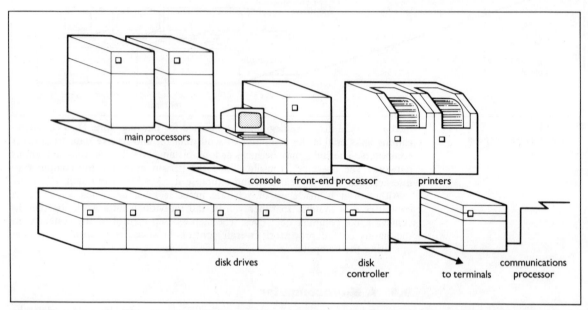

Figure 9.4
A large mainframe computer

data to and from the terminals and data communications links. There may be hundreds of terminals. A **backing store control** unit controls the passage of data to and from the various backing store units.

The front-end processor, communications processor and backing store control unit are powerful processors in their own right. They have facilities for storing a certain amount of data, routing data to the required channel, and transferring data from one code to another.

An essential unit in all mainframe computers, although it has no data links to other units, is an **uninterrupted power supply** unit. This device smooths the flow of electricity to the computer. It 'irons out' any fluctuations in voltage, and has batteries to ensure that there is no break in the electricity supply to the computer should there be a power failure. The batteries are sufficient to keep the computer going until standby generators can be started.

9.6 Conclusion

This chapter has introduced the overall structure of computers of various sizes. Various units making up the computers have been introduced, and their relationships to the rest of the system indicated. In the next six chapters, aspects of the devices introduced in this chapter are discussed in more detail.

Although these units are all part of the same system, it must be noted that they have very different operating characteristics, particularly with regard to speed. In general, processors are many times as fast as peripheral devices. This causes problems in the co-ordination of the devices in an efficient way.

The main points of this chapter are as follows:

- Computers consist of input, output, processing and backing store devices, and may include communications links.
- Computers can be roughly categorised as mainframes, minicomputers and microcomputers.
- The units of a computer are modular in design; many may be unplugged and replaced by more powerful versions in order to increase the capacity of the computer system as a whole.

Exercise 9

1 Briefly define the following terms: plug-compatible; peripheral; front-end processor; front panel; mainframe; minicomputer; microcomputer; supercomputer.
2 Discuss the concept of a module in relation to the structure of a computer system.
3 Extend the lists of mainframes, minis and micros quoted in Section 9.2.
4 Note the overall structure of one or more computers known to you. In each case, make a sketch of the units and their inter-connection, similar to the diagrams in this chapter.
5 It is becoming increasingly common for manufacturers to produce peripheral devices which are plug-compatible with processors made by other manufacturers. Find out the names of some companies producing such equipment, and discuss the advantages and disadvantages of this practice.

10
Processor Architecture

This chapter is concerned with the architecture of the processor of a computer. The objectives of a processor are discussed, together with various aspects of the structure of a typical processor. To simplify this discussion, a model computer, specially designed for this course, is used.

It must be mentioned at this point that the term 'processor' is not very precise. In some contexts it means the whole central processing unit of a computer, including the memory. In other cases, it means the processing circuits only. In other cases, it means one chip within a processing unit - a **microprocessor**.

10.1   Objectives of a Processor

The primary objective of a processor is to carry out the steps of a data processing task. In order to become familiar with the level at which a processor operates, this objective needs some clarification.

In Chapter 3 the point is made that data is a representation of information, in a binary code. You will also recall that data and instructions (also in a binary code) are stored together in a computer memory, and no distinction is made between them. Accordingly, a step of a data processing task involves the manipulation of one or more items of data, in a binary code, in response to an instruction, also in a binary code. The manipulation is carried out by logic circuits on individual bits of the data items. This, then, is the level at which a processor operates.

In addition to accomplishing its primary objective, a processor must work as quickly as possible, using as little electricity as possible, while avoiding errors and breakdowns. These objectives sound rather a tall order, but in practice they are attained to a remarkable extent. Thirty years of intensive research and development have led to processors which are fast, powerful, reliable, efficient and cheap. Nevertheless, the basic design principles of processors, formulated just after the Second World War, have, until very recently, remained the same. It is these design principles which are the subject matter of this chapter.

10.2   The Structure of a Processor

As explained in the previous chapter, computers come in all shapes and sizes. Although the design principles are similar in most cases, these principles are implemented in a variety of ways. It is therefore impossible to choose one computer as a representative, and discuss various features of the structure of its processor. To overcome this problem, a model computer has been designed, specifically for this course. It is used in this chapter to introduce the important features of a processor. It is also used in subsequent chapters, to help explain how a processor operates, and to introduce the program languages used to control a computer.

The following sections introduce the overall structure of a processor, using the model computer as an example.

10.3   A Model Computer - the AMC

The **A-level model computer**, or **AMC**, has been designed to assist in the teaching of a number of topics in this book, the first being processor architecture. The design of the AMC reflects a compromise between the requirements of Computing Science syllabuses and the features of a number of actual computers. Design principles are implemented in as straightforward a manner as possible.

In common with most processors, the AMC may be thought of as a number of functional units, connected by one or more **buses**, as well as control links. Figure 10.1 shows the overall block structure of the AMC. Control links are omitted for simplicity.

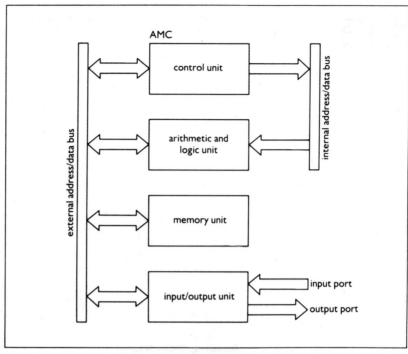

Figure 10.1
AMC block structure

A bus is a pathway along which data, address and control signals pass within a processor. The two buses in the AMC are both 16 bits wide, and are used for both data and addresses. The input and output ports are, however, 8 bits wide, as most input/output devices work in units of 8 bits.

The AMC is a **16 bit processor**. This means that all operations are performed on 16 bit quantities and internal transfers of data are in units of 16 bits. In the context of the AMC, a 16 bit quantity is called a **word**, and an 8 bit quantity a **byte**. The four functional units in Figure 10.1 each contain a number of **registers** (introduced in Section 8.7) and other logic circuits. Most of the registers are 16 bits wide, and most AMC logic circuits process 16 bit quantitiies in parallel.

10.4 The AMC Memory Unit

The AMC memory unit consists of the **memory address register**, **address decoder**, **main store** and **memory data register**. See Figure 10.2. The function of the memory unit is to store and retrieve data and instructions. The interface between the memory unit and the rest of the AMC is the external address/data bus.

The **main store** of the AMC is an **immediate access store**. The store is partitioned into a number of locations or **cells**, each of which is identified by a number called an **address**. Each location stores one byte. Given its address, any cell may be accessed immediately.

Like most AMC registers, the **memory address register** holds 16 bits. This means that there can be 2^{16} ($=65536$) distinct addresses - the **address space** of the AMC. A unit of memory size commonly used is the K unit, where $1K = 2^{10}$ $= 1024$. The AMC address space is $65536/1024 = 64K$ locations.

The 16 bit **memory data register** holds data during transfer to or from main store. Data may be stored or retrieved in units of bytes or words. A word occupies two consecutive store locations. The lower byte address is always used to locate a word.

The concept of addressing is fundamental to the way a computer works. Several techniques of addressing are used in the AMC. These are discussed in Chapter 12.

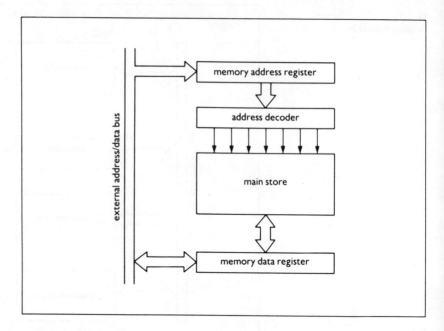

Figure 10.2
AMC memory unit

Reading from Store

When a data item is accessed, or **read from** main store, the following sequence of actions takes place:

1 The address of the data item is placed in the memory address register.
2 The address decoder accesses the store location addressed.
3 If a word is being read, the byte addressed by the memory address register is placed in the most significant half of the memory data register, and the byte at the next address is placed in the least significant half.
4 If a byte is being read, it occupies the least significant half of the memory data register, and the most significant half of the register is filled with copies of the most significant bit of the byte. This process is called **sign extension**.

Writing to Store

When a data item is placed in, or **written to** main store, the following sequence of actions takes place:

1 The address of the store location to be used is placed in the memory address register.
2 The data item is placed in the memory data register.
3 If a word is being written to store, the most significant byte of the memory data register is placed in the store cell addressed by the memory address register, and the least significant byte in the next store location.
4 If a byte is being written to store, it is taken from the least significant half of the memory data register.

A Memory Cycle

The sequence of actions for reading from or writing to store are very much the same. One such sequence is called a **memory cycle**. The complexity of an operation often depends on how many memory cycles it involves, and the time taken for a memory cycle is an important factor in determining the overall speed of a processor.

10.5   Construction of Immediate Access Store

The AMC address space is 64K, which is typical of a small microcomputer. The address space of mainframe computers is measured in **megabytes** (a megabyte is one million bytes) or millions of words, if each cell holds a word rather than a byte. A supercomputer like the Cray-2 has up to 256 million words (each of 64 bits) in its main memory. In many computer systems the address space is larger than the actual number of cells available. This enables more memory to be added without altering the memory access mechanism.

Some of the largest chips in a computer system are used for main store. There are two types: **random access memory (RAM)** and **read-only memory (ROM)**. ROM holds permanent instructions and data which may be read but cannot be altered, while RAM holds temporary data and instructions which may be altered at any time. Each type of computer has its own mixture of the two types. These areas are further divided into spaces for various purposes. A **memory map** shows the various partitions. Some are fixed, such as those occupied by programs, while others, notably stacks for data, grow and shrink as a program run proceeds.

Two types of RAM chips are used: **static** RAM and **dynamic** RAM. Static RAM has the property that data is retained for as long as power is supplied to the memory circuits. In the case of dynamic (or **volatile**) RAM, data gradually 'leaks away', and must be **refreshed** periodically. Memory refresh is accomplished by reading an item from the store and writing it back into the same location. Locations are refreshed in rotation all the time that the computer is running.

Some ROM chips have their bit patterns permanently written into them when they are constructed. Others are initially blank, and can be 'blown' with a specific bit pattern using appropriate equipment. These are **programmable read-only memories** or **PROMs**. Certain PROM chips can have their bit patterns changed, again using special equipment for the purpose. These are known as **EPROMs** (for erasable programmable read-only memory). In all cases, however, ROM chips installed in a computer memory can only be read. Instructions and data in ROM remain after the computer has been switched off. However, any attempt by the computer to write data to a cell in ROM has no effect.

The capacities of ROM and (particularly) RAM chips are increasing all the time. Most chips are only one bit 'wide' - each address locates a single-bit cell, thus requiring eight identical chips to implement a memory holding a byte at each cell. At present 16K bit memory chips are the most common, with 64K and 256K bit versions becoming increasingly popular. RAM chips holding a million bits are beginning to be introduced.

10.6   The AMC Arithmetic and Logic Unit

The AMC **arithmetic and logic unit**, or ALU, consists of an **accumulator**, a set of **logic circuits**, a **result register** and four **condition codes**. These form the part of the processor concerned with the actual manipulation of data. See Figure 10.3.

The **accumulator** is the principal 'working area' of the computer. It contains the data item being processed at any time. The **logic circuits** carry out various operations on one or two data items. The logic circuits have two inputs and one output, as well as a connection to the condition codes register. They consist of a set of NOT gates, an addition unit, sets of AND, OR and non-equivalence gates, and a shift register. The **result register** is a temporary store for the output from the logic circuits. All processing is in units of 16 bits. See Figure 10.4.

This seemingly limited set of logic circuits is quite sufficient to perform all the data processing operations carried out by the computer. The reason for this is that operations are expressed as a large number of small steps, each step involving one or two of the logic circuits of the ALU. Ways in which this can be done for various arithmetic operations are discussed in Section 5.1.

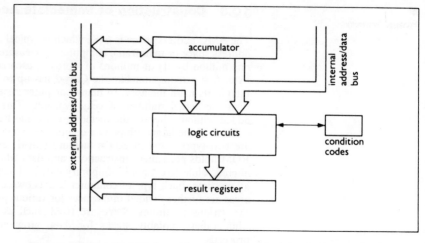

Figure 10.3
AMC arithmetic and logic unit

The **condition codes** are four bits which provide information about the most recent operation carried out by the ALU. These codes are also known as **program status bits** or **flags**. The AMC has four condition codes, as follows:

Zero (Z) is set to 1 if the output from the current operation is zero.

Negative (N) is set to 1 if the output from the current operation is negative, i.e. the most significant bit is 1.

Carry (C) is set to 1 if there is a carry out of the most significant bit during shifting or addition.

Overflow (V) is set to 1 if an addition results in an overflow. The method of determining whether overflow has occurred is discussed in Section 5.2.

Values of condition codes are used in the control of programs, and in carrying out certain operations. This is discussed in more detail in Chapter 12.

10.7 The AMC Input/Output Unit

Communication between the AMC processor and peripheral devices is via an **input** and an **output register**, and a **peripheral device selection register**. Unlike the storage, processing and control registers, these registers are only eight bits wide. They are connected to the least significant eight bits of the external address/data bus. See Figure 10.5.

All input and output to and from the AMC is assumed to be in character form. This is the case for the majority of peripheral devices. For this reason, input and output registers contain one byte, or one character. When a character is input to the AMC, the sequence of events is as follows:

1 The identification of the input device is placed in the peripheral device selection register.
2 The input device thus selected is requested to send a character to the input register.
3 When the input register has been loaded, a signal is sent to the AMC control unit.
4 The character is then copied from the input register into the AMC.

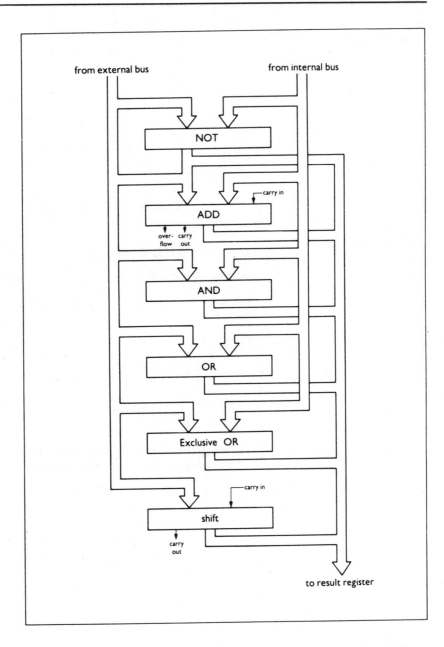

Figure 10.4
AMC logic circuits

When a character is output by the AMC, the sequence of events is as follows:

1 The character to be output is placed in the output register.
2 The identification of the output device is placed in the peripheral device selection register.
3 The output device thus selected is requested to copy the character from the output register.
4 When the character has been copied, a signal is sent to the AMC control unit.

It can be seen that there are several steps involved in the input or output of a single character. Furthermore, each step requires one program instruction. Although this is a cumbersome process, it is representative of the way some actual computers work.

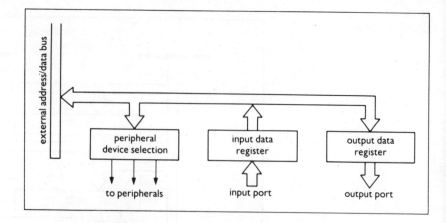

Figure 10.5
AMC input/output unit

10.8 The AMC Control Unit

The **control unit** of the AMC comprises the **program counter, instruction register** and **decoder, stack pointer** and **index register**. The control unit also contains a **clock pulse generator** which controls the timing of the whole processor. See Figure 10.6.

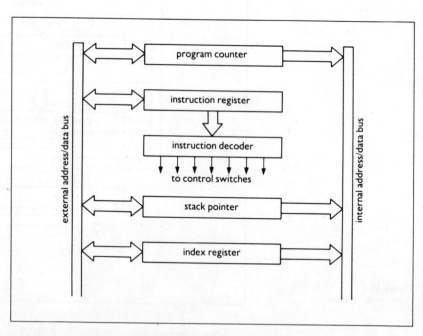

Figure 10.6
AMC control unit

The task of the control unit is to direct the step-by-step working of the processor as it carries out each instruction of a program. More specifically, the functions of the control unit are:

1 To control the sequence in which instructions are executed.
2 To control access to the main store of the processor.
3 To regulate the timing of all operations carried out within the processor.
4 To send control signals to, and receive control signals from, peripheral devices.

The **program counter** contains the address of the current program instruction. After the instruction has been fetched from the main store, the contents of the program counter is increased, ready for the next instruction. AMC instructions occupy 2, 3 or 4 bytes, thus the amount of the increase varies from one instruction to another. If an instruction transfers control to another part of the program, the address to which control is transferred is loaded into the program counter.

The **instruction register** stores a copy of the current program instruction. This register is connected to an **instruction decoder**, which in turn connects with control switches at various points throughout the processor. In this way, control switches are opened or closed according to the instruction in the instruction register.

In common with most modern processors, the AMC organises part of its main store as a stack. The stack serves a number of purposes, most of which are introduced in Chapter 12. The **stack pointer** stores the current address of the top of the stack.

The **index register** is used to implement a particular type, or **mode**, of addressing. Address modes are explained in Chapter 12.

Not shown in the diagrams is the **clock pulse generator**. This produces signals in a number of control lines, at regular intervals. These signals switch on, or **enable** various components of the AMC. In this way, co-ordination of the timing of the whole processor is achieved.

To complete the description of the AMC at register level, Figure 10.7 shows the register layout of the whole AMC processor.

10.9   The AMC and Real Processors

The AMC is a model computer: it implements a number of concepts of processor architecture in as simple and direct a way as possible. Among the differences between the AMC and real processors are the following:

1 In many processors, the program counter, index register, stack pointer and accumulator are not specific **dedicated** registers, but can be any one of a set of **general-purpose** registers. In other words, any register in the set can be used as an accumulator, index register, etc.
2 Some processors have restrictions on the storage of words in memory. In many cases words may only be stored at even addresses.
3 In many microprocessors, particularly microprocessors, input and output is done via memory locations, rather than input and output registers.
4 Many processors have far larger main stores than the AMC. Further registers are used in connection with the partitioning of these memories.
5 Some processors have special-purpose hardware for cetain operations such as floating-point multiplication.
6 The trend in processor design is towards increased parallelism, both within each processor, and the incorporation of several processing elements, operating in parallel, in a CPU.

More about the architecture of the processors of real computers is to be found in Chapter 15, which contains a number of case studies of processor architectures.

10.10   Conclusion

This chapter has introduced the architecture of a simple processor, described at the level of registers, decoders and other logic circuits. The objective is to give a feel for the structure of a computer at this level.

Several general points can now be made about the structure of a processor:

● A central processing unit consists of a control unit, an arithmetic and logic unit and a main store. Units are connected by one or more data buses.
● The structure of a processor, at register level, is quite simple, and the range of operations which can be carried out directly by the hardware of a processor is fairly limited.

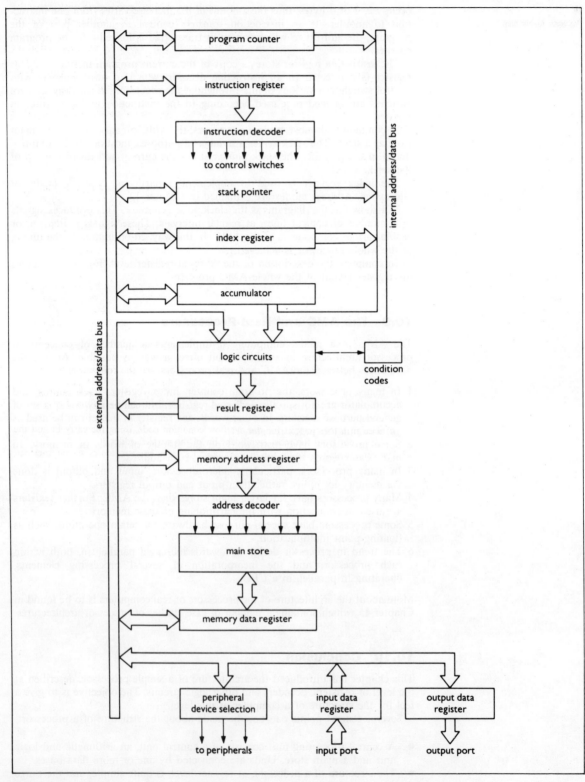

Figure 10.7
AMC register layout

- In order to be carried out by a computer, a data processing task must be expressed as a large number of simple steps, each step being an operation within the capabilities of the hardware of the processor.
- All the circuits of the processor are devoted to carrying out one program instruction at a time.
- The most important concept introduced in this chapter is the idea of an **address**. Addresses are used to locate instructions and data.

Chapter 12 shows how the registers and other functional circuits of a processor are put to work. It again uses the AMC as an example.

Exercise 10

1 Briefly define the following terms: main store; ALU; bus; control unit; immediate access store; address; address space; memory map; cell; RAM; ROM; PROM; EPROM; volatile memory; memory cycle; accumulator; condition codes; program counter; enable; dedicated register; sign extension; program status bits.

2 a) In your own words, explain the concept of an address.
  b) State why addresses are so important to the functioning of a processor.

3 In a particular type of computer, addresses are 24 bits.
  a) Calculate the address space of the computer.
  b) The precise value of the M unit is $2^{20} = 1048576$. Express the answer to part (a) in M units.
  c) Express the M unit in terms of the K unit ($1K = 2^{10} = 1024$).
  d) Calculate, in M units, the address space of a computer with a 32-bit address register.

4 Discuss the concept of a **module** in relation to the architecture of a processor.

5 Briefly distinguish between static and dynamic memory.

6 a) Draw a logic circuit to show how the zero (Z) condition code is determined from the output of the AMC logic circuits. The output carries 16 bits.
  b) Design a logic circuit to perform the process of sign extension mentioned in Section 10.4. It requires a control link which enables the circuit when it is required.
  c) Design a logic circuit for the overflow condition code, using the carry in and the carry out from the most significant bit of the parallel adder.

7 The chips which make up the processing and storage components of a computer can be made in several different ways. Popular types include **metal oxide semiconductor (MOS), transistor-transistor logic (TTL)** and **emitter coupled logic (ECL)**. Write short notes on each of these types and their relative advantages and disadvantages.

8 What problem can occur when part of the address space of a computer is used for a stack?

11

Processor Fabrication

This chapter covers the steps involved in the design and construction of chips and computers. It shows how the theory introduced in the previous three chapters is put into practice. It describes the work done at a number of chip fabrication plants and computer manufacturing factories throughout the world.

11.1 Transistors and Chips

A chip is a solid-state device containing a number of individual elements, the most important of which are **transistors**. A **transistor** can be used to amplify a signal or to act as a switch. It has three external connections, as shown in Figure 11.1. A small signal at one connection causes a large change in the flow of current between the other two: the current can be stopped entirely, or allowed to flow unhindered. This is due to the electrical properties of the **semiconductor** material (silicon or gallium arsenide) from which transistors are made. A semiconductor is a substance which conducts electricity better than an insulator such as porcelain, but not as well as a conductor such as copper.

The silicon crystals from which transistors and integrated circuits are made are extremely pure. To this pure crystal are added small, precisely controlled quantities of impurities, a process known as **doping**. Two kinds of semiconductor are created: dopants such as arsenic or phosphorus give rise to **n-type** semiconductor, with an excess of electrons. A dopant such as boron makes **p-type** semiconductor, with a shortage of electrons (it is said to have **holes**). It is the electrical properties of the junction between the two types of semiconductor (known as a **p-n junction**) which gives a transistor its switching and amplification powers.

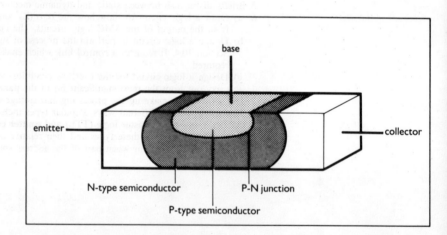

base

emitter

collector

N-type semiconductor

P-N junction

P-type semiconductor

Figure 11.1
A transistor

The size of a p-n junction has little effect on its operation - it can be microscopically small and still work perfectly well. For this reason individual transistors are a very inefficient way of making use of the capabilities of a p-n junction. It is preferable to combine large numbers of them, together with other electrical elements such as resistors and capacitors, into integrated circuits.

There are a number of methods of chip fabrication, which give rise to chips with different electrical properties. These include:

- **Transistor-transistor logic (TTL)**, which is relatively fast, but uses more power than the others.
- **Metal oxide silicon (MOS)**, which uses less power than TTL, but, apart from the **CMOS** variation, is somewhat slower.
- **Emitter-coupled logic (ECL)**, the fastest chip technology, but the one with the highest power consumption. Special systems are needed to cool densely packed ECL chips.

At present, the majority of computer chips are made by the TTL technique. MOS chips are used for systems where low power consumption is important. ECL chips are used in very fast computers such as the Cray-2.

11.2 Chip Design

There are two overall stages of chip design: **logic design** and **circuit design**. The logic design is derived from the functional requirements of the chip: it may be a processing chip, a memory chip, a graphics support chip, etc. The logic design is drawn up as a network of logic circuits, as described in Chapter 6. Simplification techniques are used extensively to ensure that the required logic functions are achieved with the minimum number of gates, or only with gates of certain types. The final logic design is checked very carefully before it is approved.

The logic design is then transformed into an equivalent circuit design, using gates and other electrical components for the logic elements. This design is separated into a layout for each layer of the chip, in terms of the areas of n-type and p-type semiconductor, and the layer of metal interconnections. P-n junctions are almost always formed between two adjacent layers in the chip.

The entire operation is done with the aid of a **computer-assisted design (CAD)** system. This includes some form of electronic drawing board, with a light pen to do the drafting of the logic circuits, and large libraries of common elements which can be called up and included in the design. Designs are stored on disk and printed on flat-bed plotters when they are complete. The checks on the logical operation of the chip are carried out semi-automatically, the CAD system being able to simulate the operation of a design for given input signals.

The translation from a logic circuit to a physical arrangement of gates is becoming increasingly automated. Some CAD systems can perform the entire operation automatically, others give varying degrees of assistance to the designer. Once a gate layout has been produced, the CAD system adjusts it in order to minimise the lengths of the connections between the gates, as this is one of the determining factors of the speed of operation of the chip. The complete design is again checked very carefully, with the aid of simulation programs which are part of the CAD system. Large diagrams (about 500 times the actual size of the chip) are produced, one for each layer of the chip. These diagrams - the **artwork** - are then reduced photographically to make the **masks** used in the fabrication of the chips.

The eventual goal of the CAD systems is to enable a designer to specify the functional requirements of the chip: its logical properties, speed of operation, electrical parameters and the external connections required. The CAD system will then carry out all the design stages, to the point of producing the masks for the chip layers, automatically. The development of CAD systems of this nature is an integral part of the fifth generation computer programmes, discussed in Chapter 34.

11.3 Chip Fabrication

The raw material of a chip is a crystal of pure silicon or gallium arsenide. These are grown under precisely controlled conditions to cylindrical shapes approximately one metre in length and between 100 and 150 millimetres in diameter. The level of impurities in the crystal is so low as to be negligible. The crystals are cut into circular slices or **wafers**, 1 millimetre thick and polished on one surface so that it is perfectly flat. On each wafer are formed several hundred identical chips.

Chips have up to ten layers, each containing a pattern of areas of either p-type or n-type semiconductor. As shown in Figure 11.2, each layer is built up in four stages: **oxidation**, **masking**, **etching** and **doping**:

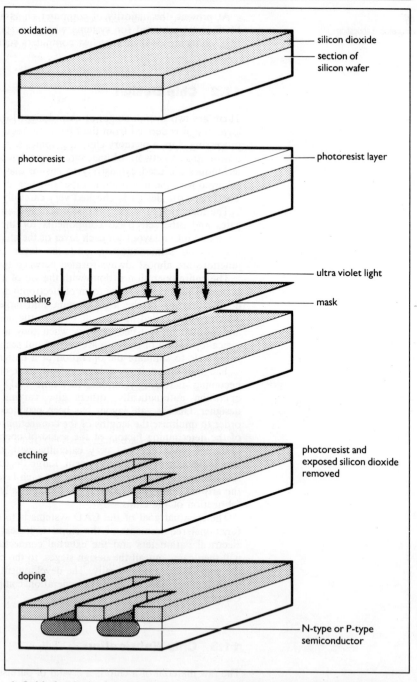

oxidation
silicon dioxide
section of
silicon wafer

photoresist
photoresist layer

ultra violet light
masking
mask

etching
photoresist and
exposed silicon dioxide
removed

doping
N-type or P-type
semiconductor

Figure 11.2
The stages of forming a layer on
a chip

1 Oxidation is the formation of an insulating layer of silicon dioxide. The silicon dioxide also forms a barrier for the later diffusion stages. Oxidation is done by heating the wafer in a furnace containing a controlled amount of oxygen.

2 Masking involves coating the wafer with **photoresist** - a substance which is hardened on exposure to light. The mask with the layout of the particular layer is placed on top of the wafer. The wafer is then exposed to ultra-violet light. The areas not covered by the mask are hardened.

3 The mask is removed and the unexposed photoresist is dissolved away. The pattern it has created is etched with acid into the silicon dioxide layer of the chip, exposing the silicon below.

4 The exposed silicon areas are doped by a **diffusion** process to produce n-type or p-type semiconductor. The heated wafer is placed in an atmosphere containing a vapour of the dopant at precisely the required temperature and concentration. This process generally oxidises the chip as well, performing the first step of the formation of the next layer. An alternative method of **ion implantation**, using an electron gun, is used to dope larger chips.

After all the layers have been formed, windows are etched at appropriate positions through the oxide to provide electrical contact points for each element on the chip. A further mask is used for this process. The wafer is then **metallised**, by evaporating a layer of a conductor (usually aluminium) onto it. The metal is masked and etched to produce the required network of connections within the chip. Many of the conducting paths are less than a micron (one millionth of a metre) wide.

The chips on the wafer are then tested by touching the connecting pads on the edge of each one with fine probes, and carrying out a complete, computer-controlled check on all the required chip functions. Any chips not passing these stringent tests completely are marked with an ink spot and later discarded. The percentage of acceptable chips is known as the **yield** of the wafer. Yields can vary from close to 100% to 0% if something has gone wrong.

After testing, the wafer is scribed with lines on the boundaries of the chips, using a diamond cutter. It is then broken into individual chips. The ones which have passed the initial tests are given a visual inspection before being mounted onto their carriers. Fine wires, generally made of gold, are bonded onto the connector pads on the chip edges and run outwards to the external chip connections. The tops of the carriers are then sealed on, and the packaged chips are again rigorously tested. Most chips are cased in plastic, but ceramic is used for applications requiring more rugged chips.

The fabrication steps are carried out under very precisely controlled conditions. The air in the fabrication rooms is constantly filtered. All workers wear protective clothing including gloves and face masks. The temperature required for each step is finely adjusted, as are the quantities of the various chemicals involved. The masks are aligned with extreme care, typically to an accuracy of a quarter of a micron, as only a very slight error will ruin the whole wafer.

The chips are now ready for despatch and use. Because of the high standards of construction and testing, the chances are that they will work perfectly for years. Figure 11.3 shows the overall stages of chip design and fabrication.

11.4 Computer Manufacture

The process of designing and manufacturing a complete computer is long, complex and very expensive. It involves the work of teams of highly skilled computer architects, engineers and systems software writers. In the case of mainframe computers, it can take several years. It is very seldom a continuous sequence of steps from the original concept to the final product. In most cases, problems are encountered at various stages which require designs to be modified and earlier stages repeated. The techniques of computer design used by most companies take account of these requirements for modification.

11.5 Computer Design

Computer design starts with an overall concept of what the complete computer will do. It may be a general-purpose personal computer, a special-purpose computer such as a word processor, a minicomputer or a large mainframe for scientific use. Whatever type of computer it is, it will be intended for a certain market and a certain price range. In most cases it will compete with existing computers from other manufacturers. A certain amount of **market research** is undertaken to find out more about the requirements of the prospective users,

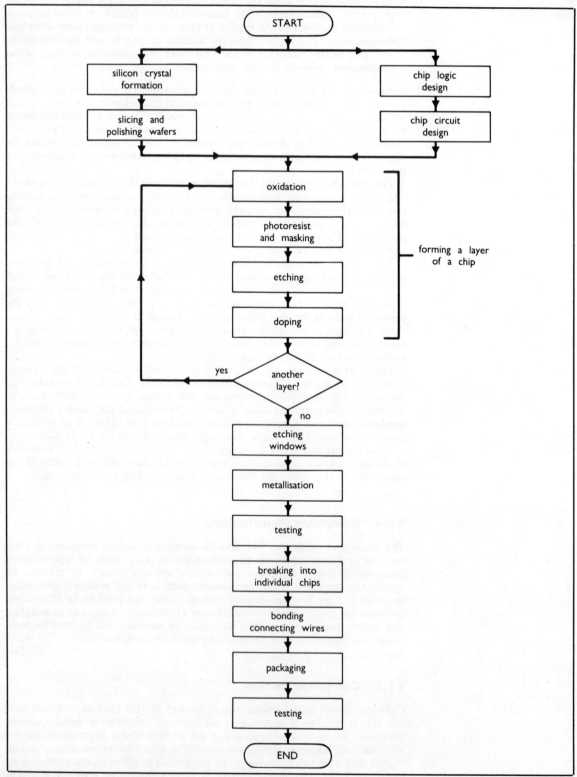

Figure 11.3
Chip fabrication

and the extent to which these are being satisfied by existing products. This latter process is referred to as searching for a gap in the market.

The overall configuration and performance characteristics of the new computer are clarified, and stated in some detail in a **functional specification**. This document describes the features of the computer, its levels of performance, processing power, memory capacity, external interfaces and projected price. It generally requires a number of revisions before the designers, salesmen and managers of the computer manufacturer are satisfied with it. It is generally revised further as design and manufacture progress.

Once the functional specification has been established, teams of designers set to work on the various components of the computer - the processing unit, the input, output and backing store devices and the data communication equipment. A start is also made on the computer software, often using an existing computer to simulate the new machine. In most cases, complete sub-systems such as display screens, keyboards and disk drives are bought in from outside suppliers. The design work is precisely scheduled, with target dates set for completion of various stages, and for checking the compatibility of different units. The management of the design process requires some skill, to ensure that the schedule is adhered to, in spite of the inevitable revisions.

11.6 Printed Circuit Boards

Computer processors are constructed internally from one or more **printed circuit boards (PCBs)**. A PCB is a rectangular fibreglass board, with metal **tracks** providing connections between the chips, which are soldered into holes in the board, or pressed into chip carrier sockets which are soldered to the board. Standard PCBs have two layers of tracks, one on each side of the board; multi-layer boards have up to eight layers of tracks. The external connections of a PCB are generally **edge connectors** which plug into sockets on other boards, or on the racks in which PCBs are mounted. Edge connectors are sometimes made of gold. The normal layout inside a computer is a **baseboard**, sometimes called a **motherboard**, with boards for various functions plugged into it at right angles. (Small microcomputers generally have a single PCB with areas for processor, memory, disk control, etc.)

There are similarities between the design of printed circuit boards and chip design. Each starts with a specification of the required operation of the unit, which is then translated into a physical arrangement. In both cases, computer aided design systems are used. In the case of printed circuit boards, the chips required to perform the various operations are selected, and their interconnections specified. For certian operations custom-designed chips are required, generally based on uncommitted logic arrays (ULAs). The layout of the board is then determined, with the tracks linking the chips via the shortest possible routes and with the minimum number of crossovers.

When the design is complete, a **prototype** printed circuit board is constructed, filled with chips and tested. After all the errors have been identified and corrected, the boards are ready for bulk production.

11.7 Computer Assembly

The final stage of the design of a computer system is the construction and assembly of a complete working **prototype**. The newly developed systems software is loaded into the hardware, and the entire system, both hardware and software, is tested very thoroughly. When all the required modifications have been made to the first prototype, a small production run is generally made. These units are sent to potential users for **beta tests**, during which they are made to run operational software, and their performance is carefully monitored. When the reports from the beta tests have been analysed and faults rectified, the new computer is ready for volume production. Mainframe and minicomputers are produced to order; microcomputers are generally produced in large volumes and sold from stock.

Printed circuit boards are constructed in the required quantities, and chips, display screens, disk drives and all the other components are purchased. All vital components such as processor chips are **second sourced** - two independent suppliers are nominated, and components from both suppliers are evaluated in prototypes. This is to ensure that a shortage or delivery delay of a vital component will not hold up production of the whole computer.

Assembly is done at a series of **workstations**, at each of which one set of operations is performed, before the intermediate product is passed to the next workstation. The first stage is to insert the chips and other components into the printed circuit boards. Machines or robots are sometimes used for this operation, although it is still most frequently done by hand. Printed circuit boards are labelled with the identity of each component to be inserted. PCBs with all their components are sent to a **flow soldering machine**, which solders all the chips onto the PCB in one operation. It passes the board over a bath of molten solder which adheres to all the points where connections are to be made. The PCBs are then inserted into their racks or baseboards, which are in turn mounted in the casings of the various units. All the external connections are wired up, and the units are now ready for testing.

11.8 Testing, Commissioning and Maintenance

The various units of the computer are connected together and the computer is switched on. It is then thoroughly tested, both by hand and by means of special software designed for the purpose. Manual checks include tests with an oscilloscope at various points inside the computer to ensure that the waveform at the point is of the required shape and size. Software tests include **soak tests** which try out every function of the new computer repeatedly, generally over a period of several days. For example, the computer memory is filled with a known bit pattern, which is then read back and compared with the original. In a similar way, disks are written to and then read from. All faults are automatically logged, and appropriate remedial action taken. When all tests have been passed, the computer is approved for delivery.

On delivery to the user, the computer is **commissioned**. In the case of mainframes and minicomputers, this is done by field engineers from the suppliers; microcomputer purchasers generally have to commission the computers themselves. Commissioning involves unpacking the various units and connecting them together, by cables under the computer room floor in the case of a mainframe. The computer is started, often using special commissioning software, and tested thoroughly. When suppliers and users are satisfied that the new computer is working properly, it is handed over to the user, ready for productive operation.

All computers require some form of **maintenance**. This is either carried out by the manufacturer under a maintenance agreement signed with the user, or by an independent maintenance company. Routine checks are carried out periodically, and maintenance engineers are called out if a fault occurs. Most computer systems have enough duplication of units to ensure that the majority of failures do not halt the entire system. From time to time the computer is **upgraded** with new peripherals, a larger memory or more powerful processing facilities.

The useful life of most computers seems to be between five and ten years. Most spend very little time out of service due to faults, and the majority of large computers operate round the clock, seven days a week. When the time comes to replace them they are unplugged and sold as scrap, in almost every case in perfect working order. The most common reason for their replacement is that they are obsolete, and their place is being taken by another computer which is smaller, faster, more powerful, and cheaper.

The overall process of computer design and construction is shown in Figure 11.4.

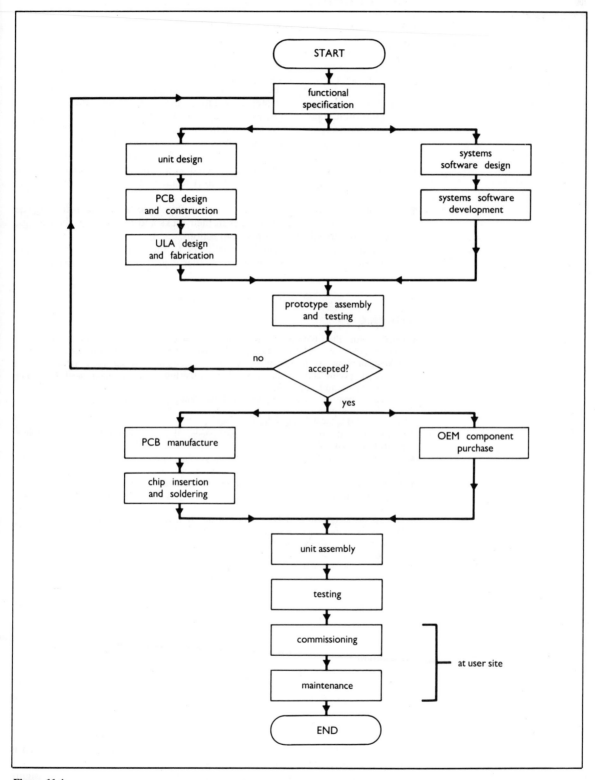

Figure 11.4
Computer manufacture

11.9 Conclusion

The main points of this chapter are as follows:

- Chips are semiconductor devices made from silicon which has been treated by the addition of precisely controlled quantities of impurities. They have up to ten layers of active elements.
- Chips are made from wafers of pure silicon or gallium arsenide crystal. Each layer is built up in four steps: oxidation, masking, etching and doping. A metallisation stage completes the chip, which is then tested and cased.
- Computer design starts from a functional specification. Work on the printed circuit boards in each unit, as well as the systems software, then proceeds in parallel. At the end of the design stage, a working prototype is constructed.
- Further prototypes are then constructed and sent for beta testing. When final modifications have been made as a result of the tests, volume production commences.
- A computer is assembled by inserting the chips into the PCBs, soldering the connections, mounting the boards in their racks and the racks in the casings, and wiring up all the external connections.
- Computers are commissioned on delivery to the user, and require periodic maintenance. The useful life of a computer is generally between five and ten years.

Exercise 11

1 Briefly define the following terms: transistor; semiconductor; p-type and n-type semiconductor; p-n junction; ECL; TTL; MOS; artwork; wafer; oxidation; masking; etching; photoresist; doping; diffusion; ion implantation; metallisation; yield; functional specification; track; flow soldering machine; second source; soak test; beta test; commissioning; upgrade.
2 a) What steps are taken to ensure the high standard of cleanliness in chip fabrication plants?
  b) Why is this level of cleanliness necessary?
3 Comment on the the significance of the concept of a module in relation to chips and printed circuit boards.
4 Discuss the uses of computer-aided design systems in chip and printed circuit board manufacture.
5 At what stages are robots used in the manufacture of computers? List any other stages of chip and computer manufacture where you think robots may be used in the future.
6 Discuss the significance of ULA chips in the design and construction of computers.
7 Discuss the importance of beta testing of new computers.
8 Discuss the similarities and differences between chip fabrication and:
  a) steelmaking
  b) motor car production.

12
Processor
Operation

This chapter describes the way in which the processor of a computer operates. The instructions which control the step-by-step working of a processor are introduced, and the sequence of actions needed to carry out one instruction is explained. The AMC model computer is used as an example throughout the chapter. Some features of actual computers, which are not found in the AMC, are outlined at the end of the chapter.

This chapter relates closely to Chapter 10, which describes the structure of a processor. It is essential to an understanding of several subsequent chapters, notably the following chapter, on advanced processor features, and Chapter 16, on assembly languages.

12.1   Machine Language

The instructions which control the step-by-step working of a processor are in a language called **machine language**. Machine language instructions are closly related to the architecture of a computer. There is one machine instruction for each operation performed directly by the hardware of the computer. Consequently, each type of processor has its own machine language.

The length and composition of machine language instructions vary considerably from one processor to another, but all have certain features in common. These include the following:

1 Machine instructions are in a binary code.
2 Machine instructions relate directly to registers and functional units of the processor.
3 Every machine instruction includes an **operation code**. This specifies the type of operation to be carried out.
4 Some machine instructions refer to the main store of the computer. Ways of doing this are discussed in the next section.
5 All the instructions in the machine language of a processor make up the **instruction set** of that processor.

12.2   Addressing

Some machine instructions refer to the main store of the computer. This is accomplished by specifying, in some manner, the **address** of the particular memory location. Addressing can be done in a number of ways, some of which are quite complex. Only the essential features of addressing are dealt with here.

The Number of Addresses
The number of addresses in a single machine instruction can vary. Computers can be classified according to the maximum number of addresses they permit in a machine instruction. One- and two-address computers are the most common, but three- and four-address computers have been constructed as well as zero-address computers, where the entire main store is regarded as a stack.

Examples of machine instructions with various numbers of addresses are given below. They are not taken from the instruction sets of any actual processor, and are written in English, rather than in machine code.

One-address instruction
ADD J   Add the number in memory location J to the number in the accumulator, and store the sum in the accumulator.

Two-address instruction
ADD J,K   Add the numbers in memory locations J and K, and store the sum in location J.

Three-address instruction
ADD J,K,L Add the numbers in memory locations J and K, and store the sum in location L.

Zero-address instruction
ADD   Pop the two top numbers from the stack, add them together, and push the sum onto the stack.

The instruction set of a particular computer can contain more than one of the above types of instructions. A common combination in microcomputers is zero-address and one-address instructions.

Addressing Modes
Each address in a machine instruction may refer to a memory location in one of several different ways. These methods of addressing are called **addressing modes**. Part of the machine instruction is a specification of the addressing mode used. Addressing modes vary between different types of computers. The following modes are, however, common to most types.

Absolute or direct address
This is the simplest addressing mode. The number in the address part of the machine instruction is the number of the memory location holding the data item.

Indexed address
The number in the address part of the machine instruction is added to the contents of a register, called the **index register**, in order to obtain the address of the memory location. This mode is particularly useful when a set of data items is stored in consecutive memory locations. The machine instruction contains the address of the first element in the set, and the index register contains the number (or **offset**) of the particular element in the set.

Indirect address
The address in the machine instruction does not locate a data item, but the address of the data item. The latter address is used to locate the data item. In theory, this principle can be extended to several layers of indirect addresses, although this is not very common. Indirect addressing is particularly useful if data is structured into linked lists or trees. The address of the data item, which is located by the machine instruction, is a **pointer** to the data item.

Relative address
The address in the machine instruction indicates the offset of the data item from the machine instruction, i.e. the address of the data item relative to the machine instruction. In order to locate the data item, the value of the program counter is added to the relative address (the program counter stores the address of the current instruction). Relative addresses are used if a block of instructions and data must be moved from one place to another in the computer memory, without alteration to the addresses being needed. Such a block is called **relocatable code**. Addresses within it are valid wherever it is in memory.

Immediate operand
An immediate operand is a data item located in the address part of a machine instruction. In this case, the memory is not accessed at all. Immediate operands are a useful way of including constants in a program.

The above are the most common addressing modes, implemented on most types of computers. The phrases **address modification** or **address transformation** are used to describe indexed, indirect and relative addressing. Other, more complex addressing modes may be formed by combining two or more of the above modes. An example is indexed indirect addressing. Such addressing modes are, however, beyond the scope of this course.

The reason for having these various addressing modes is that they enhance the power of a computer, and make it easier to program at machine language level. They also make it easier to program the data structures described in Chapter 4. On the other hand, complex addressing modes mean that several memory cycles and passes through the addition unit are needed before the data item required by a machine instruction is obtained. This slows down the computer.

12.3 AMC Machine Language

The AMC is a one-address computer. In other words, instructions which refer to the main store contain at most one address. Addressing modes available are immediate operand, absolute, indirect and indexed.

AMC machine instructions occupy one word (16 bits), followed, in some cases, by a word containing an address, or a word or a byte containing a data item. Hexadecimal notation is used to describe the instructions, being far more compact than binary. You will recall from Chapter 3 that one hexadecimal digit represents four bits. Thus four hexadecimal digits will describe an AMC instruction.

The AMC instruction set is divided into **groups**. All the instructions within a group perform similar operations. The first hexadecimal digit of the instruction identifies the group. The second identifies the operation within the group. Taken together, the first two hexadecimal digits of the machine instruction form the **operation code**. The interpretation of the remaining two hexadecimal digits in an instruction depend on its group.

Three of the AMC registers are under program control. They are the **accumulator**, **index register** and **stack pointer**. These registers are numbered 1, 2 and 3, respectively, in machine instructions. In most cases the third hexadecimal digit of the machine instruction identifies the register used. The fourth digit indicates the addressing mode.

Figure 12.1 shows the layout of the different groups of AMC instructions. The table in Figure 12.2 contains the complete AMC instruction set. The instructions in a group perform similar operations, and have the same layout. Figure 12.2 also specifies the effect of each instruction on the condition codes. This is explained in more detail later.

Memory Addressing Group
All the instructions which refer to the AMC memory are in this group. Each operation can be applied to a word or a byte of data. An instruction in this group consists of an operation code, register identifier, and addressing mode, followed by an address word, or a data word or byte. For example:

1312 423B	operation code **13**:	add word
	register identifier **1**:	accumulator
	addressing mode **2**:	absolute address
	address **423B**	

This means means: add the word (i.e. 16 bit number) at (absolute) address **423B** to the accumulator.

2234 17B5	operation code **22**:	store byte
	register identifier **3**:	stack pointer
	addressing mode **4**:	indexed
	address **17B5**	

This means: store the (least significant) byte from the stack pointer at memory address **17B5** plus contents of index register.

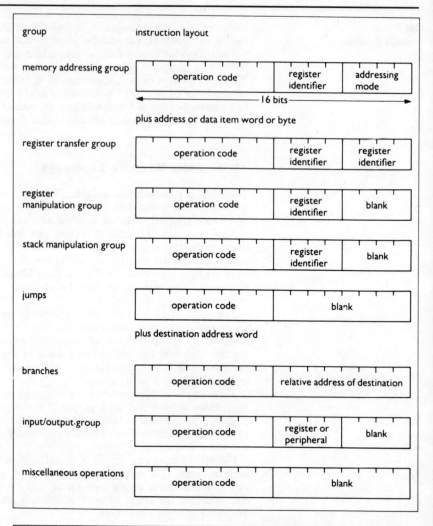

Figure 12.1
Bit layout of AMC machine instructions

M addressing mode:
- 1 immediate operand
- 2 absolute address
- 3 indirect address
- 4 indexed address

R register identifier:
- 1 accumulator
- 2 index register
- 3 stack pointer

P peripheral device:
- 1 terminal

XX relative address of destruction of branch

Effects on condition codes:
- S set (becomes 1)
- C cleared (becomes 0)
- N no effect
- D conditional upon result

condition codes:
- Z zero
- N negative
- C carry
- V overflow

Figure 12.2
AMC instruction set (see also Figure 12.2 continued)

machine instruction (hexadecimal)	interpretation	Z	N	C	V
memory addressing group					
11RM	load data word to register	D	D	N	N
21RM	load data byte to register	D	D	N	N
12RM	store register word in memory	D	D	N	N
22RM	store register byte in memory	D	D	N	N
13RM	add data word to register	D	D	D	D
23RM	add data byte to register	D	D	D	D
14RM	add data word and carry bit to register	D	D	D	D
24RM	add data byte and carry bit to register	D	D	D	D
15RM	subtract data word from register	D	D	D	D
25RM	subtract data byte from register	D	D	D	D
16RM	subtract (data word plus carry bit) from register	D	D	D	D
26RM	subtract (data byte plus carry bit) from register	D	D	D	D
17RM	AND data word with register	D	D	C	C
27RM	AND data byte with register	D	D	C	C
18RM	OR data word with register	D	D	C	C
28RM	OR data byte with register	D	D	C	C
19RM	NEQ (exclusive OR) data word with register	D	D	C	C
29RM	NEQ (exclusive OR) data byte with register	D	D	C	C
1ARM	compare register with data word	D	D	D	D
2ARM	compare register with data byte	D	D	D	D
register transfer group					
31R_1R_2	move word from register 1 to register 2	D	D	N	N
register manipulation group					
01RO	clear register	S	C	C	C
02RO	increment register (increase by 1)	D	D	D	D
03RO	decrement register (decrease by 1)	D	D	D	D
04RO	rotate register right, 1 bit, via carry bit	D	D	D	D
05RO	rotate register left 1 bit, via carry bit	D	D	D	D
06RO	arithmetic shift right, 1 bit	D	D	C	C
07RO	arithmetic shift left, 1 bit	D	D	C	C
08RO	complement register	D	D	D	D
09RO	negate register (NOT operation)	D	D	C	C
stack manipulation group					
41RO	push register word onto stack	D	D	N	N
42RO	pop top of stack word to register	D	D	N	N
jumps					
5100	unconditional jump to specified address	N	N	N	N
5200	jump to subprogram, stack return address	N	N	N	N
branches					
61XX	unconditional branch	N	N	N	N
62XX	branch if zero (Z = 1)	N	N	N	N
63XX	branch if non-zero (Z = 0)	N	N	N	N
64XX	branch if greater than or equal to zero (Z = 1 or N = 0)	N	N	N	N
65XX	branch if greater than zero (Z = 0 and N = 0)	N	N	N	N
66XX	branch if less than or equal to zero (Z = 1 or N = 1)	N	N	N	N
67XX	branch if less than zero (N = 1)	N	N	N	N
68XX	branch if carry clear (C = 0)	N	N	N	N
69XX	branch if carry set (C = 1)	N	N	N	N
6AXX	branch if overflow clear (V = 0)	N	N	N	N
6BXX	branch if overflow set (V = 1)	N	N	N	N
6CXX	branch if input not complete	N	N	N	N
6DXX	branch if output not complete	N	N	N	N
input/output group					
71PO	signal peripheral device to load input register	N	N	N	N
72RO	copy byte from input register to register R	D	D	N	N
73PO	signal peripheral device to unload output register	N	N	N	N
74RO	copy byte from register R to output register	D	D	N	N
miscellaneous operations					
3100	set carry bit	N	N	S	N
8200	clear carry bit	N	N	C	N
8300	return from subprogram (unstack return address)	N	N	N	N
8400	no-operation	N	N	N	N
8500	halt	N	N	N	N

Figure 12.2
(continued)

2111 BB   operation code **21**:   load byte
              register identifier **1**:   accumulator
              addressing mode **1**:   immediate operand
              data item **BB**

Because the addressing mode indicates an immediate operand, the instruction is followed by a data item, rather than an address. The instruction means: load the byte **BB** into the accumulator.

All the instructions in this group affect the Z (zero) and N (negative) condition codes. For example, if an addition results in a negative number, then Z becomes 0 and N becomes 1. Addition, subtraction and comparison operations affect the C (carry) and V (overflow) codes as well. The three logic operations clear these codes, while load and store operations leave them unchanged.

Register Transfer Group

The single instruction in this group copies the contents of one register into another register. For example:

3123	operation code **31**:	move
	register identifiers **2**:	index register
	3:	stack pointer

This means: copy the contents of the index register into the stack pointer. This instruction affects the zero and negative condition codes, but does not alter the carry and overflow codes.

Register Manipulation Group

This group of instructions operates on the contents of one of the registers. The clear, increment, decrement and negate instructions are obvious enough, but a word or two of explanation is needed about the others.

The complement instruction forms the twos complement of the contents of the register. As explained in Chapter 3, this is done by negating the bits and then adding 1.

The rotate operations include the carry bit, and are best explained by means of a diagram. See Figure 12.3.

The arithmetic shift operations preserve the most significant bit of the word (the sign bit) and shift the rest. The arithmetic shift left has the effect of multiplying by 2, and the arithmetic shift right has the effect of dividing by 2. In the latter case the sign bit is copied into the next position. See Figure 12.4.

An example of a machine instruction in this group is:

0320	operation code **03**:	decrement
	register identifier **2**:	index register

This means: decrease contents of index register by 1.

All the instructions in this group affect all the condition codes.

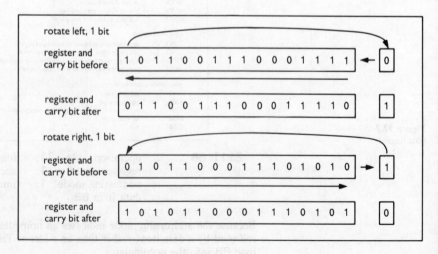

Figure 12.3
Rotate instructions

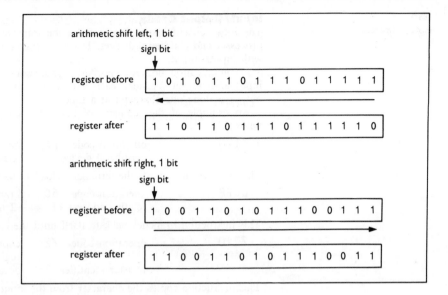

arithmetic shift left, 1 bit

sign bit

register before | 1 0 1 0 1 1 0 1 1 1 1 0 1 1 1 1 1

register after | 1 1 0 1 1 0 1 1 1 0 1 1 1 1 1 0

arithmetic shift right, 1 bit

sign bit

register before | 1 0 0 1 1 0 1 0 1 1 1 0 0 1 1 1

register after | 1 1 0 0 1 1 0 1 0 1 1 1 0 0 1 1

Figure 12.4
Arithmetic shift instructions

Branches

The branching instructions transfer control to another part of the program, using relative addressing. The first instruction in the set is an unconditional branch, the remaining 13 transfer control depending on the value of one or more condition codes. These enable a branch to be made depending on the outcome of some previous operation.

For example, suppose that a branch has to be made if two numbers are equal. One number is loaded into the accumulator, and compared with the other. The compare operation in the memory addressing group is used. It subtracts the numbers, sets the condition codes depending on the result, but does not retain the result. If the numbers are equal, the difference is zero, and the Z code is set to 1. The branch if zero instruction is then used.

The address of the destination of the branch is contained in the second byte of the instruction word. This byte is interpreted as a twos complement integer, and can thus have a value in the range −128 to 127. This limits the range of the branches, which are sometimes called 'short' branches. This address is relative to the current value of the program counter. By the time the branch instruction is executed, the program counter has been reset to contain the address of the next instruction. Thus the destination of the branch is the address of the next instruction plus the relative address contained in the branching instruction. For example:

678A   operation code **67**:   branch if less than zero
                    relative address **8A**:   138 in base ten

If this instruction is at address 0049 (=73 in base ten), then the program counter contains 004B (=75 in base ten), the address of the next instruction. The destination address of the branch is 138 + 75 = 213 in base ten, or 00D5 in hexadecimal. Accordingly, if condition code N = 1 (i.e. less than zero), control will be transferred to the instruction at address 00D5. If N = 0, control passes to the next instruction, at address 004B.

The reason for having this rather awkward addressing mode in branching instructions is to save memory space. Instructions of this type occupy only one word, whereas a jump to an absolute address occupies two words. Although these instructions depend on values of various condition codes, they do not alter these codes in any way.

Input/Output Group

The input/output instructions control the transfer of data between the AMC processor and peripheral devices. Two branching instructions are also concerned with input/output.

Communication between the AMC processor and peripheral devices is via input and output registers, each with a capacity of one byte. All input and output is done one character at a time.

An example of the sequence of instructions to input a character is given below:

| 7110 | operation code 71: | input request |
| | peripheral device 1: | terminal |

This instruction requests the terminal to load a character into the input register.

| 6CFE | operation code 6C: | branch if input not complete |
| | relative address FE = −2 in base ten | |

This instruction branches back to itself until the character has been loaded.

| 7210 | operation code 72: | copy character from input register |
| | register identifier 1: | accumulator |

This instruction copies the character from the input register to the accumulator.

This example shows the number of instructions needed for the input of a single character. The second instruction causes the processor to wait until the input has taken place. Although it is very inefficient, it is one way of synchronising a processor with a slower peripheral device.

The instructions in this group which relate to peripheral devices have no effect on condition codes. The instructions which move data to or from input/output registers affect the zero and negative condition codes.

12.4 Example Program 12.1

The objective of this program is to input a sequence of characters and store them in consecutive memory locations. The end of the input is marked by a special character, with hexadecimal code FF. The address of the memory location to contain the first character is known when the program is written.

The program uses the technique of indirect addressing. The address of the first character is loaded into a convenient memory location. A character is input, and compared with the end-of-input marker. If the character is not the marker, it is stored at the address specified in the memory location, using indirect addressing. This address is then increased by 1, and the next character is input. When the end-of-input marker is found, the program ends. For convenience, the program is written starting at address 0000.

Program

Address	Instruction	Comments
0000	001F	Address of first character, later of current character.
0002	7110	Signal terminal to load character into input register.
0004	6CFE	Branch back to this instruction if input not complete.
0006	7210	Copy character from input register to accumulator.
0008	2A11 FF	Compare character with end-of-input marker.
000B	6210	Branch if equal, to address 001D.
000D	2213 0000	Store character at address in location 0000.
0011	1112 0000	Load address of current character to accumulator.
0015	0210	Increase contents of accumulator by 1.
0017	1212 0000	Store address of next character in location 0000.
001B	61E5	Branch to address 0002, to input next character.
001D	8500	Halt.
001F		First character.

Points to Notice

- Location **0000** initially contains the address of the first character, namely **001F**. After each character has been input, the contents of this location is increased by 1. In this way, characters are stored in consecutive memory locations.
- The first program instruction is at address **0002**; the previous word is used for data. Program instructions occupy 2, 3 or 4 store locations. The length of an instruction determines the address of the next instruction.
- The relative address in the first branching instruction is **FE** ($=$ -2 in base ten). This instruction has the effect of branching back to itself repeatedly, until a character has been input. In this way, the processor 'waits' for the terminal.
- Three different addressing modes are used in this program. They are immediate operand (at address **000B**), indirect address (at address **000D**) and absolute address (at addresses **0011** and **0017**).
- The characters are stored immediately after the program. If a different memory area is required for them, all that needs to be changed is the address in location **0000**.
- The portion of program from address **0002** to address **001B** is repeated, once for each input character. A portion of a program which is repeated is called a **loop**.
- The relative addresses in branching instructions are the differences between their destination addresses and the addresses of the instructions which follow them.

12.5 Stack Manipulation and Subprogram Calls

Since the AMC stack is an essential part of its subprogram calling mechanism, the two aspects are dealt with together.

Stack Manipulation Group

The two instructions in this group implement the **push** and **pop** operations introduced in Chapter 4.

Any part of the AMC memory may be used for the stack. Before the stack is built, the stack pointer is loaded with the address of the stack base. As the stack is used, it points to the next available space above the stack top. The stack grows 'upwards' in the memory, from high addresses to low addresses. Stack elements are words, occupying two memory locations.

The **push** operation involves the following steps:

1 The data item is copied from the register specified in the push instruction, into the two memory locations addressed by the stack pointer.
2 The contents of the stack pointer is reduced by 2, so that it again contains the address of the memory location into which the next stack element is to be pushed.

See Figure 12.5.

The **pop** operation is as follows:

1 The contents of the stack pointer is increased by 2. It now addresses the top element of the stack.
2 The word addressed by the stack pointer is copied into the register specified in the pop instruction.

See Figure 12.6.

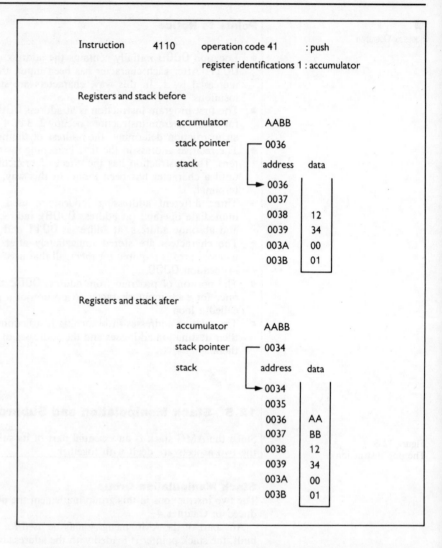

Instruction   4110   operation code 41   : push

register identifications 1 : accumulator

Registers and stack before

accumulator   AABB

stack pointer   0036

stack	address	data
	0036	
	0037	
	0038	12
	0039	34
	003A	00
	003B	01

Registers and stack after

accumulator   AABB

stack pointer   0034

stack	address	data
	0034	
	0035	
	0036	AA
	0037	BB
	0038	12
	0039	34
	003A	00
	003B	01

Figure 12.5
The push instruction

Jumps and Subprogram Calls

The two instructions in this group transfer control to another part of the program. Unlike the branching instructions, these instructions are followed by the (absolute) address of the destination of the jump, in a separate word. For example:

5100 341A   operation code **51**: jump
                    destination address **341A**

This instruction transfers control to the instruction at address 341A. Because a complete word is used for the destination address, any location in the AMC memory can be reached.

The second instruction in this group introduces the idea of a **subprogram**. A subprogram is a set of instructions, carrying out a specific task, which is called from any other part of the program. When the subprogram is complete, control returns to the point in the program from which the subprogram was called. See Figure 12.7.

From a machine language point of view, the problem with subprograms is how to remember the address to which control returns after the subprogram is complete. In the AMC, and in many other modern computers, this problem is solved by means of the system stack.

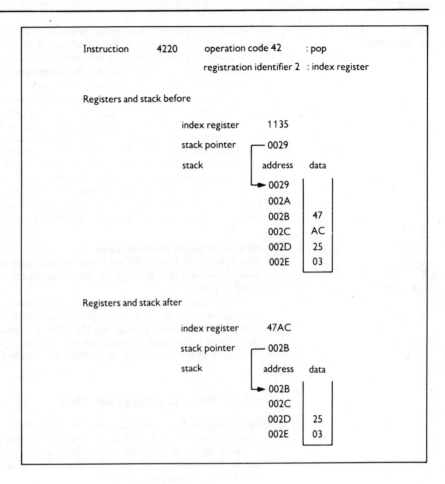

Figure 12.6
The pop instruction

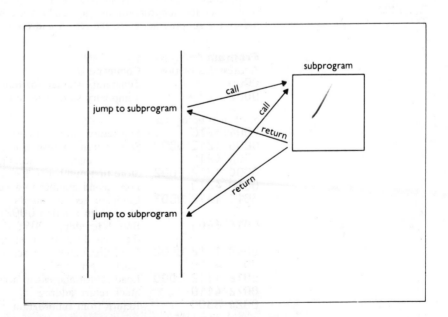

Figure 12.7
Calls to and returns from a
subprogram

When a jump to subprogram instruction is executed, the program counter contains the address of the next instruction (it has already been reset). This is the required return address. It is loaded onto the stack, and the stack pointer is updated. Control then passes to the subprogram, by loading the destination address of the jump to subprogram instruction into the program counter.

The last instruction in the subprogram is a **return** instruction. Although it is in the miscellaneous instructions group, it is discussed here. This instruction causes the return address to be popped from the stack to the program counter. Control thus returns to the instruction following the jump to subprogram instruction. Although the stack may be used by the subprogram, it is important that the return address is at the top of the stack when the subprogram ends.

Dealing with return addresses in this way means that subprograms may contain calls to other subprograms, or even calls to themselves, a technique known as **recursion**. The use of the stack ensures that control returns in the reverse order to that of the subprogram calls.

Miscellaneous Instructions

The remaining few AMC machine instructions are grouped together in the miscellaneous instructions group. Only the operation code part of the instruction word is used.

Apart from the return from subprogram instruction, which is discussed in the previous section, the only instruction which deserves special mention is the **no-operation** instruction. This causes the AMC processor to 'idle'. It may be used to slow down a program, to synchronise the processor with a peripheral device, or to reserve space in a program so that other instructions can be inserted later.

12.6   Example Program 12.2

This program illustrates the use of a subprogram, and shows how information can be passed to and from a subprogram by means of the stack.

The purpose of the subprogram is to decide which of two given numbers is larger. The numbers are passed to the subprogram on the stack, and the larger number is returned on the stack.

You will recall that the return address is placed on the stack when the subprogram is called. This address must be stored in the memory during the running of the subprogram, as the numbers are beneath it on the stack. Just before the subprogram ends, the return address is again placed on the stack.

Program

Address	Instruction	Comments
0000		Temporary storage for return address.
0002		Temporary storage for one number.

Start of subprogram

Address	Instruction	Comments
0004	4210	Pop return address to accumulator.
0006	1212 0000	Store return address in location 0000.
000A	4210	Pop first number to accumulator.
000C	1212 0002	Store first number in location 0002.
0010	4210	Pop second number to accumulator.
0012	1A12 0002	Compare second number (in accumulator) with first number (in location 0002).
0016	6404	Branch to address 001C if greater than or equal to zero (i.e. second number is larger, or numbers are equal).
0018	1112 0002	Load first number to accumulator.
001C	4110	Stack larger number.
001E	1112 0000	Load return address to accumulator.
0022	4110	Stack return address.
0024	8300	Return from subprogram.

End of subprogram, start of main program

0026 1131 007F	Initialise stack pointer (to 007F).
002A 1111 4135	Load second number (4135) to accumulator.
002E 4110	Stack second number.
0030 1111 62A4	Load first number (62A4) to accumulator.
0034 4110	Stack first number.
0036 5200 0004	Jump to subprogram.
003A 4210	Pop larger number to accumulator on return.
003C 8500	Halt.

Points to Notice

- The return address is stored in location **0000** for the duration of the subprogram.
- In the main program, the numbers are stacked in reverse order. The last number pushed onto the stack is the first number popped from the stack in the subprogram.

12.7 The Instruction Cycle

The sequence of actions required to carry out one machine instruction is called the **instruction cycle**. The instruction cycle of a computer depends on its register architecture and the nature of its machine instructions. Consequently, the actions carried out for a machine instruction vary from computer to computer. Nevertheless, the overall pattern is much the same in all cases. The general pattern of the instruction cycle is discussed below, with the AMC used as an example.

Fetch

The first action is to fetch the machine instruction from the memory. The program counter contains the address of the instruction. The address is used to locate the instruction. If the instruction occupies more than one memory location, several memory cycles are needed to fetch it. The instruction is loaded into the instruction register.

Reset

As soon as the current instruction has been fetched, the contents of the program counter is updated so that it contains the address of the next program instruction. The amount by which it must be increased depends on the length of the current instruction.

Locate Operand

If the instruction contains an address, or an immediate operand, the data item, or **operand**, referred to by the instruction must be located. Details of the way this is done depend on the addressing mode of the instruction. Apart from the immediate operand mode, all modes require at least one access to the memory. The number of memory locations occupied by the operand also influences the number of memory cycles required.

Execute

The operation required by the machine instruction is carried out. In most cases, one or more registers are involved, as well as the operand from memory. The arithmetic and logic unit carries out the process involved. In some cases a data item is stored in memory. Condition codes are set or cleared according to the result of the operation.

Timing

An instruction cycle involves at least one memory cycle, to locate the instruction

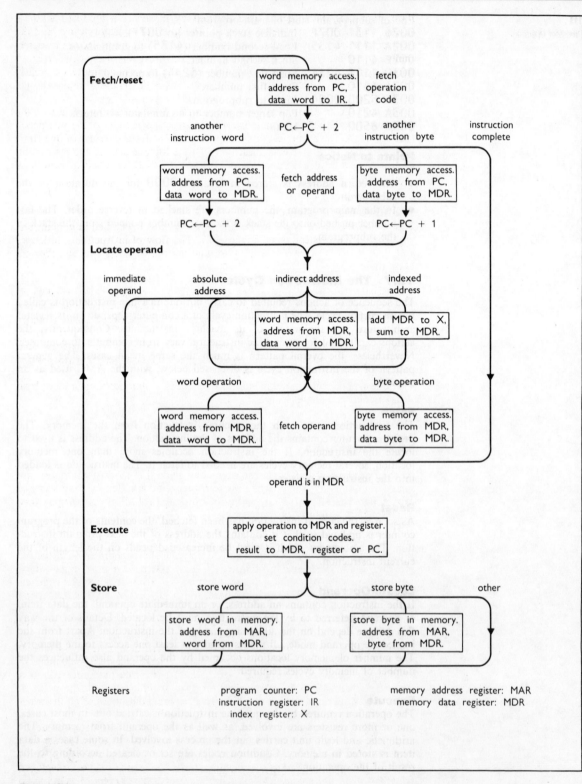

Fetch/reset

word memory access.
address from PC,
data word to IR.

fetch
operation
code

another
instruction word

PC←PC + 2

another
instruction byte

instruction
complete

word memory access.
address from PC,
data word to MDR.

fetch address
or operand

byte memory access.
address from PC,
data byte to MDR.

PC←PC + 2

PC←PC + 1

Locate operand

immediate
operand

absolute
address

indirect address

indexed
address

word memory access.
address from MDR,
data word to MDR.

add MDR to X,
sum to MDR.

word operation

byte operation

word memory access.
address from MDR,
data word to MDR.

fetch operand

byte memory access.
address from MDR,
data byte to MDR.

operand is in MDR

Execute

apply operation to MDR and register.
set condition codes.
result to MDR, register or PC.

Store

store word

store byte

other

store word in memory.
address from MAR,
word from MDR.

store byte in memory.
address from MAR,
byte from MDR.

Registers

program counter: PC
instruction register: IR
index register: X

memory address register: MAR
memory data register: MDR

Figure 12.8
The AMC instruction cycle

itself. If a long data item is used, located by means of a modified address, several more memory cycles are involved. The speed of a memory cycle, and the number of memory cycles per instruction cycle, are important factors in determining the duration of an instruction cycle. This duration is typically from 10 microseconds (μs) to 10 nanoseconds (ns), over the range of computers currently in operation (1μs = 1 millionth of a second, 1ns = 1 thousand millionth of a second).

The steps of an instruction cycle are controlled by the timing circuits of the computer, and either by outputs from the instruction decoder or by microcode (Section 12.9). The timing circuits provide a signal at fixed intervals of one **clock cycle**. A clock cycle is the smallest unit of time for one step of the instruction cycle, and is generally the duration of one memory cycle, or a half or quarter of the length of a memory cycle.

The AMC Instruction Cycle

Figure 12.8 shows the AMC instruction cycle. It must be studied in conjunction with the AMC register layout, Figure 10.7. The flow of instructions, addresses and data items between the main store and various registers can be followed. Note that:

1 The fetch and reset phases are combined. The program counter (PC) is updated more than once if the instruction comprises more than one word.
2 The locate operand phase results in the operand being placed in the memory data register (MDR), no matter what addressing mode is in the instruction.
3 Accordingly, execution of the operation only involves the memory data register, and one of the program-controlled registers (accumulator, index register or stack pointer).
4 The last part of the cycle is only carried out if a store word or a store byte instruction is being executed.

12.8 Interrupts

At the beginning of this book, the point was made that modern computers are seldom controlled by one program. Rather, they are controlled by a hierarchy of programs. At the top of the hierarchy is a program called an **operating system**, which forms the subject of Chapter 21.

There are two methods of transferring control from one of these programs to another. One is when one program **calls** another, as a program calls a subprogram. The other is a mechanism whereby the running of a particular program can be **interrupted**. An interrupt is an external event or signal which causes the running of a program to be suspended. This interrupt signal is generally placed on one or more **interrupt lines**, which are part of the bus connecting the processor to peripheral devices.

When an interrupt occurs, the current contents of all the registers are saved and control passes to an **interrupt service routine**, which is part of the operating system. See Section 21.7. The interrupt service routine determines the source of the interrupt, generally by examining a number of **flags**, and transfers control to a routine to handle the particular type of interrupt which has occurred. At a later stage, running of the interrupted program is resumed, from the point at which it was interrupted. This is achieved by restoring the values of all the registers which were saved when the interrupt occurred.

Common causes of interrupts include the input or output of data, the detection of an error in a program, or the fact that a program has exceeded the time allocated to it. The instruction sets of most computers include instructions which **disable** interrupts, effectively switching them off, and **enable** interrupts, switching them on. On most computers, inperrupts have levels of priority, so that high-priority interrupts can supercede the handling of lower priority interrupts. Interrupts are not implemented in the AMC for simplicity.

12.9 Microcode

In the AMC, and a number of actual computers, the step-by-step control of each instruction cycle is carried out directly by the instruction decoder and the timing circuits of the control unit. Such computers are said to have **hard-wired control**.

In contrast to this method of control, many other computers have another level of instructions, beneath that of machine language. These are **micro-instructions** or **microcode**. Micro-instructions are stored in a special read-only memory known as the **control memory**, and control the detailed steps of each machine instruction. Each machine instruction accesses a set of micro-instructions, which control the opening and closing of control switches as the machine instruction is carried out.

There are several advantages of microcode. One is that the instruction set of a computer does not have to be 'frozen'. Changes at microcode level enable different instruction sets to be used. In this way one type of computer can be made to **emulate** another type of computer, by adopting its machine code. Another advantage is cost. Control circuits of microcoded computers are generally simpler, and therefore cheaper, than those of hard-wired computers. Most microprocessors use microcode control.

The major disadvantage of the use of microcode is speed. Microcoded computers are generally slower than hard-wired computers with similar instruction sets.

12.10 Conclusion

The main points of this chapter are as follows:

- The program language which controls the step-by-step working of the processor of a computer is called machine language.
- Machine language instructions refer directly to the hardware of a computer.
- All machine instructions include an operation code, which specifies the type of operation to be carried out.
- Some machine instructions refer to the main store of the computer. Data is located by specifying the address of the required store location.
- A number of different addressing techniques are in common use. Some require address transformation before the data item, or operand, is located. Common addressing modes are absolute address, indexed address, indirect address and immediate operand.
- The AMC is a one-address computer. AMC machine instructions occupy one word, sometimes followed by a word containing an address, or a word or byte containing an operand.
- AMC machine instructions are divided into groups. The instructions in each group have the same bit layout, and perform similar operations. The operation codes of instructions in the same group have the same initial hexadecimal digit.
- The sequence of actions required to carry out one machine instruction is called an instruction cycle. Instruction cycles include fetch, reset, locate operand, and execute phases.
- All computers have a mechanism to enable the running of a program to be interrupted by some external signal.
- Two ways of controlling the steps of an instruction cycle are hard-wired control, and micro-instructions.

Taken together, this chapter and Chapter 10 describe what might be called a traditional computer architecture. A distinguishing feature of this type of architecture is that only one step takes place at a time. This limits the speed and processing power of the computer. The next chapter introduces some advanced processor features. Most of these are ways of permitting various operations inside a processor to take place in parallel.

Exercise 12

1 Briefly define the following terms: machine language; operation code; instruction set; addressing mode; offset; pointer; address modification; subprogram; recursion; instruction cycle; clock cycle; interrupt; micro-instruction; hard-wired control; emulate; loop.

2 Describe one use for each type of addressing mode mentioned in this chapter.

3 Consider the following three locations of AMC main store:

Address	Contents
2A61	1113 49B6
3521	AB02
49B6	3521

State clearly the result of carrying out the instruction in location **2A61**.

4 For each of the following decimal numbers: 16, 56, −128

a) Express the number as a 16 bit twos complement integer.

b) Apply the operation arithmetic shift left to the 16 bit integer, and convert the result to a decimal number.

c) Apply the operation arithmetic shift right to the 16 bit integer, and convert the result to a decimal number.

Comment on your findings.

5 Calculate the destination addresses (in hexadecimal) of these AMC branching instructions:

Address	Instruction
0024	6120
0120	61E4

6 Show the contents of the AMC stack after the following sequence of instructions:

Address	Instruction	Comments
0100	1131 0200	Initialise stack pointer (to **0200**).
0104	1111 AABB	Load **AABB** to accumulator.
0108	4110	Push contents of accumulator to stack.
010A	1111 CCDD	Load **CCDD** to accumulator.
010E	4110	Push contents of accumulator to stack.

Also write down the value of the stack pointer after the instructions.

7 If the byte **80** (hexadecimal) is copied into a sixteen bit AMC register, the contents of the register is **FF80** (hexadecimal). Explain why this is so (convert both of above quantities, regarded as twos complement integers, via binary to decimal to assist your explanation).

8 The program shown below, written in AMC machine language, is designed to add up the corresponding numbers in two arrays, and store the results in a third array. In other words, the first number in the third array is the sum of the first number in the first array, and the first number in the second array.

In the program, each number occupies one word, i.e. two storage locations, and each array contains four numbers. The length of each array is thus eight bytes.

The index register serves a dual purpose. It is used to locate array elements via the indexed addressing mode, and also to count the number of additions which have been made. Processing starts at the back of the arrays, working towards the front. Because the numbers occupy two storage locations, the index is decreased by two for each addition.

The part of the program which adds together two array elements is repeated four times. Such a portion of a program is called a **loop**.

Program

Address	Instruction	Comments
0000	08	Length of arrays, 8 bytes or 4 words.
0001		Array 1, assumed
to 0008		already loaded.
0009		Array 2, assumed
to 0010		already loaded.
0011		Array 3.
to 0018		

Start of program
```
      0019          2122  0000
```
Start of loop to add each pair of numbers
```
      001D          0320
      001F          0320
      0021          670E
      0023          1114  0001
      0027          1314  0009
      002B          1214  0011
      002F          61EC
```
End of loop
```
      0031          8500
```

a) Copy down the program, and write an appropriate comment next to each instruction. The comment must state clearly, in a few words, precisely what the instruction does.
b) What is the value of the index register at the end of the program?
c) Will the program instructions need to be altered if arrays of a different length are to be added? If so, what changes must be made?
d) Replace one instruction in the program, so that array elements are subtracted rather than added.

You will see in Chapter 15 that some computers have a single machine instruction to add corresponding elements of two arrays.

9 Write a program in AMC machine language to output a set of characters, stored in consecutive memory locations. The character with hexadecimal code 7E is used to mark the end of the set. The memory area used to store the characters can be immediately after the output program. Next to each machine instruction write a comment which explains clearly what the instruction does.

10 The following extract is taken from the manufacturer's literature accompanying a popular range of minicomputers. Read the extract carefully and then answer the questions.

MAJOR REGISTERS

Accumulator (AC)

The AC is a 12-bit register in which arithmetic and logic operations are performed. Under program control the AC can be cleared or complemented or its contents can be rotated right or left. The contents of the Memory Buffer Register can be added to the contents of the AC (via the adder circuit), and the result stored in the AC. The contents of both of these registers can be combined by the logical AND operation with the result remaining in the AC. The inclusive OR may be performed between the AC and the switch register (on the programmer's console), and the result left in the AC. The AC also serves as an input/output register; all programmed information transfers between the core memory and an I/O device are passed through the AC to data lines located on the (input/output) bus line.

Program Counter (PC)

The PC is a 12-bit register that is used to control the program sequence; that is, the order in which instructions are performed is determined by the PC. The PC contains the address of the core memory location from which the next instruction is taken. Information enters the PC from the core memory via the memory buffer register and from the memory address register. Information in the PC is transferred into the memory address register to determine the core memory address from which each instruction is taken.

Memory Address Register (MAR)

The MAR is a 12-bit register that contains the address in core memory that is currently selected for reading or writing. All of core memory can be directly addressed by the MAR. Data can be transferred into the MAR from the memory buffer register, from the program counter and from the switch register on the operator's console.

Memory Buffer Register (MBR)

The MBR is a 12-bit register that is used for all information transfers between the central processor registers and the core memory. Information can be transferred and temporarily held in the MBR from the AC or the PC....

i) What is the difference between an arithmetic operation and a logic operation?
ii) The program counter receives information from core memory or from the MAR. Under what circumstances will the PC be loaded from each of these two sources? How else would the PC contents normally be altered?
iii) The MAR can receive data from the switch register. How could this facility be of use?
iv) Draw a diagram of the registers described above, showing the flow of data between them.
v) Describe how an indirectly-addressed unconditional transfer of control makes use of the registers described above.

UL 78 I

11 Figure 12.9 includes five of the registers found in the central processor of a computer. Explain the function of each of the named registers:

i) AC: Accumulator,
ii) SCR:Sequence control register,
iii) SAR:Store address register,
iv) SDR:Store data register,
v) IR: Instruction register.

Describe how these registers are used in the execution of the 'fetch cycle' when an instruction is retrieved from store.

In principle, it is necessary to have information about four storage addresses, in order to execute an add instruction:

i) and ii) the addresses of the two operands,
iii) the address where the result is to be placed,
iv) the address from which the next instruction is to be taken.

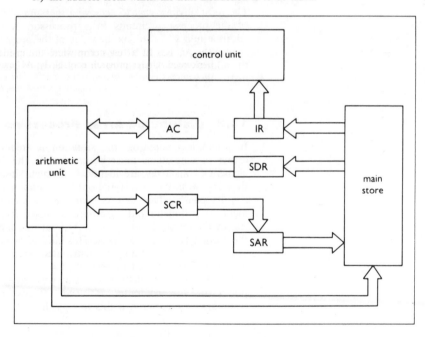

Figure 12.9

Explain how the registers in Figure 12.9 above, and a re-organisation of the computation, enable addition of two numbers to be carried out in a computer that can only hold **one** address in each instruction word.

UL 80 I

13

Advanced Processor Features

The principles of the design of digital electronic computers were first set out in 1946, by John von Neumann. These principles lead to a computer architecture like that described in the previous four chapters. A great many computers have been built in accordance with these principles, and no doubt many more will be built in the future.

The advantages of the 'traditional' Von Neumann design are its simplicity and versatility. A Von Neumann processor operates on a fixed cycle of fetching an instruction from store, and then executing it, before fetching another instruction. The major disadvantage is that only one action is performed, inside a processor, at any one moment. Many of the advances from Von Neumann architecture are centred around attempts to introduce a measure of **parallelism** into the design of computers. Parallelism means that several actions can be performed simultaneously within a processor. It is essential in coping with the demands for data throughput placed on modern computers, and for such applications as voice recognition and image processing, both of which require the simultaneous processing, at a number of levels, of very large amounts of data.

This chapter examines a number of advanced processor features which have been incorporated into contemporary computers. Each is an attempt to enhance the processing power of a computer in some way. Some are only suitable for special-purpose computing, particularly scientific computing. Others are suitable for computers of all types. The features are discussed in broad outline only, as the details of some of them are extremely complicated. Developments in computer architecture which are part of the fifth generation initiative are discussed in Section 34.3.

13.1 Duplicate Processing Circuits

The most obvious way to achieve a measure of parallelism is to duplicate some of the processing circuits in a processor. A common example is a simple addition unit which resets the value of the program counter while an instruction is being executed. In a few computers, the entire mechanism which deals with the address part of an instruction is separate from the circuits which execute the instruction.

13.2 Distributed Array Processing

In scientific computing, the situation is frequently encountered where large arrays of data items must be processed. The operations carried out on each element of an array are identical. In such situations, a significant amount of time can be saved by carrying out the operations on all the elements of an array simultaneously. This can be done by a computer with a large number of identical arithmetic and logic units arranged in parallel, and circuits which can supply the required data to each ALU at the same time, and similarly deal with the outputs from all the ALUs. This kind of processing is called **distributed array processing**. A variation on distributed array processing, known as **vector processing**, is discussed in Section 15.4.

The problem with distributed array processing is to ensure that the processing power of the computer is used effectively. Sophisticated programming techniques are required if this to be achieved.

13.3 Advanced Memory Architectures

One of the slowest aspects of the operation of a computer is the transfer of data between processing units and peripheral devices. In a conventional computer, all the steps of such transfers are controlled directly by the program. Peripheral devices are much slower in operation than processors. This often involves 'idling' a processor while a peripheral device completes the transfer of a data item.

Several techniques have evolved to deal with this problem. The most common is **autonomous peripheral operation**, with the peripheral having direct access to the main store of the processor. This technique is also known as **direct memory access** or DMA. It requires hardware known as **DMA controllers**.

Data is input or output under DMA, not as individual characters, but in blocks of characters. The DMA controller is supplied with the start address of the data in main store, and the number of characters to be transferred. The controller then proceeds independently of the processor, until the transfer of the data is complete. Memory cycles are 'stolen' from the processor whenever they are required by the DMA controller. Because the processor works much faster than the peripheral which governs the speed of the DMA controller, this does not slow the processor down very much.

A further development, which eliminates the need for cycle stealing, is the **multi-port** memory. A large common main store has a number of high-speed read/write channels which operate in parallel. These enable several data items to be stored or accessed simultaneously. See Section 15.4 for an example.

The memory of most large computers is not regarded as a single unit, but as a series of areas, each allocated to one process. In order to ensure that a process does not exceed its allocated area, there is a **base register** which holds the address of the start of the area, and a **limit register** which holds the address of the end of the area. All addresses used by the process are checked to ensure that they lie within these two bounds.

A smaller subdivision of memory is into **pages**, of fixed length, and which are transferred to and from backing store in one unit, generally by DMA. This enables the main memory and the backing store of the computer to be regarded as a single entity known as a **virtual store**. See Section 15.2 for an example. The concept of virtual store is important in the study of operating systems: see Section 21.7.

13.4 Pipelining

The feature which has contributed the most towards improving the performance of a processor is a technique known as **pipelining**. Pipelining is widely used, even among fairly small computers.

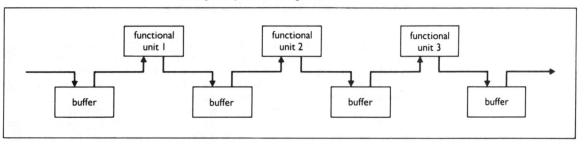

Figure 13.1
A pipeline

Pipelining can be used whenever an operation can be expressed as a sequence of steps. A functional unit is constructed for each step. These are connected by storage areas, or **buffers**, which hold the items as they pass through the pipeline. See Figure 13.1. A requirement of a pipeline is that each step takes the same length of time. During this time interval, called a **beat**, each item in the pipeline moves from a buffer, through a functional unit, into the next buffer. At any one time, a number of items are at different stages of processing, each only one beat behind the previous item.

Another requirement of a pipeline is that each step in the process is independent of all other steps. This means that separate functional circuits can be constructed for each step, and items are not held up at any step because information from some other step is not available. This requirement of independence of steps is not always met in practice, and causes problems in the design and operation of pipelines.

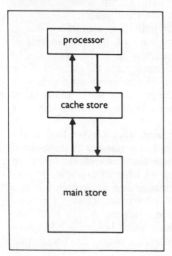

Figure 13.2
A cache store

The concept of pipelining is implemented in two ways in computers. These are **instruction pipelines** and **arithmetic pipelines**. In an instruction pipeline, each functional unit carries out one step in the instruction cycle of the computer. Items moving through the pipeline are instructions. Each instruction is only one beat behind the previous instruction. Problems arise when the results from one instruction are needed by the next instruction, and when a branching instruction is encountered. Details of the way in which these problems are dealt with are beyond the scope of this course.

An arithmetic pipeline is especially useful when dealing with floating point numbers, and for multiplication of all types of numbers. In this case items in the pipeline are numbers, and each functional unit carries out one step of the calculation.

13.5 Cache Stores

One of the slowest activities taking place within a processor is access to memory. As a memory access can occur a number of times during one instruction cycle, the speed of memory access is a major factor in determining the speed of the processor.

One way of improving the speed of memory access is to use a **cache store**, also known as a **slave store**. This is a small store, with a very fast access time, situated between the main store and the rest of the processor. See Figure 13.2. The arrangement of cache store, main store and backing store is known as a **three level memory**.

The use of the cache store is based on the assumption that, for most of the time, processing requires data and instructions close to each other in main store. Areas of main store surrounding the current machine instruction and data item are loaded into the cache store. This is generally done independently of the operation of the processor, at the maximum speed of the main store. Data and instructions required by the processor are then accessed from the cache store. From time to time the processor is slowed down when an item it requires is not in the cache store. A cache store is frequently used in conjunction with an instruction pipeline.

13.6 Content-Addressable Memory

The fundamental principle of the operation of a computer memory is that an address is used to locate a data item. However, for certain operations it is very useful to have a portion of store which works the other way round - a data item is used to locate an address. A portion of store which works in this way is called a **content-addressable memory**, or **associative store**.

The most common application for a content-addressable memory is looking up an item of data in a table. What is required is the position of the item in the table. The table is loaded into content-addressable memory, and the data item is compared, simultaneously, with all the entries. The address of the location at which a match is found is returned. This process is illustrated in Figure 13.3.

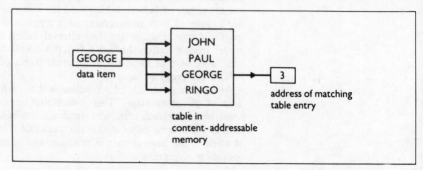

Figure 13.3
A content-addressable memory

13.7 Conclusion

This chapter has shown some of the ways in which computer architecture is evolving away from the traditional 'one step at a time' concept. Some of the ideas presented, such as pipelining and cache stores, are fairly well established, while others, such as distributed array processing, are relatively recent. The fifth generation (Chapter 34) may see radical departures from Von Neumann architectures. In all cases, the motivation for these new developments is the same: faster, more powerful and more versatile computer systems at a lower cost.

Exercise 13

1 Briefly define each of the following terms: parallelism; distributed array processing; direct memory access; DMA controller; multi-port memory; base and limit registers; page; pipelining; cache store; three level memory; content-addressable memory.
2 The overall steps of the AMC instruction cycle are fetch, locate operand, execute and store. Briefly describe how an instruction pipeline could be used to implement these steps, and some of the problems which would be encountered.
3 A particular computer has an instruction cache with a capacity of 256 instructions. Explain the benefits of this facility when executing program loops of less than 256 instructions.
4 A multiplication pipeline has a beat time of 10 microseconds, and contains 32 stages.
   a) How long does it take for one complete multiplication operation?
   b) How long does it take for 32 multiplication operations?
   c) How long does it take for n multiplication operations?
5 To what extent, if at all, do the advanced CPU features in this chapter alter the concept of a computer, discussed in Chapter 1?
6 Example Program 12.1 can be generalised to input data from any peripheral device, to AMC main store. Assume that it is used to read data from a disk drive, and the speed of the disk drive is such that the instruction at address 0004 must be executed 10 times per data item.
   a) Count the number of memory cycles per data item transferred.
   b) Use this figure to estimate the number of memory cycles needed to transfer 1K of data from the disk drive.
   c) If a DMA controller requires 32 memory cycles to set up, and thereafter steals one memory cycle per data item, calculate the number of memory cycles needed for 1K of data.
   d) Comment on your results from parts (b) and (c).

14
Peripheral Devices

Peripheral devices carry out six of the seven types of operation which characterise a computer: input, output, storage, retrieval, transmission and reception. As their name implies, they are on the 'outside' of the computer system, and provide its external interfaces. This chapter describes the commonest of the large number of input, output and storage devices which are now in use, and how they are connected to, and controlled by, a processor. (Data communication is described in Chapter 29.) The devices are described in outline only, and precise figures of speeds of operation and storage capabilities are not given. This is because the technology of peripheral devices is constantly changing, and improved performance figures are being attained all the time.

At the start of this chapter it is important to clarify the terms **medium** and **device**, and recall the terms **module** and **interface**. A medium is a material used for the storage of data. An example of a medium is magnetic tape. A device is a machine which transfers data, generally to or from a storage medium. The majority of peripheral devices may be regarded as modules. What they do is important, whereas how they do it is less significant. A peripheral may be unplugged and replaced by one which carries out the same task in a different way, without affecting the computer system as a whole in any way at all. The interface between a processor and its peripherals, and the external interfaces of the peripherals, are important aspects of computer system design.

In the early days of computing, the processor was the largest, most important and most expensive item of equipment in a computing installation. In many cases, the present-day situation is almost the opposite. The processor is the smallest and cheapest item, and may sometimes be regarded merely as a control device for the peripherals.

14.1 Terminals

A **terminal** is the simplest and most common way of gaining access to a computer. A terminal may be an integral part of the computer, as in the case of small microcomputers, connected directly to the processor, or be linked to the processor by telephone or radio from a very long distance. A terminal is used for both input and output.

The most popular form of terminal consists of a keyboard, resembling that on a typewriter, and a display screen, also known as a **monitor**, similar to a television screen. A terminal of this type is called a **visual display unit**, or **VDU**. Input is typed at the keyboard, and output appears, in character form, on the display screen. Some modern terminals are fitted with a **mouse** - a hand-held device which is moved by the user over a flat surface. As the mouse moves, a pointer moves in a corresponding way on the display screen. Pressing a button on the mouse selects the data item or control option at the pointer. Some computer systems allow their terminals to display **windows** which show the output from several programs simultaneously.

An enhanced version of a VDU is a **graphics terminal**. In addition to characters, a graphics terminal allows shapes and patterns to be displayed on the screen. Diagrams, maps, animated cartoons and graphs may be generated by these patterns. The patterns are formed by closely-spaced rows of dots or **pixels** on the screen. Many graphics terminals work in colour, and some permit **high resolution graphics**, with a much finer level of detail (the closer the spacing of the pixels, the higher the resolution). Some graphics terminals are fitted with a **light pen** which allows the user to 'draw' directly on the screen. Others have a **digitising pad** which allows the user to 'trace' from the pad onto the screen. (A mouse can be used to achieve a similar effect.)

An older and less popular type of terminal does not have a display screen, but produces printed output. Terminals of this type are called **teletypewriters**, or teletypes.

A terminal may perform a variety of tasks in a computer system. In an application such as word processing, a terminal is a **workstation** where text is entered, edited, stored and retrieved. The processor is dedicated to the support of the terminal. In a number of computing systems, terminals are used for **direct data entry**. Data input at the terminal is stored on magnetic disks until ready for processing. See Section 27.1 for details on data capture using terminals. Terminals are used to enter and edit programs. In most modern computers the **operator's console** is in the form of a terminal. A **software front panel** enables the contents of registers and key memory cells to be displayed when necessary. In most microcomputers, a terminal has the role of input/output device and operator's console.

14.2 Input Devices

Input devices transfer data from an external medium to a computer processor. They interpret the data, in the representation used by the input medium, and send it to the processor, often having changed the data to a code used by the processor.

In the early days of computing, the commonest input media were punched cards and paper tape. They have now been superseded by direct data entry at terminals, and a number of methods of reading data directly from its source. These include **optical character recognition, magnetic ink character recognition** and the use of **magnetic strips** and **bar codes**.

Optical Character Recognition

Optical character recognition (OCR) makes use of a data input device which can recognise printed or typed characters by a light scanning process. Many commercial documents such as gas, electricity and telephone bills, have a row of figures across the bottom which are read by an OCR scanner. A special typeface is used for the characters, to enable them to be read more easily. (Some OCR equipment can read ordinary typeface, and some, such as that used by the Post Office for sorting letters, can even read neat handwriting.) A simpler variation of this system is **mark sensing**. Mark sense equipment can recognise whether certain areas of a document have been shaded in pencil. Mark sense documents include football pool coupons, forms used to record gas and electricity meter readings, and multiple choice question papers. OCR and mark sensing have the advantage of being able to read directly from source documents, but are slow and error-prone by comparison with other methods.

Magnetic Ink Character Recognition

Magnetic ink character recognition (MICR) is the process of reading characters which are printed in magnetic ink. It is used almost exclusively within the banking system for the automatic clearing of cheques, and is fairly fast and relatively error-free. Cheques have a row of figures printed along the bottom in magnetic ink. These are read by the automatic equipment which sorts the cheques and inputs the data from them.

Bar Codes

Bar codes are becoming the standard way of displaying machine-readable information on merchandise, particularly in supermarkets. A bar code consists of a number of vertical stripes, in black (or dark) ink or paint on a white (or light) background. Characters are coded by combinations of thick and thin stripes, and check characters are always included. The commonest type of bar code used outside the USA is the **European Article Number (EAN)** code. Every item is allocated a unique, twelve-digit number, together with a parity digit. The digits are printed below the bars to allow for visual checks if necessary. The bar codes incorporate a number of checks to detect errors in reading, and to allow them to be read in either direction.

A **bar code reader** interprets the pattern of stripes and produces the equivalent character code. Bar code readers are either hand-held, similar to pens, or larger devices incorporating a window against which the bar code is held. Laser beams are used in the latter type. Bar code readers are generally incorporated into terminals, such as the most recent type of cash terminal used at supermarkets. Experience to date indicates that bar code input is fairly fast and acceptably reliable.

Magnetic Strips

Magnetic strips are used on such things as credit cards, building society passbooks and product labels. They hold identifying data such as account numbers or product codes, prices, etc. These strips are read, either by hand-held readers resembling pens, or by detectors in slots into which the credit card, passbook or label is inserted. The advantage of this form of data entry is that the data is almost impossible to alter, once it has been written to the strip. This provides a security check against data printed on the credit card or passbook.

Voice Recognition

Voice recognition has been the subject of intensive research for a long time. Although success has been limited, this is a promising growth area for the future. It is now a central theme in the development of fifth generation computers. See Chapter 34.

Current voice recognition systems can respond to a fairly small number of words or phrases from a person whose voice has been 'learned'. Recognition rates are fairly high, but not yet adequate for a wide variety of applications. Speed of input is, of course, limited by the rate at which a person can speak coherently.

14.3   Output Devices

Output devices transfer data from a processor to an external medium or visual display. As in the case of input devices, the data code used by the output device is sometimes different from the internal code used by the processor. Changing to the output code is generally done by the processor.

Printers

Printers are one of the commonest form of output device, with a wide variety currently available. They produce a permanent copy (**hard copy**) of the output. The largest and fastest printers are **line printers** which print all the characters in an entire line in one operation. Lines generally contain one hundred and twenty characters, and speeds vary from three hundred to twelve hundred lines per minute. At the top of the range are **laser beam printers**, which achieve up to twenty thousand lines per minute.

More suited to microcomputers and word processors are **character printers**, which print one character at a time. Some models speed up the operation by printing alternate lines in alternate directions. The commonest character printers are **dot matrix printers**, **daisy wheel printers** and **ink jet printers**. Dot matrix printers form characters by combinations of dots, produced by an array of needles in the print head. Daisy wheel printers have a print wheel with one or two characters on each 'petal'. The wheel is rotated in order to select the characters to be printed. Ink jet printers spray a fine stream of ink onto the paper, using a dot matrix pattern. Some models can print in more than one colour. Character printers are slower but cheaper than line printers, with print speeds of between twenty and one hundred lines per minute.

Computer Output on Microfilm

Computer output on microfilm (COM) is an output technique gaining wide acceptance. COM is now used by banks for their daily records of account balances. It avoids the bulk and expense of the large quantities of paper produced by printers.

A 'page' of output is displayed on a screen and photographed by a special camera. The film image of one page measures less than a quarter of an inch square. The film is cut into postcard-sized **microfiches**, which contain the images of approximately one hundred pages. A **microfilm reader** is used to project the enlarged image of a page onto a screen.

Digital Plotters

Computer-aided design (CAD) applications in areas such as chip and PCB design, engineering and architecture use **digital plotters** for output. These devices produce plans, engineering drawings, chip layouts and maps. A digital plotter has a pen whose motion across the surface of the paper is controlled by a computer. Some models work in a range of colours. Digital plotters are very slow output devices, and require special software to control them. In some applications they have been replaced by graphics terminals.

Some character printers can produce hard copy of graphics displays by printing dotted patterns of varying intensity. The quality is not very high, and the speed of output is very slow, but it is adequate for certain applications.

Speech Synthesis

Speech synthesis output is the counterpart of voice recognition input. Like voice recognition, speech synthesis is currently the subject of intensive research. A few speech synthesis output devices have been implemented, but the full potential of this technique is far from being realised. See Chapter 34.

Speech synthesis works by storing a digitally coded form of a number of key sounds. Words are constructed by combining these codes, and then decoding the digital patterns through a suitable set of circuits connected to a speaker.

14.4 Backing Store

Permanent copies of data in machine readable form are kept on **backing store**. In many computer applications, a bank of stored data is the most important element in the system. Backing store technology is being developed all the time. Improvements in speed and storage capacity, and reductions in cost, are frequently announced.

Magnetic Disks

Magnetic disks are the commonest way of storing data for access by computer. A magnetic disk is made of metal or plastic, coated with a layer of a magnetisable substance. Data is stored as small spots of magnetisation in one direction or the other.

Magnetic disks are made in a number of different sizes. At the top end of the range are **exchangeable disk packs**, with a number of large disks mounted on a common shaft. In the middle of the range are **single disk cartridges**, used mainly by minicomputers. Microcomputers generally use **floppy disks**, which are small, flexible disks made of plastic. A recent development is the **Winchester** disk. A Winchester disk is a small high precision hard disk, with an extremely high storage capacity. It is permanently mounted in its drive. Storage capacities range from a thousand **megabytes** for a large disk pack to one megabyte for a floppy disk (1 megabyte = 1 million bytes).

Magnetic disks generally store data on both surfaces. On each surface, data is arranged in concentric rings, or **tracks**. Corresponding tracks, directly above and below each other in a disk pack, form a **cylinder**. All the data in a cylinder can be reached without moving the read-write head of a magnetic disk drive. Each track is divided into units called blocks or **sectors**. Data is transferred to or from the disk in complete sectors. The gaps between the sectors allow for movement of the read-write head. See Figure 14.1. To locate a block of data on a disk, it is necessary to know which surface it is on, which cylinder it is in, and the position of the block around the circumference of the disk. This information, generally expressed as a sequence of numbers, forms the **address** of the block.

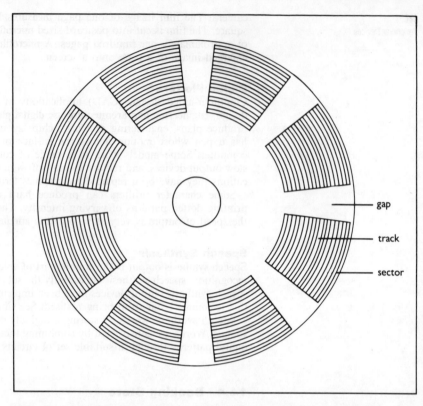

gap

track

sector

Figure 14.1
Data layout on a magnetic disk

This disk address is very similar to the idea of an address in the main store of a computer.

Magnetic disk drives transfer blocks of data to or from a magnetic disks. The disk rotates at a high speed, and a **read-write head** moves very close to the surface of the disk to detect magnetised areas, or create them. Speeds of data transfer vary from a few thousand characters per second for floppy disk drives to a million characters per second for large disk drives. There is, however, a delay in locating the data before transfer can commence. This delay has two components: the **seek time** while the read-write head moves to the required track, and the **latency** while the disk rotates until the required sector reaches the head. Latency is eliminated by transferring data to or from consecutive sectors, and seek time is reduced by transferring data to or from adjacent tracks or cylinders. Many disk drives have controllers which optimise head movements by careful control of the arrangement of data in tracks and cylinders, and handling requests for transfers in such a way as to reduce head movement.

The biggest problem affecting the use of magnetic disks is dust. Large disks are made of metal, machined to a very high precision. The gap betwen the surface of the disk, which rotates at a high speed, and the read-write head is very small. If a speck of dust is caught in the gap, it can cause a **disk crash**, damaging both the disk and the read-write heads. Floppy disk drives have read-write heads which rub against the surface of the disk. Dust can cause the disk to be scratched. Winchester disks are sealed in dust-free environments in their drives.

Magnetic Tape
Magnetic tape is the cheapest medium for storing large quantities of data. The tape is made of plastic, coated with a magnetic substance, and resembles ordinary sound recording tape. Magnetic tapes vary in length from several hundred to a few thousand feet. The longest tapes can store one hundred million characters. **Cassette tapes**, resembling ordinary sound cassettes, are used by some microcomputers. Other microcomputers use tape **cartridges** which contain

a continuous loop of tape. A recent development is simple, cheap magnetic tape units called **streamers**, whose sole purpose is to provide backup copies of magnetic disks, particularly Winchester disks.

Magnetic tape units transfer data to and from magnetic tape. They include spools for the tape, a read-write head, and, in many cases, **vacuum columns** to allow the tape to be started and stopped rapidly. Many magnetic tape units can read from or write to a tape when it is running in either direction.

The unit of transfer of data to and from a magnetic tape is a **block**. Like a disk sector, a block is a physical unit of data, of a fixed size for any particular computer system. Between successive blocks on a tape is a blank area known as an **inter-block gap**. The reason for this arrangement is that data can only be read from or written to a tape when it is running at full speed. The inter-block gaps are for the tape to be started up, slowed down or reversed.

Optical Disks

The most recent development in backing store technology is **optical disks**. These are made of plastic, coated with a transparent layer. The surface beneath the transparent layer has data encoded by very small indentations, which can be read by a laser beam in an optical disk reader. Storage capacities are in the **gigabyte** range (one gigabyte is a thousand megabytes). At present, optical disks are read-only media, but development of read/write optical disks is under way. If these prove successful, they could make magnetic disks obsolete.

14.5 Serial and Random Access to Data

There is a significant difference between magnetic disks and magnetic tape, which determines which is more suitable for a particular application. Magnetic tape is a **serial** access medium, while magnetic disks and optical disks are **random** or **direct** access media.

On a magnetic disk, blocks of data can be accessed (more or less) equally quickly, regardless of their positions on the disk. However, data items in the same cylinder or consecutive tracks can be accessed more quickly than data items in different cylinders. Nevertheless it is true to say that any block of data on a disk can be accessed in an acceptably short time for most purposes. Together with the fact that blocks of data can be located by address, this means that files of a far more complex structure can be stored on magnetic disks than on magnetic tape.

On magnetic tape, the time taken to access a block of data depends on its position on the tape. The quickest way to access all the data on the tape is in the order in which it was written to the tape. This has a number of implications as far as the structure of files which can be stored on magnetic tape is concerned.

14.6 Interfacing Processors to Peripherals

Linking peripherals to a processor can be a complicated task. Several characteristics of a peripheral must be taken into account, in particular:

- the character code used by the peripheral
- the rate of transfer of data
- the number of characters transferred in one operation.

Changing from the character code of the peripheral to that used by the processor is done either by the peripheral or the processor. In some cases a considerable amount of data conversion is required. For example, a bar code is detected as a sequence of wide and narrow bars, and is decoded into a thirteen-digit number, stored in most cases as a character code. Conversion to and from analogue data requires special hardware (analogue-to-digital converters) and software to control it.

In most cases the peripheral device works much more slowly than the processor. The aim of peripheral control systems is to transfer data in such a way as to minimise the delay and disruption to the processor. Many peripherals and their control systems now incorporate microprocessors and memory of their own. Large computers have separate front-end processors to handle transfers to and from peripherals.

The three main approaches to peripheral control are **polling**, **interrupts** and **autonomous peripheral operation**. If polling is used, the processor repeatedly checks the status of the peripheral to see whether it has an item or a block of data to transfer, or has completed a previous transfer. Interrupt-driven control allows the peripheral to operate at its own speed, and interrupt the operation of the processor when it has an item or a block of data to transfer to or from memory. Peripherals which operate autonomously have direct access to memory (DMA) and, once instructed by the processor, carry out a transfer entirely independently of it. Most disk drives operate in this way.

Data **buffers** are used to store blocks of data at various stages of transfer to or from a peripheral. A portion of main store is generally set aside for peripheral buffers, and most devices contain buffers of their own. In many cases the data passes through a series of buffers during a transfer. The size of the buffer generally corresponds to the number of characters passed to or from the peripheral in one operation. For example, the buffer for a line printer generally contains the number of characters in one line. Disk buffers hold one block of data. Rapid transfers are achieved by **double buffering**, where the peripheral transfers a block of data to or from the one main store buffer while the processor deals with the other. The peripheral and processor then swap buffers to deal with the next block.

The synchronisation and step-by-step control of peripheral devices is carried out by single-bit registers known as **flags**. A flag may be **set** (value 1) or **cleared** (value 0). For example, two flags may be used in the control of a line printer. When the printer buffer has been filled by the processor, one flag is set, to signal the printer to start printing the contents of the buffer. When the printing is complete, the printer sets the other flag. The flags are cleared once the signal has been noted.

Most microcomputers handle input and output in the following way. There is a special **parallel input-output (PIO)** chip to deal with all peripheral devices except for the monitor. The monitor is linked directly to a certain area of main store. The characters on the screen are copies of the characters in this memory area, which is known as a **map** of the screen. In other words, when a character is to be displayed on the screen, it is written in to the memory location corresponding to the desired position for the character on the screen. This is a simple but extremely powerful method of interfacing the display screen to the processor. An extension of this technique is the **bit map** where a portion of the memory holds bits which correspond to the pixels on the graphics screen. Writing a pixel to the screen is equivalent to setting the corresponding bit in memory.

14.7 Automatic Checking During Data Transfer

Transfer of data to and from backing store media is a relatively error-prone operation. Accordingly, on most computer systems a number of checks are carried out automatically during these operations. In addition to **parity checks**, discussed in Chapter 3, these checks include **read-after-write checks**, the use of **block sums**, and self-correcting codes such as **Hamming codes**.

A read-after-write check is carried out on most disk systems. After a block has been written to the disk, it is read back again and compared with the original, which is still in the transfer buffer. If the two versions do not match exactly, the data is written again. If the error persists, it is reported.

When a set of data items, such as a block, is transferred, a **block sum** or **check sum** is formed from the numeric value of the code for each data item. After the set of data and its check sum have been read, the check sum is again calculated. If the new value does not match the transferred value of the sum, then an error has occurred during transfer. In some cases an error is recorded as soon as this occurs. In other cases, the set of data is re-transferred and checked again. If a number of transfers are all unsuccessful, then an error is reported.

Hamming codes are binary codes, used to represent data items, which have a number of extra bits for checking purposes. The check bits are assigned in such a way that it is possible to detect and correct an error in the transmission of a single bit, and detect errors in the transmission of more than one bit. This is known as **single error correction, double error detection or SECDED**. See Exercise 29.

14.8 Conclusion

The most important point in this chapter is that the transfer of data between a processor and a peripheral device is a complicated process. In many computer applications, it is the most time consuming activity carried out by the system. The speed of input and output, or the speed of transfer to or from backing store, is very often the limiting factor in the performance of a computer system. In most systems, the details of the transfer of data to and from peripheral devices are taken care of by the **operating system**. Operating systems are discussed in Chapters 21 and 22.

The main points of this chapter are as follows:

- Terminals are general-purpose input/output devices.
- Graphics terminals can display pictures as well as text on the screen. They can include light pens, digitising pads and mice.
- Methods of input include optical character recognition, magnetic ink character recognition, bar codes, magnetic strips and voice recognition.
- Output techniques include printers, digital plotters, computer output on microfiche and speech synthesis.
- The commonest backing store media are magnetic disks (random access) and magnetic tape (serial access). In both cases, data is stored and transferred in blocks. Disk data is arranged in tracks and cylinders.
- Peripherals are controlled by polling, interrupts or autonomous peripheral operation, and data is transferred to or from them via buffers.
- A number of checks are carried out during transfer of data to or from peripherals.

Exercise 14

1 Briefly define the following terms: medium; device; terminal; block; track; sector; cylinder; microfiche; disk crash; serial access; random access; polling; interrupt; buffer; flag.
2 A line printer outputs 600 lines per minute, each line comprising 120 characters. What is the average rate of output in characters per second?
3 A twenty megabyte disk is to be dumped onto magnetic tape, i.e. the entire contents of the disk is to be copied onto a magnetic tape. The data is in blocks each containing 1K of characters.
   a) How many blocks are there on the disk? (Assume that 1 megabyte = 1000K of characters).
   b) A 1K buffer is used for the transfer. At a transfer rate of 500K characters per second, how long does it take to fill the buffer from the disk? (Give your answer in microseconds, where 1 second = 1000 microseconds).
   c) At a transfer rate of 20K characters per second to the magnetic tape, how long does it take to empty the buffer to the tape?
   d) If there is an additional 15μs overhead on the transfer of each block, how long does the whole copying operation take?
   e) How much time is saved if a double buffer is used, so that one is being filled at the same time as the other is being emptied?

4 The transfer of a data item from a processor to a peripheral device is controlled by three flags, labelled A,B and C. The data item is loaded into a buffer by the processor, and removed from the buffer by the peripheral.

Algorithms for the functioning of the processor and of the peripheral are as follows:

Processor

Repeat
 If flag A = 1, then set it to zero and continue else wait.
 If flag B = 1, then set it to zero and continue else wait.
 Load data item into buffer.
 Set flag B to 1.
 Set flag C to 1.

Peripheral

Repeat
 If flag C =1, then set it to zero and continue else wait.
 If flag B =1, then set it to zero and continue else wait.
 Copy data item from buffer.
 Set flag B to 1.
 Set flag A to 1.

Initially, flags A and B are 1, and flag C is zero.
 a) Write down the steps involved in transferring one character from the processor to the peripheral. State the values of the flags at each step.
 b) By studying the algorithms, and from your answer to part (a), you will realise that the purpose of flag B is to protect the buffer while it is being loaded or unloaded. Briefly state the purposes of flags A and C.
 c) If the peripheral works much more slowly than the processor, at which point will most of the waiting occur?
●**5** Write a program, in AMC machine language, to accept ten characters as input, and store them in consecutive memory locations. The first eight characters are data, the last two together are the check sum of the numeric value of the previous eight characters.

Having input the data, re-calculate the check sum and compare it with the input value. Output 1 if the check is successful, and 0 if the check fails.
 6 Find out more details about some of the peripheral devices mentioned in this chapter, particulary ones which are relatively recent, such as voice recognition and speech synthesis systems, and optical disks.
 7 A method of checking data, in addition to those mentioned in the text, is the cyclic redundancy check (CRC). Find out how this checking method works, and how it is used.

15
Processor
Case Studies

This chapter examines the topic of computer hardware from a practical aspect, by presenting case studies of a selection of computer processors. In choosing the case study computers, an attempt has been made to give an idea of the range in size and complexity of processors, while selecting ones which are up-to-date, widely used and regarded as having a sound architecture. Accordingly, the following four computers have been selected:

Research Machines Nimbus microcomputer,
Digital Equipment VAX minicomputer,
ICL 2900 Series mainframe computer,
Cray-2 supercomputer.

In the sections which follow, each computer is described in general terms, and then its register layout and machine language are discussed. The intention is to present the overall design features of each processor, without going into too much detail, and to show how the principles of processor architecture are put into practice in each case.

15.1   Research Machines Nimbus Microcomputer

The Research Machines Nimbus range is a family of microcomputers based on the sixteen-bit Intel 80186 processor chip. It was launched in 1985, and is intended for business, research and educational computing. It is available as a stand-alone unit or as a network workstation or fileserver.

The 80186 processor has a clock cycle time of 125 nanoseconds, and an instruction throughput rate of 1 million instructions per second. Memory sizes range from 512K bytes to 1 megabyte of RAM for the user, with an additional 64K bytes dedicated to screen graphics. ROM is used for system firmware, and external ROM packs may be plugged in for programs and read-only data. External EEROM packs may be plugged in for reading and writing of data. Backing store is one or two 3.5 inch disk drives, each with a capacity of 720K bytes, or a 3.5 inch disk and an internal Winchester disk, which may have a capacity of 10 or 20 megabytes. Up to four external Winchester disks may be added. (Alternatively, network workstations may have no backing store.) A second high-speed mathematical processor, the Intel 8087, may be included. Input is by keyboard or mouse, and output is on an integrated text-plus-graphics screen, with a printer as an optional extra. Sound and voice output are also provided.

Overall Configuration

Figure 15.1 shows the overall configuration of the Nimbus processor. The 80186 processor chip is connected by the sixteen-bit address/data bus to the other system elements. As one megabyte of memory requires twenty address bits, the additional four address bits are carried on a separate bus to the memory control chip. There are three custom-designed ULA chips: Gate Array 1 for memory control, Gate Array 2 for graphics and Gate Array 3 for input/output control.

Gate Array 1 performs part of the address decoding, and also provides a direct link between memory and the serial output chip. Gate Array 2 is a high-speed graphics processing chip, with direct access to the 64K graphics screen memory. The display is bit-mapped onto the graphics memory, and supports windows showing portions of different programs. Gate Array 3 performs a number of tasks associated with input and output, controlling access to the rompacks, mouse, network (Znet) and a communications system for a range of digital electronic control systems known as Piconet. A dedicated serial input/output chip controls access to the keyboard and printer.

If an 8087 co-processor is fitted, it is linked directly to the 80186 chip, and carries out all machine instructions for arithmetic operations. The 8087 chip has 80-bit registers which can represent numbers in integer (using 64 bits) or floating point form, and can process them directly in these forms.

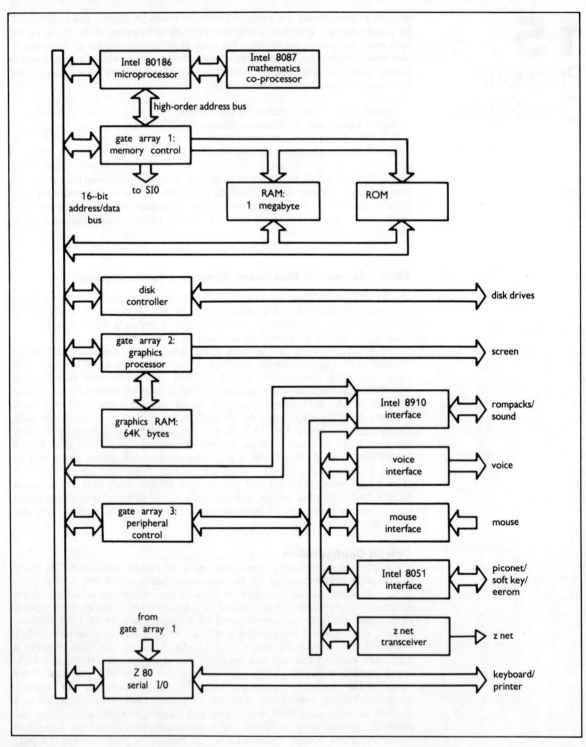

Figure 15.1
RM Nimbus processor configuration

Register Structure

Figure 15.2 shows the registers in the 80186 chip, and how they relate to the memory. All registers are sixteen bits wide; some may be regarded as two eight-bit registers for certain operations. There is a single accumulator, a base and a count register for accessing arrays, and a data register. Local stacks are defined by a stack base and stack pointer. There are two index registers, one for the source of data transfers, and the other for the destination of the transfers.

The one megabyte address space (from hexadecimal address **00000** to address **FFFFF**) is organised as **segments**. Each segment is a sequence of up to 64K bytes, and is accessed by one of four segment base registers (code, stack and two data registers) which contain the address of the start of the segment. The offset address, or **displacement** of a data item in its segment is added to the address of the base of the segment in order to obtain the physical address of the data item. Note from Figure 15.2 the alignment of the displacement and the segment registers in order to produce a twenty-bit physical address.

Figure 15.2
Intel 80186 microprocessor:
register configuration

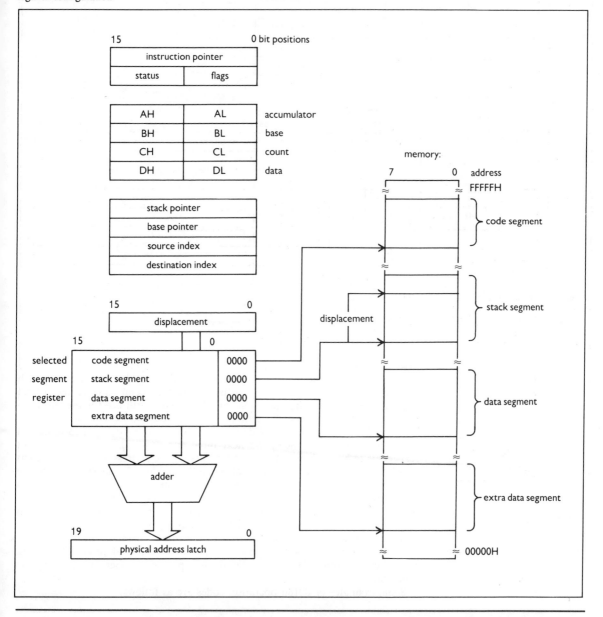

Figure 15.3 shows the registers of the 8087 co-processor chip, and how they relate to the 80186 registers. The eight main registers each hold 80 bits, and have a two-bit tag field associated with them. Numbers are stored in integer, packed decimal or floating point form in these registers. There is a sixteen-bit control register which provides details of how mathematical operations are to be carried out, and a status register which reports on the success or otherwise of operations. The instruction register (32 bits) holds the address of the current machine instruction, and a copy of its operation code. The 20-bit data pointer register holds the physical address of the data item being processed at the time.

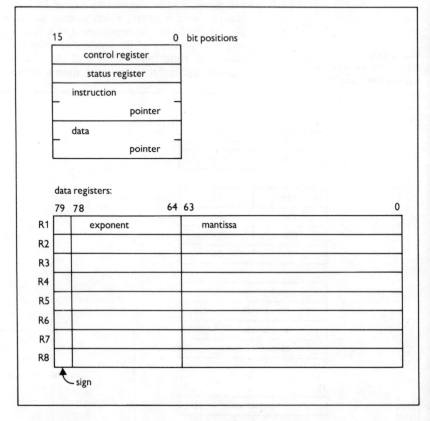

Figure 15.3
Intel 8087 mathematics co-processor: register configuration

Instruction Set

Figure 15.4 shows the general format of an 80186 machine instruction, which may occupy up to six bytes. The first byte is for the operation code, the second specifies the mode of the operation, the third and fourth are for the displacement part of the address of the data item, if required, and the fifth and sixth are for immediate operands. The mode byte has the first two bits for a specification of the address displacement, the next three bits denoting which of the eight registers is to be used, and the final three bits for the addressing mode. All eight addressing modes generate a physical address by adding the displacement to the value of one or more of the base and index registers.

The 80186 instruction set has 250 operations, including addition, subtraction, integer multiplication and division, Boolean operations, stack push and pop operations, string manipulation, register interchanges and branches. There are separate instructions for word, byte and immediate operands. Instructions for the 8087 chip have a more complex format, and include addition, subtraction, multiplication and division on the three types of numbers which may be represented.

Some examples of 80186 operation codes are as follows:

- Op Code   Modifier   Displacement
                  Mod   Reg   Mode
  00000011   **10**   **000**   **111**   **00000000 00000001**

Interpretation:

Operation Code **00000011**: Add
Modifier **10**: 16-bit displacement follows
Register **000**: Accumulator
Address Mode **111**: Add displacement to Base Register

Add data item at (Base Register + Displacement) to Accumulator,
placing result in Accumulator.

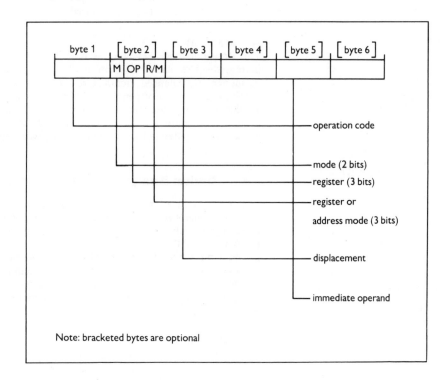

Note: bracketed bytes are optional

Figure 15.4
Intel 80186 instruction format

- Op Code   Displacement

  11101001   **00000000 10000000**

Interpretation:

Operation Code **11101001**: Jump

Jump by relative amount specified in Displacement. The Displacement is
added to the Instruction Pointer to obtain the address of the next instruction.

- Op Code   Modifier   Displacement
                  Mod   Reg   Mode
  11111111   **10**   **110**   **100**   **00000000 00000001**

Operation Code **11111111**: Push a word onto the stack
Modifier 10: 16-bit displacement follows

Register 110: Part of the Operation Code in this instruction
Mode 100: Add Source Index to Displacement

Reduce the Stack Pointer by 2, then transfer the word at (Source Index + Displacement) to the address indicated by the Stack Pointer.

Links to Peripheral Devices

The Nimbus has a DMA channel for disk access, and several layers of interface circuits in order to link to a wide range of peripherals as efficiently as possible. The graphics system has a separate memory for the bit-mapped display, and an autonomous graphics processor. This means that graphics operations do not take up any memory allocated to the user, and do not hold up the operation of the main processor. The wide range of peripheral links built into the main processor help to give it the versatility required of a general-purpose microcomputer.

Assessment

The Research Machines Nimbus is a state-of-the art microcomputer, consolidating advances made by a number of other manufacturers in the years prior to its launch. Its balanced architecture - fast processing, large memory, powerful graphics and variety of peripheral links - gives it a very wide range of potential applications. It is designed to support either of the operating systems which are becoming standard for microcomputers: CP/M or MSDOS (Section 22.1). Its use either as a stand-alone unit or in a network gives further flexibility.

15.2   Digital Equipment VAX Minicomputer

The VAX range of minicomputers manufactured by Digital Equipment is a series of general-purpose computers, designed for commercial, industrial and research applications. The range was first introduced in 1980 as a successor to the popular PDP-11 series.

The name VAX - for **Virtual Memory eXtension** - emphasises the main architectural feature of the processor: the virtual memory, which gives each computer in the range a virtual address space of 4096 megabytes. The computers are designed to run in a multiprogramming environment, with any number of active processes loaded at any time.

Virtual Memory

The VAX computers have 32-bit virtual addresses, which mean that programs and data can be designed as if they were accessing a main store of 2^{32} bytes (4096 megabytes). This relieves designers of applications of the need to swap program and data segments between backing store and memory under program control. Although the physical memory of the computer is considerably less than its virtual address space, all memory transfers required to support the virtual memory are carried out by the memory management mechanism, under control of the operating system.

Both virtual and physical memory are regarded as sets of **pages**, where one page is 512 bytes. Each process running in the computer has a **page table** which relates virtual addresses to physical addresses. The virtual page number is used as an index to this table, which supplies the physical page address. The offset within the virtual page is the same as that within the physical page, and is appended to the physical page address to locate the memory location. The process of translating from a virtual to a physical address is illustrated in Figure 15.5.

The virtual memory also has a protection mechanism, based on four levels of privilege assigned to processes: kernel, executive, supervisor and user. The first two levels are reserved for the operating system, the third is for certain users only, and the lowest level, user mode, is for applications. All memory accesses (to read or write data, or to execute code) are checked to ensure that they are

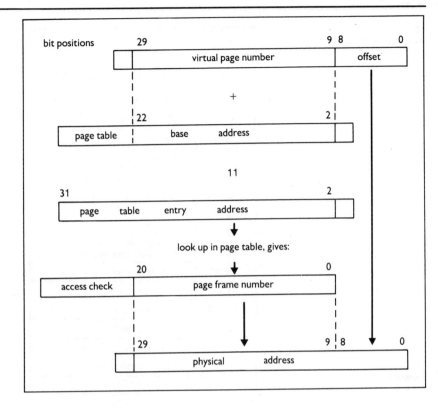

Figure 15.5
Translating from a virtual to a physical address

permitted according to the level of privilege of the process requesting the memory access.

Data Representation

Seven types of data are represented directly on the VAX hardware: integer, floating point numeric, packed decimal, numeric string, character string, variable length bit field and queue. The lengths of the data items vary considerably: from 1 to 16 bytes for integers and packed decimal numbers, from 4 to 16 bytes for floating point numbers, and up to 64K bytes for character strings. Queues are equivalent to the linked list data types described in Section 4.8, with forward and backward pointers.

Register Structure

VAX computers have sixteen 32-bit registers, as illustrated in Figure 15.6. Some are used for special purposes, such as the Program Counter and Stack Pointer, others are for general use. The general-purpose registers may be regarded as accumulators, index registers, registers for indirect addressing, or any combination of these.

Instruction Set

The 256 machine instructions cover a wide range of numeric and string processing operations. The **operation code** occupies one or two bytes, and may be followed by one or more **operand specifiers**, each occupying between one and four bytes. The operation code implicitly specifies the type(s) of the operands, and each operand specifier includes the addressing mode to be used for that operand.

Addressing Modes

There are sixteen addressing modes, which are **orthogonal** to the operation code. In other words, any operand may have any addressing mode (apart from a small

		Conventional Software Use
R15:PC	program counter	program counter
R14:SP	stack pointer	stack pointer
R13:FP	frame pointer	frame pointer
R12:AP	argument pointer	argument pointer
R11	general-purpose register	general purpose
R10	general-purpose register	general purpose
R9	general-purpose register	general purpose
R8	general-purpose register	general purpose
R7	general-purpose register	general purpose
R6	general-purpose register	general purpose
R5: AC	address counter	general purpose
R4: LC	length counter	general purpose
R3: AC	address counter	general purpose
R2: LC	length counter	general purpose
R1: AC/R	results/address counter	results of functions
R0: LC/R	results/length counter	results of functions

Figure 15.6
VAX register structure

number which are logically impossible, and which are checked for by the hardware). Addressing modes include direct, indirect and indexed addressing, addresses relative to the program counter, and several which use a register for an index or indirect address and then increase or decrease the contents of the register. The latter are known as **autoincrement** and **autodecrement** addressing modes.

Some examples of VAX machine code instructions are as follows:

- Op Code   Operand 1   Operand 2
  00001000   0101 0001   0101 0010

Interpretation:

Operation Code: **00001000**: Move word
Operand 1: Address Mode **0101**: Register
       Register Number: **0001**
Operand 2: Address Mode **0101**: Register
       Register Number: **0010**

Move the word in Register 1 (the least significant 16 bits) to the least significant 16 bits of Register 2.

- Op Code   Operand 1   Operand 2
  11010000   1000 0001   0101 0010

Interpretation:

Operation Code: **11010000**: Move long word
Operand 1: Address Mode **1000**: Autoincrement
       Register Number: **0001**

Operand 2: Address Mode **0101**: Register
Register Number: **0010**

Move the long word (32 bits) whose address is in Register 1 to Register 2, and then increase the contents of Register 1 by 4 (the number of bytes in a long word). Register 1 now points to the next long word in memory.

Links to Peripheral Devices

Access to peripheral devices is provided by memory locations which contain control instructions to the peripheral and the data items being transferred. Device controllers transfer data to and from these locations by means of **interrupts**; programs can initiate transfers by means of **exception calls**. In both cases, control is transferred to a handling routine in the operating system, which runs at a higher priority than a user program. This routine supervises the data transfer, before returning control to the user program.

Assessment

The distinguishing features of the VAX range are the very large virtual address space, the flexible combination of special- and general-purpose registers, and the orthogonality of operation codes and addressing modes. Programs written for the PDP-11 computers can run on the VAX range, in most cases without any modifications.

In its time, the PDP-11 range was the most successful series of minicomputers available; the VAX series has continued in this vein. VAX computers are very widely used, either running under the operating system supplied by Digital Equipment, or the Unix operating system (Section 22.2) which is becoming increasingly popular.

15.3 ICL 2900 Series Computers

Designed and manufactured by International Computers Limited, the **ICL 2900** series has the aim of creating a mainframe architecture which is the basis of a powerful, versatile hardware and software system. A particular objective is the efficient processing of machine code translated from a program in a high level language.

The design principles of the processor are implemented over a range of models in the 2900 series. The largest computers in the range are many times as powerful as the smallest. The largest models use hard-wired control, cache stores and pipelining, while smaller models make extensive use of microprogramming. Computers in the series can be configured in a number of ways. Large configurations have more than one processor. In all cases, peripheral devices and processors have independent access to main store, via **store multiple access controllers**. Figure 15.7 shows a large 2900 series configuration, including two processors.

Register Structure

Figure 15.8 shows the processor register structure and logical main store layout of the ICL 2900 series. The single accumulator can store 32, 64 or 128 bits, other registers are 32 bits wide. Broadly speaking, the ICL 2900 has a 32-bit wordlength.

The main store is partitioned in a fairly complex manner, because it is designed to be occupied by a number of programs (more properly called **processes** in this context) at the same time. Each process is allocated a separate portion of store, structured as a stack. Most addressing is relative to the base of the stack belonging to the particular process. Stacks are 32 bits wide.

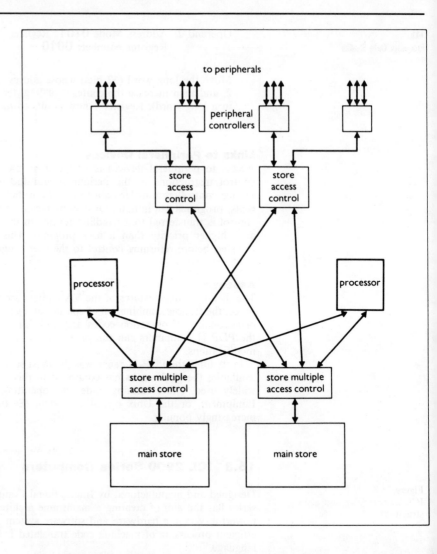

to peripherals

Figure 15.7
ICL 2900 series multiprocessor
configuration

Instruction Set

An ICL 2900 is basically a one-address computer, though a few two-address instructions are available to move data from one store location to another. Most addressing modes refer to various portions of the stack allocated to the particular process. Any data items not in this stack are accessed via a **descriptor register**. All addressing modes are available to all instructions. In this way, the address transformation hardware is kept separate from the instruction decoding hardware in the instruction pipeline.

Machine instructions are available for a wide range of fixed and floating point operations, including multiplication and division. Floating point numbers can occupy up to 128 bits. Packed decimal representation, using four bits per BCD digit, may also be used for the storing and processing of integers.

Memory Protection

Because the ICL 2900 main store is designed to be occupied by a number of processes at any time, it incorporates a sophisticated protection mechanism. This allows portions of processes to be shared, under strictly controlled conditions, while preventing errors in one process from corrupting the store area allocated to other processes, and making it almost impossible to 'break into' a process without authorisation.

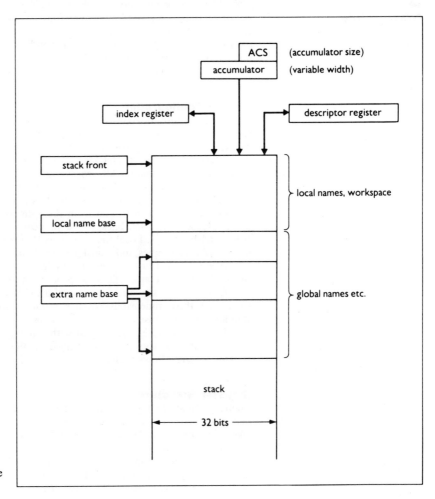

ACS (accumulator size)

accumulator (variable width)

index register

descriptor register

stack front

local names, workspace

local name base

extra name base

global names etc.

stack

← 32 bits →

Figure 15.8
ICL 2900 register and main store
structure

The question of protection is discussed further in Chapters 21 and 22, on operating systems.

Assessment
The most significant features of the ICL 2900 processor architecture are its single accumulator, stack-oriented addressing and extensive use of cache stores and pipelining. The 2900 series architecture is an attempt to design a 'high level language' processor, suitable for multi-purpose configurations and interfacing to data communications networks. It reflects advanced concepts in computer design in these areas.

15.4 Cray-2 Supercomputer

The **Cray-2** is a supercomputer designed for scientific and engineering applications. First marketed in 1985, Cray-2 computers are used for such diverse applications as weather forecasting, nuclear physics research, defence systems, structural analysis, economic modelling, electrical power distribution and very high resolution animated graphics.

A Cray-2 offers both **scalar processing** on individual numbers, and **vector processing** on arrays of numbers, wherever possible carrying out identical operations on each element of an array simultaneously. A number of the registers in a

Cray-2 are **vector registers** - banks of registers, each containing a number. The vector register is regarded as a single unit in many operations. Most functional circuits are duplicated, and many processing operations take place in parallel. A number of pipelines are provided, for multi-stage operations such as floating point multiplication. A very high transfer rate to and from memory is achieved, with a similar input/output transfer rate, to match the computational speeds.

Overall Configuration

A Cray-2 mainframe consists of a **foreground processor** and four identical **background processors** working in parallel. The foreground processor is in overall control, sharing work amongst the background processors, and providing the external interface to backing store and the front-end processors which control other peripherals. All processors have access to a common memory of 256 million 64-bit words. Four high-speed data channels connect the common memory to the processors, disk controllers and front-end interfaces. The total rate of transfer of data to and from the common memory is one billion 64-bit words per second. Each background processor has a local memory containing 16K of 64-bit words. Local memory is used as a programmable cache store, and has faster access times and transfer rates than those of the main memory. Each background processor operates at a cycle time of 4.1 nanoseconds. Figure 15.9 shows the overall configuration of processors and memory.

A Cray-2 processor uses a quarter of a million VLSI chips, closely packed on some 750 three-dimensional carrier modules. All carrier modules are of a standard size. Because of the close packing of components, Cray processors are liquid cooled, using an inert liquid with a high thermal capacity. The computer continuously monitors the performance of all its components. A maintenance control console allows faults to be monitored and rectified.

Register Structure

Figure 15.10 shows the registers, functional units and memory links of a Cray-2 background processor. The processor is divided into an **instruction section**, an **address section**, a **scalar section** for individual data items, and a **vector section** for arrays of data items. Each section has its own registers and functional units, and uses the local memory as a cache store. All functional units operate independently of each other, and are all internally pipelined. This configuration provides several dimensions of parallelism.

The significant features of the Cray-2 architecture are its very large common memory, parallel processors and the vector processing circuits within each processor. Each of the eight vector registers holds an array of 64 data items, each 64 bits in length. Successive elements from a vector register enter a functional unit in successive clock periods. The vector and scalar registers share the floating point functional units, which do addition and multiplication, and calculation of reciprocals and square roots. The vector length register holds the number of elements (between 1 and 64) to be processed in a vector operation. The vector mask has 64 bits, each corresponding to one element of a vector register. In a vector test instruction, each bit is set according to the result of the test for the corresponding element. The bits also control the selection of vector elements for logical operations.

Each of the eight buffers in the instruction cache can contain 64 consecutive instructions. Instructions occupy 16 bits; addresses, which may be stored either in the instruction buffers, or in the address registers, comprise 32 bits. This means that program loops, provided that they are reasonably short, can be executed without reference to main store.

The common memory consists of 128 banks, each of which has independent access to each of the four memory ports. The ports in turn are linked to the four high-speed data channels which connect the various elements of the system. In the common memory, each 64-bit word has an additional eight check bits. The check bits enable a single error to be corrected and a double error to be detected in the word (SECDED - see Section 14.7).

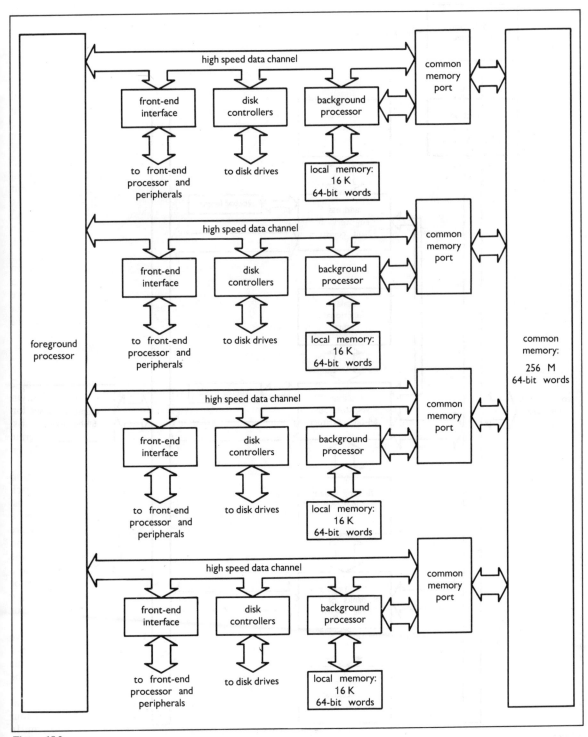

Figure 15.9
Cray-2 processor configuration

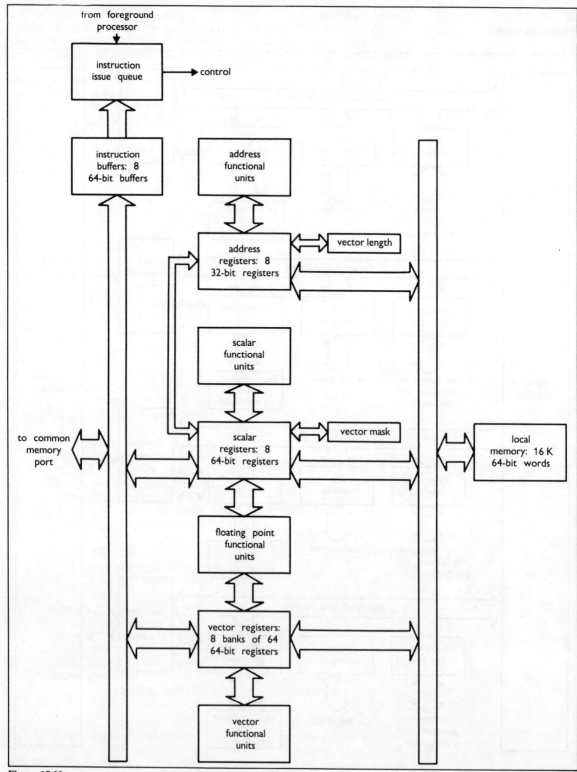

Figure 15.10
Cray-2 background processor: register configuration

Instruction Set

The Cray-2 has 128 machine instructions in 11 groups, each instruction comprising a 16-bit operation code, some of which are followed by up to four 16-bit address or data specifications. Data items referred to by instructions may be addresses, scalars or vectors.

Instructions which transfer data to or from local memory are one-address instructions; those transferring to or from common memory may be one- or two-address. Data may be transferred as single items (scalars) or arrays of items (vectors). It is possible to gather data from different parts of memory into one set of vector registers, and to scatter the data in a vector to different memory addresses. Instructions which process data refer to scalar or vector registers only. Arithmetic operations include addition, subtraction, multiplication and calculation of reciprocals, on integers and floating point numbers. Logical and shift operations are also provided.

Some examples of Cray-2 machine instructions are as follows:

Instruction (Octal)	Interpretation
014xjx <Address>	Branch to the address following the operation code if the contents of Scalar Register j is zero.
036xxk	Set the Vector Length Register (VL) to the value of the contents of Address Register k. All subsequent vector operations will use this value until VL is next altered.
070ijk	Read VL words from common memory, starting at the address in Address Register j, taking items at address intervals specified in Address Register k, and transferring the data items to Vector Register i.
072ijk	Gather from the VL memory locations at addresses with base in Address Register k, and offsets in Vector Register j, placing the data items in Vector Register i. (The address of the first data item is the sum of Address Register k and the first element in Vector Register j.)
155ijk	Multiply the VL corresponding floating-point numbers in Vector Registers j and k, placing the products in Vector Register i.

The Cray-2 may be programmed in its assembly language, or in Fortran (Section 19.1), Pascal (Section 19.5) or C (Section 19.6). The compilers for the high level languages are written to produce machine code which makes the best use of the vector architecture of the processors. Programmers may provide additional information to assist the compilers (Chapter 20) in producing optimal machine code. Multitasking facilities are available so that programs can include modules which are executed in parallel on different background processors.

Links to Peripheral Devices

The four high-speed communication channels provide direct access by disk controllers to foreground and background processors and common memory. Other peripherals are linked to the system through the front-end interfaces, and may use separate front-end processors. All transfers of data between common memory and peripherals are carried out independently of the foreground and background processors.

Assessment

Distinguishing features of the Cray-2 are its multiple processors containing vector registers and processing circuits, the high degree of parallelism in its design, and its extensive use of pipelining. Its very large common memory, with four parallel access ports, means that most computation takes place using data already loaded into memory. Its flexibility of use - a program may use any or all of the background processors - broadens its potential range of applications. The Cray-2 is a specialised numerical processing computer. Static data structures like arrays can be handled directly at machine level, but there is little hardware provision for dynamic structures such as trees or linked lists.

The Cray-2 is the most powerful computer of its time. It is a milestone in scientific computing, and its architecture indicates clearly the prevalent trends in large computer systems design.

15.5 Conclusion

This survey of a few selected computer architectures has given some idea of the wide variety of ways in which the principles of computer design are put into practice. It shows the range in size and complexity, from a microcomputer to a supercomputer. It also brings to light a few differences of opinion on issues of computer design. For example should registers be dedicated to a specific task, or general-purpose?

However, there are a number of underlying similarities, common to these (and most other) contemporary processor architectures. These include the following:

- A centralised main store, from which both instructions and data can be drawn.
- An addressing mechanism, whereby instructions and data items are located in the main store.
- A place where instructions are decoded, to become sequences of pulses along control lines.
- Functional circuits which perform arithmetic and logical operations.

These general principles may not, however, remain the same when fifth generation computers come into use. See Chapter 34.

This chapter concludes the part of the book concerned with computer hardware. This part has described the structure and functioning of a computer at the very lowest level, namely registers, processing circuits and machine language. The next part of this book works outwards from this 'core' level, describing the various layers of software which surround the hardware of a computer, transforming it into a useful machine.

Exercise 15

1 Distinguish between general-purpose and dedicated registers. For each of the case study computers in this chapter, list the general-purpose and special-purpose registers.
2 State whether each case study computer is a one-address or a two-address computer.
3 Which features of the case study computers are also to be found in the AMC? In the light of your study of the AMC, state why you think each feature is included in its architecture.
4 Which of the case study computers use pipelining?
5 Consider the following Cray-2 machine instruction:

Instruction (octal)	Interpretation
161123	Add corresponding integers in Vector Register 2 and Vector Register 3, and store the sums in Vector Register 1.

In Exercise 10 there is a program , in AMC machine language, which performs an equivalent process on vectors in the AMC memory.

a) How many AMC instructions are equivalent to this Cray-2 instruction?

b) The Cray-2 instruction takes (number of array elements + 3) clock periods to execute. Assume that AMC instructions take 8 or 16 clock periods to execute, depending on whether they occupy one or two words.

If each array contains 64 elements, work out the number of clock periods required by each processor. Comment on your results, bearing in mind that a Cray-2 clock period is about one hundredth of the length of a feasible AMC clock period.

6 Which of the case study computers makes the most extensive use of a stack in its memory arrangement? Suggest which of the design objectives of the particular computer is the reason for this.

7 Discuss the extent of parallelism in the architecture of each of the case study computers. In each case, describe how parallel processing assists in achieving the design aims of the processor.

●8 Find out the current prices of the four case study computers. Comment on their relative prices by comparison with their relative performancees.

●9 By obtaining manufacturer's literature, carry out a case study of your own on a suitable computer. Write a report on the processor, in about as much detail as the ones in this chapter. Some suggested computers are:

Microcomputers: IBM PC-AT, Apple Macintosh.
Minicomputers: Prime series, Data General Eclipse.
Mainframes: IBM 3000 series, Burroughs 6000 series.
Supercomputers: CDC Cyber 205.

16
Assembly Languages

This is the first chapter in the part of the book devoted to computer software. An item of software, or a program, is a set of instructions to a computer, which transforms it from a general-purpose collection of hardware into a machine dedicated to a particular task. As you will see during this and the following chapters, the task of some programs is to set up a computer to be able to run other programs. Accordingly, software may be regarded as layers, surrounding the hardware of a computer, and bridging the gulf between the hardware and a user-oriented machine. Figure 16.1 illustrates this idea.

This chapter concerns a class of programming languages called **assembly languages**. It explains their nature and objectives, and outlines their development. Features of assembly languages are introduced, using the assembly language of the AMC as an example.

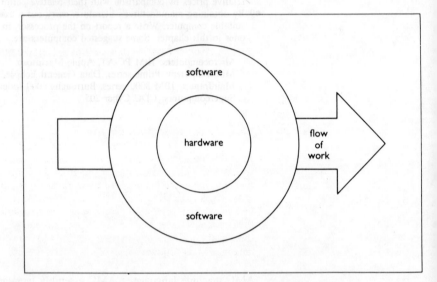

Figure 16.1
Hardware and software

16.1 The Nature and Objectives of Assembly Languages

In Chapter 12, a class of programming languages called machine languages was introduced. The step-by-step control of a computer is achieved through instructions in the particular machine language of the computer. Having studied this chapter, and having tried out some machine language programs, you will realise how slow and difficult it is to program a computer in its machine language.

Assembly languages have come into being to overcome these difficulties. Broadly speaking, the objective of an assembly language is to simplify the programming of a particular computer, while still enabling the programmer to control the hardware of the computer directly. An assembly language may be defined as a programming language whose data structures correspond to the physical structure of the registers and main store of its host computer, and whose instructions are closely related to the machine instructions of the computer.

From this it follows that each type of computer has its own assembly language, which is not too far removed from its machine language. Machine languages and assembly languages are together known as **low level languages**. This is because they are both close to the architecture of the computer which supports them.

16.2 The Development of Assembly Languages

In their most primitive form, assembly languages are almost as old as digital electronic computers. The first computers, produced in the period 1945 to 1950, could initially only be programmed in machine language. Although programming in those days was confined to a small group of specialists, writing out programs in binary code and personally allocating each memory cell soon proved far too cumbersome and error-prone.

Assembly languages quickly began to evolve out of machine languages, with additional features being added as time went by. At first they were just a character representation of machine code. Then features such as symbolic addressing, automatic conversion of data, directives and macro-instructions were added, in different ways on different computers. The confusion caused by the piecemeal development of assembly languages was one of the incentives for the development of high level languages, starting in about 1955. Since then, the nature and objectives of assembly languages have become better understood. These languages have generally been simplified and their structure improved.

16.3 Features of Assembly Languages

Although assembly languages differ considerably from one type of computer to another, they generally have the following features in common: **mnemonic operation codes, symbolic addresses, automatic data conversion, directives** and **macros**.

Mnemonic Operation Codes

To preserve a close relationship to the architecture of its host computer, an assembly language includes a set of instructions which are in one-to-one correspondence with the machine language of the computer. In other words, for every machine language instruction, there is an assembly language instruction.

Whereas machine language instructions are written in binary, octal or hexadecimal notation, assembly language instructions use a group of letters for the operation code. This group of letters is known as a **mnemonic**. For example, the instruction to stop a program in AMC machine language and assembly language is as follows:

AMC machine language   AMC assembly language
      8500   **HLT**

Symbolic Addresses

In machine language, the address of a data item or instruction is expressed as a number, in binary, octal or hexadecimal notation. This involves great inconvenience, particularly when indexed or relative addressing is used, or when the location of the program in the computer memory is not known. Assembly languages overcome this problem by the use of **symbolic addresses**. A symbolic address is a group of characters which represents the address of an instruction or data item. For example:

AMC machine language	AMC assembly language	Interpretation
1312 00AB	**ADD A NUM**	Add the number at address **00AB**, symbolic address **NUM**, to the accumulator.

Notice how the accumulator is also identified by a symbol, the letter A.

In order to associate the symbolic address with the data item or instruction to which it refers, the address is used to **label** the data item or instruction. The following program segment illustrates the idea of a label.

AMC machine language	AMC assembly language	Interpretation
	NM1 WRD	Location storing a number.
1A12 0002	**CMP A NM1**	Compare number in accumulator with number at address **NM1**.

6404		BGE	DWN	Branch to instruction labelled **DWN** if greater than or equal to zero.
1112 0002		LOA	NM1	Load number at **NM1** to accumulator.
4110	DWN	PSH	A	Push number in accumulator onto stack.

Notice how the symbolic address **NM1** labels the memory location storing the number, and the symbolic address **DWN** labels the instruction to which control is transferred by the **BGE** instruction.

The above program segment compares a number in the accumulator with one at address **NM1**, and pushes the larger of these numbers onto the stack.

Automatic Data Conversion

If the value of a data item is used in a machine language program, for example, as an immediate operand, then this value must be in the same notation as the rest of the machine language, namely binary, octal or hexadecimal code. In assembly languages, the value of a data item can generally be expressed as a decimal number, or as a set of characters. The characters are interpreted in a character code such as ASCII. For example:

AMC machine language	AMC assembly language	Interpretation
1121 0010	LOA X N +16	Load the number 16 to the index register.
1111 4243	LOA A N /BC/	Load the characters **BC** to the accumulator.

Notice how the letter N is used to denote an immediate operand.

Directives

In addition to instructions which correspond directly to the machine instruction set of the particular computer, assembly languages have certain instructions which operate at a slightly higher level. These are known as **directives**, or **pseudo-operations**, and have no direct counterpart in machine language. Directives greatly enhance the power of the assembly language, making the computer easier to program at this level.

Among the tasks performed by directives are marking the end of a program, which may be nowhere near a halt instruction, and reserving space for data items. AMC assembly language uses the directives **BTE** and **WRD** to reserve space for a byte and a word of data. For example:

AMC assembly language	Interpretation
NM1 WRD +35	Reserve a word for a data item, loaded with the value 35, and with symbolic address **NM1**.

Macros

A macro, more properly called **macro-instruction**, is a single instruction which represents a group of instructions. A macro-instruction is defined at the start of a program by listing the set of instructions which it is to represent. Whenever the macro-instruction is subsequently used in the program, it represents the entire set of instructions previously defined.

For example, supposing a certain assembly language does not have an instruction which negates the number in the accumulator, but that the following two instructions would achieve this:

STO A TMP	Store number in accumulator in location **TMP**.
NEG A TMP	Negate the number in location **TMP** into the accumulator.

A macro-instruction **NGA**, negate accumulator, could be defined in terms of these instructions as follows:

```
NGA MCD              Define a macro-instruction named NGA.
    STO A TMP
    NEG A TMP
    EDM              End of macro definition.
```

The two directives **MCD** and **EDM** are used to start and end the macro definition. Whenever the instruction **NGA** is subsequently used in the program, it is replaced by the instructions in the above definition.

Macros are an extremely powerful feature of most assembly languages, but are not implemented in AMC assembly language. Macros are also used in some operating system command languages. See Section 21.7.

16.4 AMC Assembly Language

AMC assembly language has been specifically designed for this course. It is simple, but fairly powerful, and illustrates the principal features of assembly languages.

M	addressing node:	N	immediate operand (blank) absolute address
		I	indirect address
		D	indexed address
R	register identifier:	A	accumulator
		X	index register
		S	stack pointer
ADR			symbolic address
OPD			operand
P	peripheral device	T	terminal
	effects on condition codes:	S	set (becomes 1)
		C	cleared (becomes 0)
		N	no effect
		D	conditional upon result
	condition codes:	Z	zero
		N	negative
		C	carry
		V	overflow

Figure 16.2
AMC assembly language (see also Figure 16.2 continued)

Mnemonic Operation Codes
The operation code for an AMC assembly language instruction consists of three letters. A complete list of these codes is in Figure 16.2. If the operation refers to a register, a further letter is used to identify the register, as follows:

```
A    accumulator
X    index register
S    stack pointer
```

For example:

```
CLR A      Clear accumulator.
MOV X S    Copy from index register to stack pointer.
```

Symbolic Addresses
In AMC assembly language, a symbolic address consists of up to three characters. The first character must be a letter, the others can be letters or numbers. In addition, there is a letter for the addressing mode, as follows:

instruction				interpretation	effect on condition codes			
					Z	N	C	V
memory addressing group								
LOA	R	M	OPD	load data word to register	D	D	N	N
LOB	R	M	OPD	load data byte to register	D	D	N	N
STO	R	M	OPD	store register word in memory	D	D	N	N
STB	R	M	OPD	store register byte in memory	D	D	N	N
ADD	R	M	OPD	add data word to register	D	D	D	D
ADB	R	M	OPD	add data byte to register	D	D	D	D
ADC	R	M	OPD	add data word and carry bit to register	D	D	D	D
ACB	R	M	OPD	add data byte and carry bit to register	D	D	D	D
SUB	R	M	OPD	subtract data word from register	D	D	D	D
SRB	R	M	OPD	subtract data byte from register	D	D	D	D
SBC	R	M	OPD	subtract (data word plus carry bit) from register	D	D	D	D
SCB	R	M	OPD	subtract (data byte plus carry bit) from register	D	D	D	D
AND	R	M	OPD	AND data word with register	D	D	C	C
ANB	R	M	OPD	AND data byte with register	D	D	C	C
ORR	R	M	OPD	OR data word with register	D	D	C	C
ORB	R	M	OPD	OR data byte with register	D	D	C	C
NEQ	R	M	OPD	NEQ (exclusive OR) data word with register	D	D	C	C
NQB	R	M	OPD	NEQ (exclusive OR) data byte with register	D	D	C	C
CMP	R	M	OPD	compare register with data word	D	D	D	D
CPB	R	M	OPD	compare register with data byte	D	D	D	D
register transfer group								
MOV	R_1	R_2		move from register 1 to register 2	D	D	N	N
register manipulation group								
CLR	R			clear register	S	C	C	C
INC	R			increment register (increase by 1)	D	D	D	D
DEC	R			decrement register (decrease by 1)	D	D	D	D
ROR	R			rotate register right, 1 bit, via carry bit	D	D	D	D
ROL	R			rotate register left, 1 bit, via carry bit	D	D	D	D
ASR	R			arithmetic shift right, one bit	D	D	D	D
ASL	R			arithmetic shift left, one bit	D	D	D	D
COM	R			complement register	D	D	D	D
NEG	R			negate register (NOT operation)	D	D	C	C
stack manipulation group								
PSH	R			push register word onto stack	D	D	D	N
POP	R			pop top of stack word to register	D	D	N	N
jumps								
JMP			ADR	unconditional jump to specified address	N	N	N	N
JSR			ADR	jump to subprogram, stack return address	N	N	N	N
branches								
BRN			ADR	unconditional branch	N	N	N	N
BZE			ADR	branch if zero (Z = 1)	N	N	N	N
BNE			ADR	branch if non-zero (Z = 0)	N	N	N	N
BGE			ADR	branch if greater than or equal to zero (Z = 1 or N = 0)	N	N	N	N
BGT			ADR	branch if greater than zero (Z = 0 and N = 0)	N	N	N	N
BLE			ADR	branch if less than or equal to zero (Z = 1 or N = 1)	N	N	N	N
BLT			ADR	branch if less than zero (N = 1)	N	N	N	N
BCC			ADR	branch if carry clear (C = 0)	N	N	N	N
BCS			ADR	branch if carry set (C = 1)	N	N	N	N
BVC			ADR	branch if overflow clear (V = 0)	N	N	N	N
BVS			ADR	branch if overflow set (V = 1)	N	N	N	N
BIN			ADR	branch if input not complete	N	N	N	N
BON			ADR	branch if output not complete	N	N	N	N
input/output group								
IRQ	P			signal peripheral device to load input register	N	N	N	N
INP	R			copy byte from input register to register R	D	D	N	N
ORQ	P			signal peripheral device to unload output register	N	N	N	N
OUP	R			copy byte from register R to output register	D	D	N	N
miscellaneous operations								
STC				set carry bit	N	N	S	N
CLC				clear carry bit	N	N	C	N
RTS				return from subprogram (unstack return address)	N	N	N	N
NUL				no - operation	N	N	N	N
HLT				halt	N	N	N	N

Figure 16.2
(continued)

N   immediate operand
    (blank) absolute address
I   indirect address
D   indexed address

For example:

LOB A D CHR	Load the byte at address (**CHR**+Index) to the accumulator.
STO S I RES	Store the contents of the stack pointer at the address contained in the location with address **RES**.
ADD A NM1	Add the number at address **NM1** to the accumulator.

Automatic Data Conversion

The value of a data item can be included in an AMC assembly language program in one of two ways, as follows:

1 An integer may be written as a signed decimal number.
2 A literal data item may be written as one or two characters, between the symbols //, for example /IT/. (Remember that one character occupies a byte, and two characters occupy a word.)

Data items written in this way in a program are called **immediate operands**, or **constants**. Some examples of instructions using constants are as follows:

ADD X N +32	Add 32 to the contents of the index register.
LOB A N /J/	Load the character **J** to the accumulator.

Note that if a constant is used in a program instruction, the addressing mode must be immediate operand.

Directives

AMC assembly language has three directives, with mnemonics **BTE**, **WRD**, and **END**. They are used as follows:

BTE	reserves a byte of store for a data item.
WRD	reserves a word of store for a data item.

In each case, the value of the data item may be included as a constant, as described in the previous section.

    END marks the end of the program. It must be placed after all the other directives and instructions in the program.

Instruction Format

The spacing of an AMC assembly language instruction is important. There is a specific **field** for each part of the instruction. These fields are shown in Figure 16.3. If a field is not required in a particular instruction, it is left blank.

16.5 Example Program 16.1

The objective of this program is to input a sequence of characters, and store them in consecutive locations in the AMC memory. The end of the input is marked by the character *. Apart from the end-of-input marker, this program is identical to Example Program 12.1, in AMC machine language. It enables a comparison to be made between the two levels of language. For details of the method, see Chapter 12.

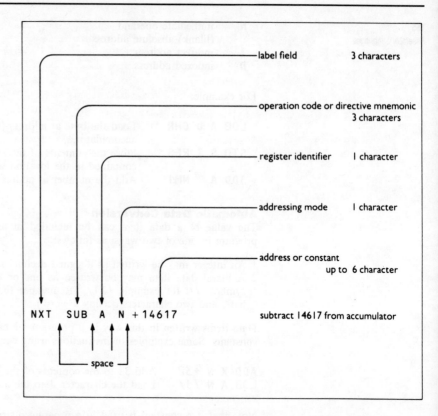

Figure 16.3
AMC assembly language
instruction format

| | | | label field | 3 characters |
| NXT | SUB | A | N + 14617 | subtract 14617 from accumulator |

Program

PTR WRD	CHR	Address of first character, later of current character.

Start of Loop

AGN IRQ T		Signal terminal to load character into input register.
HRE BIN	HRE	Branch back to this instruction if input not complete.
INP A		Copy character from input register to accumulator.
CPB A N	/*/	Compare character with end-of-input marker.
BZE	OUT	Branch if equal, to instruction labelled OUT.
STB A I	PTR	Store character at address in location PTR.
LOA A	PTR	Load address of current character to accumulator.
INC A		Increase contents of accumulator by 1.
STO A	PTR	Store address of next character in location PTR.
BRN	AGN	Branch to instruction labelled AGN, to input next character.

End of Loop

OUT HLT		Halt.

Start of Data Area

CHR BTE	Space for first character.
END	End of program.

Points to Notice

- It is most likely that this program is much easier to follow than its machine language equivalent.
- The address of the current character is in a location labelled **PTR**, short for **pointer**. This address may be said to point to the current character.

- Notice how the assembly language program is set out in columns.
- Apart from the directives, there is a one-to-one correspondence between instructions in assembly language and instructions in machine language.

16.6 Example Program 16.2

As discussed in Section 4.8, one method of constructing a list of data items is as follows:

data item   data item   data item
pointer   pointer   end-of-list marker

Each element of the list consists of a data item and a pointer. The pointer holds the address of the next list element. The last element in the list has an end-of-list marker for its pointer value.

This example program assumes that a list, structured in this way, has been loaded into the AMC memory. Each list element consists of a byte storing the data item (one character), and a word storing the pointer to the next list element. The end-of-list marker is a zero pointer.

The objective of the example program is to output the data items in the list, given the address of the start of the list. The method is to output a data item, and then use the next word in store as an indirect address to locate the next data item.

Program

PTR	WRD	LE1	Address of first list item, later address of current list item.

Start of Program Loop

NXT	LOB A	I	PTR	Load current list item to accumulator, using location **PTR** as an indirect address.
HRE	BON		HRE	Branch to this instruction if output not complete.
	OUP A			Copy current list item to output register.
	ORQ T			Request terminal to output current list item.
	LOA A		PTR	Load address of current list item to accumulator.
	INC A			Increment accumulator, to become address of pointer part of current list item.
	STO A		PTR	Store address of pointer part of list item.
	LOA A	I	PTR	Load pointer part of list item to accumulator.
	BZE		OUT	Branch to end of program if pointer is zero.
	STO A		PTR	Store pointer part of list item, i.e. address of next list item.
	BRN		NXT	Branch to instruction labelled **NXT** to continue.

End of Program Loop

OUT	HLT	Halt.

Data Area

LE2	BTE	/B/	Second list element.
	WRD	LE3	Pointer to third element.
LE1	BTE	/A/	First list element.
	WRD	LE2	Pointer to second element.
LE3	BTE	/C/	Third list element.
	WRD	+0	End-of-list marker.
	END		End of program.

Points to Notice

- Notice carefully how indirect addressing is used to go from one list item to the next.
- The pointer part of each list element contains the address of the next list element.
- The portion of program from the instruction labelled **NXT** to the instruction **BRN NXT** is repeated once for each list element. This loop is ended when a zero pointer is found in a list element.

16.7 Example Program 16.3

In Chapter 5, an algorithm is given for the multiplication of two unsigned integers, by a process of shifting and addition. This program puts the algorithm into practice.

The algorithm is given again below, using slightly different notation. The layout of the working areas used by the program is shown in Figure 16.4. Three words of store are used for these working areas in the program, but it is helpful to imagine them set out as in the diagram.

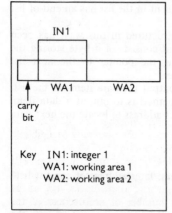

Key IN1: integer 1
    WA1: working area 1
    WA2: working area 2

Figure 16.4
Working areas for multiplication algorithm

Algorithm

Initially, the carry bit and working area 1 contain zeros, while integer 1 and working area 2 contain the two numbers to be multiplied.

Repeat, for each bit of the numbers

Mask out all but the least significant bit of working area 2.

If the least significant bit is 1, then add integer 1 to working area 1, placing the sum in working area 1, and the carry in the carry bit.

Shift all the bits in the carry bit, working area 1 and working area 2 one place to the right.

When this process is complete, the product of the two numbers is in working area 1 and working area 2.

Program

IN1	WRD	+31465	Integer 1, with value declared.
WA1	WRD	+0	Working area 1: initially zero, finally most significant word of product.
WA2	WRD	+15437	Working area 2: initially integer 2, finally least significant word of product.

Start of Program

	LOA X N	+16	Initialise index register to 16. The index register is used to count the number of bits processed.
	LOA A	WA2	Load accumulator with working area 2.

Start of Loop

NXT	AND A N	+1	Mask all but least significant bit of accumulator.
	BZE	OVR	Branch if result is zero, to instruction labelled **OVR**.
	LOA A	WA1	Load accumulator with working area 1.
	ADD A	IN1	Add integer 1 to accumulator.
	BRN	DWN	Branch to instruction labelled **DWN**.
OVR	LOA A	WA1	Load accumulator with working area 1.
	CLC		Clear carry bit.
DWN	ROR A		Rotate accumulator right, 1 bit, via carry bit.
	STO A	WA1	Store new value of working area 1.
	LOA A	WA2	Load working area 2 to accumulator.

ROR A		Rotate accumulator right, 1 bit, via carry bit.
STO A	WA2	Store new value of working area 2.
DEC X		Decrease index register by 1.
BGT	NXT	Branch if index is still positive, to continue shifting and adding.

End of Loop

HLT		Halt.
END		End of program.

Points to Notice

- The carry bit is used to pass a bit from working area 1 to working area 2 during the rotation operation. In the first rotation operation, the least significant bit of working area 1 moves into the carry bit. In the second rotation, the same bit moves from the carry bit into the most significant bit position of working area 2.
- This program contains a loop from the instruction labelled **NXT** to the instruction **BGT NXT**. The index register is used to count the number of times the loop repeated.

16.8 Example Program 16.4

This program scans a set of characters, and counts the number of occurrences of a given character. It is assumed that the set of characters is already loaded into the AMC memory, and is terminated by the character *.

The program is written as a subprogram, called from a main program. The address of the start of the set of characters is passed from the main program to the subprogram, together with the character whose occurrences are to be counted. On return from the subprogram, the number of occurrences of the character is passed back to the main program. Registers are used to pass the information to and from the subprogram.

Within the subprogram, indirect addressing is used to locate each character in the set. The algorithm for the subprogram is as follows:

Set the number of occurrences of the character to zero.

Repeat

Load a character from the set to the accumulator.

If the character is the required character, increase the number of occurrences by 1.

Until the end-of-set marker is reached.

Program

CHR BTE		Character whose occurrences are to be counted.
LOC WRD		Address of current character in set.
CNT WRD		Number of occurrences of character.

Start of Subprogram

SBP STB X	CHR	Store required character, passed to subprogram in index register.
STO A	LOC	Store address of first character in set, passed to subprogram in accumulator.
CLR A		Clear accumulator.
STO A	CNT	Set character count to zero.

Start of Loop to Inspect One Character

BGN	LOB	A I	LOC	Using indirect addressing, load current character to accumulator.
	CPB	A N	/*/	Compare with end-of-set marker.
	BZE		OUT	Branch to end of subprogram if equal.
	CPB	A	CHR	Compare with required character.
	BNE		DWN	Branch to instruction labelled **DWN** if not equal.
	LOA	A	CNT	Load character count to accumulator.
	INC	A		Increment character count.
	STO	A	CNT	Store new value of character count.
DWN	LOA	A	LOC	Load address of current character to accumulator.
	INC	A		Increment address of current character.
	STO	A	LOC	Store new address of current character.
	BRN		BGN	Branch back to repeat loop.

End of Loop

OUT	LOA	A	CNT	Load character count to accumulator.
	RTS			Return to main program.

End of Subprogram, Start of Main Program

	LOB	X N	/T/	Load character to be counted, T, to index register.
	LOA	A N	SET	Load start address of character set to accumulator.
	LOA	S N	+127	Initialise stack pointer to 127.
	JSR		SBP	Jump to subprogram.
	HLT			Halt on return to main program.

End of Main Program, Start of Data Area

SET	BTE	/T/
	BTE	/H/
	BTE	/E/
	BTE	/ /
	BTE	/C/
	BTE	/A/
	BTE	/T/
	BTE	/*/
	END	End of Program.

Points to Notice

- The accumulator and index register are used to pass data to the subprogram. The accumulator is also used to pass data back from the subprogram.
- The branching instruction **BNE DWN** is designed to skip the next three instructions if the current character is NOT the one which is being counted. Branching in this manner, on a negative condition, is an efficient way of constructing a portion of a program such as this.
- The test for the end-of-set marker must be made before the test for the required character.

16.9 Example Program 16.5

This program takes a data structure in the form of a binary tree (Section 4.9), and scans the structure in a systematic way. The data item at each node is output, and the left subtree is scanned, followed by the right subtree. The process is known as **tree traversal**. It is a **depth-first** scan, since the left subtrees of all the nodes are scanned before any right subtrees are examined.

Each node of the tree is represented as a data item (one byte) followed by two pointers (one word each), holding the addresses of the left and right subtrees respectively. Null pointers have a value zero. The tree traversal program is written as a **recursive** subprogram - it repeatedly calls itself until the entire tree is scanned. The algorithm is as follows:

> Traverse tree (tree pointer) is:
> Output data item at node
> If left subtree pointer is non-zero then
>   Traverse tree (left subtree pointer)
> If right subtree pointer is non-zero then
>   Traverse tree (right subtree pointer)

The subprogram requires as a **parameter** a pointer to the tree each time it is called. This parameter is passed to the subprogram in the accumulator. During the subprogram, it is stored on the stack, since it needs to be used again after recursive calls.

Program

Storage for Tree Pointer

TPR	WRD		Tree pointer

Tree Traversal Subprogram

TTR	STO A		TPR	Store tree pointer in location **TPR**.
	PSH A			Push copy of tree pointer to stack.
	LOB A	I	TPR	Load data item at tree node.
	OUP A			Copy data item to output register.
	ORQ T			Request terminal to output data item.

Left Subtree

	LOA A		TPR	Load tree pointer to accumulator.
	INC A			Increment tree pointer, now holds address of left subtree pointer.
	STO A		TPR	Store address of left subtree pointer.
	LOA A	I	TPR	Load left subtree pointer to accumulator.
	BZE		RST	Branch if zero to deal with right subtree.
	JSR		TTR	Traverse left subtree.

Right Subtree

RST	POP A			Pop original tree pointer to accumulator.
	ADD A	N	+3	Add 3 to tree pointer, now holds address of right subtree pointer.
	STO A		TPR	Store address of right subtree pointer.
	LOA A	I	TPR	Load right subtree pointer to accumulator.
	BZE		OUT	Branch if zero to end of subprogram.
	JSR		TTR	Traverse right subtree.
OUT	RTS			Return from subprogram.

Main Program

	LOA S	N	+127	Initialise stack pointer to 127.
	LOA A	N	TRE	Load tree pointer to accumulator.
	JSR		TTR	Call tree traversal subprogram.
	HLT			Halt on return.

Data

TRE	BTE	/A/	Top tree node: data item.
	WRD	T1A	Left subtree pointer.
	WRD	T1B	Right subtree pointer.
T1A	BTE	/B/	Second level left node: data item.
	WRD	T2A	Left subtree pointer.
	WRD	T2B	Right subtree pointer.
T1B	BTE	/C/	Second level right node: data item.
	WRD	T2C	Left subtree pointer.

	WRD	T2D	Right subtree pointer.
T2A	BTE	/D/	Third level first node: data item.
	WRD	+0	Left subtree pointer.
	WRD	+0	Right subtree pointer.
T2B	BTE	/E/	Third level second node: data item.
	WRD	+0	Left subtree pointer.
	WRD	+0	Right subtree pointer.
T2C	BTE	/F/	Third level third node: data item.
	WRD	+0	Left subtree pointer.
	WRD	+0	Right subtree pointer.
T2D	BTE	/G/	Third level fourth node: data item.
	WRD	+0	Left subtree pointer.
	WRD	+0	Right subtree pointer.
	END		End of program.

Points to Notice

- Indirect addressing is used several times to locate data items from their pointers.
- Before the subprogram is called, the pointer to the tree or subtree to be traversed is loaded into the accumulator.
- The data for the program is shown in Figure 16.5. The order of traversal is also shown in the diagram.

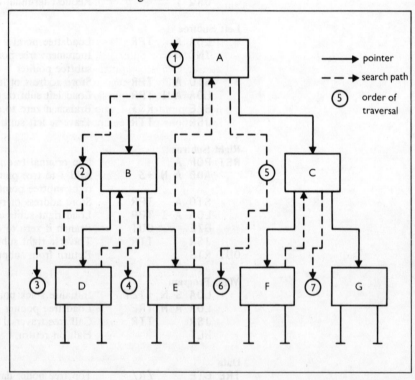

Figure 16.5
Tree traversal for Example
Program 16.5

16.10 Uses of Assembly Languages

With the development of high level languages (Chapter 18), there has been a gradual reduction in the relative importance of assembly languages. However, they still have a variety of uses, notably in the writing of **systems software**, and in the programming of microcomputers.

Systems software is a name given to the layers of software which transform the raw hardware of a computer into a machine which can be programmed in a straightforward way. Systems programs include operating systems and language translation programs, both of which are discussed in later chapters. Most systems software is written, at least in part, in a low level language, though high level languages are becoming increasingly popular in this area.

The advent of microcomputers has given low level languages a new lease of life. Some microcomputers are too small to support anything but the most primitive subset of a high level language. Most computer games are written in assembly language. Furthermore, a significant proportion of microprocessors are dedicated to the performance of a single task, such as controlling a camera. The only program which these microprocessors require is permanently stored on read-only memory. Such programs are almost always written in a low level language.

16.11 Conclusion

This chapter has introduced the concept of an assembly language, outlined the objectives and features of assembly languages, and then used AMC assembly language to demonstrate a number of techniques of low level language programming. The main points of the chapter are as follows:

- The objective of an assembly language is to simplify the programming of a particular computer, while still enabling the programmer to control the hardware of a computer directly.
- An assembly language is a programming language whose data structures correspond to the physical structure of the registers and main store of its host computer, and whose instructions are closely related to the machine instructions of the computer.
- Characteristic features of assembly languages include mnemonic operation codes, symbolic addresses, automatic data conversion, directives and macros.
- Assembly languages are used principally in the writing of systems software and in the programming of microcomputers.

Exercise 16

1 Briefly define the following terms: assembly language; mnemonic; symbolic address; label; directive; macro-instruction; low level language; immediate operand; pointer; recursive; tree traversal.

2 Write short sequences of instructions, in AMC assembly language, for each of the following operations:
   a) Set a store word, labelled DT1, to zero.
   b) Store the decimal value 16291 in a word labelled CS1.
   c) Increase the contents of a byte of store, labelled CTR, by 1.
   d) Test whether the contents of two store locations with addresses AB1 and AB2 are equal.
   e) Create a stack containing the code for the following ASCII characters:

```
| AB
| CD
| EF
```

3 Rewrite Example Program 12.2 in AMC assembly language.

4 Rewrite the program in Exercise 14, Question 6, in AMC assembly language.

5 A 'double length' integer may be stored in two consecutive words of AMC store, as follows:

The first word stores the high order part of the number, with the most significant bit representing a negative quantity. The place value of this bit is $-2^{31} = -2147483648$. The least significant bit in this word has the place value of $2^{16} = 65536$.

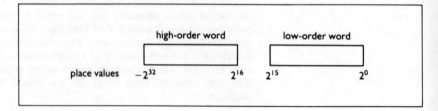

Figure 16.6
A double length integer

The second word stores the low order part of the number, with all bits representing positive quantities. Place values range from $2^{15} = 32768$ to $2^0 = 1$. See Figure 16.6.

For example, if the high order part of the word contains the decimal value 10000 and the low order part contains the decimal value 8763, then the double length number represented is $2^{16} \times 10000 + 8763 = 655368763$.

Addition of two double length integers is as follows: the low order words of the two numbers are added first, and the sum stored. The high order words are then added, together with the carry from the low order addition. The program shown below carries out this process:

Program
Data areas

HI1	WRD	+10000	High order word of integer 1.
LI1	WRD	+ 8763	Low order word of integer 1.
HI2	WRD	+20000	
LI2	WRD	+14261	
HSM	WRD		High order word of sum.
LSM	WRD		Low order word of sum.

Start of program
```
LOA A LI1
ADD A LI2
STO A LSM
LOA A HI1
- - - -
STO A HSM
HLT
END
```

Make a copy of this program, and
a) Fill in the missing instruction in the program.
b) Write suitable comments next to each program line.
c) Write a program to add three double length integers.
●d) Write a program to subtract two double length integers.

6 Write a program in AMC assembly language to locate the end of a list of data, structured as in Example Program 16.2. The program is given the address of the first list element, and scans the list until the last element is located. The program halts with the address of the last list element in the accumulator.

● **7** Write a program in AMC assembly language which scans a tree, structured as in Example Program 16.5, in order to locate a given character. If the character is found at one of the nodes, a pointer to the node is returned, otherwise a zero value of the pointer is returned.

8 Write a program in AMC assembly language to divide two unsigned integers by a process of shifting and subtraction.

9 The simplest form of integer multiplication is by a process of repeated addition. For example, to multiply 4 by 9, add 4 nine times. This process was used on early computers. An algorithm for this method of multiplication is as follows:

To multiply positive integers **IN1** and **IN2**, using working areas **WA1** and **WA2**,

> Clear **WA1**, and load **IN2** to **WA2**.
> While **WA2** is greater than zero, repeat
> Add **IN1** to **WA1**
> Reduce **WA2** by 1.

Write a program in AMC assembly language to implement this algorithm. Either use data numbers which are small enough for the product to be accomodated in one word (**WA1**), or use a double length word for **WA1**, and add the carry arising from the addition into the high order word.

10 Integer division may be carried out by a process of repeated subtraction. For example, to divide 40 by 7, count the number of times 7 may be subtracted from 40.
   a) Write an algorithm for division by this method.
   b) Write a program in AMC assembly language to implement your algorithm.

11 Explain what is wrong with the following AMC instruction

   STO A N /AB/

12 The least significant bit of a 16 bit word is an even parity bit. This means that the parity of the word is correct if the total number of 1s is an even number.

Write a program, in AMC assembly language, to check the parity of the word. Use repeated shifting, masking, and addition to obtain the total number of 1s in the word.

Assume that, at the start of the program, the word to be checked is loaded into the accumulator. At the end of the program, the accumulator contains 0 if the parity is correct, and 1 if it is not correct.

13 Explain fully the reasons for the use of the stack in the subprogram in Example Program 16.5.

14 a) Describe briefly what is meant by indexed addressing.
   b) A certain computer has one accumulator and one index register, and no indirect addressing capability. Thirty small integers are stored in addresses **ARRAY**, **ARRAY + 1**, ... Show, by means of a description, a flowchart or a section of assembly code (use a real or an imaginary language, explaining the notation used) how the sum of the thirty values may be evaluated and stored in the address **SUM**.

UCLES 81 Specimen I

17
Assemblers

This chapter concerns the process of translating a program written in an assembly language to an equivalent program in machine language. The item of software which performs this task is called an **assembler**. The nature and objectives of an assembler are discussed, together with a brief examination of some of the techniques of assembly used in practice. As in previous chapters, AMC machine and assembly language are used as examples.

17.1 Nature and Objectives of an Assembler

The objectives of an assembler are to translate a program from the assembly language to the machine language of a particular computer, and to assist programmers in writing programs in assembly language. In addition to their translation function, assemblers perform other tasks, for example the detection and reporting of errors in programs which they are translating. Accordingly, an assembler may be defined as follows:

> An assembler is a program which translates from the assembly language to the machine language of a particular computer, and provides additional facilities to assist in the development of low level language programs for the computer.

A more general objective of an assembler is to provide a programmer-oriented interface to the hardware of a particular computer. In other words, the assembler enables the programmer to 'see' the hardware of a computer in a simple, useful way. It must enable the hardware of the computer to be used in the most effective manner. In addition to these general objectives, an assembler must be acceptably short, and carry out its tasks quickly and efficiently. In practice, this objective must be balanced against the desire to include a large number of non-essential features in an assembler.

17.2 Tasks Performed by an Assembler

This section examines some of the tasks carried out by an assembler in the process of translating from assembly language to machine language. Most of these tasks are associated with the features of assembly languages described in the previous chapter. Although the details of the ways these tasks are performed vary from one assembler to another, the general nature of the tasks is common to all assemblers. The tasks are analysis of the structure of an assembly language program, decoding mnemonic operation codes, dealing with symbolic addresses, automatic data conversion, interpreting directives and macro expansion.

Analysis of the Structure of an Assembly Language Program
The first task of an assembler is to analyse the structure of an assembly language program, and determine the nature of each part of the program. Each assembly language has a set of rules which govern the structure of programs written in the language. These rules determine both the overall structure of a program, and the detailed structure of each program line. In most cases these rules are fairly simple. Programs generally consist of one instruction or directive per line. Lines either have fixed-length fields for specific purposes, or use punctuation marks to separate fields. AMC assembly language is an example of the first type.

The assembler uses these rules in the analysis of a program. The rules enable each group of characters to be interpreted as a mnemonic operation code, symbolic address, etc. Once the nature of a group of characters has been determined, more detailed work can be done, as outlined in the following sections.

If the structure of any portion of a program does not match the requirements of the rules, then an error is detected by the assembler. An error message is displayed.

Decoding Mnemonic Operation Codes

This is a very straightforward procedure. As there is a one-to-one correspondence between assembly language mnemonics and machine instruction codes, a table is used to store each mnemonic together with its equivalent machine language operation code. Each mnemonic operation code in a program is looked up in this table, and the corresponding machine language operation code placed in the machine language program. If a mnemonic operation code is not in the table, then an error is recorded, and an error message is displayed.

Dealing with Symbolic Addresses

The objective here is to replace each symbolic address by a machine language address. The procedure is more complicated than decoding operation codes, and several stages are involved.

Every symbolic address used in a program must occur in one, and only one, position in the program as a label. As the assembler works through the program, the address of each instruction or directive is determined. If the instruction or directive has a label, then the address is associated with that label. Part of the task of an assembler is to build up a table of all the labels used in a program, together with the addresses at which they occur. If identical labels are encountered at different addresses, then an error is reported.

The table thus created is used to relate each symbolic address in a program to a machine address. If a symbolic address is not in the table, then an error is detected. In some assemblers, the process of creating the table is completed before symbolic addresses are looked up in it. In others, the two processes occur concurrently. This point is dealt with again in the section on the structure of assembler programs.

In some cases, the machine addresses allocated to symbolic addresses at this stage are the final ones which are used when the machine language is run. In other cases, they are relative addresses, generally relative to the start of the program. They are changed into absolute memory addresses at a later stage, when the machine language program is loaded into its position in memory for running.

Automatic Data Conversion

If an assembly language permits the representation of data values in various number bases and character codes, then conversion algorithms and tables are used to change these representations to machine code format. This is generally a very straightforward process.

Interpreting Directives

As mentioned in the previous chapter, directives are assembly language instructions which do not have a counterpart in machine code. An assembler acts upon a directive as soon as it is recognised. The nature of the action depends upon the particular directive. For example, if, in AMC assembly language, the directive **WRD** is encountered, the assembler reserves a word of store.

Macro Expansion

You will recall from the previous chapter that a macro-instruction is a single instruction which is defined, within a program, to represent a set of instructions. When an assembler encounters the definition of a macro-instruction, it decodes the set of instructions which the macro-instruction represents, and records the mnemonic of the macro-instruction in a table. When the macro-instruction is encountered in the body of a program, the set of instructions is inserted at the corresponding position in the machine language program. In this way, the macro-instruction is **expanded** to the full set of instructions in the machine language program.

17.3 The Structure of an Assembler Program

Assembler programs consist of a number of modules, one for each task mentioned previously. The structure analysis module is in overall control. Once the nature of a set of characters in an assembly language program has been recognised, the appropriate module is called to carry out whatever detailed work is required.

There are, broadly speaking, two approaches to the analysis of the structure of an assembly language program. The traditional method involves scanning the assembly language program twice. Assemblers using this method are called **two-pass assemblers**. The more modern approach involves only one scan of the assembly language program. Assemblers of this type are called **single-pass** or **incremental assemblers**.

17.4 The AMC Assembler

The program which translates from AMC assembly language to AMC machine language is an example of a two-pass assembler. The tasks performed during each pass through an assembly language program are as follows.

First Pass
1 Break down the current assembly language program line into its constituent parts (label, operation code mnemonic, etc.)
2 If the label field is non-blank, store the label and its corresponding machine address in the symbolic address table.
3 Decode the operation mnemonic, register identifier and addressing mode, or directive.
4 Insert the operation code into the current machine language program instruction, and record the address of this instruction.
5 From the number of words used by the current machine instruction, calculate the address of the next machine instruction.

Second Pass
1 If the current assembly program line contains a symbolic address, look this address up in the symbolic address table. Insert the equivalent machine code address into the current machine code instruction.
2 If the current assembly program line contains the value of a data item as a decimal number or set of ASCII characters, obtain the hexadecimal equivalent of this value and insert it into the current machine code instruction.
3 If the current assembly program line is a relative branching instruction, calculate the relative offset and insert it into the current machine code instruction.

If an error is detected during any of these steps, an error message is displayed. Assembly continues to the end of the current pass.

17.5 Language of Assemblers

Assemblers are programs which translate from the assembly language to the machine language of a particular computer. But in what language is the assembler program itself written? In the early days of computing, the answer was obvious: in the machine language of the particular computer. This is still the case for a some present-day assemblers, particularly those used by microcomputers.

However, a significant proportion of assemblers are written in the assembly language which they translate. Others are written in high level languages, which are introduced in the next chapter. Some assemblers are designed to run on a different computer from the one whose language they translate. Such assemblers are called **cross assemblers**.

17.6 Conclusion

The main points of the chapter are as follows:

- An assembler is a program which translates from the assembly language to the machine language of a particular computer, and provides additional facilities to assist in the development of low level language programs for the computer.
- Tasks performed by an assembler include:
  analysis of the structure of an assembly language program
  decoding mnemonic operation codes
  dealing with symbolic addresses
  automatic data conversion
  interpreting directives
  macro expansion.
- The overall control of an assembler is carried out by the structure analysis module. Other tasks are performed by modules called from this module.
- The two approaches to the analysis of an assembly language program are the two-pass method and the single-pass or incremental technique.

Exercise 17

1 Briefly define the following terms: assembler; symbolic address table; two-pass assembler; cross assembler.
2 Summarise, in about one hundred and fifty words, the tasks carried out by an assembler.
3 In addition to language translation, what other function does an assembler perform?
4 Why can a symbolic address be used as a label in only one position in a program?
5 If the machine and assembly languages of a computer were altered to include a new instruction, what changes would have to be made to the assembler program?
6 The machine code corresponding to the following AMC assembly language program is shown after the first pass of the AMC assembler. The table of symbolic addresses is also shown.

AMC assembly language		AMC machine language		Interpretation
	LOA X N +1	0000	1121 ____	Use index register as loop counter, initial value 1.
NXT	CMP X N +27	0004	1A21 ____	Compare index register with 27.
	BGT OUT	0008	65__	Exit loop if greater than 27.
	LOA A N +100	000A	1111 ____	Load 100 in accumulator.
	STB A D W	000E	2214 ____	Store contents of accumulator in W + index.
	INC X	0012	0220	Increment index register.
	BRN NXT	0014	61__	Continue loop.
OUT	HLT	0016	8500	Halt.
W	BTE	0018		Data item.

Table of symbolic addresses
```
NXT 0004
OUT 0016
W   0018
```

Make a copy of the program, and complete the machine language version by carrying out the steps of the second assembly pass. Remember that the relative address in a branching instruction is calculated from the address of the following instruction. For example, the relative address in the machine language version of BGT OUT is calculated from address 000A.

7 Select a program in AMC assembly language from Chapter 16, and convert it to AMC machine language. Start the machine language version at address 0000. Include a table of the symbolic addresses used in the program, together with their machine addresses.

18
High Level Languages

This chapter is concerned with a class of programming languages called **high level languages**. It explains the nature of high level languages, outlines their development, discusses their objectives and features and assesses their significance.

18.1 What is a High Level Language?

A high level language is a **problem oriented** programming language, whereas a low level language is **machine oriented**. In other words, a high level language is a convenient and simple means of describing the information structures and sequences of actions required to perform a particular task.

A high level language is independent of the architecture of the computer which supports it. This has two major advantages. Firstly, the person writing the programs does not have to know anything about the computer on which the program will be run. Secondly, programs are **portable**, that is, the same program can (in theory) be run on different types of computer. However, this feature of **machine independence** is not always achieved in practice.

In most cases, programs in high level languages are shorter than equivalent programs in low level languages. However, conciseness can be carried too far, to the point where programs become impossible to understand. More important features of a high level language are its ability to reflect clearly the structure of programs written in it, and its readability.

18.2 The Development of High Level Languages

Work started on the development of high level languages in the mid-1950s, about ten years after the emergence of digital electronic computers. During those ten years it had become evident that the major shortcoming of computers was not their hardware performance but their software performance. Writing correct, useful machine and assembly language programs for the computers of the day was a difficult, time-consuming and expensive process.

During this period, advances in computer languages consisted of additional features to increase the capabilities of assembly languages. Although these features provided a few short cuts, they increased the complexity of the assembly languages. The languages lacked a clear, coherent overall structure.

There was resistance to the idea of high level languages on the grounds of inefficiency. High level languages require compilers to translate the programs into machine language before they can be run. It was feared that the machine language programs produced by compilers would be extremely inefficient, compared with programs written directly in machine language. Considering the small size and low speed of computers in those days, this fear had some justification. Despite these objections, the period from 1954 to 1960 saw the development of three major high level languages, namely Fortran, Algol 60 and Cobol. Some details about the development of these languages are provided in the next chapter.

In spite of the problems mentioned above, once high level languages became available, their use spread very rapidly. Many more languages were written, and compilers were produced to implement these languages on the various computers currently in use. It has been estimated that there were about 1700 programming languages by 1965, but two of the first three are still among the most popular.

Work on the development of high level languages still continues today. Existing languages are modified in the light of experience, and sometimes substantially revised. For example, a new version of Algol, Algol 68, was introduced in 1968. From time to time, new high level languages are produced, the latest prominent example being Ada, in 1979.

18.3 Types of High Level Languages

High level languages may be broadly classified as **general-purpose** or **special-purpose**. General-purpose languages are intended to be equally well suited to business, scientific, engineering or systems software tasks. The commonest general-purpose languages are Algol 68 and PL/1. The language Ada also falls into this category. Because of their broad capabilities, these languages are large and relatively difficult to use.

The commonest categories of special-purpose languages are commercial, scientific and educational. In the commercial field, Cobol still reigns supreme, while Fortran is still the most widely used scientific language. In the computer education field, Basic is widely used in schools, with Logo and Prolog gaining popularity. Pascal is the most popular language at universities. Pascal is a powerful general-purpose language in its own right.

Another way of classifying high level languages is as **procedural** and **declarative** languages. Procedural languages state how a task is to be performed, often breaking programs into **procedures**, each of which specifies how a particular operation is to be performed. All the early high level languages are procedural, with Algol (Section 19.2), Pascal (Section 19.5) and Ada as typical examples. Declarative programming languages describe the data structures and relationships between data relevant to a particular task, and specify what the objective of the task is. The process by which the task is to be carried out is not stated explicitly in the program. This process is determined by the language translation system. Prolog (Section 19.8) is an example of a declarative programming language.

18.4 Objectives of High Level Languages

Before going on to discuss the features of high level languages, it is essential to be clear about what high level languages are trying to achieve. The defining characteristics of a high level language are **problem-orientation** and **machine independence**. These are taken for granted in the following discussion.

The first objective of a high level language is to provide a convenient means of expressing the solution to a problem. There are two other common ways of doing this - mathematics, and natural languages, such as English. Most high level languages borrow, without much modification, concepts and symbols from mathematics. The problem with natural languages is that, in their full richness and complexity, they are quite impossible to use to instruct a computer. Nevertheless, high level languages use words from natural languages, and allow these words, and mathematical symbols, to be combined according to various rules. These rules create the structure of programs written in the language. The result, in a good high level language, is a clear structure, not too different from our customary ways of thinking and expressing ourselves.

This discussion leads to the second objective of high level languages - **simplicity**. Simplicity is achieved by a small set of basic operations, a few clear rules for combining these operations, and, above all, the avoidance of special cases.

The third objective of a high level language is **efficiency**. Programs in the language must be able to be translated into machine code fairly quickly, and the resulting machine code must run efficiently. This objective almost always conflicts with the first two. Most high level languages reflect a compromise between these objectives.

The final objective is **readability** of programs. Many languages allow for the inclusion of comments or additional 'noise' words, to make programs easier to read. However, a good high level language should enable programs to be written which are clear to read without additional comments. Regrettably, some high level languages ignore this objective altogether.

18.5 Features of High Level Languages

The next few sections outline the features common to most high level languages. In this chapter, these features are discussed in general terms. The next chapter shows how these features are implemented in some popular high level languages.

Character Set and Reserved Words

The **character set** used by a language is the set of all characters which may be used in programs written in the language. Almost all languages use letters and decimal digits; differences arise in the use of special characters such as punctuation marks.

Most high level languages use **reserved words**. These are words which have a specific meaning in programs, and may not be used by the programmer for any other purpose. For example, in Pascal, reserved words include **read, if ... then ... else** and **write**. Some languages permit abbreviations of reserved words. The size and complexity of a language can be measured by the number of reserved words it uses. For example, Occam (Section 34.4) has 28 reserved words, while Ada uses more than sixty.

Program Structure

Perhaps the most important feature of a high level language is the way in which programs in it are structured. The structure of a program is specified by a set of rules, called **rules of syntax**. Different languages have different ways of expressing these rules. In some, the rules are written in concise English. Others use **syntax diagrams**, while others (notably Algol) use a notation originally called **Backus-Naur form**, now known as **BNF**. See Section 20.3.

Much attention has been devoted, in the development and use of high level languages, to the way in which programs are split up into **blocks** or **modules**, each module doing a specific task. In some languages, notably Fortran, these blocks are called **subroutines**, in others such as Algol and Pascal, these blocks are called **procedures** or **functions**. Because of the careful structuring of programs into blocks which they permit, Algol, Pascal and similar languages are called **block-structured languages**.

Procedures, functions or subroutines are activated via **calls** from other parts of the program. For example, if a program contains a function to calculate the square root of a given number, this function is called every time a square root is required in the rest of the program. Most languages permit a procedure or function to call itself, a feature known as **recursion**. This is an extremely powerful feature for handling such data structures as lists, stacks and trees, and for such tasks as analysing the structure of arithmetic expressions. See Sections 16.9 and 19.5 for examples of the use of recursion.

Data

An important aspect of high level languages is the way in which they handle the data items and data structures used in a program. Broadly speaking, data items fall into two categories: **variables**, which can change their value during the running of a program, and **constants**, which keep the same value. In most program languages, variables are given names, or **identifiers**. In some languages, such as Fortran and Basic, constants are referred to by their values, while in others, such as Algol and Pascal, constants are also given identifiers.

Some program languages require that all variables be **declared** before they are used. Generally, variables are declared by listing them at the start of the procedure or subroutine in which they are to be used. An attempt to use a variable which has not been declared results in an error.

This gives rise to the idea of the **scope** of a variable. The scope of a variable is the part of a program in which it may be used. Variables which are declared for use in one procedure only are called **local** variables. Their scope is limited to that procedure. Variables which are declared for use in the whole program are called **global** variables. Their scope is the whole program. The intention of providing each variable with a scope is to enable a program to be broken up into 'watertight' blocks, or modules. Each block uses only the information it requires. This simplifies the task of designing, writing and testing programs, and limits the effects of errors.

Almost all high level languages include the notion of **data types**. In Basic language, the standard data types are **numeric** and **character strings**. These types can be incorporated into **arrays**, which are tables of items of the same type. In most high level languages, numbers can be **integers** or **real** numbers (generally stored in floating point form). PL/1 even permits the number of significant figures in a number to be declared. Another common standard data type is **Boolean**, with the range of values 'true' and 'false'. Data types can contain single elements, or be structures such as arrays, stacks, lists, trees, etc.

A **pointer** is a data type which contains the address of another data item. Pointers can be used to construct such data structures as lists and trees. For example, a list of people's names could be constructed as follows:

name pointer → name pointer → name pointer → etc.

Pointer types are only available in certain high level languages, notably Algol and Pascal. The problem with pointers is that careless use of them can result in program errors which are very difficult to detect and correct.

Some languages permit the programmer to declare his or her own data types, built up from standard data types. **Records** can be constructed, containing data of different types. The following section of a Pascal program shows how this can be done.

```
type name=array [1. . .20] of char;
     day=(mon, tues, wed, thur, fri, sat, sun);

     pay_record=record
                    employee_name: name;
                    payrate: real;
                    hours_worked: integer;
                    pay: real;
                    payday: day
                end;
```

In the above example, **char** is a standard data type. Variables of type **char** have values consisting of a single character. The data type 'name' is an array of twenty characters. Variables of the data type 'day' can have one of the values listed in the brackets.

The purpose of data types is to make programs more meaningful, and to provide additional checks for errors. For example, if an attempt is made to add an integer variable to a character variable, then an error will be caused.

Operations

The operations included in a high level language enable data items and data structures to be manipulated in various ways. Almost all program languages permit arithmetic operations. Many allow expressions of any degree of complexity to be evaluated in one statement. Most languages include the logical operations AND, OR and NOT, again combined to form expressions if necessary. Some program languages, notably Fortran and PL/1, have instructions to manipulate entire data structures such as matrices. In these languages, multiplying two matrices, for example, requires only one program instruction.

All program languages have rules of **precedence** which specify the order in which operations are carried out within the same expression. Arithmetic operations follow the usual rules: multiplication before addition, etc., but languages differ over the precedence of logic operations over arithmetic operations in the same expression.

The process whereby a variable takes on a value is called **assignment**.

Different languages express assignment in different ways. For example, assigning the value of a variable Y to a variable X is expressed in Basic and Fortran as

```
X = Y
```

Algol 60, Algol 68 and Pascal would express it as

```
x:= y
```

while in Cobol it would be written as

```
MOVE Y TO X
```

Input and Output

High level languages vary considerably in their treatment of input and output. The intention in all cases is to hide from the programmer the problems which surround input and output at machine level, although in many cases these problems are taken care of by the operating system.

Most high level languages provide a simple, logical method of transferring data to or from the computer. Some languages, notably Fortran and Cobol, pay considerable attention to the layout, or **format** of the data. Other languages deliberately 'play down' this aspect, to simplify matters for the programmer.

Control Structure

All program languages, both low level and high level, have ways of transferring control from one part of a program to another. In procedural high level languages, there are generally three aspects of the question: **sequencing, looping** and **branching**. Control is transferred to procedures and functions by **calling** - see previous section.

Sequencing is the flow of control from one instruction to the next. In most program languages this is achieved by writing instructions one after the other, separated by semi-colons, or on consecutive lines. Basic language is an exception, with instructions being executed in order of line number.

Looping is concerned with repeating instructions or groups of instructions. Most high level languages have instructions for performing loops a certain number of times, using one variable as a counter. Some languages allow loops to be repeated while some condition is true, or until a condition becomes true.

Branching concerns transferring control to one part of a program if a condition is true, and to another if the condition is false. The most general form of a branching instruction is as follows:

if <condition> **then** <instructions to be executed if condition is true>
           else <instructions to be executed if condition is false>
endif

A more sophisticated version of the conditional branching instruction is available in many languages. This is the **multi-way branch** instruction. In Pascal, the multi-way branch is implemented as the **case** statement. For example:

```
case operator of
      add       : a:=a+b;
      subtract  : a:=a-b;
      multiply  : a:=a*b;
end;
```

Depending on the value of the variable **operator**, one of the statements is executed.

There is some controversy about the use of the **unconditional branching** instruction, of the form:

```
go to <statement number>
```

in high level languages. Its use cuts across the structures created by the use of looping, branching and conditional transfers of control. It can also spoil the scoping of variables. **Go to** is regarded as a low level language feature, to be avoided in well-written high level language programs.

18.6 An Assessment of High Level Languages

A high level language is a programming language which is problem-oriented and machine independent, and has the objectives of a clear structure, simplicity, efficiency and readability. How well do high level languages match these criteria in practice?

Problem-orientation is generally well achieved, especially in special-purpose languages such as Cobol and in block-structured languages like Pascal. Machine independence does not score so highly. A 'standard' version of most popular high level languages has been published, but machine-dependent features persist in most implementations. Basic language is particularly bad, with different computer manufacturers offering different enhancements to the language on their own computers.

A clear structure of programs is achieved on many high level languages. Perhaps the best example of this is the fact that several large operating systems have been successfully written in high level languages. Simplicity is certainly possible in most high level languages, but it is limited by the complexity of the problem being programmed. Program readability is still very much a matter for the individual programmer.

The main success of high level languages has been their transformation of the art (or science...) of computer programming from the domain of a few highly skilled computer experts to a much wider group of people, including researchers in a wide range of fields, some businessmen and school pupils. With computers becoming cheaper, and programmers' time becoming more expensive, high level languages are appearing more and more cost-effective, at least from the point of view of the data processing system as a whole.

However, there is still a place for programming in low level languages. Systems software must still be written, at least in part, in a low level language. Many microcomputers are too small to support anything more than a simple subset of a high level language. If a microprocessor is to be dedicated to a specific task, such as word processing, all the software required is usually written in assembly language.

At present there is a move towards an even higher level of programming languages, which might be called **specification languages**, and an increasing use of **software development tools**. These are discussed in Chapter 23. The profession of programming is evolving into **software engineering** (Chapter 24) as the fifth generation of computers approaches (Chapter 34). These developments are challenging the current dominance of high level languages for the development of applications software, and may make them obsolete during the next decade.

18.7 Conclusion

The main points of this chapter are as follows:

- High level languages are application-oriented, machine-independent programming languages.
- High level languages may be classified as special-purpose or general-purpose, or as procedural or declarative.
- Desirable features of high level languages are a clear structure, simplicity, efficiency and readability.
- Features of high level languages are their character set and reserved words, facilities for structuring programs and data, the processing operations they perform, input and output facilities and their control structures.

● The state of the art in programming is beginning to move beyond high level languages to the use of software development tools as programming evolves towards software engineering.

Exercise 18

1 Briefly define the following terms: high level language; portable; general-purpose language; procedural language; declarative language; character set; reserved word; syntax; block; subroutine; call; recursion; variable; constant; declaration; scope; local variable; global variable; data type; Boolean variable; pointer; rule of precedence; assignment; format.

2 What are the two distinguishing features of high level languages?

3 What factors were the driving force behind the development of high level languages?

4 Summarise the objectives of high level languages.

5 What similarities and differences are there between natural languages (such as English) and high level programming languages?

6 Below is a complete program in Pascal language. It inputs a set of ten numbers and outputs them, together with their squares and reciprocals. Functions are used to calculate squares and reciprocals.

```
program   question_6 (input,output);          (*line 1*)

var   x: real;                                 (*line 2*)
   count: integer;                             (*line 3*)

function square (y:real): real;               (*line 4*)
var w : real;                                  (*line 5*)
begin w := y*y;                                (*line 6*)
      square := w                              (*line 7*)
end;                                           (*line 8*)

function reciprocal (z:real): real;           (*line 9*)
var v:real;                                    (*line10*)
begin if z=0.0 then v:= 0.0                    (*line11*)
              else v:= 1.0/z;                  (*line12*)
      reciprocal := v                          (*line13*)
end;                                           (*line14*)

begin for count :=1 to 10 do                   (*line15*)
          begin readln(x);                     (*line16*)
              writeln(x,square(x),reciprocal(x))  (*line17*)
          end                                  (*line18*)
end.                                           (*line19*)
```

This program has three blocks, namely the two functions and the main program. The scope of a variable is the block within which it is declared. In Pascal, variables are declared by a **var** instruction, or in a **function** declaration. Thus the scope of variable w is the function square, from line 5 to line 8.

a) Write down the scope of the variables x, count and v.

b) Is it permissible to refer to variable x in line 7?

c) Is it permissible to refer to variable w in line 13?

d) Which variables are local variables, and which are global variables?

e) From which program line are the two functions called?

7 Consider the following segment of a Basic program, containing two assignment statements:

```
105 LET Y = X
110 LET X = Y
```

a) If X and Y initially have the values 3 and 4, what are their values after this segment of program?

b) Write a sequence of three assignment statements which will interchange the values of X and Y.

8 In Fortran, a **FORMAT** statement specifies the layout of input and output data. It contains a number of codes, for integers, spaces, real numbers, etc. For example, to input three integers, set out as follows:

314 2175 46629

the program segment below can be used:

```
     READ (1,100)I,J,K
100 FORMAT (I3,1X,I4,1X,I5)
```

where I3 means a 3 digit integer and 1X means a space.
a) Write a **READ** and **FORMAT** statement to input the following data:

41 23 16 4117 2234 1697

b) Write a set of data which would be read by:

```
     READ (1,120) K,L,M1,M2,N
120 FORMAT (I4,2X,I4,2X,I2,1X,I2,1X,I8)
```

c) Comment on the advantages and disadvantages of this type of input.
9 Consider this statement from a Pascal program:

```
if (x<0) or (x>9) then y:=10
                   else y:=9-x;
```

Write down the value of y in each of the following cases:
a) x = 4
b) x = 10
c) x = -2
d) x = 0
e) x = 9
●f) Write a segment of a Basic language program to achieve the same effect as the Pascal statement above. Comment on similarities and differences between it and the Pascal language instruction.
10 Identify some shortcomings of many implementations of high level languages.
●11 Examine the low level language introduced in Chapter 16. To what extent (if at all) does it satisfy the objectives of high level languages?
●12 John Backus, leader of the team which developed Fortran, has the view that conventional programming languages are still far too closely tied to the general ideas of computer architecture, such as addresses, sequences of operations etc. In the light of your knowledge of computer architecture, and of high level languages, comment on this view.

19
High Level Language Case Studies

This chapter takes the general ideas from the previous chapter and relates them to eight significant high level languages: Fortran, Algol 60, Cobol, Basic, Pascal, C, Lisp and Prolog. Each language is discussed under the following headings: development, objectives, features and an assessment. Also included is a short example program in each language. The program is designed to illustrate the distinguishing features of the language.

The reasons for choosing the languages are as follows: Fortran, Algol 60 and Cobol are three of the oldest high level languages, Cobol and Fortran being two of the most popular programming languages currently in use. Algol 60 is the forerunner of a long line of high level languages, notably Algol 68, Pascal and Ada. Pascal, Basic and C are more recent languages, developed in the light of earlier experience. Lisp and Prolog are associated with artificial intelligence and the development of fifth generation computers.

As a group, these case studies cover a wide spectrum of high level languages, from special-purpose to general-purpose, from from scientific to commercial, and from procedural to declarative. The group represents a class of computer languages whose members number over a thousand.

19.1   Fortran

The name Fortran comes from **For**mula **Tran**slation. Fortran, developed between 1954 and 1957, is a programming language designed for scientific and engineering applications.

Development

In December 1953, John Backus, an employee of IBM, proposed the idea of Fortran. At the time virtually all programming was in assembly language. Although some work had been done in the direction of high level languages, there was much scepticism about the efficiency of **'automatic programming'** as it was then called.

Backus was motivated by an economic factor - the cost of programmers' time, as they laboriously wrote assembly language programs. His proposal was accepted, and in January 1954 a Fortran team was set up in New York, by IBM. The main objective of the team was to produce a language which could be translated into efficient machine code. The details of the language were made up as the team went along. In November 1954, the team produced a preliminary report. In early 1955, work started on the huge task of producing a Fortran compiler. The computer for which the compiler was written was the newly-released IBM 704. The compiler was reportedly 'always six months to completion', and was finally finished in April 1957.

From its first release, Fortran was very popular. From time to time, the language has been revised. The version in common use today is **ANSI 77 Fortran**, the version standardised by the American National Standards Institute. Fortran is available on most computers. Simple versions have been written for small computers, and very powerful versions, with a significant degree of parallel processing, have been written for large computers.

Objectives

Fortran is designed for use in mathematical, scientific and engineering applications. The prime objective of Fortran is to produce programs which can be translated into efficient machine code. Other objectives include ease of use, and close resemblance to ordinary mathematical notation.

As Fortran was originally sponsored by IBM, not much thought was initially given to the objective of machine independence. However, time has shown that Fortran is easy to implement on other computers. Most implementations conform to the ANSI 77 standard.

Character Set and Reserved Words

The character set used by Fortran includes capital letters, decimal digits and a few special characters. Fortran has a fairly large set of reserved words, including data type declarations (**INTEGER**, **REAL**, etc.) and instruction words (**READ**, **WRITE**, **CALL**, **RETURN**, etc.) All statements except calculations start with an instruction word.

Program Structure

A Fortran program consists of a **main program** and a number of subprograms, called **subroutines**. Subroutines can be called from the main program, or from other subroutines. Recursive calls from a subroutine to itself are not permitted.

Subroutines are compiled separately from each other, and from the main program. The scope of all variables is thus limited to the subroutine in which they occur, unless they are declared to be in a **COMMON** block. Within each routine, a program consists of a number of statements, each written on a separate line, with various columns having special purposes. Line numbers are optional, and do not have to be in order.

Data

The data types available are integer, real, double precision, complex and logical (Boolean). Variable names consist of up to six alphanumeric characters, the first of which must be alphabetic. Unless otherwise declared, variables starting with any of the letters from I to N are integers, and the rest are real. Variables do not have to be declared at the start of the routine in which they are used.

The **DIMENSION** statement is used to create arrays. The elements of an array may be any of the above data types. Most versions of Fortran allow at least three dimensions of arrays. For example, the statement:

```
DIMENSION LOAD (10), STRESS (10,4)
```

declares **LOAD** to be a one-dimensional array of ten items, and **STRESS** to be a two-dimensional array of forty items.

Operations

All the usual operations of arithmetic are available, with rather complicated rules for combining variables (or constants) of different types in the same expression. The standard arithmetic functions (sin, cos, tan, etc.) are available, as well as user-defined functions. Relational operators (greater than, less than, etc.) are included, for use in logical expressions which may appear in **IF** statements.

Input/Output

The methods of input and output provided are very powerful, but rather cumbersome. At the start of the program, all peripheral devices required are listed, together with their **channel number** for the duration of the program. Each input or output statement specifies a channel number, a list of variables to be transferred, and a **FORMAT** statement. The **FORMAT** statement specifies the precise layout of the data on the input, output or backing store medium. For example:

```
      READ (1,100) NPART, NSTOCK, PRICE
  100 FORMAT (I6, 2X, I6, 2X, F6·2)
```

inputs the integers **NPART** and **NSTOCK** and real variable **PRICE** from channel 1. The integers each have six digits, and the number contains six characters, with two digits after the decimal point. The data items are separated by two spaces.

Control Structure

Two types of conditional branching statement are available, namely the arithmetic **IF** and the logical **IF**. The **arithmetic IF** statement includes an expression and three statement numbers. The expression is evaluated. If the result is negative, control passes to the first statement, if the result is zero, control passes to the second statement, and if the result is positive, control passes to the third statement. For example:

```
IF (X+Y) 10, 20, 30
```

branches to statement

> 10 if $X+Y<0$
> 20 if $X+Y=0$
> 30 if $X+Y>0$.

The **logical IF** statement includes a logical expression, and an unconditional statement. If the logical expression is true, the unconditional statement is executed, otherwise control passes to the statement after the **IF** statement. For example:

```
IF (AMOUNT.LE.20.00) CHARGE=5.00
```

assigns the value 5.00 to **CHARGE** if **AMOUNT** is less than 20.00. Unconditional branching (**GO TO**) is available, as is multi-way branching.

Program loops can be constructed by means of the **DO** statement. The **DO** statement includes the statement number of the end of the loop, a variable to be used as a counter, its initial and final values, and (optionally) a step size. For example:

```
DO 20 MONTH = 1, 12, 1
```

causes the program segment ending at statement 20 to be repeated for all values of **MONTH** from 1 to 12 in steps of 1. Loops controlled by **DO** statements are always performed at least once. This is regarded by some as a shortcoming of Fortran.

Example Program

The subprogram shown below accepts two 10x10 matrices, and multiplies them together. The formula used is as follows:

If

> $C=A\times B$ where A, B and C are matrices

then

> $c_{ij} = a_{i1}\times b_{1j} + a_{i2}\times b_{2j} + ...a_{i10}\times b_{10j}$

The subprogram uses three nested loops. The outer and middle loops work through the rows and columns of the product matrix C, the inner loop adds up the terms which form the product as shown in the formula.

```
      SUBROUTINE MATMULT (A,B,C)
      REAL A(10,10), B(10,10), C(10,10)
C OUTER LOOP WORKS THROUGH ROWS OF PRODUCT
      DO 100 I =1,10
C MIDDLE LOOP WORKS THROUGH COLUMNS OF PRODUCT
      DO 100 J =1,10
C SET PRODUCT ELEMENT TO ZERO
      C(I,J)=0.0
C INNER LOOP ADDS UP TERMS OF PRODUCT
      DO 100 K =1,10
```

```
100 C(I,J) = C(I,J)+A(I,K)*B(K,J)
    RETURN
    END
```

Notes

1 The lines starting with the letter C are comments.
2 The statement numbered 100 is the end of all three loops.
3 The dimension of the matrices are declared in the second line of the subprogram.

Assessment

Fortran was designed as a scientific and engineering language and in general it is excellent for tasks of this nature. The only major shortcoming is the difficulty experienced by many programmers with input and output. To overcome this, some versions of Fortran have simplified input/output statements.

Fortran's weaknesses become apparent when handling non-numeric data. Input, output, storage and manipulation of data in character form is extremely cumbersome, even compared to a language such as Basic. In addition, the range of data types is limited, pointers are not implemented, and user-defined data types are not allowed.

In spite of these shortcomings, Fortran remains as popular as ever. It has even survived attempts by its original sponsor, IBM, to replace it with a supposedly superior language, PL/1.

19.2 Algol 60

The name Algol comes from the phrase **Algorithmic Language**. Algol 60 is a structured general-purpose language developed between 1957 and 1962.

Development

During the mid 1950s, the idea of a 'universal programming language' was expressed by a number of people, in Europe and the USA. They envisaged a language that was clearly structured, general-purpose and machine independent. Fortran, which became available at this time, did not measure up to these requirements.

During 1957, the first steps towards designing such a language were taken by the USA **Association for Computing Machinery (ACM)** and its European counterpart, **GAMM**. In October 1957 a letter from GAMM to ACM suggested a combined approach. Accordingly, during May and June 1958, a joint working conference was held in Zurich. Delegates were from computer manufacturers, users, universities and governments on both sides of the Atlantic, but did not formally represent these institutions. This conference produced a preliminary draft of the language, which became known as Algol 58.

Algol aroused considerable interest, but by 1959 it was already clear that Fortran, with IBM backing, was going to be more widely used, certainly in the USA. As the concepts of language design became clearer, it soon became evident that Algol 58 could be improved. A meeting was held in Paris, in January 1960, at which a new version of the language was drafted, to incorporate all the improvements which had been suggested. Prominent delegates at this meeting were John Backus, of Fortran fame, and Peter Naur. Naur, with assistance from Backus, devised the notation, now known as BNF, in which the syntax of the revised language, called Algol 60, was expressed.

Algol 60 was appreciated, almost immediately, as a 'rounded work of art'. Its clear, consistent structure had a significant influence on the design of subsequent high level languages, and on the architecture of many computers. Compilers were written to implement Algol 60 on a number of computers. Algol 60 was written and revised during a few short, intensive meetings attended by approximately fifteen people. There was no formal voting procedure, design decisions being reached by consensus. Algol 60 represents a degree of international co-operation hardly ever achieved in any field.

Objectives

Algol was originally conceived as a 'universal programming language'. As various drafts were written, it acquired an algebraic bias, and thus an orientation towards scientific and engineering problems. However, it is certainly more general-purpose than Fortran.

The objective of machine independence is achieved in an interesting way. No less than three versions of the language have been defined, namely a **reference language**, a **publication language** and various hardware **implementation languages**. The reference language is the standard 'official' version, used in the revised Algol 60 report. It forms the basis of the other versions. The publication language permits a wider range of characters and notations, and is intended for the publication of algorithms. Each hardware version is the language implemented on some computer. It contains a set of rules for translating from the reference language to the hardware representation.

The other objective which is very well achieved is that of a simple, clear structure with a minimum of special cases.

Character Set and Reserved Words

In any hardware representation of Algol 60, the character set depends on the computer being used. Unlike Fortran, most current representations permit the use of lower case letters. Algol 60 has a slightly larger set of reserved words than Fortran. For example, the pair of reserved words `begin...end` are particularly important.

Program Structure

An Algol 60 program has the following structure, called a block:

```
Label: begin
            declarations;
            statements
       end
```

The **label** is a general form of a statement number, and is optional. **Declarations** are lists of the **types** and **identifiers** of all the variables used in the block. **Statements** are simple statements, or complete blocks, having the same structure as above. Blocks within a program are called **procedures**, and correspond roughly to the idea of subroutines in Fortran. A procedure may be called from any other procedure, or recursively from itself.

Data

Data **types** are **integer**, **real**, **Boolean** and character **strings**. Arrays may be created out of these types. Identifiers are sequences of letters or digits, starting with a letter. All variables must be declared at the start of the block in which they are used. The scope of each variable is the extent of the block in which it is declared. This includes any sub-blocks declared inside the block. Any reference to a variable which has not been declared, or is outside its scope, is invalid.

Operations

All the operations of arithmetic are available, with rules for combining different types in the same expression. Some standard functions (sin, cos, tan, etc.) are available on most hardware representations of the language. User-defined functions are written as procedures. Relational operations are available for use in logical expressions.

Input/Output

The reference language contains no provisions for input or output. Input/output operations have subsequently been standardised. These are much simpler, but less powerful, than those in Fortran.

Control Structure

Two conditional branching constructions are available:

    if <condition> then <statement>

and

    if <condition> then <statement 1> else <statement 2>.

Since each statement may be a complete block, this is an extremely powerful construction. In most cases, it eliminates the need for the **go to** statement, which is, however, available.

Loops are constructed as follows:

    for count: = c1 step c3 until c2 do <statement>

where the counter variable starts at value $c1$, and is increased in steps of $c3$ until it reaches $c2$. The statement may be a complete block. The counter variable is tested before each execution of the statement, and thus the loop may be repeated no times, if $c1$ is greater than $c2$ at the start.

Sequencing of instructions is achieved by placing a semi-colon between two consecutive statements. Statements do not have to start on new lines.

Example Program

The factorial of a number n may be written as:

    factorial (0) = 1
    factorial (n) = n x factorial(n − 1).

This is a recursive definition of factorials. It is used in the following program which calculates and outputs the factorials of five input numbers.

```
begin
     integer number, fact, count;
          integer procedure factorial (n);
               value n; integer n;
               begin integer i;
                    if n = 0 then factorial:= 1
                              else begin i:= factorial (n-1);
                                        factorial:= n*i
                                   end
               end
     for count: = 1 step 1 until 5 do
          begin ininteger (0, number);
               fact: = factorial (number);
               outinteger (1, fact)
          end
end
```

Notes

1 The variables declared in the outer block are

number: input number
fact: factorial of input number
count: counter

Their scope is the whole program.

Working variables **n** and **i** are declared in the inner blocks. Their scope is limited to these blocks.

2 The instructions `ininteger` and `outinteger` are for input and output respectively. The numbers 0 and 1 refer to particular input and output channels of the computer.

3 The recursive call to the factorial procedure is in the statement:

```
i: = factorial (n-1)
```

Assessment

The original objective of Algol 60 was to be a 'universal programming language'. This objective has not been achieved, as Algol has turned out to be scientifically oriented, with virtually no character handling facilities. Machine independence has been well achieved by the use of a separate reference language. A specific criticism of Algol is that its input/output facilities are very clumsy and weak. Algol 60 has not been used very widely.

Algol's biggest contribution has been to the theory of the design of computer languages. Ideas which were first used in Algol, such as a block, the scope of a variable and the if..then..else construction, have been copied by many other languages. The clear structure of the language is one of its strongest points. Algol has given rise to a whole family of computer languages, notably Pascal and Ada, often referred to as **Algol-like languages**.

19.3 Cobol

The name Cobol comes from the phrase **Common Business Oriented Language**. Cobol is a language designed for commercial data processing, and was developed between 1959 and 1960.

Development

In the late 1950s, computer manufacturers and users began to realise the need for a common, machine-independent, business-oriented programming language. In April 1959 a meeting was held at the University of Pennsylvania to discuss these views. At this meeting it was agreed that the sponsorship of the new language should be independent of any computer manufacturer. Accordingly, the USA Department of Defense was asked to co-ordinate the project. In May 1959, a meeting was held at the Pentagon in Washington. Present were representatives of all major computer manufacturers, prominent users and USA government departments. The meeting agreed on the desirable characteristics of a common business language, and set up a number of committees to carry out the development work. The overall steering committee was called **Codasyl** (Conference on data systems languages).

After a short, intensive period of formal meetings, with decisions being taken by vote, the initial specification of the language was completed. It was accepted by the Codasyl committee in January 1960, and published soon afterwards under the name of Cobol 60. By the end of 1960, Cobol programs were running on several different types of computer. Various revisions of Cobol were introduced during the 1960s. A standard version was accepted in 1968 by the American National Standards Institution (ANSI).

Objectives

The primary objectives of Cobol are machine independence, and a correspondence with current business practices. In addition, the following 'desirable characteristics' were identified at the initial planning meetings: maximum use of simple English; ease of use, even if less powerful than other languages; and 'to broaden the base of those who can state problems to computers'.

Character Set and Reserved Words

The Cobol character set includes capital letters and digits, and is implementation dependent. The set of reserved words is very large, including 'noise' words which can be included to improve the readability of programs, but are not acted on by the computer.

Program Structure

All Cobol programs consist of four **divisions**. These are:

Identification division: This identifies the program, its author and its purpose.
Environment division: This specifies the computer environment of the program, particularly peripheral devices used.
Data division: This specifies the nature and organisation of all the data used in the program. The identifiers of data items are declared, together with certain information about the data.
Procedure division: This specifies the operations to be carried out on the data.

Each division is organised into **sections**, **paragraphs**, **sentences** and **words**.

Data

The identifiers for data items can be up to thirty alphanumeric characters, containing hyphen (−) characters if required. For example `GROSS-PAY` and `PAY-RATE` are valid data names. Data items are declared using **picture clauses** which specify the number and type of characters in the data item. For example:

```
77 NET-INCOME IS PICTURE 999V99
```

declares a data item containing five digits, two of which are after the decimal point.
   Arrays are declared as follows:

```
01  PRICE-LIST
    02 ITEM-PRICE PIC 99V99 OCCURS 20
```

declares an array named `PRICE-LIST` of twenty `ITEM-PRICE`s.

Operations

Separate words (known as **verbs**) are used for each arithmetic operation. For example:

```
MULTIPLY ITEM-PRICE BY NUMBER-SOLD GIVING SALE-VALUE
```

However, the `COMPUTE` verb may be used if an expression is to be evaluated. A very useful verb is the `SORT` verb which causes a set of data items to be sorted into numerical or alphabetical order.

Input/Output

All input and output data is structured in **files**, composed of records. The verbs `READ` and `WRITE` are used to input and output records. The layout of input and output data is carefully specified, including `FILLER` items for spacing.

Control Structure

Both `IF..THEN` and `IF..THEN..ELSE` constructions are available for conditional branching. The `GO TO` statement is available for unconditional branching.
   The `PERFORM` verb is used for loops. A paragraph can be repeated until a certain condition is true, or a specified number of times. Examples of each type are:

```
PERFORM WAGE-CALCULATION-PARAGRAPH
    UNTIL END-OF-FILE MARKER='X'
```

and

```
PERFORM PRICE-CALCULATION VARYING ITEM-NUMBER
     FROM 1 BY 1 UNTIL ITEM-NUMBER =20
```

Example Program
The following program inputs a file of names, addresses and telephone numbers. The file is sorted into alphabetical order of names, and then output on a line printer.

```
IDENTIFICATION DIVISION
PROGRAM-1D.
    DIRECTORY-SORT.
DATE WRITTEN.
    16 MAY 1980.

ENVIRONMENT DIVISION.
INPUT-OUPUT SECTION.
FILE CONTROL.

    SELECT DIRECTORY-FILE-IN ASSIGN TO INPUT-DISK
    SELECT DIRECTORY-FILEASSIGN TO WORK-DISK
    SELECT DIRECTORY-FILE-OUT ASSIGN TO LINE-PRINTER.

DATA DIVISION.
FILE SECTION.
SD DIRECTORY-FILE
01 ENTRY
    05 SURNAME              PIC X(20).
    05 INITIALS            PIC X(5).
    05 ADDRESS             PIC X(60).
    05 TELEPHONE-NUMBER    PIC 9(7).

FD DIRECTORY-FILE-IN
01 ENTRY-IN
    05 SURNAME-IN          PIC X(20).
    05 INITIALS-IN         PIC X(5).
    05 ADDRESS-IN          PIC X(60).
    05 TELEPHONE-NUMBER-IN PIC 9(7).

FD DIRECTORY-FILE-OUT
01 ENTRY-OUT
    05 SURNAME-OUT         PIC X(20).
    05 INITIALS-OUT        PIC X(5).
    05 ADDRESS-OUT         PIC X(60).
    05 TELEPHONE-NUMBER-OUT PIC 9(7).

WORKING STORAGE SECTION.
01 MORE-ENTRIES-REMAIN-FLAG
    88 MORE-ENTRIES-REMAIN          PIC XXX VALUE'YES'
    88 NO-MORE-ENTRIES-REMAIN               VALUE'YES'
                                            VALUE'NO'

PROCEDURE DIVISION.
SORTING SECTION.
    SORT DIRECTORY-FILE
        ASCENDING KEY SURNAME
        ASCENDING KEY INITIALS
        INPUT PROCEDURE LOAD-FILE
        GIVING DIRECTORY-FILE-OUT.
```

```
        STOP RUN.

LOAD-FILE SECTION.
        OPEN INPUT DIRECTORY-FILE-IN
            OUTPUT DIRECTORY-FILE-OUT.
        READ DIRECTORY-FILE-IN
            AT END MOVE 'NO' TO MORE-ENTRIES-REMAIN-FLAG.
        IF MORE-ENTRIES-REMAIN
            MOVE ENTRY-IN TO ENTRY
            RELEASE ENTRY.
```

Notes

1 There are three data files: an input file, a working file used by the **SORT** verb, and an output file. All three files have the same structure.
2 The sort is in ascending order of surnames, and ascending order of initials for the same surname.
3 The sorting section calls the loading section to input each directory entry. As soon as an entry has been loaded, it is released to the sort.

Assessment

One of Cobol's stated objectives is to 'broaden the base' of the people who can write computer programs. As Cobol is one of the world's most popular programming language, there is no doubt that this objective has been achieved.

Another objective is the 'maximum use of simple English' in programs. This is indeed achieved, although it has led to criticisms that Cobol is verbose and cumbersome. Undoubtedly, the overall structure of a Cobol program is clear, though there are some awkward features, such as the construction surrounding the sort verb.

The major setback to an even wider acceptance of Cobol has been the negative view of it taken by the university-based computing science community. In spite of this, Cobol's future seems secure for the time being, partly through the enormous investment in existing software, and partly because simple versions of Cobol are available for microcomputers. The main challenge to Cobol is the increasing use of software development tools (Chapter 23).

19.4 Basic

The name Basic comes from the phrase **B**eginner's **A**ll-Purpose **S**ymbolic **I**nstruction **C**ode. Basic is designed to introduce students, particularly those not studying science or mathematics, to computer programming. Basic was developed between 1963 and 1964.

Development

Basic language was developed by Thomas E. Kurtz and John Kemeny at Dartmouth College, USA. Dartmouth College is a small institution, with the main teaching emphasis on the humanities. Computing is taught as a supporting subject to other disciplines. During the early 1960s, several attempts were made to produce a simple, introductory programming language.

Basic language was designed as part of an overall plan to make it easier for students to use the college's computer. In the summer of 1963, John Kemeny began work on a Basic compiler, for a General Electric 225 computer. On 1st May 1964, at 4a.m., the first Basic program was run.

From the outset, Basic was used on an interactive, multi-access computer system. Work continued at Dartmouth on improvements and extensions to the language. Six Dartmouth editions of Basic have been released.

Basic was well received from its first release. Over the years it has established itself as the world's most popular educational programming language. Many microcomputers use Basic as their standard language. In addition, Basic has been extended to become a powerful scientific and commercial programming language in its own right.

Objectives

The prime objective of Basic is ease of use, even at the expense of machine efficiency. In the words of Thomas Kurtz: 'The system would be designed to save the time of the user, even if it appeared that the computer was being "wasted".' Those were very brave words in an era when computer time was much more expensive than user time. Today, in a world of cheap microcomputers, the situation has been reversed, and the objective makes sound commercial sense.

Character Set and Reserved Words

The character set used by Basic includes capital letters, digits and a few special symbols. Early versions of Basic use a very small set of reserved words, a minimal set numbering about a dozen. Extended versions of Basic require much larger sets of reserved words.

Program Structure

A Basic program consists of a set of numbered statements, which are executed in order of statement number. Subprograms may be written, but they are not clearly differentiated from the main program, with no local variables or parameter passing.

Data

The data types available are **numeric** and **character string** variables and constants. Arrays may be constructed out of either variable type. Identifiers consist of a single letter, optionally followed by a single digit. Character string variable identifiers end with a $ symbol. Thus valid identifiers are:

X, A3, M$** and **J3$.

Although this is a very simple notation, it is rather restrictive. Some versions of Basic permit long identifiers. Data items need not be declared before use, and the scope of all variables is the whole program.

Operations

Arithmetic operations, standard functions and user-defined functions are available. Relational operators may be used in **IF** statements. One of the strengths of Basic is the number of character string operations and functions which are available. These make manipulation of non-numeric data extremely simple. For example, if A$ = "CAT" and B$ = "FISH", then the instruction:

LET C$ = A$ + B$

assigns to **C$** the value **"CATFISH"**, using the joining operator **+**.

Input/Output

The input and output operations combine simplicity with considerable power. Unless otherwise specified, printed output is automatically arranged in columns. Many versions of Basic permit data transfer to or from named data **files** on backing store. This enables programs to manipulate large sets of data, and pass this data from one program to another.

Control Structure

Conditional branching is achieved by a simple form of the if..then construction, namely

IF <condition> THEN <statement number>.

Control passes to the statement specified if the condition is true, otherwise it passes to the statement after the if statement. For example:

IF A>5 THEN 60

passes control to statement 60 if A is greater than 5.

Recent versions of Basic permit compound condition joined by AND or OR, and complete statements after THEN. Some editions extend the construction to include ELSE. A GO TO statement is available for unconditional branching.

The FOR...NEXT construction is used for program loops. A counter is used to control the number of times that the loop is repeated. For example:

10 FOR K = 1 TO 20 STEP 1

part of program to be repeated twenty times

100 NEXT K

In most versions of Basic, the loop is repeated zero or more times.

Example Program

The subprogram shown below is part of a word processing program. The subprogram takes a line of text, stored as the string variable T$, and inserts the string A$ into the line, immediately before the string B$. For example, if the line of text T$ is:

NOW IS THE TIME FOR ALL GOOD TO COME TO THE AID OF THE PARTY

and the character string A$ is MEN, and B$ is TO, then the result is:

NOW IS THE TIME FOR ALL GOOD MEN TO COME TO THE AID OF THE PARTY

The subprogram uses some of the string manipulation functions available in Basic. Firstly, the position of the string B$ in the text is located. Then the text is split into two parts, the second starting with the characters in B$. Finally the string A$, followed by a space, is inserted between the two parts.

```
1000 REM SUBPROGRAM TO INSERT INTO LINE OF TEXT
1010 REM
1020 REM LOCATE POSITION OF STRING B$ IN TEXT T$
1030 LET P = POS (T$, B$)
1040 REM IF P = 0, STRING IS NOT IN TEXT, GO TO END OF
     SUBPROGRAM
1050 IF P = 0 GO TO 1130
1060 REM SPLIT LINE T$ INTO TWO PARTS
1070 LET U$ = MID$ (T$, 1, P-1)
1080 LET V$ = MID$ (T$, P, LEN (T$))
1090 REM U$ IS THE FIRST PART, V$ IS FROM B$ TO THE END
1100 REM INSERT STRING A$ BETWEEN THE TWO PARTS
1110 LET T$ = U$ + A$ + " " + V$
1120 REM
1130 RETURN
```

Notes

1 Lines starting with the word REM are remarks.

2 Most of the work is done by the Basic functions **POS** and **MID$**, and the joining operator **+**.

3 The line numbers of the statements go up in steps of 10. This is normal practice in writing programs in Basic.

4 In some versions of Basic, the **MID$** function is called by a different name, and the joining operator is not **+**, but **&**.

Assessment

In its primary objective of simplicity, Basic has undoubtedly been extremely successful. In 1978, one of the authors of Basic, Thomas Kurtz, estimated that five million schoolchildren had learned Basic language. This simplicity is achieved through simple yet powerful instructions, particularly for character handling and input/output. Basic is particularly well suited to interactive computing, games and simulations, as well as to its original application area - teaching programming to beginners.

A number of criticisms of Basic language can be made, and as time goes by, its popularity is diminishing because of them. The most serious is that Basic gives very little assistance in the writing of well-structured programs. It is quite easy to develop bad programming habits through the careless use of Basic. Subprograms are not clearly separated from each other, with no mechanism for parameter passing. And, perhaps the most serious problem, there is no widely accepted standard version of Basic available.

19.5 Pascal

Pascal language is named after the French mathematician and philosopher, Blaise Pascal. It was developed between 1968 and 1971.

Development

By contrast with Fortran, Algol 60, Cobol and Basic, Pascal is the work of one person - Niklaus Wirth, a university professor in Zurich, Switzerland. Using Algol 60 as a basis, Wirth set out to design a language suitable for teaching computer programming to university students. The first draft of the language was made in 1968. A compiler for Pascal, also written by Wirth, was operational in 1970. Pascal was first published in 1971, and a revised report appeared in 1973.

Since its publication, Pascal has gained increasingly wide acceptance at universities and for scientific and engineering applications. Pascal is available on some microcomputers. Its use may yet spread to schools and to the business computing community.

Objectives

The primary objectives of Pascal are best expressed by its author, Niklaus Wirth: 'The development of the language Pascal is based on two principal aims. The first is to make available a language suitable to teach programming as a systematic discipline based on certain fundamental concepts clearly and naturally reflected by the language. The second is to develop implementations of this language which are both reliable and efficient on presently available computers.'

Pascal is a compromise between these aims. On the one hand, it has a concise, consistent abstract structure. On the other hand, it is sufficiently close to modern computer architectures to be easily and efficiently implemented. An international standard version of the language has been agreed on.

Character Set and Reserved Words

Most implementations of Pascal use upper and lower case letters, digits and a number of special characters. Pascal has a fairly large set of reserved words, including a few not found in other programming languages.

Program Structure

Like Algol 60, Pascal is a block structured language. However, a Pascal block is slightly more restricted than one in Algol 60. In outline, the structure of a Pascal program is as follows:

A **program** is a **program heading** followed by a **block**.

A **block** is a number of **declarations** (of labels, constants, data types, variables, **procedures** and **functions**), followed by a set of **statements**.

A **procedure** is a **procedure heading** followed by a **block**.

A **function** is a **function heading** followed by a **block**.

A **statement** is a simple statement or a set of statements enclosed by the words **begin** and **end**.

Statements are separated by colons, and do not have to be on separate lines. It can be seen that a program may contain a number of procedure and function blocks, which may themselves contain procedure and function blocks. A procedure or function may be called recursively from itself.

Data

One of the strengths of Pascal is the variety of **data types** available, and the provision for user-defined data types. This means that a person writing a Pascal program can construct data types, either by combining the standard types, or by listing all the values a data item can have. Pascal permits the use of **pointers**, which are data items holding the address of other data items. Pascal is unusual in having the operations **new** and **dispose** which create and delete data items pointed to in this way. In addition to individual data items, **arrays**, **sets** and **records**, Pascal language contains the concept of a **file**. All input and output takes place via a few simple operations on files. **Enumeration literals** can be used in conjunction with arrays.

Like Algol 60, Pascal includes the concept of **scope**. The scope of a data item is the block within which it is declared, and any sub-blocks contained in that block.

Operations

Pascal contains all the arithmetic (except raising to powers), relational and logical operations. In addition, the set operations **union**, **intersection** and **set difference** are available. In all cases, the types of the data items used must be compatible with the operations. In addition to the usual arithmetic functions, there are a number of functions to handle non-numeric data. For example, there are functions to find the successor and predecessor of a given data item in its set of values.

Input/Output

All input and output, as well as transfers to and from backing store, take place via files of data. A few simple operations enable data items to be transferred to or from these files. Each file is associated with a particular peripheral device.

Control Structure

Like Algol 60, Pascal has both `if..then` and `if..then..else` constructions for conditional branching. The `go to` statement is available, but its use is discouraged. Pascal has three different constructions for program loops. If a loop is to be repeated a certain number of times, the statement is:

```
for count : = startvalue to endvalue do <statement>
```

The counter variable is automatically increased in steps of 1. If a loop must be repeated at least once, until a certain condition becomes true, the construction is:

repeat <statement> until <condition>

If a loop must be repeated none or more times, while a certain condition holds, the construction is:

while <condition> do <statement>

In this case, the condition is tested before each repetition of the loop. In the previous case, the condition is tested after each repetition. In all of the above examples, 'statement' may be a set of statements, enclosed by the words begin..end.

Example Program
The following procedure of a program shows how a list can be constructed using pointers. The program inputs the names of twenty-five people, and stores them in a list, structured as in Figure 19.1. Note that there is a pointer called **first** pointing to the start of the list. The pointer at the end of the list does not point to anything - it has the value **nil**.

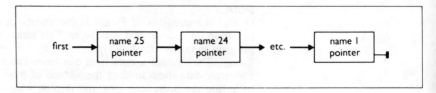

Figure 19.1

```
procedure makelist;
type
    list = ↑person;                    (* pointer to person *)
    person = record
        name: array [1..20] of char;
        next: list                     (* pointer to next person *)
    end;

var first, newperson: list;            (* front pointer and list element *)
    count: integer;                    (* loop counter *)
    newname: name;
begin
    first: = nil;
    for count:= 1 to 25 do
        begin
            readname (newname);        (* procedure,not shown,to
                                          to read a name *)
            new(newperson);            (* create storage space for
                                          new list element *)
            newperson↑.next:= first;
                                       (* link pointer to existing list *)
            newperson↑.name:= newname; (* fill in name of new person *)
            first:= newperson;         (* change front pointer to
                                          new list element *)
        end
end
```

Notes
1 Diagramatically, the sequence of operations is as follows:

Create storage space for new list element: Figure 19.2.

Link pointer of new list element to existing list, and fill in new name: Figure 19.3.

Change front pointer to point to new list element: Figure 19.4.

2 Notice how comments can be inserted in the program.

3 The notation '**newperson**↑' means 'the data item to which the pointer **newperson** points'.

The notation '**.next**' refers to the field called '**next**' in the record.

Thus '**newperson**↑**.next**' means the field called '**next**' in the record pointed to by '**newperson**'.

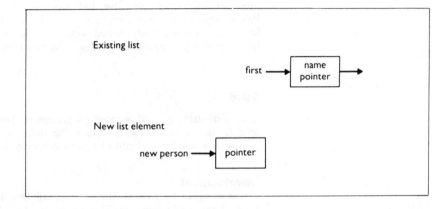

Figure 19.2

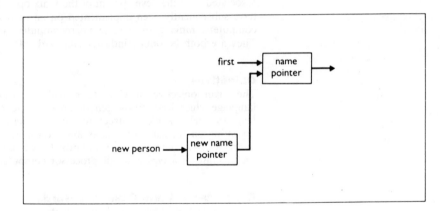

Figure 19.3

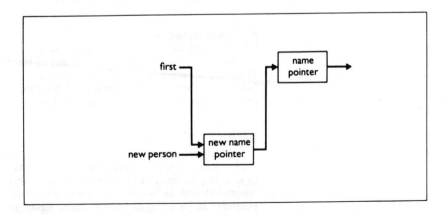

Figure 19.4

Assessment

Pascal was designed to illustrate certain key concepts in programming, such as structured programming, and various types and structures of data. In general, Pascal achieves this objective very well. It combines simplicity with considerable power. Pascal generally tries to provide one mechanism to implement each programming concept. Short cuts are deliberately discouraged. While this sometimes makes programs somewhat longer than they might be in other languages, it does help identify, isolate and eliminate program errors.

Particular strengths of Pascal are its handling of data types and structure, and its disciplined use of pointers. Some people would criticise its input/output facilities as being rather restrictive, but they do have the advantage of simplicity. Pascal language has been developed in the light of experience in other high level languages. It has already gained wide acceptance, and is currently one of the fastest-growing computer languages in terms of numbers of users.

19.6 C

C is a modern, general-purpose programming language which combines high level features such as block structure, the ability to handle data types and recursion with a number of features more commonly found in low level languages.

Development

C was designed by Dennis Ritchie, originally for use on the Digital Equipment PDP-11 range of computers. The development of the language has been closely associated with the development of the Unix operating system. Both Unix and C have subsequently been implemented on an increasingly large number of other computers, ranging from large microcomputers to the Cray-2 supercomputer. They are both becoming industry standard software items.

Objectives

The main objective of C is to provide a powerful, versatile programming language which leads to the generation of efficient object code. C has high level features such as block structures and modern control constructions, while operating on the same objects as low level languages: characters, numbers and addresses. By contemporary standards, C is a small language, and close to the architecture of a typical single-processor computer.

Character Set and Reserved Words

C uses upper and lower case letters, digits and a small number of special characters. C has a fairly small set of reserved words.

Program Structure

Like Algol 60 and Pascal, C is a block structured language. A program consists of a main program, which calls a number of functions to perform specific tasks. There are no procedures in C, and functions may not be defined within other functions. Statements are terminated by colons, and do not have to be on separate lines. A function may be called recursively from itself.

Data

C concentrates on a small range of data types. These include characters, integers (which may be short or long) and floating point numbers (which may be single or double precision). Arrays, structures (corresponding to records in most other languages) and unions may be constructed from these elementary types, and pointers can be set up to point to them. Functions may return any single-valued data type. Although every variable in a program must be declared to be of a particular data type, the rules of types are not as strict as they are in Pascal. For example, pointers may be used to access array elements, and for some purposes characters may be regarded as integers. All data items must be declared before use, and the scope of a data item is the function or program segment in which it is declared.

Operations

C contains all the arithmetic (except raising to powers), relational and logical operations. It also contains the Boolean operations AND, OR, exclusive OR and shift, and the **auto-increment** and **auto-decrement** operations commonly found in machine and assembly languages. For example, if n has the value 5, the assignment:

```
x = n++ ;
```

sets x to 5 and then adds 1 to n. If n is 9, the assignment:

```
x = --n ;
```

decreases n by 1 and then sets x to its new value (now 8). These operations enable very concise programs to be written to count through data structures. There is a 'shorthand' way of writing such expressions as:

```
i = i + 2 ;
```

which may instead be written as:

```
i += 2 ;
```

again leading to very compact code.

Input/Output

C has no built-in facilities for input and output; these are created by using the library of standard input/output facilities which is provided with every implementation of C. This library includes functions to get individual characters and numbers from the keyboard, print data with a specified format and read from and write to files on backing store.

Control Structure

C has the if..then..else construction for conditional branching, and the case construction for multi-way branches. Statements may be bracketed into blocks for use with these constructions. The go to statement is available, but its use is contrary to the design principles of C. There are three types of loop construction. The while construction tests the condition to continue the loop at the start of each repetition; the do ... while construction has the test at the end. The for construction is more general than that in most other languages. The loop:

```
for (expression_1; expression_2; expression_3)
    statement ;
```

is equivalent to:

```
expression_1 ;
while (expression_2) {
    statement ;
    expression_3 ;
}
```

Example Program

The program below, consisting of a main program and a function, reads a set of
words from input and sorts them in alphabetical order into a tree structure.
Each node of the tree contains a pointer to the word at the node, and left and
right subtree pointers. See Sections 4.9 and 16.9. The program starts with a
declaration of the data structure required.

```
struct tree_node {                      /* tree node structure */
    char *word;                         /* pointer to word */
    struct tree_node *left;             /* pointer to left subtree */
    struct tree_node *right;            /* pointer to right subtree */
}

main ()                                 /* start of main program */
{
    struct tree_node *root, *load_tree();
                                        /* declares data item root and
                                           function load_tree
                                           as pointers to trees */
    char word[20];                      /* declares an array of 20
                                           characters */
    int test_word, get_word();          /* declares integer variable
                                           test_word and function
                                           get_word */
    root = NULL;                        /* start with a null tree
                                           pointer */
    while ((test_word = get_word(word)) != EOF)
                                        /* input next word and test for
                                           end-of file */
        root = load_tree(root, word);
                                        /* load next word into tree */
}                                       /* end of main program */
struct tree_node *load_tree(tree_ptr, wrd)
                                        /* function to load word into
                                           tree */
struct tree_node *tree_ptr;             /* tree_ptr is pointer to a tree */
char *wrd;                              /* wrd is a pointer to a character
                                           array */
{
    struct tree_node *tree_allocate();
                                        /* function tree_allocate returns
                                           a pointer to a tree */
    char *string_save();                /* function string_save returns a
                                           pointer to a character array */
    int str_compare();                  /* function str_compare returns
                                           an integer */
    if (tree_ptr == NULL) {             /* a new word is to be appended */
        tree_ptr = tree allocate();     /* allocate a new pointer */
        tree_ptr->word = string_save(wrd);
                                        /* link wrd to the node pointer */
        tree_ptr->left = tree_ptr->right = NULL;
                                        /* make null left and right subtree
                                           pointers */
    } else if (str_compare(wrd, tree_ptr->word) < 0)
        tree_ptr->left = load_tree(tree_ptr->left, wrd);
                                        /* look at left subtree */
    else tree_ptr->right = load_tree(tree_ptr->right, wrd);
                                        /* look at right subtree */
    return (tree_ptr);
}
```

Notes

1 Brackets **{ }** are used to create blocks of statements.
2 Notice how comments can be inserted in the program.
3 The functions `get_word`, `string_save` and `str_compare` are called from this program, but not defined in it.
4 The notation `!=` is used to mean 'not equal to'.
5 The notation `*var` means that var is a pointer to some other object.

Assessment

C is a concise, efficient programming language with facilities for the creation of carefully-structured programs and data. It is not as elegant as Pascal, but is rapidly emerging as an alternative to it for a wide range of commercial, industrial and research applications. A particular strength of C is its suitability for the writing of systems software: almost all of the Unix operating system is written in C, as are all Unix utility programs. Discussions are at present under way to agree on an international standard version of C.

19.7 Lisp

Lisp is a programming language designed for artificial intelligence work. Until quite recently its use was restricted to a small group of researchers, but at present, with the fifth generation computer projects now under way, Lisp is being used much more widely.

Development

Lisp originated in 1959 in the artificial intelligence group at MIT under John McCarthy. It is intended for problems which involve symbol manipulation and recursion. Most artificial intelligence work falls broadly into this category, hence the popularity of Lisp for these purposes.

Objectives

The aim of Lisp is to provide a vehicle for the writing of programs which are based on symbol manipulation. The most common programming tasks are generating and testing alternatives, and searching large bodies of information for patterns. Lisp is a small, concise language ideal for these purposes. It bears very little resemblance to any other programming language.

Character Set and Reserved Words

Lisp uses upper and lower case letters, digits and special characters, and has a small number of reserved words.

Program Structure

Lisp is a functional programming language. A top-level function calls lower-level functions in order to compute its result. Library functions may be called for elementary operations.

Data

The fundamental data element in Lisp is the **atom**, which may be an identifier or a number. Atoms are built into **lists** by the use of brackets. For example, **(A B C)** is a list of three atoms, and **(A (B C) D)** is a list containing two atoms and a sublist **(B C)**. The notation **(A | B)** indicates a list with atom **A** at the head and the list **B** as the tail.

Operations

Processing in Lisp is in terms of functions, of which there are five elementary ones:

```
car[(A B C)] = A              ... the head of the list
cdr[(A B C)] = (B C)          ... the tail of the list
cons[A; (B C)] = (A B C)      ... the constructor function
eq[A; A] = T          (for True)   ... equality of atoms
atom [(A B C)] = Nil  (for False)  ... test for an atom
```

(The function names car and cdr are derived from associated assembly language instructions on the first computer on which Lisp was implemented. They are sometimes re-named head and tail respectively.)

Arithmetic operations are expressed as functions: sum[A; B] gives the sum of the atoms A and B. Arithmetic relations are expressed as Boolean-valued functions, or **predicates**: lessp[A; B] is true if A is less than B.

Control Structures

The conditional construction is:

```
[p1 -> e1; p2 -> e2 ... pn -> en]
```

where p1, p2 ... pn are predicates and e1, e2 ... en are expressions. The construction is scanned sequentially, and the first expression corresponding to a predicate which is true is evaluated. There is also a more conventional if ... then ... else construction, structured as a list:

```
(if A B C)
```

If predicate A is true then the value of B is chosen, else the value of C is selected.

A program in Lisp is written as a top-level function which invokes lower-level functions in its implementation. Functions may be processed by other functions, giving Lisp programs endless possibilities for self-modification.

Example Program

The recursive function defined below tests whether the data item elt is a member of the list lst. The logic of the function is as follows:

```
if lst is non-empty
     then if elt is the head of lst
                then the function is true
                else check whether elt is a member of
                     the tail of lst
     else the function is false
```

The program is as follows:

```
(define member (elt lst)
   (if (consp (lst))
        (if eq (elt car (lst))
             T
             (member (elt cdr (lst))))
        Nil ))
```

Assessment

Lisp has been the mainstream artificial intelligence programming language for many years, and almost without exception the AI programs of any significance have been written in Lisp. Lisp has been the starting point for a number of more recent non-procedural programming languages, notably Prolog.

An early problem with Lisp was that it did not run very efficiently on most computers. In recent years a number of dedicated Lisp workstations have appeared, with hardware and low-level software designed to support Lisp very efficiently. It seems quite likely that Lisp, or a derivative of it, will be a fifth generation programming language. Although the 'upper' layers of software of a fifth generation computer are likely to be declarative in nature (see Section 18.3), at lower levels there is a need for a procedural language which can operate on large, complex data structures. One possible evolution of Lisp is into an applicative language (Section 18.3), with no destructive assignments, which will bring it into line with dataflow and graph reduction architectures.

19.8 Prolog

Prolog is a declarative programming language which has recently become increasingly popular. It is a logic-based language, suitable for a wide variety of database and artificial intelligence applications.

Development
Prolog was developed by Alain Colmerauer and his colleagues at Marseilles University in 1972. Research and development has continued in the UK, notably at Imperial College under Robert Kowalski, and in Japan at the Icot centre (Section 34.2).

Objectives
The objective of Prolog is to provide a rigorous logical basis for the development of a wide range of computer applications. Prolog allows a programmer to state a computing task in terms of a description of the data objects required, and their logical relationships, rather than a 'recipe' of processing steps which the computer must carry out. An important application of Prolog is in education, where it can be used to teach logic, problem-solving or programming, and be used with a variety of educational databases.

Character Set and Reserved Words
Prolog uses upper and lower case letters, digits and a small number of reserved words.

Features
There is no clear distinction, in Prolog, between data, processing operations and control facilities. A Prolog program consists of a set of declarations, all of which are valid simultaneously. A simple declaration, also known as a **predicate**, is of the form:

```
topic-of(Computing, Logic)
```

Predicates may be combined into **Horn clauses** of the form:

```
teaches(x, y) if topic-of(z, y) and assigned-to(x, z)
```

(This means that teacher x teaches topic y if y is a topic of subject z and teacher x is assigned to teach subject z.)

Because predicates can contain constants or variables, both the processing and data structuring aspects of conventional programming are expressed in Prolog in a uniform notation based on logic. The data in predicates can be single items or lists with the same rules for construction as used in Lisp (Section 19.7). For example, membership of a list is defined by the clauses:

```
member-of(x, (x|z))
member-of(x, (y|z)) if member-of(x, z)
```

(In other words, a data item x is a member of a list if it is the head of the list or if it is a member of the tail of the list. This is the Prolog equivalent of the example Lisp program.)

A Prolog program is activated by queries of the form:

```
which(x, causes-deformity(x, stunted growth))
```

This causes the Prolog interpreter to check the predicate in the query against those in the program, examining lower-level predicates and 'cancelling out' those known to be true or false, until a result is obtained, or a contradiction arises, in which case the query has no result.

Input/Output

Prolog has a number of standard predicates for input and output. Many implementations have predicates for graphics output and some include control facilities.

Example Program

An example of a Prolog program which uses a simple aircraft flight database is as follows:

```
calls-at(BA11, (London Bombay Singapore Sydney Melbourne))
calls-at(BA23, (London New-York))
calls-at(BA67, (London Madrid Las-Palmas Buenos-Aires))
calls-at(BA39, (London Berlin Moscow))
calls-at(BA27, (London Madrid Cairo Nairobi))

member-of(x, (x|z))
member-of(x, (y|z)) if member-of(x, z)

destination-of(x, y) if calls-at(y, z)
                    and member-of(x, z)
```

The last clause is interpreted as x is a destination of flight y if y has a list of calling points z and x is a member of the list z.

A query such as

```
which(y, destination-of(Madrid, y))
```

meaning 'Which flights have Madrid as a destination?' produces the results:

```
BA67
BA27
no (more) answers.
```

Assessment

Prolog has gone very rapidly from being a fringe programming language to being one of the key elements in the fifth generation computer programmes. There are still some problems to be ironed out, notably in the way Prolog deals with negative information. Recent work includes Parlog, a parallel implementation of Prolog, and various attempts to synthesise elements of Prolog and Lisp, or Prolog and a procedural language.

19.9 Conclusion

This small sample from the rapidly increasing population of high level languages shows some of the similarities and some of the differences that exist between these languages. Each language studied has its strengths and weaknesses, and each is best suited to a certain class of computer applications.

When choosing a high level language for a particular application, the following criteria are taken into consideration:

- The nature of the application: whether it is a commercial, industrial or scientific task, whether it is real-time, batch processing, transaction processing, an expert system or primarily a control application. In each case, there are certain special-purpose languages which may be particularly suitable.
- The computer(s) on which the application is to run, and whether the software is to be developed on these computers. If the software is not to be developed on the ultimate host computers, cross-compilers (Section 20.2) and associated software tools are needed.
- The software development tools available: if the program is a standard commercial application, for example, most of the software can probably be developed using a program generator (Section 23.7).
- Whether the software is to be developed within the company or organisation which is to use it, or whether an outside software house is to be commissioned to do the work. In the latter case, the choice of languages is wider.
- The budget for the software development, and the time allocated to do the work. If time and money are short, a language which is familiar to the company is more likely to be chosen.

Exercise 19

1 Select any two of the languages described in this chapter. Answer the following questions, comparing the selected languages.
  a) Compare the input and output facilities provided by the languages. State, with reasons, which language is simpler and which language is more powerful in this respect.
  b) Compare the provisions for calculation provided by the languages. State, with reasons, in which language complicated calculations can be expressed more concisely.
  c) Compare and contrast the provisions for conditional and unconditional branching in the languages.
  d) Compare the facilities for making decisions based on rules, and for handling data in structures such as lists.
2 Of all the languages described in the chapter, Algol 60 is probably the least widely used. In the light of your studies of the chapter, suggest some reasons for this.
3 Give your own views on the idea of a universal programming language.
4 What is the main difference between the objectives of Algol 60 and those of Pascal? What difference do you think this has made in the relative popularity of the two languages?
5 Which of the languages mentioned in this chapter come closest to being a general-purpose language, suitable for scientific, commercial and educational computing? Give reasons for your choice.
6 Suggest at least two reasons for the persistent popularity of Fortran, and two for that of Cobol.
7 Select a programming language not discussed in this chapter. Using suitable references, write a concise account of the language, under the same headings as those used in this chapter. Some suitable languages are Algol 68, Simula, Modula, PL/1, Logo, Comal, Occam, Hope and Ada.
●8 Consider the problem of printing the digits of a number in reverse order. One method is as follows:

```
reverse digits is:
    output last digit of number
if digits remain
    then reverse remaining digits.
```

This method is recursive, because it uses itself repeatedly until there are no more digits to reverse. A procedure of a Pascal program to carry out this process is as follows:

```
procedure reverse (n:integer);
begin
    write (n mod 10);          (* the remainder when n is
                                  divided by 10 *)
    if n div 10<>0             (* the integer part of n
                                  divided by 10 *)
        then reverse (n div 10)  (* recursive call *)
end;
```

a) Write down the steps carried out by this procedure if it is supplied with the number 8271.

A portion of a program in Basic language, to carry out the same task, is as follows:

```
1000 REM PRINT DIGITS OF NUMBER N IN REVERSE ORDER
1010 LET X = INT (N/10): REM INTEGER PART OF N DIVIDED BY 10
1020 PRINT N-10*X        : REM REMAINDER WHEN N IS DIVIDED BY 10
1030 IF X = 0 THEN RETURN
1040 LET N = X
1050 GO TO 1010
```

b) Dry run this program segment, using the number 8271.

c) In your opinion, which program segment is easier to understand? Give reasons for your answer.

d) Write an equivalent program segment in one of the other languages introduced in this chapter. Comment on similarities and differences between it and the above program segments.

9 Comment on the relative emphasis on arithmetic operations in the eight languages studied.

10 Rank the case study languages in order of ease of readability of programs. Compare your ordering with that of others and comment on it.

20
Compilers and Interpreters

This chapter concerns the process of translating a program written in a high level language to an equivalent program in a machine language. The two major approaches to language translation, namely **compilation** and **interpretation**, are discussed. Also discussed are some of the other software items which are used in conjunction with language translators in the development of applications programs.

20.1 The Objectives of Language Translation

The main objective of a language translation program is to convert a program or part of a program in a high level language into an equivalent program in a machine language, sometimes via one or more intermediate languages. The input language is called the **source language**, and the output language the **object** or **target language**. The translation program itself is written in a **base language**. A language translation program can be represented as a **T diagram**, shown in Figure 20.1. An example of the T diagram for a Basic language compiler, written in Z80 assembly language, producing Z80 machine code, is shown in Figure 20.2.

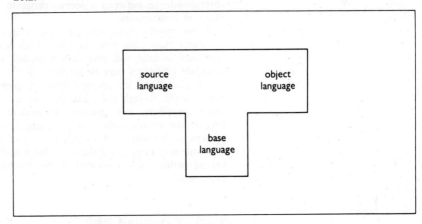

Figure 20.1
A T diagram of a language translation program

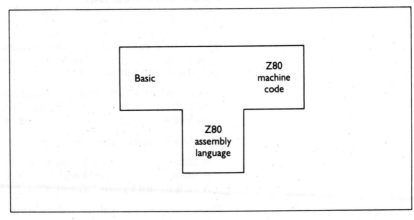

Figure 20.2
An example of a T diagram

A second objective of a translation program is to identify any errors in a source program. **Diagnostic** error messages are output, to assist the programmer to correct the errors.

Thirdly, many language translators attempt to produce object code which is as efficient as possible. The process of making the code more efficient is known as **optimisation**.

Fourthly, a language translator is a part of a set of software development tools, and one of its aims is to integrate its workings with the other tools as well as possible.

Finally, the translation program itself should be efficient. It should not take too long to translate a source program, and must not occupy too much space in the main store of the computer. This objective conflicts to some extent with the other objectives, particularly the third one. Most translation programs represent a compromise betwen this and the other objectives.

20.2 Principles of Compilation and Interpretation

Compilers and interpreters represent two very different approaches to the task of enabling programs written in a high level language to be run.

A **compiler** translates a source code module (which may be a complete program, or part of one) in a high level language into an equivalent object code module in a machine language. The object code may then be linked to other object code modules to form a complete program which can be executed. The translation process is applied to the source code module as a whole. Source statements may be separated or combined, and there is not always a direct correspondence between a source program statement and one or more object program instructions.

An **interpreter** transforms a computer into a high level language machine. The computer then runs programs in a high level language. Each source program statement is analysed, and then executed. Object code is not produced. Only complete programs may be interpreted.

Compilers and interpreters have in common the process of analysing the source code, though the methods they use differ. Having analysed the source code, compilers then generate equivalent object code, whereas interpreters execute the source code directly. Compilers are more sophisticated than interpreters, as the latter can do little by way of optimisation. Simple languages such as Basic and Logo, and the logic language Prolog, are more commonly interpreted rather than compiled. Early microcomputers were too small to run compilers.

20.3 Extended BNF

One of the most useful ways of describing the syntax of a programming language is to express it as a set of rules, using a notation known as **extended BNF**. A BNF rule shows how one syntactic structure of a language is made up of other structures. For example, a very small class of English sentences can be specified by the following BNF rules:

```
<sentence>::= <noun> <verb>
<noun>     ::= John|Paul|George|Ringo
<verb>     ::= eats|sleeps|sings
```

In ordinary English, these rules are:

A sentence is a noun followed by a verb.
A noun is "John" or "Paul" or "George" or "Ringo".
A verb is "eats" or "sleeps" or "sings".

These rules can be used to produce sentences like:

John eats
Paul sings
Ringo sleeps

On the other hand, the sentence:

John eats George

is not in accordance with the rules.

A much larger class of sentences is obtained by adding the following rules:

```
<sentence>   ::= <sentence> <conjunction> <sentence>
<conjunction>::= and|or
```

The first of these rules is called **recursive** since the same element, namely <sentence>, appears on the left and the right of the `::=` symbol.

These rules allow the production of sentences such as:

John eats and Paul sings or Ringo sleeps

However, the sentence:

John or Paul sings

is not in accordance with the rules.

The folowing BNF rules specify the structure of a fairly wide class of decimal numbers:

```
<decimal number>::= <decimal point> <number>|
                    <number> <decimal point> <number>
<number>         ::= <digit> | <digit> <number>
<digit>          ::= 0 | 1 | 2 | 3 | 4 | 5 | 6 | 7 | 8 | 9
<decimal point> ::= .
```

A formal way of using these rules to analyse a number is as follows:

Example 1: 97.652

```
         9       7                         6       5       2
rule 3: <digit> <digit>            .      <digit> <digit> <digit>
rule 4: <digit> <digit> <decimal point>   <digit> <digit> <digit>
rule 2: <digit> <number> <decimal point>  <digit> <digit> <digit>
rule 2:    <number>      <decimal point>  <digit> <number>
rule 2:    <number>      <decimal point>     <number>
rule 1:                  <decimal number>
```

Example 2: 3.

```
                         3                    .
   rules 3 and 4:     <digit>          <decimal point>
```

No further rules can be applied. This is not a valid decimal number as defined by the above rules.

Two extensions are now used to the above BNF notation, hence the name extended BNF. The first is for optional elements, which are enclosed in curly brackets: { }. The second is for zero or more repetitions of an element, which is enclosed in square brackets: [ ]. For example, the syntax of a signed integer may be written as:

```
<signed integer> := {<sign>} <digit> [<digit>]
```

This means that a signed integer is an optional sign, followed by a digit, followed by zero or more additional digits. The definition of a decimal number given above may be re-written in extended BNF as:

```
<decimal number> ::= {<number>} <decimal point> <number>
<number>         ::= <digit> [<digit>]
<digit>          ::= 0 | 1 | 2 | 3 | 4 | 5 | 6 | 7 | 8 | 9
<decimal point>  ::= .
```

Rules in extended BNF, or **syntax diagrams,** which are a diagramatic representation of the same constructions, are used to specify the structure of high level languages, and correspond closely to the code of the syntax analysis portions of the compilers for the languages.

20.4 Editing

The first stage of software development is to enter and edit the source code. For this purpose, an **editor** is used. The editor enables source code segments to be typed and amended, and has text manipulation facilities to speed up the process. To an increasing extent, word processing packages are used for editing source code.

Some assemblers include an interactive editor. As soon as a line of program has been edited, it is translated into machine code, and any necessary amendments are made to the machine code version of other program lines. In this way the program remains in an assembled state during editing. It is ready to run throughout the process.

20.5 The Steps of Compilation

The main steps of compilation are **lexical analysis, syntax analysis** and **code generation.** These are now discussed, together with three other important features of compilers, namely a **dictionary, optimisation** and **error handling.** All compilers include these features, though in some they are more distinct than in others.

Lexical Analysis

Lexical analysis is the first stage in the processing of a source program by a compiler. It may be regarded as 'tidying up' the source program, ready for more detailed analysis. Lexical analysis generally has to perform three tasks:

- Changing the source code into a form which is independent of the input device.
- Removing redundant information such as spaces and comments.
- Dealing with reserved words and composite symbols such as ':=', replacing them with **tokens** which are used during syntax analysis.

For example, consider the following segment of a program in Basic language:

```
200 FOR I = 1 TO N STEP 1
210 LET X (I) = 0 :REM INITIALISE ARRAY
215 NEXT I
```

A lexical analysis might produce the following:

```
[L45] [T16] I = 1 [T17] N [T18] 1 \
[L46] [T09] X(I) = 0 \
[L47] [T19] I
```

where the character \ marks the end of the line, and the tokens, in square brackets, are of the following types:

L45, L46 and L47 are the internal line numbers
T16, T17, T18, T09 and T19 are the tokens for the reserved words.

Note that the comment (:REM INITIALISE ARRAY) in the source code is deleted by the lexical analyser.

Syntax Analysis

Syntax analysis is where the structure, and, to some extent, the meaning, of a source program is determined by the compiler. The overall source program is analysed into blocks, the blocks are analysed into instructions, and the individual items such as instruction words, variables and constants in each instruction are identified.

As discussed in Section 20.3, the syntax of a high level programming language can be expressed as a set of rules. Each rule specifies how one structure in a program is composed of smaller structures. The compiler applies the rules, in a systematic way, to the source program, to determine its structure. The process is known as **parsing**. For example, one of the syntax rules of Basic language can be written, in BNF notation, as follows:

```
<program line> :: = <line number> <instruction word>
                        <rest of instruction>
```

This rule analyses the line:

```
100 LET X = 0
```

(or, strictly speaking, the tokenised form produced by the lexical analyser) as follows:

```
<line number>              : 100
<instruction word>         : LET
<rest of instruction>      : X = 0
```

and, therefore:

```
<program line>             : 100 LET X = 0
```

A common technique of syntax analysis involves the use of **state tables**. These are discussed in the exercise at the end of this chapter.

The Dictionary

A large amount of information about a program is accumulated as compilation proceeds. This information is stored in a data structure known as a **dictionary**. The information is loaded into the dictionary during the early stages of compilation and used during later stages.

Much of the information in the dictionary concerns the use of variables in the source language. As each variable in a source program is encountered, an entry for it is made in the dictionary. This entry includes the name of the variable, its type, and the address of the memory location where its value is to be stored. The dictionary entry for the variable X in the Basic program line above might be as follows:

variable name	type	address
X	N	3A2F

where N represents numeric, and the address is a hexadecimal number.

The tokens for line numbers and constants generated by the lexical analyser would also be references to entries in the dictionary. For example, a Basic program might include the lines:

```
70 GO TO 100        tokenised as [L21] [T19] [L34]
...
100 LET X = 0       tokenised as [L34] [T09] X = [C04]
```

An entry in the dictionary is created for the line number 100. The token [L34] identifies the entry, which contains the address of the translated code for the line. It might be as follows:

source name	type	address
100	L	2B1A

where L represents line number, and the address is a hexadecimal number. This entry enables the branching instruction in line 70 to be translated completely, by providing the destination of the branching instruction.

Code Generation

Having analysed the structure of the source program, and having transformed it into an intermediate tokenised form, it is now possible to generate the object code. The intermediate code is scanned, and each token is looked up in the dictionary. The entry in the dictionary is used to form the machine code instruction. For example, if the token for a variable name is recognised, then the dictionary is used to find its address. This address is inserted into the machine code instruction being generated.

In most cases, a statement in a high level language generates more than one machine code instruction. To give an example of this, a short section of a Basic program is shown below, together with the equivalent code in AMC assembly language. It must be remembered that compilers generally produce machine code, but assembly code, together with comments is shown here for simplicity.

Basic		AMC assembly language		
200 FOR I = 1 TO N		LOA X N + 1		Use index as loop counter.
	NXT	CMP X	N	Compare with N.
		BGT	OUT	Exit loop if greater than N.
205 LET Y(I) = 0		CLR A		Clear accumulator.
		STO A D Y		Store contents of accumulator in Y + index.
210 NEXT I		INC X		Increment index.
		BRN	NXT	Continue loop.
	OUT			

Optimisation

One of the objections to high level languages, when they were first introduced, was that the object code they produced would be less efficient than machine code written by hand. Accordingly, much attention has been paid, especially in the early days of compilers, to increasing the efficiency of object code.

Optimisation can take place before or after code generation, and sometimes at both places. Either the source or the object code is manipulated to produce a more efficient end product. In most cases, 'more efficient' means object code which will run more quickly when it is executed. (An alternative objective is object code which is as compact as possible. This is seldom the fastest possible version.)

Optimisation can be attempted on almost any part of the code of a program, but loops are one of the most fruitful areas. Here the objective is to do as much as possible outside the loop, and reduce the number of times that the test for the end of the loop is carried out.

As an example, consider the portion of assembly code in the previous section. The instruction to clear the accumulator can be taken outside the loop. Furthermore, if the loop limit N is an even number, then the body of the loop can be performed twice before the test for the end of the loop is carried out. These optimisations lead to the following AMC code:

	CLR A		Clear accumulator.
	LOA X N + 1		Use index as loop counter.
NXT	CMP X	N	Compare with N.
	BGT	OUT	Exit loop if greater than N.
	STO A D Y		Store contents of accumulator in Y + index.
	INC X		Increment index.
	STO A D Y		Store contents of accumulator in Y + index.
	INC X		Increment index.
	BRN	NXT	Continue loop.
OUT			

Although the object code now contains more instructions, it will be executed more quickly.

One problem with optimisation is that it increases the size and complexity of the compiler. There are two solutions to this problem. One is is to allow machine code instructions to be combined with high level language statements in a source program. This allows the programmer to optimise crucial areas of the program, and simplifies the task of the compiler. The other technique is to allow the programmer to provide the compiler with information about the program before it is compiled. This specifies how the optimisation is to be carried out, and which modules require particular attention.

Error Handling

In all of the previous sections it has been assumed that the source program input to the compiler is correct. Unfortunately, this is not always the case. Errors detected during compilation are generally of two types. The first type are **syntax errors,** when a source program does not conform to the rules of syntax of the source language. The other type (**semantic errors**) includes transfers of control to statements which do not exist, and duplicate labels on statements.

When an error is detected, most compilers attempt to locate the position of the error and determine its cause. This process is called **diagnostics.** A message, called a **diagnostic error message,** is output, together with some indication of the position of the error.

In most cases, when an error is detected, compilation cannot be completed. The usual practice is to continue to the end of the syntax analysis phase, in case any more errors are encountered. Code generation does not take place. In some cases it is difficult to continue syntax analysis, as assumptions have to be made about the correctness of code near the error. Analysis generally re-commences from the start of the next source program statement. A few compilers make an attempt to correct certain errors such as mis-spelt instruction words. This practice does not, however, meet with widespread approval.

20.6 Linkage

In many cases, the output from a compiler or assembler is a set of separate modules (known as **segments**) of machine code, corresponding to groups of subprograms in the source code. These segments relate to each other, via call and return instructions, and may share common data. They also contain calls to library modules (Section 20.7) which are part of the software development system. The segments produced by the compiler are generally in **relocatable code** – they contain relative machine addresses, and cannot be run until these are replaced by absolute machine addresses. The task of a **linkage program,** also known as a **linkage editor,** is to plant the appropriate addresses in all the external call and return instructions, so that all the modules are linked together properly. The linker also enables blocks of data, which are declared to be common to more than one segment, to be accessed by all those which use it.

Some linkage editors enable a single object program to be built up from segments which may originate from different high level languages, or a combination of high and low level languages. Some replace the relative addresses in the relocatable code with absolute addresses; in other cases this is done by the loader (Section 20.8)

20.7 Library Modules

Compiled code for common operations such as arithmetic, file handling and graphics control are kept as separate modules in the **library** associated with a compiler. The particular library modules required by an application program are linked with the other code segments by the linkage editor. Some software development systems have **indexing** and cross-reference facilities which enable new code modules to be added to the library.

These programs considerably reduce the length of applications programs, and relieve programmers of the task of writing large portions of identical code for different programs.

20.8 Loading

When a program has been compiled or assembled, and all the object code modules linked together, the resulting machine code program is generally written to backing store. In many cases, all the addresses in the program are relative to the start of the program. They do not yet contain the absolute addresses of the store locations to which they will refer when the program is loaded into the computer memory.

A loading program thus performs two functions. It copies the object code of a program into the main store locations in which it will reside during execution, and changes the addresses in program instructions to match the addresses into which the program has been loaded. This process is known as **relocation**. Execution of the program can then commence.

Some compilers and assemblers are called **load-and-go** systems because they include linkage and loading modules. As soon as language translation is complete, the machine language version of the program is linked, loaded and run. The language translation system remains in control throughout. In other cases, linkage and relocation are performed by the link editor, and loading is done by the operating system. Figure 20.3 shows the process of language translation, linkage and loading. For an interpretation of the symbols used, see Figure 25.1.

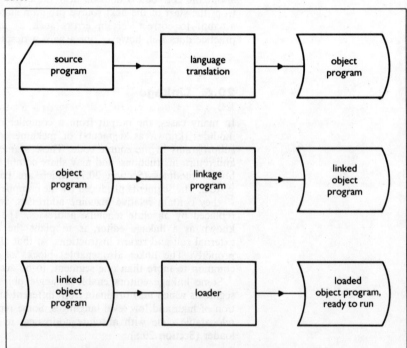

Figure 20.3
Language translation, linkage and loading

20.9 Run-Time Diagnostics

During the process of developing and testing a program, it is extremely useful to know precisely what is happening at each step while it is running. Some compilers have **run-time diagnostics packages** which enable this to be achieved. The way these packages work is generally as follows.

The programmer creates a **breakpoint** at every stage where he or she wants to investigate the state of the program. This is done by inserting a special instruction or directive at each breakpoint. The program is then compiled or assembled, and run. When a breakpoint is reached, control passes to the run-time diagnostics package. The program is suspended, but the contents of all registers is preserved. The diagnostics package enables registers and store locations to be displayed and altered if necessary. Execution of the program can then be continued from the instruction following the breakpoint. Some run-time diagnostics packages allow **single stepping,** where the program pauses after every single instruction. A run-time diagnostics facility can save one of the most expensive elements of a software development system, namely programmer's time.

20.10 Interpreters

An interpreter is a program which analyses and runs a source program, statement by statement. Like compilers, interpreters analyse the structure of each source program statement. However, lexical and syntax analysis are not always distinguished. Interpreters also create and maintain a dictionary of variable names and statement labels. Instead of generating object code for each source program statement, the interpreter carries out a sequence of actions equivalent to the instructions in the statement. Object code is not generated in the process.

As a consequence of this, optimisation is virtually impossible, and error diagnostics are limited, by comparison with compilers. Only one copy of the program being translated is kept, in source code. On the other hand, interpreters are generally shorter and simpler than compilers. Some interpreters have run-time diagnostic facilities. For these reasons, interpreters are particularly popular on small microcomputers.

20.11 Case Study: Prospero Pascal Compiler

To show how the general ideas introduced in this chapter can be put into practice, the chapter concludes with a case study of a compiler system used extensively on microcomputers, and describes the stages of the compilation of a typical program. The compiler chosen is the Pascal compiler from Prospero Software, which runs on a variety of microcomputers using the CP/M or the MSDOS operating systems. The version of Pascal is that approved by the International Standards Organisation (ISO), making it fully portable across the range of computers. The compiler system consists of the following programs:

- The compiler, Propas, which has three linked modules to perform the three stages of compilation. It accepts source code produced by a text editor or word processor such as Wordstar, and produces relocatable code segments in the machine code of the target computer. The source code can be an entire program, or a segment of a program which is to be linked to other segments at a later stage. Program segments can share common data, and call procedures and functions in other segments, or in the library modules.
- The linker, Prolink, which links the relocatable code segments from the compiler and produces executable code, ready to be loaded and run. The linker will combine segments compiled from Pascal or Fortran source code, or assembled from the assembly language of the target computer.
- A set of library modules, including Paslib, the general-purpose library, and Hrglib, the library of high-resolution graphics routines. The high-resolution graphics library is supplied by the computer manufacturer, and not by Prospero, since it is machine dependent. These library modules are in relocatable machine code, ready to be combined with segments of applications programs. Procedures and functions in the library routines may be used selectively by other programs.
- The librarian utility, Prolib, which links relocatable code modules into library routines, and allows them to be used selectively. It can produce a set of cross-references, showing which procedures and functions are in which

segments, and from which segments they are called. Prolib enables new library modules to be created by programmers for subsequent use.

● The run-time diagnostics utility, Probe. It is in the form of a relocatable code module, to be linked with the other segments of an application program before execution. It shows the source program lines as they execute, and provides a breakpoint at the start of each line. Values of all variables can be inspected and changed before running of the program continues.

To illustrate the workings of the compiler, consider a typical application program, written in Pascal, with the overall structure shown in Figure 20.4. There is a control module (the main program), three operation modules, each comprising a number of procedures and functions, and a set of service modules, which contain procedures and functions used by a number of operation modules. There are also calls to external modules for file handling and graphics operations. The program is entered as four segments: the first containing the main program and the service modules, the other three each containing an operation module.

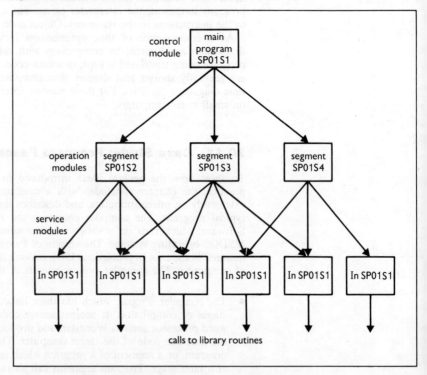

Figure 20.4
Example program: segment structure

The compiler is used to produce the relocatable object code for the four segments. The instruction to compile the first segment is:

PROPAS SP01S1/LN

where SP01S1 is the name of the program segment being compiled, and the letters L and N specify the compilation options chosen. The letter L creates a listing of the source code, with line numbers added, and N causes a record of the source file and line number to be kept of each machine instruction produced. This information is written to separate files on disk, for use by the run-time diagnostic program.

When all the compilation errors have been corrected in the first segment, the others are compiled by a similar process. The instructions are:

PROPAS SP01S2/LN
PROPAS SP01S3/LN
PROPAS SP01S4/LN

When all the segments have been compiled, each has a corresponding segment of relocatable object code on disk, ready for linking. The linker is called up by the instruction:

```
PROLINK SP01S1, SP01S2, SP01S3, SP01S4, PROBE,
                                    PASLIB/S, HRGLIB/S
```

The linker combines the four segments of the application program, the run-time diagnostic module, Probe, the general Pascal library, Paslib, and the high-resolution graphics library, Hrglib. The letter S used with the last two modules means that only procedures and functions required by the other segments will be linked from them.

The linker produces a single (large) executable module in machine code, which has the run-time diagnostic facilities built into it. This program is then run, and tested by checking the values of variables at breakpoints, etc. Changes are made to source code segments, which are then re-compiled and linked, until all the run-time errors in the program have been identified and corrected. The program is then re-compiled without the L and N options, and linked without the Probe module. The resulting machine code program is then ready for use.

This process, which in practice takes several weeks or months, shows how the facilities of the compiler system are used at the various stages of software development. The program is developed in segments, rather than as a complete entity, and the error detection facilities in the compiler, linker and run-time diagnostics package help the programmer to identify and correct errors as quickly as possible.

20.12 Conclusion

Over the last twenty years, language translators have become an indispensable part of computer systems. Some microcomputers go to the lengths of having a language translator permanently stored in read-only memory. Many of these computers can only be programmed in a high level language.

Language translation is a very active area in computing. Work is in progress improving existing compilers and interpreters, and writing translators for new languages or new computers. Much attention is currently being paid to the problem of writing translators for large languages on small computers. One line of development, however, might make language translation programs obsolete. This is the design of computers which have a machine instruction set in a high level language.

The main points of this chapter are as follows:

- A compiler converts a source program or program segment in a high level language into an object code module in machine language. The compiler itself is written in a base language.
- Linkage editors combine code segments produced by compilers into single executable programs in machine code.
- Loaders replace the relative addresses in relocatable code with absolute addresses, and load these programs into memory, ready to be run. (Many linkers perform the address conversion as part of the linkage process, making separate loaders unnecessary.)
- Library modules contain compiled code for common operations such as graphics and file handling. These modules may be linked to segments in applications programs.
- Run-time diagnostics utilities enable the workings of a program to be examined while it is running.
- An interpreter analyses a source program in a high level language, and executes each instruction as it is analysed. No object code is produced.

Exercise 20

1 Briefly define the following terms: compiler; interpreter; source language; object language; base language; editor; lexical analysis; token; syntax analysis; parsing; optimisation; diagnostics; dictionary; linkage editor; module library; loader; load-and-go compiler; run-time diagnostics; breakpoint.

2 Compare and contrast the processes of compilation and interpretation.

3 Why is interpretation more suited to small computers than compilation?

4 a) Construct some more correct and incorrect English sentences according to the rules in Section 20.3. In each case, analyse the sentence using the rules, to prove whether or not it is correct.

   b) Analyse the following numbers according to the rule for a decimal number given in Section 20.3. State whether each is a valid number in terms of these rules:

      469.31
      .734
      4325
      45.6.7
      846.

   c) Modify the extended BNF rule for <decimal number> so that both 4325 and 846. become valid numbers.

   d) Write a set of extended BNF rules to specify the structure of a **signed decimal number.** Test each of the following numbers according to your rules:

      +2.345
      −14.37
      456.8
      +99
      −.543
      +398.

5 Summarise the tasks performed by a load-and-go compiler.

6 An applications program, written in a high level language, requires the use of two library routines for its execution. The library routines are regarded as subprograms by the applications program. Machine code versions of the utility programs are kept on backing store. Describe in outline all the events which occur before running of the applications program can commence.

7 A much simplified form of the Basic language `IF...THEN` statement is specified by the following syntax rules, written in BNF notation:

```
<conditional statement>::=<line number> IF <condition>
                                                THEN <line number>
<condition>::=<variable> <relation> <constant>
<relation>::= <= | < | >= | > | =
```

Using these rules to analyse a statement, the steps are as follows:

Example: `200 IF A>10 THEN 300`

```
        200     IF    A          >       10      THEN    300
rule 3: <line number>IF<variable><relation><constant>THEN<line number>
rule 2: <line number>IF            <condition>        THEN<line number>
rule 1:                          <conditional statement>
```

Use these rules to analyse the folowing statements. Some are valid and some are invalid.

   a) `50 IF J=1 THEN 75`
   b) `95 IF K>L THEN 100`
   c) `100 IF 100=M THEN 50`
   d) `30 IF T<−5 THEN 20`
   e) Modify Rule 2 so that the statement in part (b) becomes a valid statement.

8 An alternative method of analysing the syntax of a program is the use of **state tables.** The program is examined character by character. The state table contains a row for each state, and a column for each character which may be encountered. An entry in the table contains either a jump to another state, an exit instruction or an error condition. An exit instruction indicates that the structure defined by the table has been recognised.

The state table below is for the recognition of signed decimal numbers. The symbol * indicates that the end of the number has been reached.

state	next character				
	+	-	digit	.	*
1	2	2	3	4	error1
2	error2	error2	3	4	error3
3	error2	error2	3	3	exit
4	error2	error2	4	error4	exit

The use of this table is illustrated by some examples:

Example 1 −59.6

	state	next character	new state
Start in state 1:	1	−	2
	2	5	3
	3	9	3
	3	.	4
	4	6	4
	4	*	exit

As an exit is reached, −59.6 is a valid signed decimal number.

Example 2 7.8.9

	state	next character	new state
Start in state 1:	1	7	3
	3	.	4
	4	8	4
	4	.	error 4

An error condition is reached. This error might carry the message 'More than one decimal point in number'.

Use the state table to analyse the following numbers:
a) 796
b) 5.2
c) +59
d) +7.3−6
e) ++8
f) −
g) Supply suitable messages for the other error conditions.
●h) Extend the state table to recognise floating point numbers like 3.6E9 and 4.7E-5.

9 Generate code in AMC or some other suitable assembly language for the following segments of Basic programs:
a) `100 LET L=J+K`
b) `50 IF C>10 THEN 200`
c) `100 FOR K=1 TO 20`
   `110 LET J(K)= J(K)+1`
   `120 NEXT K`

10 Consider the following portion of code, written in Basic and in AMC assembly language:

Basic	AMC assembly language		
`500 FOR J=1 TO 27`		`LOA X N +1`	Use index register as loop counter, initial value 1.
	`NXT`	`CMP X N +27`	Compare index with 27.
		`BGT    OUT`	Exit loop if greater than 27.
`510 LET W(J)=100`		`LOA A N +100`	Load 100 to accumulator.
		`STB A D W`	Store contents of accumulator in W + index.
`520 NEXT J`		`INC X`	Increment index register.
		`BRN    NXT`	Continue loop.
	`OUT`		

Optimise the AMC assembly code so as to speed up the execution of the loop.

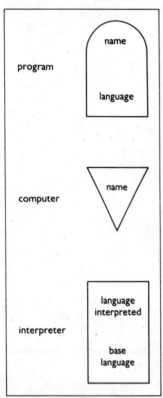

Figure 20.5
Additional symbols used with T
diagrams

Figure 20.6
Compiling and running a Pascal
program on a PDP-11 computer

11 Write a short program in a high level language and test it until it is free of errors.
Run your program a number of times, in each case introducing a single, simple error. For each run, make a note of the error you have introduced and the diagnostic error message you obtain. Comment on your findings.

If possible, repeat the process using exactly the same errors, on a different computer, or on a different compiler or interpreter on the same computer. Compare the error messages you receive in each case.

12 Some additional symbols used in conjunction with T diagrams are shown in Figure 20.5.

Figure 20.6 shows how these symbols may be combined to depict the compilation and running of a program. The example chosen uses a source program in Pascal being compiled and run on a PDP-11 computer.

Draw similar combinations of these symbols for the following situations:
a) Compiling and running a Fortran program on an IBM 370.
b) Interpreting a Basic program on a Z80 based microcomputer.
c) Assembling a Basic compiler written in Z80 assembly language to produce a compiler written in Z80 machine language. Note that a T diagram can also be used for an assembler.
d) A Pascal compiler for an Intel 8086-based microcomputer is written in Pascal. It is **cross-compiled** on a PDP-VAX, using a Pascal compiler written in VAX machine code, producing 8086 machine language.

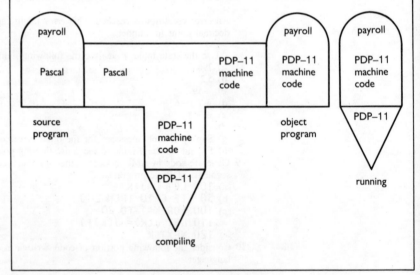

13 A number can be recognised by a procedure which uses a device called a 'state table'. The procedure used in a computer program is as follows:
i) at the start of the recognition process the table is entered at state 1;
ii) a character appearing on the input causes a change in state as specified by the state table (e.g. if the process is in state 3 and the character + appears the recogniser changes to state 6 (entry 3 in column '+ or −') and proceeds to consider the next character on the input);
iii) successful recognition is achieved if an **EXIT** position is reached;
iv) a blank entry signifies non-recognition;
v) the symbol * is used to signify any other character which is not an integral part of the number and is therefore used as a number terminator (e.g. space).

State name and number	Symbol				
	+ or −	Digit	.	E	*
1 <root>		4	2	3	
2 <dec>		5			
3 <exp>	6	7			
4 <int>	4	2	3	EXIT	
5 <frac>	5		3	EXIT	
6 <exp-1>		7			
7 <exp-2>		7			EXIT

Given the state table above:
a) indicate which of the following numbers will not be recognised and the state at which non-recognition occurs:
   (i) 21·3   (ii) −12   (iii) 2·3E−2
   (iv) 3·4E6   (v) 97·
b) define the syntax of numbers which can be recognised;
c) draw a program flow chart for the recognition process described above.

UL 79 I

14 A particular computer system compiles Basic programs into executable code. Describe the effect of the following Basic statements on (a) the storage requirements of the program (executable code and data), and (b) the likely execution of the program.

   i) REM
   ii) DIM
   iii) FOR . . . . . . NEXT
   iv) END

In the light of your answers, why is the number of lines in a Basic program compiled by this system a poor guide to the amount of storage used, and/or the execution time?

   What are the advantages of compiling a Basic program, as opposed to interpreting it? What are the advantages of interpreting?

UL 80 I

15 Normally an assembler translates a reference to a label into a reference to a numeric address relative to the start of the segment being assembled. Why is this address relative to the start of the segment instead of being a physical address in immediate access memory? Your answer should include a brief explanation of relocation.

JMB 80 I

21
Operating Systems

This chapter describes the item of software which transforms the hardware of a computer into a useful machine: the operating system. A few of the concepts introduced in earlier chapters are re-examined here. Many of the ideas introduced in this chapter pave the way to an understanding of data processing and computer applications, which form later chapters in this book.

At the beginning of this book, a computer is defined as follows:

A computer is a collection of resources, including digital electronic processing devices, stored programs and sets of data, which, under the control of the stored programs, automatically inputs, outputs, stores, retrieves and processes the data, and may also transmit data to and receive it from other computers. A computer is capable of drawing reasoned conclusions from the processing it carries out.

For the purposes of this chapter, it is important to emphasise the view of a computer as a set of **resources**. These resources may be hardware, software or a combination of both. Together they provide such facilities as input, processing, output, etc. For example, a compiler is a software resource which provides the facility of language translation. This concept of a resource is used extensively in this chapter.

21.1 Types of Computer Operation

Computers vary considerably in size, capability and type of application. Similarly, there is a wide variety of ways in which they can be operated. Each type of computer operation requires a different type of operating system.

Most microcomputers and some minicomputers can only process one program at a time. This is **single program operation**, and it requires only a simple operating system. The operating system supervises the loading and running of each program, and the input and output of data. Any errors occurring are reported.

Next in complexity is **batch processing**. A number of programs are batched together, and then run as a group. Although the programs are actually run one at a time, input and output from various programs can overlap to some extent. Programs are normally queued up for batch processing, and the operating system starts the next program in the queue as soon as sufficient computing resources are available for it.

Similar to batch processing, but much more sophisticated, is **multiprogramming**. At any one time, a number of programs are on the computer at various stages of completion. Resources are allocated to programs according to the requirements of the programs, and in order to maximise the usage of the different resources of the computer.

Both batch processing and multiprogramming can permit **remote job entry**, where programs are submitted for processing at sites remote from the computer. A particular type of multiprogramming, which is becoming increasingly popular, is **transaction processing**. Transaction processing is designed for systems which must run large numbers of fairly small programs very frequently, where each program run deals with a single transaction such as a withdrawal from a cash terminal. In many cases more than one copy of the same program is running at the same time.

The most sophisticated type of computer operation is **multi-access**, where a number of users can interact, via terminals, with programs while they are running.

Looking at computer operation in a slightly different way, one can classify some computer applications as **real-time processing**. Real-time processing requires that the computer keep pace with some external process. In many real-time systems, computers interact directly with other equipment. A common example is computers controlling machines. Real-time processing is generally restricted to computers with multiprogramming (and particularly transaction processing) or multi-access capability, though it is becoming more common in the case of microcomputers under single program operation. Real-time processing places an additional burden on an operating system, since there is a deadline associated with every action performed by the computer.

21.2 The Nature of an Operating System

Like the question 'What is a computer?', the question 'What is an operating system?' can be answered at several levels.

Firstly, an operating system is a program, or set of programs. Operating systems vary in size from very small to very large, but all are pieces of software. In the past, almost all operating systems were written in a low level language. Currently, many operating systems are partly or completely written in a high level language.

Secondly, an operating system is, by virtue of its name, a system. It is a collection of parts, working together towards some common goals. The goals, or objectives, of an operating system are discussed below.

Thirdly, a computer may be regarded as a set of devices, or resources, which provide a number of services, such as input, processing, storage and output. The operating system of the computer may be regarded as the manager of these resources. It controls the way in which these resources are put to work.

Finally, an operating system is the lowest layer of software on a computer. It acts directly on the 'raw' hardware of the computer. It supports other layers of software such as compilers and applications programs. Part of the task of an operating system is to 'cushion' users from the complexities of direct use of the computer hardware.

In summary, an operating system is a program, or set of programs, driving the raw hardware of a computer, which manages the resources of the computer in accordance with certain objectives, providing higher layers of software with a simplified computer.

21.3 The Development of Operating Systems

Operating systems are as old as electronic computers. It was realised from the start that the hardware of a computer on its own is very difficult to use. Various **supervisor**, **executive** or **monitor** programs were written to make aspects of using a computer easier. As time went by, these programs became larger, more complex, and, unfortunately, more cumbersome and less reliable.

Gradually the objectives and functions of these supervisory programs became clearer, and the term 'operating system' came into use. Better program design led to improvements in efficiency and reliability of operating systems. Sophisticated operating systems made very large computers and networks of linked computers a practical possibility. Today big operating systems face a new challenge, from cheap, plentiful microcomputers, which require only the simplest of monitor programs for their operation.

21.4 Objectives of Operating Systems

All operating systems have two major objectives. These are to make it possible for the resources of the computer to be used efficiently, and to conceal the difficulties of dealing directly with the hardware of the computer.

The first objective, of efficient resource utilisation, is made especially difficult by the fact that some devices of a computer work much more quickly than others. Part of the task of an operating system is to ensure that fast devices such as processors are not held up by slow peripheral devices.

To achieve the second objective, of simplifying the use of the hardware of the computer, the operating system creates a **virtual machine**. A virtual machine is a simplified computer, with all difficult details taken care of by the operating system. People writing other software for the computer need only know about the virtual machine, and not about the actual hardware of the computer.

21.5 The Functions of an Operating System

The tasks performed by an operating system depend to some extent on the type of computer operation in question. The functions of a multi-tasking operating system on a large computer are somewhat different from those of a single program operation monitor on a microcomputer. Nevertheless, some general points can be made. These apply to a greater or a lesser extent depending on the type of computer operation.

The functions of an operating system may be loosely classified as **time allocation**, **resource control**, **input/output control**, **error handling** and **protection**, **operator interface** and **accounting**. These are discussed below, and again mentioned in the context of the structure of a typical operating system, later in the chapter.

Time allocation involves the scheduling of all the various activities going on in the computer. Resource control is the allocation of the resources of the computer in a rational way. Major resource control tasks include partitioning the computer memory between programs, allocating disk space to programs and data and queuing output for printers. Input/output control involves channelling data to and from the peripherals of the computer. Error handling and protection involves the detection and reporting of errors, and minimising their effect. The operator interface is the communication with the person operating the computer. Accounting involves charging users, according to a scale of costs, for their use of the resources of the computer.

This is a diverse list of functions. At this stage it is worth remembering that they must all be performed in accordance with the objectives of the operating system, outlined in the previous section.

21.6 Desirable Features

Operating systems have certain objectives, and must perform a number of functions. In addition, they must have some desirable features. These include **efficiency**, **reliability**, **maintainability** and **small size**.

Efficiency implies that an operating system must carry out its tasks promptly. Time spent on operating system functions is productive computing time wasted. Reliability is crucial, as a failure in an operating system can render the host computer useless. Maintainability means that modifications to the operating system are easy to make. A clearly written, well structured program for the operating system is essential for this.

Finally, in spite of all the things it must do, and all the other desirable features it must have, the program for an operating system must be as small as possible. A small operating system does not occupy very much main or backing store on the computer, is less error prone, and runs more quickly. Other desirable features tend to increase the size of an operating system. In practice, a compromise has to be reached between them and the requirements of small size.

21.7 The Structure of a Typical Operating System

This section gives a description of the structure of the program for a typical, or perhaps ideal, operating system. It must be emphasised that in practice the program structure varies according to the size and complexity of the operating system. Nevertheless, the features mentioned here are all present in some form.

The program structure is presented as a series of modules. The first module, called the **nucleus**, is a service module for the others. Each of the other modules performs one or more of the operating system functions mentioned previously. The other modules are **memory management, input/output control, backing store management, resource allocation** and **scheduling**, and **protection**.

The Nucleus

The lowest-level module of an operating system is known as the **nucleus**. It is supported directly by the hardware of the computer, and provides a number of services required by the other layers of the system. Tasks carried out by the nucleus include handling interrupts (Section 12.8), allocation of work to the processor and providing a communication mechanism between different programs.

When the hardware of the computer detects that an interrupt has occurred, control is transferred to the interrupt handler in the nucleus of the operating system. The interrupt handler determines the cause of the interrupt and then takes appropriate action. This action may be to transfer control to another module of the operating system, to start up some other program, or to resume the program that was interrupted. As many interrupts are caused by requests for input or output, the input/output handler is one of the modules most commonly called.

In allocating work to the processor, the nucleus transfers control to the program which the scheduler has determined should be the next to run. Communication between programs is achieved by maintaining a queue of messages waiting for each program in the system. The nucleus receives a message from a program, and adds it to the queue of its destination program.

Most computers have certain machine instructions whose use is restricted to the nucleus of the operating system. These restricted instructions include ones which transfer control from one program to another, and ones which access restricted registers. Restricting these instructions in this way is a very efficient means of controlling the overall running of the computer, and limiting the effects of errors.

Memory Management

The main store of most computers is far too small to handle all the programs and data on the computer at any one time. The memory management module of an operating system allocates main store to programs or parts of programs which need it most. Everything else is kept on backing store. When main store is allocated, it is done so in a structured, orderly way.

The commonest memory management policy is to create a **virtual memory**. This is the memory of the computer as seen by a particular user, and is much larger than the actual main store of the computer. The operating system takes care of all transfers between main and backing store. Thus, to a user, main store and backing store are all part of the same thing, namely the virtual memory of the computer.

Input/Output Control

The problem with input and output is that different input/output devices have different characteristics, and run at different speeds. For example, a line printer outputs characters one line at a time, whereas a keyboard accepts input one character at a time. A line printer transfers characters more than one hundred times as fast as a keyboard.

The input/output control module of an operating system deals with these problems by making input and output **device independent** from the point of view of the programmer. To a programmer, all devices have the same characteristics, and are instructed in exactly the same way. The operating system deals with the special characteristics of each type of device. For example, many operating systems regard all transfers to and from backing store, peripherals or communications links in terms of reading from and writing to files. The operating system deals with the physical aspects of the transfer — the blocks and sectors of the disks, etc. – leaving the programmer free to concentrate on the logical aspects of the data structure transferred – the records and fields.

These operating system facilities are activated by means of **calls** from applications programs. There is a particular call for each type of operating system function, and each call is accompanied by a set of **parameters** describing the data to be handled by the call. For example, a call to read a file from disk will have the file name as its parameter.

A very common technique, especially useful for output, is **spooling**. Data for output is held on a spool, or queue, on backing store, until the output device is ready for it. There are calls to the operating system to add an output file to the spool, and to delete files from it. Figure 21.1 illustrates this procedure.

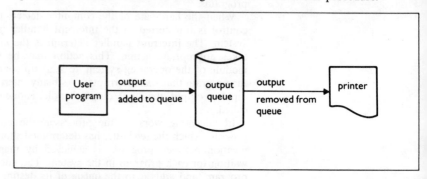

Figure 21.1
Spooling

Backing Store Management

The backing store of a computer is where the bulk of the data and programs being processed are kept. The backing store management of an operating system has the task of maintaining the structure of all this information, and ensuring that the backing store of the computer is used efficiently.

Data and programs on backing store are kept in **files**. The backing store management supervises the creation, updating and deletion of files. A directory is kept of all the files on the computer at any time. The backing store management co-operates with the memory management during the transfer of data to and from main store. If a system of virtual memory is implemented, transfers between main store and backing store are carried out in order to maintain the virtual memory.

The files on backing store have very different purposes. Some contain information which may be shared. Others are private, or even secret. Accordingly, each file has a set of **access privileges** which indicate to what extent the information in the file may be shared. The operating system checks that these privileges are not violated.

Resource Allocation and Scheduling

Most of the time that a computer is running, the demand for its resources is greater than their availability. To deal with this problem, an operating system generally has a **resource allocation policy** built into it. The resource allocation mechanism puts this policy into practice.

Matters would be very simple if a straightforward policy like 'first come, first served' could be used. The problem is that such policies can lead to a situation known as **deadlock**. This is when two programs prevent each other from continuing because each has claimed a resource which the other one possesses. Deadlock is analogous to the situation of two wide vehicles meeting half way across a narrow bridge, shown in Figure 21.2. Various resource allocation policies have been evolved, either to prevent deadlock, or to recover from it should it occur.

The **scheduler** is mainly concerned with the allocation of processor time to programs. This is done in accordance with some **scheduling policy**. Scheduling policies vary considerably from one operating system to another. Some involve the allocation of a level of priority to each program.

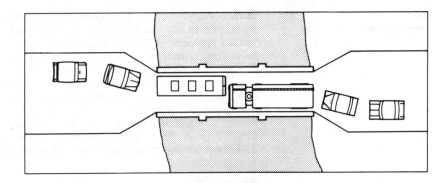

Figure 21.2
Deadlock

A very common scheduling policy on multiprogramming and multi-access systems is known as **time slicing**. Each program on the computer is allocated a short slice of processor time. If the program is not completed during its time slice, then it returns to a queue of programs waiting their turn. Figure 21.3 illustrates this method of scheduling. Scheduling policies cannot be too complicated, otherwise the computer spends far too much of its time deciding what to do next.

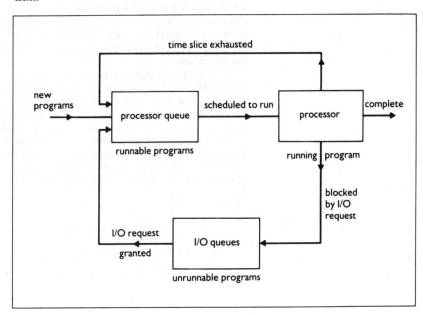

Figure 21.3
Time slicing

Protection

When a computer contains a number of items of software, accessing various stores of information, these must be protected from each other. The most essential piece of software to protect is the operating system itself.

Protection is generally against two eventualities, namely errors and deliberate abuse of the system. Although it is impossible for the operating system to prevent errors in applications programs, it is essential to detect and diagnose them as early as possible, and to limit their effects. Deliberate abuse of the system is rather more difficult to deal with. Although protection mechanisms are designed to prevent unauthorised activities from succeeding, few operating systems are regarded as completely foolproof.

Protection mechanisms are distributed throughout most operating systems, with most attention being paid to main store and backing store. Files on backing store are protected by the system of access privileges mentioned previously. Main store protection is regarded as the most important aspect of a computer, because everything that a computer does is via code or data resident in main store. The memory management system allocates portions of main store for various purposes, and then assigns these portions various levels of protection, depending on their nature. Checks are carried out to ensure that the protection of a portion of memory is not violated.

Some operating systems allocate **levels of privilege** to all programs on the computer. The nucleus of the operating system has the highest level of privilege, while applications programs have the lowest level. The use of certain machine instructions, and access to main store and backing store, is governed by the level of privilege of the program concerned. Some operating systems regard their protection mechanism as their most significant feature.

Accounting
One of the more mundane tasks that some operating systems must perform is to keep a record of the charges incurred by each user program. The most significant portion of the cost is generally for processor time. Information is passed to the accounting module from the scheduler, to establish how much processor time a program has used. Other charges are for the use of backing store media and printer paper.

User and Operator Interface
Communication between an operating system and the outside world takes the form of two interfaces, namely that between the operating system and a user of the computer, and that between the operating system and the person operating the computer.

In a batch processing system, the user interface is the **job control language** (JCL). This is the language in which instructions to the operating system are placed at the front of each program. These instructions specify, among other things, the maximum running time of the program, how much main store is required, and what peripherals are to be used. In some cases the operating system may be instructed what to do if an error is encountered in the program. Certain job control languages permit the user to define **macro-instructions**. These are single instructions which are interpreted as a group of instructions, defined previously. An example of some job control instructions is shown in Figure 21.4.

```
#job testprog umace07 lines 600 time 10
#password s021suf
#deck myfile pascal

   [program]

/*
pascal myfile
exec myfile print
#eoj
```

Figure 21.4
Job control language

They instruct an operating system to compile and run a program written in Pascal.

In reply to these job control language instructions, the operating system outputs a series of messages, indicating the progress of various stages of the program.

In a multi-access system, communication between the user and the operating system is interactive. The user can issue **commands** to the operating system from a terminal. The operating system responds to these commands, and sends messages to the user.

The interface between an operating system and the person operating the computer is also one of commands and messages. Many of the functions of the operating system can be over-ridden by the operator if necessary. This applies particularly to scheduling and resource allocation. At all times the operator is in ultimate control of the computer. A typical section of a **console log**, showing commands from the operator and messages from the operating system, appears in Figure 21.5.

```
1804 26 batch queue = 37
1804 51 job asp3 umach09 started
1804 53 job asp3 umach09 error 57
1804 55 job asp3 umach09 abandoned
1905 02 job testprog umace07 started
batch queue? 39
1905 12 job testlog umace07 time limit exceeded
1905 14 job testprog umace07 abandoned
1905 23 job at47 umach01 started
1905 25 disk vol 3721 allocated
1905 31 disk vol 3721 free
1905 37 job at47 umach01 ended
1905 39 batch queue = 38
disk vol 3721? free
```

Figure 21.5
A console log

21.8 Bootstrap Loaders

A very important item of systems software on every computer is the one which loads the first program into the computer after it has been started up. These programs have been given the name **bootstrap loaders**, from the phrase 'to pull oneself up by one's bootstraps'. The origin of this name is explained below. In some computer systems, the bootstrap loader is part of the operating system; in others it is part of the **firmware** of the computer, at a lower level than the operating system.

In the early days of computing, a bootstrap loader worked in the following manner. Hand keys on the operator's console of the computer were used to load a very short, simple program into a few memory locations. This program was sufficient to activate a peripheral device, often a paper tape reader, and to load a longer, more sophisticated loading program. This loading program would then be run, to load other items of software, generally starting with the operating system. Bootstrap loaders frequently used the technique of **self-modification**. This technique is demonstrated in the exercise at the end of the chapter.

The advent of semiconductor memories, containing portions of read-only store, has put an end to the early morning routine of hand keyed instructions and paper tape. In most modern computer systems, including microprocessor-based systems, a sophisticated program loader is permanently stored in ROM. When the processor is switched on, control passes automatically to this loader. By the time that the visual display screen in the operator's console has warmed up, all systems software has been loaded, and the computer is ready to start work. Some computers include a **reset button** which may be pushed as a last resort when things have gone wrong. The initial loading program is again activated, and the system is able to start afresh.

21.9 An Assessment of Operating Systems

Having read this chapter, and reflected a moment, you will realise the magnitude of the task undertaken by the operating system on a medium or large sized computer. An operating system must perform a number of different tasks, in an integrated way, under very difficult circumstances. Some of the largest and most complex pieces of computer software ever written are operating systems.

Because operating systems evolved in a haphazard way, without clearly defined objectives or a respectable program structure, some of the early large systems were slow, clumsy and error prone. Job control language and operating system messages were almost incomprehensible. Time and experience have brought about a new generation of smaller, simpler and more efficient operating systems, with much better user and operator interfaces.

As mentioned at the beginning of this chapter, one of the biggest challenges to large operating systems comes from microcomputers. Most microcomputers have a very small operating system, some permanently stored on read-only memory. Microcomputer salesmen never tire of pointing out the fact that medium and large size computers spend a considerable proportion of time (often more than thirty per cent) running their operating systems. Their effective processing power is thus much less than it appears. A few microcomputers, at a small fraction of the price, would be just as powerful. . . . Over the next few years the marketplace will no doubt resolve this question.

21.10 Conclusion

The main points in the chapter are as follows:

- An operating system is a program, driving the raw hardware of a computer, which manages the resources of the computer in accordance with certain objectives. The two major objectives of an operating system are the efficient utilisation of the resources of the computer, and to conceal the difficulties of dealing directly with the hardware of the computer.
- The functions of an operating system include time allocation, resource control, input/output control, error handling and protection, operator interface and accounting. Desirable features include efficiency, reliability, maintainability and small size.
- The program for an operating system is structured into the following modules: nucleus, memory management, input/output control, backing store management, resource allocation and scheduling, protection, accounting and user and operator interfaces.
- In practice, operating systems attain their objectives with varying degrees of success. It remains to be seen whether microcomputers will erode the market for medium and large sized computers with sophisticated operating systems.

Exercise 21

1 Briefly define the following terms: resource; single program operation; batch processing; multiprogramming; remote job entry; transaction processing; multi-access; real-time processing; interrupt; spooling; deadlock; time sharing; job control language; console log; bootstrap loader.

2 The phrase 'running under an operating system' is used to describe a computer using a particular operating system. For example, one might say 'a 380Z microcomputer running under CP/M'.
   Use the concept of a virtual machine to explain the significance of this phrase for a person writing a program for the computer concerned.

3 In your own words, give a brief answer to the question 'What is an operating system?'.

4 Name a significant feature which modern microcomputers have in common with early electronic computers.

5 State some advantages of the concept of a virtual machine.

6 Operating systems are described in the text as 'some of the largest and most complex pieces of computer software ever written'. Explain why this is the case.

7 Summarise the structure of a typical operating system.

8 Why is the nucleus the most privileged part of an operating system?

9 Why is the concept of virtual memory so useful to a programmer?

10 A microcomputer has a single program operation monitor as its operating system. Summarise the objectives of this system and the features you would expect it to have.

11 Why is it essential for an operator to have ultimate control of a computer, rather than an operating system?

12 The program shown below is a simple bootstrap loader, written in AMC assembly language. It demonstrates the technique of self-modification.

```
      LOA X N +2      Initialise index register to 2.
STR   IRQ P           Request paper tape reader to input a character.
HRE   BIN       HRE   Branch to this instruction until input is complete.
      INP A           Copy character from input register to accumulator.
      CPB A N /*/     Compare character in accumulator with *.
      BEQ       GO    Branch to instruction labelled GO if equal.
INS   STB A     GO    Store accumulator contents at address labelled GO.
      LOA A D INS     Load address part of instruction INS to accumulator
                      (the index register adds 2 to the value of INS to locate
                      the address part).
      INC A           Increase accumulator by 1.
      STO A D INS     Store updated address in instruction INS.
      BRN       STR   Branch to instruction labelled STR.
GO
```

Self-modification means that the program modifies one of its own instructions, namely the address part of the instruction labelled **INS**.

This program inputs a string of characters from a paper tape.

a) At which address is the first character from the tape loaded?

b) At which address is the second character from the tape loaded?

c) What character is used to mark the end of the tape?

d) What happens when the end-of-input marker is reached?

e) Briefly describe the overall effect of the program.

•f) The technique of self-modification is now regarded as obsolete. Rewrite the program so that the index register is used to acheive the same effect as the modified instruction.

13 What is understood by the term **interrupt**? How may interrupts be used to make input/output processing more efficient in a multiprogramming system?

In a particular computer system, those devices capable of causing an interrupt do so by means of a signal placed on an **interrupt-line** shared by all the devices. This signal causes the central processor to save the current contents of the sequence control register in a special register and to transfer control to an **interrupt service routine** provided by the programmer.

In order that the device causing the interrupt may be identified, a **flag** is set at the same time as the signal is placed on the interrupt-line. There is a different flag for each device, and these flags may be tested by the interrupt service routine. The following assembly language instructions are provided for manipulating and testing the interrupt system.

DISABLE	sets the central processor to ignore any signals on the interrupt-line, and hence not to respond to any interrupts.
ENABLE	resets the central processor to recognise signals on the interrupt line.
SKPFLG (device)	causes the next instruction in sequence to be skipped unless the flag associated with the device is set. Thus, if the flag associated with the line-printer is set, **SKPFLG (PRINTER)** will cause the statement immediately following to be executed, but otherwise to be skipped.
CLRFLG (device)	causes the flag associated with the device to be reset, regardless of its present status. Thus **CLRFLG (KEYBOARD)** resets the input keyboard flag.
RETI	returns from an interrupt by simultaneously **ENABLE**-ing the interrupt system and transferring control to the address held in the special register.

Among the remaining assembly language instructions are the following:

STORE address	stores the current contents of the accumulator in location **address,** overwriting anything already stored there. Thus

STORE RATE stores the contents of the accumulator in the location with the symbolic address **RATE**.

LOAD address — loads the accumulator with the contents of **address**, overwriting the present contents of the accumulator. Thus **LOAD TIME** loads the accumulator from the location with the symbolic address **TIME**.

JUMP address — transfers control to the location **address**. Thus, after executing **JUMP LOOP**, execution continues sequentially from the instruction stored in the location with symbolic address **LOOP**.

Below are shown significant parts of an interrupt service routine, in a system where the disk-reading mechanism, the line-printer and the input keyboard can cause interrupts. The lines are numbered for ease of reference only, and symbolic labels are indicated by use of a colon, as in line 10.

```
 1              DISABLE
 2              STORE SAFETY
 3              SKPFLG(DISK)
 4              JUMP DISKROUTINE
 5              SKPFLG(PRINTER)
 6              JUMP PRNTROUTINE
 7              SKPFLG(KEYBOARD)
 8              JUMP KBROUTINE
 9              JUMP ERROR
10 DISKROUTINE:CLRFLG(DISK)
   ......
19              JUMP RETURN
20 PRNTROUTINE:CLRFLG(PRINTER)
   ......
30 KBROUTINE:CLRFLG(KEYBOARD)
   ......
40     RETURN:LOAD SAFETY
41              RETI
```

i) What is the purpose of the **DISABLE** instruction (line 1)?

ii) What is the purpose of the **STORE** instruction (line 2) and the corresponding **LOAD** instruction (line 40)?

iii) What sort of error has occurred if the **JUMP** in line 9 is executed?

iv) What is the purpose of the **CLRFLG** instruction in line 10 and under what circumstances will it be executed?

v) What would you expect the routine beginning at line 20 to accomplish?

vi) What would you expect the last instruction to be in the portion of the routine beginning at line 20?

vii) What might happen if the programmer inadvertently inserted an **ENABLE** instruction before line 41?

viii) What pair of instructions would test for a paper-tape reader interrupt (device code **PTR**) and branch to an appropriate routine?

ix) Where should these instructions in (viii) above be placed in the sequence of instructions in lines 1 to 9? Give a reason for your answer.

UL 80 I

14 a) State how and why an operating system can be constructed so that programs can produce 'spooled' output in backing store which is later sent to output devices by a system routine.

b) For this system routine
   i) show what tables of information would be required;
   ii) construct a flow diagram.

OLE 80 II

22
Operating Systems Case Studies

This chapter presents surveys of three operating systems currently in use. The intention is to consolidate the general ideas introduced in the previous chapter, and to give some idea of how the principles of operating systems are put into practice. Each of the operating systems outlined here is designed for use on one of the computers whose hardware is described in Chapter 15. Like their host computers, these operating systems are representative of the range of systems currently available, and are generally regarded as being well designed. The operating systems are as follows:

MSDOS used by the Research Machines Nimbus microcomputer.

Unix used by Digital Equipment VAX minicomputers and by the Cray-2 supercomputer.

VME/B used by ICL 2900 series mainframe computers.

22.1   MSDOS

The MSDOS operating system is a single-user operating system developed for 16-bit microcomputers. It is particularly suited to computers using the Intel 8086 family of microprocessors (which includes the 80186) and their associated co-processors, or the Motorola 68000 series. It has been implemented on a wide variety of computers, including the IBM PC, where it is known as PCDOS, and the Research Machines Nimbus.

MSDOS was developed in 1979 by Tim Paterson, working for Seattle Computer Products. It was purchased by Microsoft Corporation, which now distributes it. The second and subsequent versions of MSDOS have been extended to include certain features which are similar to Unix, notably hierarchical disk directories, which are discussed below.

General Features

The aim of MSDOS is to provide a powerful, flexible layer of systems software to control all the aspects of the operation of a microcomputer. In particular it controls the disk filing system, the transfer of data to and from all other peripherals, and the loading and running of user programs. It provides a simple interface to the user of the computer.

The overall structure of MSDOS is illustrated in Figure 22.1. It has a **command processor** which calls the **input/output system** and the **utilities.** The input/output system has three levels: the **filing system** (MSDOS), the **basic input/output system** (BIOS) and the firmware input/output routines. The filing system is in overall control of all input and output. Detailed operations, in particular the transformation from logical to physical structures, are carried out by BIOS. The firmware routines deal with the machine-dependent aspects of input and output, and provide a standard interface for the operating system routines.

The input/output system has two sets of facilities: one set for peripherals which transfer individual characters, and one set for the disk drives, which transfer data in blocks. The latter is the disk filing system.

Command Processor

The command processor has four functions: interaction with the user, interrupt handling, error handling and running the internal MSDOS commands.

The user interface of the operating system is a set of prompts and messages displayed by the command processor, and its response to the instructions typed by the user. MSDOS has a simple command line editor to enable users to correct commands they are typing. It also enables users to create files of commands. These **batch files** are a sequence of MSDOS commands which are executed one at a time when the batch file is called. The command processor transfers control to the input/output system, one of the MSDOS utilities, or (via the disk filing system) a user program, as required.

The interrupt handler has a simple priority system for dealing with interrupts from peripherals. When an interrupt has been dealt with, control is returned to

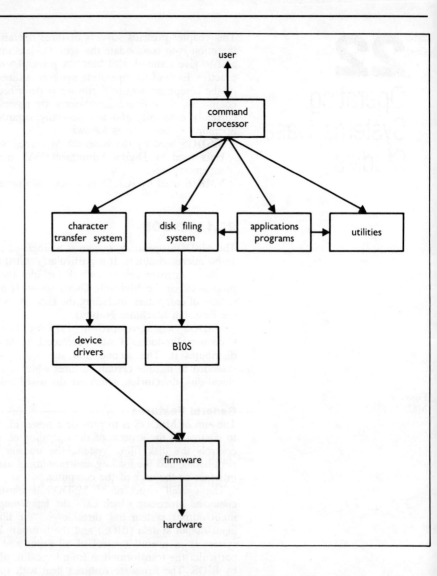

user

command
processor

character
transfer system

disk filing
system

applications
programs

utilities

device
drivers

BIOS

firmware

hardware

Figure 22.1
MSDOS overall structure

the program which was running when the interrupt occurred. The error handling system works in a very similar way, returning control to the program in which the error arose, if possible; if not, to MSDOS.

A number of MSDOS commands are dealt with directly by the command processor. These include the command which displays a disk directory, and commands to erase, rename and copy files. MSDOS keeps track of the date and the time: the command processor allows the user to set or reset these.

Backing Store Management

The most important task performed by MSDOS is managing the filing system of the computer. Each disk is given a **directory** which has details of every file on the disk, as well as the names of any **sub-directories.** In this way, the directories form a hierarchy, with a tree structure. See Figure 22.2. At any time, the user is 'logged on' to a particular directory, and unless otherwise specified, all files used are in the logged on directory. If a file outside the current directory is required, a **pathname** is used to locate the file. This contains, in order, the names of all the directories required to locate the file. For example, a letter with a filename

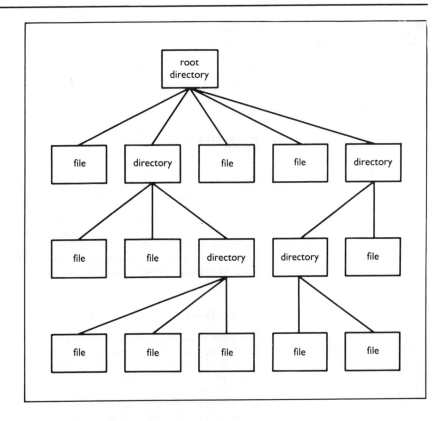

Figure 22.2
MSDOS directory structure

PBA8507.TXT, in the LETTERS sub-directory of the ADMIN directory of the disk in drive B has the pathname:

`B:\ADMIN\LETTERS\PBA8507.TXT`

The disk filing system handles this hierarchical directory system. It has facilities to create a file, open one for reading or writing, transfer information to or from files and indicate how much free space there is on a disk. Transfers take place in terms of one disk sector (512 bytes) at a time, via two or more disk **buffers** in memory. Records in files may be accessed sequentially or randomly: the programmer is concerned only with the logical structure of the files; MSDOS deals with the physical aspects. The disk filing system takes care of the details of loading and running user programs, and deals with most of the operating system calls from them.

File space in a disk is allocated by taking the next free sectors available. When a file is erased or reduced in length, unwanted sectors are freed. There is no 'tidying up' mechanism, and some files, particularly those used for word processing which change length every time they are edited, can become very fragmented. If sectors of a file are distributed throughout the disk, reading and writing can be somewhat slow.

Character-Oriented Input/Output
With the exception of the disk drives, all peripheral devices transfer data one character at a time. These include the keyboard, display screen, printer and communications links. MSDOS has a set of **device drivers,** one for each of the above types of device, which present a standard interface to the programmer. In this way, all of these devices appear to the programmer to have the same characteristics. The character-oriented input/output facilities check whether devices are ready to get or send a character, and transfer the characters.

Utilities

The MSDOS utilities are a set of programs which carry out various 'house-keeping' tasks. These include formatting disks, copying and checking disks, recovering corrupt files and a line-oriented text editor. A set of programming utilities is provided, to locate errors in assembly language programs and to link relocatable modules into executable code. There is also a sorting program to arrange lines in a text file in alphabetical order.

Assessment

MSDOS is becoming the standard operating system for 16-bit microcomputers. It is powerful and flexible, and makes good use of all the hardware features of micros of this size. However, it is compact, and fast in its own operation. The newest version, **MS Windows,** allows a number of user programs to run at the same time. It divides the computer screen into windows (hence its name), each occupied by one program. Users can transfer data from one program to another while they are running by a very simple 'cut and paste' operation. By providing the support functions for a state-of-the-art user interface of this nature, and by an increasing similarity in concept to Unix, MSDOS seems assured of a central place in systems software for some time to come.

22.2 Unix

The **Unix** operating system was originally designed for use with Digital Equipment computers. It was designed and is still supported by a team at the Bell Laboratories of the American Telephone and Telegraph Corporation (AT&T). The first version went into operation in 1971. Unix has subsequently been updated several times, and is in the process of being modified for use on a wide range of minicomputers, and some 16 bit microcomputers. Its implementation on the Cray-2 computer means that it is now regarded as being suitable for a wide range of host machines, from microcomputers to supercomputers.

General Features

Unix is a general-purpose, multi-user, interactive operating system. It supports both multiprogramming and multi-access. An assembler, a number of compilers for high level languages and a text editor are among the items of systems software available under Unix. Unix itself is written in the high level language C (Section 19.6).

Unix is designed for a number of users accessing a single processor via terminals No single user is regarded as the operator of the computer. All users may submit commands to the operating system in the course of their work. Responses to these commands are sent to the users by the system.

Memory Management

Unix implements the concept of virtual memory. Each user appears to have access to the entire memory of the computer.

Input/Output Control

Each peripheral device in the system is controlled via one or more **files.** These files are treated in exactly the same way as ordinary data files. In other words, to display an item of data, the data is written to the file associated with the VDU. This simplifies the input and output of data, and conceals all the peculiarities of the various peripheral devices from the user. Facilities also exist for the spooling of output for a line printer.

Backing Store Management

All backing store space is regarded as being partitioned into files. The contents of a file may be structured according to the wishes of a user, but the relationships between files are controlled at system level by **directories.** Directories enable files to be grouped together, and permission to be given by a user for other users to share his or her files. The operating system maintains a **root directory** via which every file in the system may be accessed. The filing system is regarded as one of the most important features of Unix.

Protection

Protection within the system is achieved via protection bits associated with each file. These enable read, write and execute permission to be established for a file, both for its owner and for other users. Different users have different levels of privilege, which determine the extent to which they may access files, and thereby use the resources of the computer. If an error is detected during the running of a program, the operating system jumps to a simple error handling subroutine. A facility is also available for a user to interrupt a program which appears to be going wrong.

User Interface

All commands to the operating system are interpreted by a program called the **shell.** One notable feature of the shell is that it enables a user to control the extent of multitasking carried out by the computer. In normal circumstances, the operating system completes its response to one command before prompting a user to input another command. However, a user may instruct the system to start work on a command, and then accept another command straight away. Actions resulting from both commands are multiprogrammed together.

Assessment

Unix combines the features of simplicity, ease of use and small size with considerable flexibility and power. It is a small, conventional operating system which has met with a wide measure of acceptance. Although it is some years old, its popularity is still on the increase. Efforts are being made to produce an internationally-agreed standard version of Unix, as there are differences between the versions for different computers. Although it was originally designed for minicomputers, Unix is being implemented on some of the more powerful 16 bit microcomputers currently becoming available. One of its chief competitors in this area is MSDOS.

22.3   VME/B

The **VME/B** (for **virtual machine enviroment**) operating system is used by the computers in the ICL 2900 series. It was designed and developed at the same time as the computers which support it.

General Features

VME/B is a sophisticated, general-purpose operating system, incorporating a number of advanced features. It supports transaction processing, multi-access and batch processing simultaneously. One of its prime objectives is to provide a simple, consistent high level interface to all users. It is flexible, in the sense that it can be tailored to the requirements of a particular installation. VME/B is written in a high level language, specially designed for the purpose. Communication with VME/B is via a language called **system control language (SCL)** which is a block structured high level language.

Virtual Machine Concept

As its name implies, VME/B is centred on the virtual machine concept. The virtual machine available to each user includes that user's program and data, and all the operating system facilities and utility programs needed by the user. To a user, a virtual machine appears completely self-contained, yet VME/B allows certain segments of data and code to be shared, to prevent unnecessary duplication of software. See Figure 22.3. A very sophisticated protection

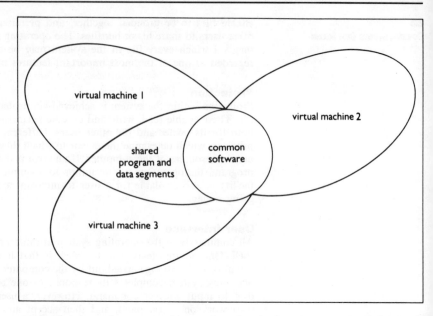

Figure 22.3
Virtual machines under VME/B

mechanism is used to ensure the security of each virtual machine, and of shared segments.

Program Structure

Like many operating systems, VME/B is built up of a number of layers. See Figure 22.4. At the centre is the **kernel,** which transforms the hardware of the computer into a number of virtual machines. Next is a layer of systems software which manages the resources of the virtual machines. The outer layer contains applications programs. Unlike older operating systems, VME/B does not have a completely rigid boundary between systems and application software.

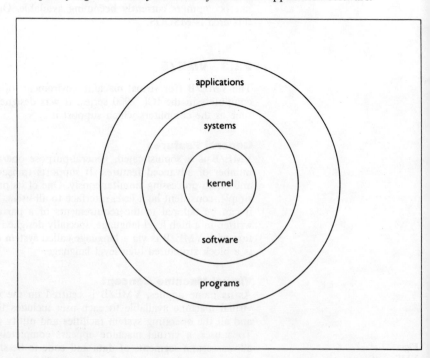

Figure 22.4
VME/B program structure

Memory Management

Each virtual machine running under VME/B is provided with a virtual store which can be much larger than the main store of the computer. VME/B manages all transfers of segments of programs and data to and from backing store in order to implement this policy. Each virtual machine makes extensive use of a hardware-driven stack. The stack simplifies the processing of programs originally written in a high level language.

Communications Management

One of the overall objectives of the 2900 series is the efficient handling of data communications. On the hardware side, a number of input/output controllers are used to link peripheral devices to processing units and main store. On the systems software side, VME/B supervises and schedules all input and output. This relieves users of this burden, and makes the best use of the hardware resources.

Backing Store Management

All aspects of the use and security of files are handled by VME/B through the use of an integrated filestore. The user may be responsible for the placement of his or her files on backing store, or may choose to leave this task to the operating system.

Scheduling

Scheduling of work takes place at several levels within the software. At the highest level, there are separate schedules for the transaction processing, batch and multi-access streams. At an intermediate level there is a scheduler for virtual machine resources, and at the lowest level the scheduler allocates the real hardware resources of the computer.

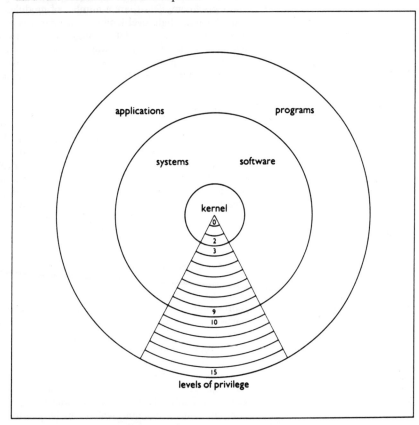

Figure 22.5
VME/B levels of priviledge

Protection

One of the most important aspects of the VME/B operating system is its protection mechanism. It is based on the concept of **levels of privilege.** Every process in the computer has associated with it a level of privilege in the range 0 to 15, 0 being the highest level, and 15 the lowest. Levels 0 to 2 are reserved for the kernel, levels 3 to 9 are for other systems software, and levels 10 to 15 are for applications programs. See Figure 22.5.

When a process is running, a register called the **access control register** contains its level of privilege. Each segment of data that the process may wish to access contains a **read access key** and a **write access key.** Each key has a value between 0 and 15. Access is only permitted if the level of privilege in the access control register is less than or equal to that of the particular key. For example, a process with privilege level 11 may read from a segment with read access key 14, but may not write to a segment with write access key 8. Furthermore, each segment has an **execute permission bit.** Only if this bit is set may the code in the segment be executed.

This is an extremely powerful and versatile protection system. It enables portions of the operating system to be protected from other portions, and users to create levels of protection within their own applications programs. It minimises the damage caused by an error at any level, and prevents the kernel from being corrupted by an error at any other level of systems or applications software.

Software Supported by VME/B

Among the systems software supported by VME/B are a Basic interpreter, Fortran, Algol and Cobol compilers, and data management software. The Basic interpreter is an interactive system which allows online syntax checking, editing and alteration of the flow of a program during execution. The Fortran, Algol and Cobol compilers share a number of modules, and produce object code in the same format. High level language programs may be written in a mixture of these three languages. The data management software is a flexible facility which allows a range of data structures to be constructed and developed by users. In particular, it provides a feature known as **data independence** (Section 28.3), which is a vital property of all large stores of data.

Assessment

VME/B is a large, complex and sophisticated operating system. Many of its design concepts are based on experience with the Atlas computer which, in its time, was the most powerful computing system in the world.

Although there have been some initial problems, these have now been resolved. Many features, especially the protection mechanism and the high level system control language, are very highly regarded. In general, VME/B is considered to be a 'state of the art' system, and a model for the development of other operating systems.

22.4 Conclusion

Although few in number, the operating systems outlined in this chapter are representative of the range of systems currently in use. Each is designed for a particular type of computer, and a particular area of application. The systems vary considerably in size and complexity, from the sophistication of VME/B to the straightforward simplicity of MSDOS. Nevertheless, they all have a number of features in common.

These operating systems represent some of the more successful attempts to write programs to the extremely demanding requirements outlined in the previous chapter. Each in its own way transforms the raw hardware of its host computer into a machine which can be put to useful work.

Exercise 22

1 Which of the case study operating systems support:
   a) Multiprogramming
   b) Multi-access
   c) Transaction Processing?
2 Which of the case study operating systems implement the concept of virtual memory?
3 Compare and contrast the protection mechanisms provided by Unix and VME/B.
4 Summarise the features provided by each operating system for the controlling of programs by users.
●**5** VM from IBM, RTL2, CP/M (and its derivative, MP/M) are the names of a few more well-known operating systems. Investigate one of these systems (or another of your choice), and summarise its features, using the same headings as contained in this chapter.
6 Discuss the significance of a single operating system which is implemented on a range of computers for:
   a) Computer manufacturers
   b) Software developers
   c) Computer users.

23
Software Development Tools

This chapter covers the most recent development in programming - the use of integrated software development tools to specify, design and generate applications software. Software tools of this nature are known as **fourth generation** languages, to distinguish them from the three previous generations of computers and their associated programming languages. Fourth generation techniques are beginning to replace the use of high level languages, for reasons which are discussed below.

23.1 Limitations of High Level Languages

High level languages were first developed in order to speed up the process of developing computer applications, and to broaden the base of the people who were able to design and program these applications. They have achieved these objectives to a great extent, but it is now becoming clear that they have severe limitations. In particular:

- High level languages are still too close to the way of working of a computer, and not close enough to the needs of the user. Although they are problem-oriented, they specify the steps of the solution to a problem in terms of the elementary processing capabilities of a computer.
- The use of high level languages, at the end of a systems analysis and design process (Section 25.3), is far too slow in today's business environment.
- The long time taken to develop software means that, in view of the costs of programming, software is very expensive.
- Software developed using high level languages is not always of a very high standard. There are no automatic checks of the correctness of program modules, and software maintenance (Section 25.3) is haphazard and can introduce new errors while correcting others.

Taken together, these shortcomings are leading many computer users, particularly commercial users, to investigate alternative techniques for software development. The majority of commercial data processing is stereotyped: an interlocking set of applications based on large files of data, or an integrated database. The software records all transactions, and enables the transaction data to be analysed and reports prepared from it. What is needed is a set of software development tools which enable applications of this sort to be developed quickly and cost-effectively.

23.2 The Objectives of Software Development Tools

The objectives of software development tools are complementary to the limitations of high level languages:

- To bring about a big improvement in the productivity of software development.
- To allow users to have more influence on the design of applications software.
- To assist in the development of integrated suites of applications software, accessing a common set of data files, or a database.
- To allow the rapid production of **prototypes** of applications from their initial specification, so that users can check whether they are actually what is needed. A prototype is a rough first draft of the software which runs on test data.
- To assist with software maintenance. The same tools which are used to develop an application in the first place are used to modify it. This reduces the possibility of introducing errors during modification.

23.3 Software Development Tools: General Structure

Figure 23.1 shows the overall structure of a typical set of software development tools. They are not a programming language in the conventional sense, although parts of them may include statements in a specification language. Instead, they are an integrated set of facilities, with a common data access mechanism. They enable applications to be developed using the same data access mechanism. The data is in the form of files, or (more commonly) a relational database (Section 28.3). The development tools have links to the file management layer of the operating system, or the database management system which maintains the database.

The common interface between the software development tools (and any applications generated by them) and the filing system is the **data dictionary**. This is a layer of software which maintains, for each file in the system, a dictionary (also known as a **descriptor file**) which describes the structure of the file as records, and the nature of each data item in a record.

There is a **screen design** module which enables the layout of the screen display for each operation to be specified, as well as the layouts of printed output. There is a **report generator** which enables summaries of the data to be extracted, analysed (by adding up totals, etc.), displayed and printed. There are **application generators**, often one for each type of application, which enable the processing of the data to be specified. Once an application has been generated, it becomes another element in the system, using the same data access mechanism as the software development tools. This is shown in Figure 23.1.

There are two broad approaches to the design of software development tools. One requires the applications designer to fill in a set of forms, on the computer screen, to specify how an application is to work. The other uses a programming language, at specification level, in order to describe how the processing is to take place. Some software development toolkits use a mixture of the approaches: the form-filling approach for the data dictionary and screen designs, and the specification language for the report generators and application generators.

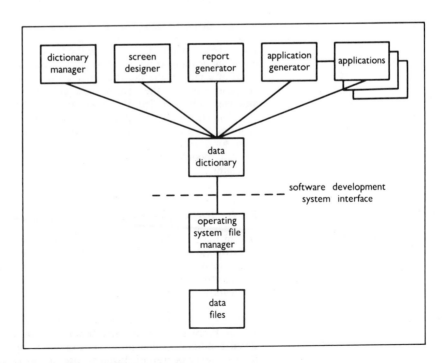

Figure 23.1
Software developments toolset:
overall structure

23.4 Data Dictionary

The data dictionary mechanism is the link between the software development tools, and the applications generated by them, and the data files on which they operate. By channeling all access to data through this single mechanism, it is possible to ensure that the data is always in a consistent state, and that the rules specifying the structure of the various files are always adhered to.

The data dictionary enables the structure of each data file in the system to be specified. A file, which may, for example, contain all the invoices raised by the company, is structured as a set of records (one for each invoice in the example), each of which has a set of fields (such as the invoice number, date, etc). The **type** of each field is specified. Types generally include characters, numbers (which may be divided into integers, fractions, currency, etc) and dates, in the format chosen. **Attributes** of each data item may also be set. For example, numbers may be in a certain range, or codes may have to be unique in the file (no duplicate invoice numbers, for example). Data items in one file may be codes for references in another file. For example, the invoice file may contain customer codes which are looked up in the client file to obtain the full name and address of the customer. These attributes are used to check data items as they are entered into the records of the file. **Default values** may also be specified in the dictionary. These are values which a field will assume if no data is entered. For example, a date may default to the current date unless the user types another.

The data dictionary facility is used to create a descriptor file for each data file in the system. One descriptor may apply to a set of data files. For example, the invoice file may hold all the invoices for a year. At the end of the year, a new invoice file, with the same structure, is created. The data dictionary allows these descriptor files to be amended, for example by the inclusion of additional fields in each record. It then supervises the conversion of the associated data files from the old format to the new format. The data dictionary is also used when data is entered into the files. It checks each entry according to the conditions for the field, and supplies default values. If an entry is a reference to another file, it checks that it is present in the other file.

23.5 Screen Design Facilities

The screen design facilities enable the layout of the screens used for each aspect of an application to be specified. If a screen is to be used for the entry of the fields in a record, the facilities enable the fields, and their associated labels, to be positioned on the screen, and additional headings, prompts and error messages to be included. If the screen is for a report, the data may be arranged in columns, with headings and footnotes. On some systems, the same design facilities are used to specify the layout of printed output.

In some software development toolkits, the screen design facilities are a separate module; in others they are an integral part of one of the applications generators.

23.6 Report Generator

One of the commonest types of commercial programs extracts data from a file and displays or prints it. For example, a program may be required to calculate and display the monthly totals of the invoices raised by a company, or the breakdown of invoices by department. The report generation module enables applications of this sort to be specified very simply.

The stages of the specification are to list the data files from which the report is to be derived, state what processing is required, and specify the format of the output. Processing includes selection of certain records in the file if fields match stated conditions, calculating totals of the records, and including only some of the records in the report. In most cases a sort is required, either before or after selection of the required records. The format of the output is specified either by reference to a screen already designed, or by formatting instructions included in the report generator.

23.7 Application Generator

Application generators are used to specify the processing which is to be carried out on the data files. Most software development toolsets have more than one application generator, for example one for transaction processing, which updates individual records, and one for batch processing, which updates all the records in a file.

An application generator allows a software designer to describe what processes are to be carried out on the data, without becoming involved in the detailed processing steps. The steps of the specification of each application are generally similar to those of report generation, but are much more flexible. The input and output files are specified, as well as any temporary files for intermediate data. The interaction with users at terminals is described, in terms of screen designs already established, or by designing the screens as part of the specification. The nature and format of any displayed or printed output is also specified. The processing operations - sorting, selection, performing calculations and carrying out conditional operations - are described. Calls to software modules written in a high level language may also be included.

When the steps of an application have been entered and checked, they are compiled, and become an integral part of the software system. The compiled application uses the data dictionary to access files, and the screen layout designs to display data. If the application is to be modified, the application generator is again used to carry out the modifications.

23.8 Case Study: Powerhouse Software Development System

Powerhouse is an integrated set of development tools for business software, designed and marketed by the Canadian company, Cognos Incorporated. It is implemented on a range of minicomputers, including the Digital Equipment VAX series.

Objectives
The principal aims of Powerhouse are the cost-effective development of error-free commercial software, with a productivity improvement from software development staff of anything up to a factor of ten. Powerhouse facilities are designed so that end users can be more closely involved with the software design process than is possible with conventional programming languages, and that prototypes can be produced very quickly. These can be run and amended using test data, and then form the basis of the operational software when the design problems have been ironed out.

The productivity improvements and greater involvement of users in the development process mean that a company will be able to develop integrated business software more closely attuned to its needs, and covering applications not previously possible, particularly in the area of data management and decision support systems.

Powerhouse Features
Powerhouse is a fourth generation language in which a wide range of file processing applications can be specified. It has a clearly defined interface, via a data dictionary, to the file management system of the operating system of the host computer. This tightly-specified interface makes it possible to implement Powerhouse on a range of computers, and enables it to access files created by

other software. This helps to ease the transition when a company with an established computer system begins to develop new applications with Powerhouse.

The data dictionary is the single, central store of information about all the file structures in the system. It is used by all the modules of Powerhouse, and by the compiled applications created by it. It ensures that all applications have identical views of the system files, and controls multiple access to the files when several applications are running concurrently, as is typically the case.

Many of the statements in Powerhouse are non-procedural. They specify what processing is to be carried out, and how the data is to be presented. An application is fully specified in a very small number of statements. The detailed processing steps, and the precise sequence of operations, are determined within the Powerhouse language processors. As far as possible, it provides default values for data and makes decisions in the absence of precise specifications according to common sense assumptions.

Powerhouse Structure

The overall structure of Powerhouse is shown in Figure 23.2. The data dictionary gives access to the system files, and there are three main operation modules: **Quiz**, **Quick** and **QTP**.

The dictionary has all the features for dictionary definition and data entry described in Section 23.4, as well as the following:

- A generic set of data attributes known as a **usage** can be defined and then applied to data items as required. For example, a set of characteristics for currency can be defined, and then attributed to all currency fields. If the application is to be run using a different currency, only the currency usage needs to be changed in order to change the presentation of all the currency items in the files.
- The use of **user modes** enables different users to access the same logical files, but to be directed to different physical files. This is particularly important during the development of an application, when it is to be run on test files, and not on operational data.

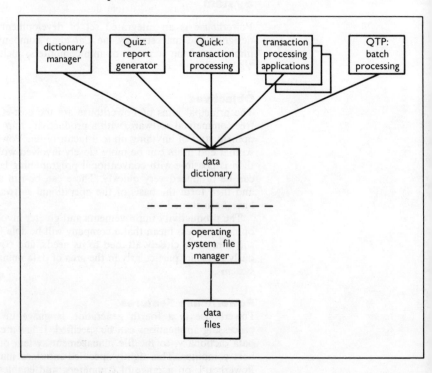

Figure 23.2
Powerhouse: overall structure

- The ability to propagate definitions from one structure to another. This facility means that once a data structure such as a record has been defined, it may be replicated for use in other files. Complementary to the replication facility is the **auto-definition** facility which supplies intelligent defaults for data items, based on what has been specified for other items.
- The provision of levels of security: **application security** which controls which users can access which files and in what way (read-only or read/write), and **dictionary security** which restricts the use of the dictionary itself. This prevents unauthorised users from altering the structure of data files.

The Powerhouse report writer, **Quiz**, has facilities to extract data and specify the format of reports. It takes statements in the Powerhouse specification language and uses them to access one or more data files, select records under given conditions, sort the records, choose fields to be displayed or printed, and send the output to a display screen, printer or file on disk. Headings and footnotes can be included. It has one major safety feature: it can only read existing data files; it cannot amend them in any way. This means that it is quite safe for users to generate reports with Quiz, with no risk of damaging operational data.

The transaction processing system generator, **Quick** is used to develop applications which create or update one record of a file at a time. They are generally interactive, based on a sequence of screens which display the data while it is being processed. Quick has two modules, one which compiles screens from information about the files to be used, and the other which runs the compiled code. Calls may be made from Quick statements to procedures in other programming languages.

Quick gives automatic protection to files during concurrent running: a transaction is carried out completely, updating all the records specified, or the files are 'rolled back' to their state prior to the transaction, and an error message is displayed. It has help facilities for users when they are running applications.

The batch processing system generator, **QTP,** is used to develop applications which update entire files, rather than individual records. The specification language it uses has many statements in common with Quick, with additional facilities to create and delete data files, and to update all the records in a file systematically. QTP does not have a screen interface, but can be used in conjunction with Quiz for report generation. QTP has locking facilities for files, either for the whole of the updating run, or while they are being accessed, and for individual records during processing.

Example Software Specification
As an example of the use of Powerhouse, suppose that the structure of an invoice file had been entered in the dictionary. An invoice contains an invoice number, date, client reference, and a series of item lines, each containing a stock reference and number ordered. The client and stock references are codes which refer to items in the client file and the stock file respectively. An application program to raise invoices might be specified as follows, using the screen design facility of Quick:

SCREEN RAISE-INVOICE	gives the application a name
FILE INVOICES	use the invoices file
FILE CLIENTS REFERENCE	also refer to the clients file
FILE STOCK REFERENCE	also refer to the stock file
TITLE 'Invoice Entry' CENTRED	gives the screen a title
GENERATE	generate the screen design
BUILD	compile the application

The Quick screen designer takes this specification, together with the descriptions of the data from the dictionaries for the invoices, clients and stock files, and generates a screen design for invoice entry.

To run the application, Quick is called, and the name of the application (RAISE-INVOICE) is supplied. A screen showing the fields of an invoice, as specified in the data dictionary, is displayed. The data for an invoice is then entered and may be edited before being written to disk and printed.

To generate a report of all the invoices raised during a particular month, with totals analysed by department, the following specification is supplied to Quiz:

ACCESS INVOICES	use the invoices file
SELECT IF DATE GT 851031 &	select invoices raised
AND DATE LT 851201	during November 1985
SORT ON DEPT	sort by department
REPORT DEPT INV-NO DATE INV-AMOUNT	include these fields
FOOTING AT DEPT 'Department Total' &	include department totals
INV-AMOUNT SUBTOTAL SKIP 2	and skip two lines
GO	

Note that the & symbol is used if a statement is to be continued on another line, and that the continuation line is indented.

Assessment

Powerhouse, and fourth generation specification languages like it, are presenting designers of business software with software development tools of unprecedented power. They are restricted to one class of applications, but this class is very broad, and software modules written in a conventional programming language can be called from generated software if necessary. Software development tools are gaining acceptance very rapidly, hindered only by the lack of knowledge of business software developers and their managers, and by the general reluctance to change from established software development practices.

23.9 Conclusion

The main points of this chapter are as follows:

● Software development tools, also known as fourth generation languages, are integrated sets of facilities which enable certain types of software to be developed very rapidly.
● Most software development toolkits are designed for the generation of commercial applications.
● Software development systems use a data dictionary to access the file management facilities of the operating system or database management system which supports them.
● There are modules for screen design, report generation and the generation of various types of application. Once an application has been compiled, it uses the same data access mechanisms as the software generation tools.
● The benefits of software generation tools include greatly increased productivity of software developers, rapid prototyping and an increased involvement of users in the software development process.

Exercise 23

1 Briefly define the following terms: software development tool; fourth generation language; prototype; specification language; data dictionary; descriptor file; report generator; application generator; attribute; default value; usage.
2 For each of the following types of application, state whether fourth generation languages of the types described in this chapter, would be suitable:
   a) stock control
   b) cinema seat reservations
   c) keeping accounts
   d) aircraft flight simulators
   e) controlling a factory robot
   f) recording and analysing examination results.

3 a) How do software development tools enable users to be more closely involved in the process of software development?

   b) What are the consequences of the closer involvement of users in software development?

4 How do software development tools bring about an improvement in the productivity of the programmers and others involved in software development?

5 Find out about other software development tools which are now in use. Write a report on one of these, using the same headings as those in the Powerhouse case study.

6 a) Give your views on the extent to which software development tools will replace the use of high level languages such as Cobol for the development of business software.

   b) Do you think that software development tools will come into use for other types of computer application? If so, list the application areas where you think this will happen.

24
Software Engineering

A number of far-reaching changes are taking place at present in the way in which computer software is developed. The causes of the changes include the following:

- The increasing costs of software development.
- Dissatisfaction from users with the quality and suitability of software.
- The increasing length and complexity of software: commercial programs have tens of thousands of lines of source code; real-time software often has hundreds of thousands of lines.
- The increased dependence of many organisations on their computer systems, with no manual backup. Banks, insurance companies and most large commercial organisations are entirely dependent on computers for their business transactions, and many scientific, engineering and, above all, military systems are now entirely computerised. A hardware or software failure in any of these systems could have very serious consequences.
- The move towards fifth generation computers, which have very different hardware and software characteristics from those in use at present, and require extensive use of concepts of artificial intelligence in their programming.

These pressures are causing a re-assessment of the methods used for the development of computer software. What is needed is a technique for the development of very large, complex software items, which satisfy strict standards of performance and correctness, in a controlled, scheduled, budgeted and cost-effective way. The approach which is evolving in response to these requirements is known as **software engineering**.

24.1 The Objectives of Software Engineering

Software engineering is the profession which is likely to replace programming and systems analysis over the next ten years. The objectives of software engineering are as stated above: the development of very large, complex software items, which satisfy strict standards of performance and correctness, in a controlled, scheduled, budgeted and cost-effective way. Software engineers require, in addition to a proficiency in programming, a knowledge of formal mathematics and logic, computing science, economics and management.

Software engineering is carried out by teams of people. When a software development project is started, the teams are set up with a management structure corresponding to the structure of the software itself. A schedule is drawn up for the project, and costs are allocated to the various portions and stages. Each team has a **team leader**, whose task is to make sure that the software developed by the team is correct, properly structured, has the right interfaces to the software being developed by the other teams, and is on schedule and within budget. This is a very difficult task, which requires a wide range of technical and management skills.

Software engineering is concerned with the entire lifecycle of a software project: design, development, testing, use and maintenance. All the work done is aimed at the highest possible standards at the lowest possible costs throughout this lifecycle.

24.2 Program Structure

It is now quite clear that the only way of achieving the required standards of correctness, performance and reliability of software is through the very careful design of the structure of a program. A well-structured program must satisfy the following conditions:

- The program must have a clear overall structure in terms of **modules**, with each module carrying out a specific task. Modules may be implemented as functions, procedures or segments, depending on the programming language used.

- There must be a clearly defined interface between modules. This is particularly important when interfaces are between modules written by different software engineers.
- Each module should be a simple combination of the elementary constructions of the programming language. Modules should be easy to read by people other than their original programmer.
- There must be a close correspondence between the structure of a module and the structure of the data on which it operates.
- Each module should leave the data structures on which it operates in a state which is consistent with their defining properties. This is particularly important with pointers: they should not be left 'hanging loose' by one module, on the assumption that another module will tidy them up.
- A module must have no **side effects**: it must not make any changes to data values, or to the state of the program, apart from those it is intended to make.

Achieving a program structure which satisfies these conditions is a very difficult task. Some help is given by the program structuring properties of the language, as discussed in Section 18.5. New programming languages are being developed which will give even greater assistance, particularly with the last two requirements of a structured program. See Section 34.4.

24.3 Program Design

Program design is the means by which proper program structure is achieved. It is the technique for going from the initial statement of the requirements of a program, which is generally vague, incomplete and contradictory, to the final structured, tested and approved code. See Figure 24.1. It is a long and difficult process, made more so by the lack of widely-accepted, tested techniques of program design. However, a number of methods of program design do exist, and their use is increasing all the time. In the foreseeable future, it is likely that all software development will be based on a formal technique of program design.

The simplest and one of the most popular methods of program design is **stepwise refinement**. It is based on the use of **algorithms**, which are written in a language somewhere between English and a programming language such as Pascal. The process itself may be described by an algorithm of this nature:

State the overall steps of a program in a brief, top-level algorithm.

Repeat

Expand each statement of the algorithm as a detailed algorithm which describes the steps required to implement the statement.

Until the task has been task has been specified in sufficient detail for the code of the program to be written.

Stepwise refinement is a **top-down** process, with details being added in an orderly fashion as the design progresses. If an algorithm turns out to be incorrect, it can be 'unplugged' and replaced by another without too much effect on the program structure as a whole.

Although stepwise refinement can bring about a great improvement in the structure of a program, it is not formal enough for many applications. In particular, there is no guarantee that data structures are left in a consistent state by the various modules. It is very difficult to prove the correctness of program modules developed in this way (Section 24.4).

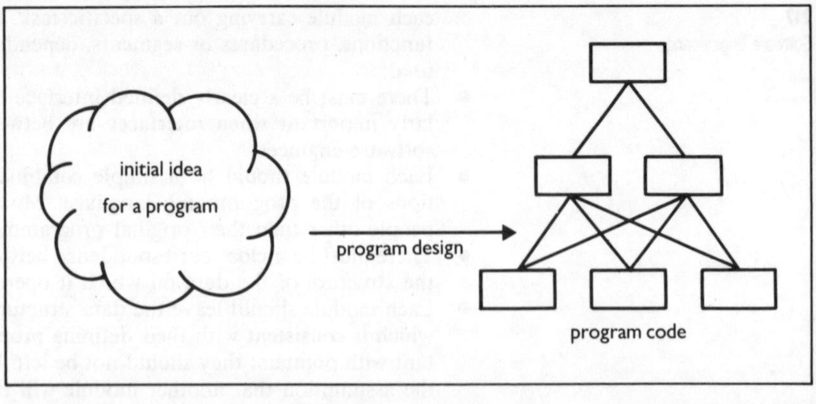

initial idea
for a program

program design

program code

Figure 24.1
Program design

A number of more formal methods of program design are coming into use, the most popular being **functional decomposition**. Like stepwise refinement, functional decomposition is a top-down method, starting with the overall requirements of a program, and adding detail in an orderly way. The difference is that at every stage, the essential properties of the data structures are specified, and each algorithm is expressed as a mathematical function which transforms these data structures. Each algorithm can be tested by various mathematical techniques, in order to prove that the properties of the data structures are not altered by the operations it performs on the data. Functional decomposition is particularly suited to some of the new functional programming languages which are being developed for fifth generation computers. See Section 34.4.

24.4 Proving the Correctness of Programs

At present, programs are tested by supplying them with a large amount of test data, in order to check that they work properly with every type of data that they are likely to encounter in practice. However, this process can never establish for certain that a program is correct, no matter how many different sets of test data are used. If a program is of critical importance, as so many commercial, industrial and military applications now are, every possible precaution needs to be taken to ensure that there are no errors in it.

The technique which is beginning to be used to ensure that program modules (and algorithms used in program design) are correct is to regard them as mathematical theorems, and apply the same methods of proof to them as are used to prove the correctness of theorems. Two types of proof are required for each algorithm or program module: the first determines that it carries out the required transformations on the data correctly, and the second checks that it leaves the defining properties of the data structures intact. This is an extremely difficult and time-consuming process, bearing in mind the length and complexity of operational software, and the complexity of the data structures commonly used. It can only be applied to software written in certain programming languages, or algorithms using a precisely-defined mathematical notation. Research is currently under way to develop semi-automatic methods of carrying out these proofs.

24.5 Software Development Environments

At present, computer programming is almost entirely a manual task. A programmer takes the specification of the program, which has been designed by one of the techniques discussed above, and writes the code to create a program which corresponds to the specification. The only change which is beginning to occur in this practice is the use of software development tools for certain types of application, as described in Chapter 23. However, the demands of software engineering, as discussed at the beginning of this chapter, mean that the traditional methods of writing programs by hand will not be adequate.

What is required is **software development environments** which form the basis of all stages of the design, development, testing and maintenance of software. They will have some features in common with fourth generation languages, such as data dictionaries, but will be much more powerful, and will be required for all types of computer application.

The likely structure of an integrated software development environment is as follows:

- A central database which includes all modules of all software under development, module libraries, and the specifications and algorithms written during software design.
- A data dictionary system giving access to all the data files for each application.
- Facilities to check specifications for completeness and correctness, and to assist in the proofs of correctness of program modules.
- Compilers and cross-compilers so that the most suitable programming language can be used for each code module, and that programs can be linked from modules written in a variety of source languages. In many cases the object code will be for different computers from the one on which the software development system runs.
- Program generators for routine modules such as file handling and screen input/output.
- Run-time diagnostic facilities and simulators for other computers, so that linked object code can be tested before it is transferred to its ultimate host computer.

A software development environment of this sort will require a large computer system to support it, with a network of terminals for the software engineers. Links are required to a range of target computers so that the final versions of the software can be transferred to them. At present, research and development work is under way as part of the fifth generation computer projects (Chapter 34) to design software development environments, but finished products are some way off, and are going to be very expensive. The Ada program support environment (Apse) is a software development environment already in existence for the support of a single high level language. Experience gained in the design and use of Apse is assisting in the design of more general-purpose software development environments, which can use a range of source languages.

24.6 Conclusion

Software engineering is an approach to software development which is steadily gaining acceptance in the computing industry. It is quite likely that during the next decade, techniques of software engineering become the norm, and **information systems factories** are set up for software development. The method of writing programs entirely by hand may go the way of the valve and the punched card.

The main points of this chapter are as follows:

- Conventional methods of designing and writing programs are becoming inadequate as programs get longer, more complex, more expensive and computer applications become increasingly important.
- Software engineering is an approach to the development of very large, complex software items, which satisfy strict standards of performance and correctness, in a controlled, scheduled, budgeted and cost-effective way.
- Software engineering is concerned with the entire lifecycle of a software project: design, development, testing, use and maintenance. All the work

done is aimed at the highest possible standards at the lowest possible costs throughout this lifecycle.

- The proper design of the structure of a program is essential if the program is to meet the software standards now required.
- Program design is a technique for going from the initial specification of a program, which may be vague, incomplete and contradictory, to the final structured, tested and approved code.
- In order to establish beyond reasonable doubt that a program module or specification algorithm is correct, mathematical techniques of theorem proving are beginning to be applied.
- An integrated software development environment is a set of development tools including data dictionaries, cross-compilers, theorem provers, module generators and run-time diagnostic aids used to assist in the development of software by methods of software engineering.

Exercise 24

1 Briefly define the following terms: software engineering; software lifecycle; program structure; side effect; program design; stepwise refinement; top-down method; functional decomposition; proof of correctness; software development environment.
2 Discuss the similarities and differences between the software development tools described in Chapter 23 and the software development environments described in this chapter.
3 Why is it so important to try to develop methods of proving the correctness of programs by mathematical techniques?
4 Describe the significance of cross-compilers for software development environments.
5 Examine the source code of a program in a high level language that you have written, or one obtained from elsewhere, and state the extent to which it satisfies each of the requirements of a well-structured program given in Section 24.2.
6 In what ways do introductory programming languages such as Basic make it difficult to satisfy the requirements for a well-structured program?
7 Give your views on the consequences for the programming profession of the trend towards software engineering.

25
Principles of Data Processing

This chapter describes the role of a computer in a practical data processing situation. It is concerned with the way in which a computerised system is set up to carry out some of the work of an organisation. In the past, the application was normally programmed by staff in the data processing department of the organisation. Today, the use of software packages, program generators or external software houses is just as common. In either case, the principles of data processing are the same.

25.1 The Nature and Objectives of Commercial and Industrial Data Processing

Data processing is a general term describing the work done by a computer. In practice its meaning is slightly more restricted. In a commercial or industrial context, data processing implies the use of a computer, or several computers, for part of the work of a company. As is customary in computing, a **system** is set up to handle each data processing application. The system includes hardware, software, collections of data and the work of a number of people.

There are several reasons for introducing a computer into a company. The commonest are to reduce costs, to take advantage of the facilities offered by computers, and to increase the volume of business. In addition, computers can supply better management information, and enable long-term forecasts and plans to be made. Also, computers enable some operations to be carried out which would be impossible without them. These reasons for introducing computers are also the general objectives of a data processing system.

The background to commercial data processing requires a few words of description. A commercial environment is characterised by large quantities of data, usually requiring identical processing. The cost of various operations are important, and it is vital that deadlines are met. Computerised systems must run smoothly, with adequate backup if anything should go wrong.

25.2 Types of Data Processing Systems

Although no two data processing applications are quite the same, it is possible to identify a number of distinct types of data processing systems. Broadly speaking, data processing systems are of three types: systems where processing is done periodically, real-time systems, and database systems. These are similar to the types of operating system discussed in Section 21.1.

Systems Where Processing is Done Periodically

These systems are characterised by large volumes of data of identical type. From time to time, batches of such data are processed in one operation. Because the data is stored in files, these systems may be called **file processing systems**. The commonest example of file processing systems is payroll systems. Once a week or once a month , a payroll system is put into action to produce the payslips for all the employees of a company. The volume of data processed is large, and each employee receives identical treatment by the system. File processing systems are now regarded as 'traditional' data processing systems. They closely resemble manual methods of data processing.

Real-time Systems

Real-time processing is data processing 'while you wait'. In other words, the computer must keep pace with some external process. Small quantities of data are processed in one operation. The delay in processing the data, which varies from a fraction of a second to a couple of minutes, is acceptable to the user of the system. Three types of real-time systems may be identified, though the distinction between them is fairly fine. The types are **process control**, **information storage and retrieval** and **transaction processing**.

Process control is an industrial application of computers. It is the continuous monitoring and controlling of an operational process by a computer. Measurements taken from the process are sent to the computer at frequent intervals, often many times a second. Control instructions are issued by the computer in response to this data. The time taken to process the data is generally very short. An example of process control is the automatic control of several aspects of oil refining. The temperature, pressure and composition of substances in various reactor vessels are monitored, and control instructions are issued accordingly.

Information storage and retrieval systems are concerned with accessing and updating data stored in files. Fairly small quantities of data are handled in one operation, and calculations or other operations on the data are minimal. An example of an information storage and retrieval system is a medical records system. The medical record of a patient can be accessed or updated by doctors, nurses or administrators from a terminal.

A transaction processing system is one which handles specifically defined transactions one at a time. Each transaction is processed to its conclusion before work on the next transaction commences. The amount of data supplied for a transaction is small, fitting into predefined categories. Processing may include a certain amount of calculation, as well as updating files. The commonest example of transaction processing is airline seat reservations. All the information required to make a reservation is supplied to the system, which then checks whether one can be made. If so, various files are updated, and passenger totals are adjusted. Other examples of transaction processing are withdrawals of money at bank cash terminals and most stock control systems.

Database Systems

Database systems use one store of information (the database) to support all the data processing activities of a particular company. The database is independent of any individual application. Applications may be of any of the types of data processing described in the previous sections. Database systems are described in detail in Chapter 28.

Data Communications Systems

Several of the types of data processing systems mentioned in the previous sections involve the transmission of data from one place to another. This aspect of data processing is discussed in Chapter 29.

25.3 The Data Processing Cycle

The **data processing cycle** is the sequence of actions carried out during the development of a new data processing application. Depending on the application, the cycle can take anything from a few weeks to more than a year. The person, or team of people, most actively involved in all stages of the data processing cycle have the job title of **systems analyst**. A description of the data processing cycle is a description of the work of a systems analyst.

The Need for Computerisation

In a variety of ways, and for various reasons, the need to computerise one aspect of the work of a company becomes apparent. Reasons for the introduction of computerised working are discussed in Section 25.1. The desire for computerisation is generally expressed by one of two groups of people within the company, namely the **management** or the **users**. Managers are concerned with turnover, profits, productivity and growth. The users are the people whose work will be done, partially or completely, by computer. They have detailed knowledge and experience of how the work is done at present.

The decision to investigate the possibility of changing to computerised working is generally taken at the appropriate level of management, in consultation with the users. But the way ahead is fraught with difficulties. How will the work be done by computer? What equipment will be needed? What changes will there be in staffing? What effects will the change to computers have on the company as a whole?

This is where a systems analyst comes in. The data processing cycle is a systematic process of answering these questions. The cycle may be terminated at several stages if it becomes obvious that it would be unwise to change to computers after all. There are four overall phases in the data processing cycle. These are **system design**, **system development**, **system implementation** and **system maintenance**. Each phase consists of several steps.

System Design

This phase is concerned with deciding whether it is feasible to do a piece of work by computer, and outlining a way in which the work can be done. The first stage of system design is a **feasibility study**. This is a preliminary survey, carried out by a systems analyst, to determine whether a full scale investigation should be carried out. The survey is generally conducted by consultation with management and users. A **feasibility report** is prepared, outlining the objectives and constraints of the proposed system, estimating some of the costs involved, and recommending whether or not to continue with the project.

If the feasibility report is favourable, and approved by the managers, then a detailed **system investigation** is undertaken. This takes the form of interviews, surveys, questionnaires and sometimes the systems analyst working with the users for a while. The two objectives are to gain a thorough knowledge of the current way of working, and analyse, in a fair amount of detail, the steps involved in computerised working.

The result of the system investigation is a detailed **system specification** (or **functional specification**) of the proposed data processing system. This includes a summary of the overall working of the system, and more detailed sections on the files of stored data required, the input and output data and the various types of processing to be done. The system specification generally includes a **systems flowchart**, (Section 25.5) which is a diagram showing the overall flow of data through the system, and the various operations carried out. The system specification is submitted to the managers for approval. It may be accepted, modified or rejected. When agreement has been reached, it marks the end of the system design phase of the data processing cycle.

System Development

Once the specification of a new data processing system has been accepted, the detailed work on the development of the system can begin. **System development** is concerned with specifying, writing, testing and documenting the programs for the new system.

Using the relevant portion of the systems flowchart, together with various file specifications, the **specification** of each program required is set out in detail. Several programs are generally required, and these are further broken down into **modules**, each module performing a specific task. It is usual to specify what must be done by each module of each program, without stating how it is to be done. The method used in each module is at the discretion of the programmer writing the module. If a software package is to be used for the application, the criteria for the selection of the package are set out, and the package is selected, or a short list of potential packages is drawn up. See Section 25.7.

If a new program is to be written for the system, a team of **programmers** sets to work, writing each module of each program. Modules are written separately, often by different programmers, and combined at a later stage. If an existing software package is to be adapted for use, the way of using the package is determined by the systems analyst. See Section 25.7.

Experience has shown that it is very unlikely for a newly-written or newly-adapted program, no matter how carefully specified, to work correctly first time. All the modules of the new programs are tested seperately, and then combined, or **built**, into complete programs. **Program testing** generally uses specially prepared **test data**. This contains all the data errors and awkward cases that are likely to arise, and is designed to try to make the new programs fail. Testing continues in this way until all the errors in the programs have been identified and corrected, and the programmers and systems analyst are satisfied.

System testing is to try out the running of the data processing system as a whole. The programs are run in their intended sequence, and the various manual parts of the operation are carried out. The passing of data from one stage to the next is checked, as are security and backup features. When these tests are satisfactory, the system is ready to be tried out by the users.

Acceptance testing is carried out by the users. They see if the system performs to their satisfaction, and again try to 'break' the system with awkward cases and incorrect data. Modifications are made to the system until the users are satisfied.

System Implementation

The final phase of the data processing cycle concerns putting the new system to work. Pilot running, with the new system doing part of the work, is often used. It is also common, though not always possible, to run the new and the old system in parallel for a while. Finally, often a year after the new system was proposed, it is in full productive operation. As can be imagined, the cost of the whole design, development and implementation process is considerable.

System Maintenance

Once a system is in operation, it is unlikely that it remains entirely satisfactory for long. On the one hand, experience in using the system brings to light shortcomings and suggests improvements. On the other hand, the requirements of the system change as time goes by. For these reasons, the system requires periodic **maintenance**. Maintenance requires re-specification of portions of the system, and amendments to programs and documentation accordingly. A certain amount of testing is also involved.

25.4 What Can Go Wrong?

The above description of the data processing cycle makes it sound like a textbook operation, with no problems likely to arise. In practice this is not always the case. A few of the commonest sources of problems are outlined below.

Changing Specifications

For a variety of reasons, it is often necessary to change the specification of a system while it is under development. Changes can arise from altered business circumstances, new hardware becoming available, or because someone has thought of an 'improvement' to the system. The amount of disruption caused by a change depends on the nature of the change. In some cases, large amounts of detailed work have to be done again.

Increasing Costs

At today's levels of inflation, it is certain that almost all costs will increase. Estimates of these increased costs are generally made at the start of a project, but they can never be totally accurate. Unforeseen costs almost always arise. Occasionally, increased costs lead to the abandonment of a new system. However, in most cases, cost increases tend to trip the balance in favour of computers, where hardware prices are still coming down.

Delays

The feasibilty report generally contains estimates of the duration of the various stages of data processing cycle. A series of deadlines is usually set up. Depending on the circumstances surrounding the project, these are or are not met. In general, the data processing industry has quite a good record for meeting deadlines. Delays can be a nuisance or a disaster, depending on how vital it is to have the new system in operation. Delays always have the effect of increasing the development cost of the system.

Resistance to Change

Changing to computerised working implies new work practices, new equipment to operate, and, in some cases, transfers to different jobs or redundancies. Most people, familiar with one way of doing a job, are reluctant to change their working habits. Very few people are happy about being made redundant. Trade unions are likely to raise objections if the welfare of their members is being threatened. Inter-union disputes over new work practices are particularly difficult. All these factors must be taken into account when a new data processing system is being planned. Unfortunately, lack of consideration of the welfare of employees, lack of consultation and inflexible attitudes have sometimes led to serious problems in this area.

25.5   Systems Flowcharts

This section provides details about **systems flowcharts**, and introduces some common data processing operations. Figure 25.1 shows the systems flowchart symbols in common use. Notice that there is one set of symbols for stored data, and another set for various types of processing.

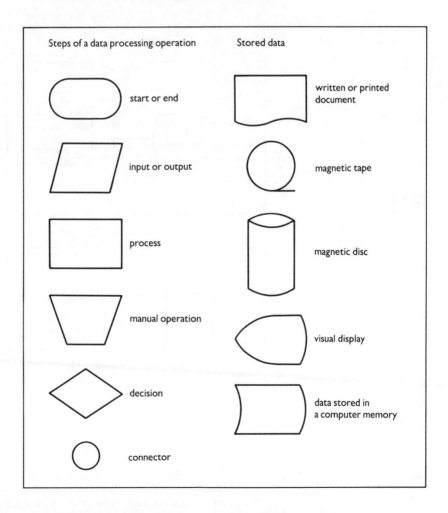

Figure 25.1
Systems flowchart symbols

Many data processing operations are concerned with **files**. A file is a large collection of data, with a definite logical structure, held on a physical medium such as magnetic tape or magnetic disks. See Chapters 26 and 27. Systems flowchart segments are discussed below for a few common operations on files.

File Creation
Data is transferred from an external medium, such as OCR forms, to a file on a magnetic tape or disk. In most data processing systems, data is typed directly from data entry terminals to a file. See Figure 25.2.

Data Validation
The data in a file is subjected to various tests. Incorrect data is printed on an **error report**; correct data is stored on another file. See Figure 25.3. This process is called **validation**. In most transaction processing systems, input data is validated as it is entered. Invalid items are rejected and must be retyped.

Updating a File
A file of amendments is used to bring the data on another file up-to-date. A new file is produced of the **updated** information. See Figure 25.4. In transaction processing systems, updating is done for each transaction as soon as it is entered.

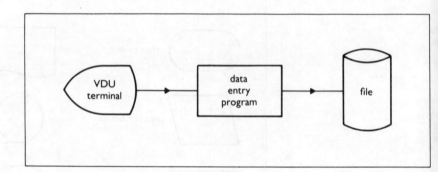

Figure 25.2
File creation

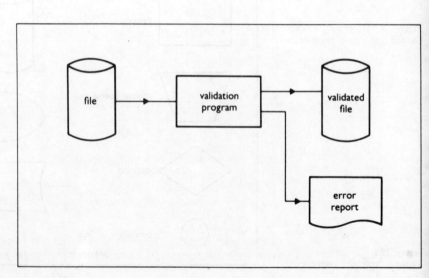

Figure 25.3
File validation

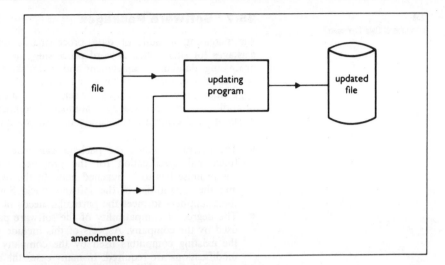

Figure 25.4
File updating

Output and Report Generation

Data selected from a file is output, and a **report** is **generated**, summarising the information contained in the file. See Figure 25.5.

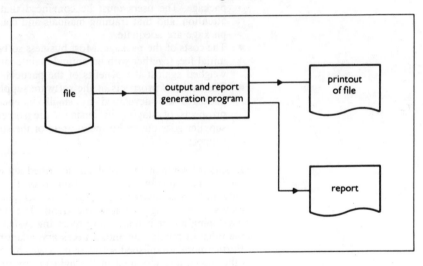

Figure 25.5
Output and report generation

25.6 System Documentation

Documentation is a written description of how a program works, how it is to be used, or how it is to be run on a computer. Several types of documentation are prepared during the development of a data processing system.

The **functional specification** is a written description of the requirements of a program, produced at the end of the systems design phase. **Program documentation** is a detailed account of how each module of a program works. It is for the use of anyone who wishes to understand the detailed working of a program, in order to test it or modify it. **User documentation** is an account of how a program is to be used. It is written in non-technical language, and does not contain any details of how the program works. **Operator documentation** is a description, for computer operators, of how a program is to be run. It states which devices are needed and which data files must be loaded, and any special stationery required. It also specifies what is to be done should the program fail.

25.7 Software Packages

An increasing amount of data processing is done using standard **software packages** for such tasks as word processing, accounting, stock control, payroll processing, database management and spreadsheets. If a software package is to be used, the systems flowcharts and functional specifications for the proposed application provide the criteria for selection of a particular package. Most types of application are covered by a number of competing packs.

The general criteria for selection of a software package are as follows:

- The extent to which the package can match the systems flowcharts and functional specification for the proposed application. In most cases, a compromise has to be reached between the requirements of the application and the capabilities of the software pack. Some packs can be tailored by their suppliers to meet the particular needs of users.
- The degree of compatibility of the software package with existing software used by the company. Aspects of this include whether the pack will run on the existing computers used by the company, and whether any hardware modifications are required. In many cases the new software must be able to use existing data files, or transfer data to and from existing data files. The user interface of the package must not be too different from those of existing software.
- The level of support and user training offered by the supplier of the software package. The users must be convinced that problems will receive prompt attention, and that training manuals and courses provided with the software package are adequate.
- The costs of the package. Most business software packs are purchased for an initial fee, together with an annual maintenance charge. The costs have to be weighed against the benefits of the particular software package.
- The business prospects of the software supplier. Regrettably, many software packages are developed by small, independent software houses, whose prospects of staying in business are sometimes uncertain. If a software supplier goes out of business, users of the software package are left with no support.

In spite of some of the problems described above, the use of software packages for commercial computer applications is on the increase. Most small businesses base all their computer applications on such packages, and many larger companies are beginning to follow the trend. The main reason is cost: the cost of developing a commercial data processing system internally is very much higher than that of purchasing and, if necessary, adapting an existing software package. Furthermore, established software packages have been proved in use by all their other users, and modified in the light of any problems that have occurred.

25.8 Conclusion

This chapter is intended to give a 'feel' for the way in which computers are put to work in commerce and industry. It is worth stressing that data processing in this area is strongly influenced by business practices, and that a relatively small proportion of the data processing cycle is spent actually writing programs.

The main points of the chapter are as follows:

- Data processing systems are generally set up in order to reduce costs, increase the volume of business of the company and to take advantage of the facilities offered by computers.
- Data processing systems may be classified as file processing systems and real-time systems. Real-time systems include process control systems, information storage and retrieval systems and transaction processing systems. Some of these systems use databases, some involve data communication.

- The data processing cycle is the sequence of activities required to bring a new data processing system into operation.
- The overall steps of a data processing cycle are system design, system development and system implementation. Each of these steps can be broken down into more detailed steps.
- A systems flowchart is used to illustrate the overall steps of a data processing system.
- In spite of careful planning, a number of things can go wrong during a data processing cycle. Common problems include changing specifications, increasing costs, delays and resistance to change.
- Criteria for the choice of a software package for a business application include its suitability for the task, its compatibility with existing hardware and software, the degree of support provided, and cost.

Exercise 25

1 Briefly define the following terms: data processing; file processing system; real-time system; process control system; information storage and retrieval system; transaction processing system; database system; data communications system; data processing cycle; systems analyst; user; system design; system development; system implementation; feasibility study; system investigation; system specification; systems diagram; program specification; program testing; test data; system testing; acceptance testing; system maintenance; validation; report generation; documentation; functional specification; program documentation; user documentation; operator documentation; software package.

2 a) Summarise the objectives of a data processing system.
  b) What are the characteristics of the environment of a commercial data processing system?

3 Classify the following data processing systems according to the types of data processing described in the chapter:
  a) An accounting system, where accounts are brought up-to-date once a month.
  b) An order processing system, where each order is processed as soon as it is received.
  c) A bank accounting system, where accounts are brought up-to-date every night.
  d) The on-board navigation system on a rocket.
  e) The book index at a library.

4 Summarise, in about 100 words, the most significant features of the data processing cycle.

5 At what stages may a data processing cycle be terminated before the new system is put into operation?

6 A small company, which already has a computer, intends to computerise another part of its operations. It intends to buy an applications package to run the new work on its computer. Outline an approach which could be used by managers in dealing with this problem.

7 Why is it not adequate to use sets of real data during program testing?

8 State some effects of delays in meeting deadlines during a project.

9 At which point in the data processing cycle is it most likely that resistance to change on the part of employees will become apparent? Discuss some approaches which could be used by managers in dealing with the problem.

10 A chain of retail shops wishes to implement a point-of-sale transaction recording system. The overall specification of the system is as follows:
  i) Cash registers are to be replaced by data entry terminals, linked to a microcomputer within each shop.
  ii) When a sale is registered, the stock number for each item sold is entered. The price of the item is displayed. The total for the sale is displayed and the amount paid by cash, cheque or credit card is entered. The amount of change is displayed.
  iii) At the end of each day, the microcomputer produces a printout showing the total cash, cheques and credit card slips collected at each till. A file is produced on a floppy disk, showing the number sold of each stock item. This file can be inspected on the display screen.
  iv) The file of stock movements is then transmitted via a telephone link to a central mainframe computer.

a) Draw one or more systems flow diagrams showing the overall steps of this system.
b) Identify the applications programs required for this system.
c) Write out a specification for each application program.
d) Identify any potential problems in the implementation of this system.

11 A stock control system is to be devised for a wholesale supplier of electrical goods. Suggest a suitable computer configuration and give reasons for your choice of equipment. Indicate how data capture will be organised and what files will be necessary. Draw outline system flow charts.

UL 78 II

12 A large hotel has installed a minicomputer to control the reservation of rooms. The management decide to implement an online system which enables the reception clerks to use terminals to access the system to make bookings, or cancellations, or enquiries. The management require reports on advance bookings, the present state of room occupation and a monthly report on the statistics of bookings.

Draw an outline system flow chart for the system.

Specify an appropriate hardware configuration and explain why each item was chosen.

How might the hotel protect itself against the breakdown of the computer or its inoperability due to a power cut?

UL 79 II

26
File Structure

This chapter is concerned with the way in which data files are structured on backing store. It deals with the logical structure of the data, as opposed to the physical structure which is discussed in Section 14.4. Users and programmers are concerned only with the logical structure of files; the conversion between logical and physical structure is done by the operating system.

26.1 Files, Records, Fields and Keys

Computers inherited files and file processing from manual data processing systems. Many of the ideas and terms used in connection with computer files are derived from the terminology of manual files. Whether it is stored in a filing cabinet, on a magnetic disk or on any other form of storage, a **file** is an organised collection of data. Files are generally large, contain related items of information, and are strictly arranged according to some structure. Files may have **subfiles** which contain part of the data in the file, and have the same general structure as a file.

The unit of data which makes up a file is a **record**. A record corresponds roughly to a card in a card index, or a single sheet of paper in a manual file. A record contains a number of data items, and each record in a file generally has the same structure. Records are not always the same length: in a file of invoices, for example, the number of item lines in an invoice (one record) is not constant. However, if the file is a random-access file (Section 14.4), where records can be accessed and updated individually, then a fixed amount of space must be allocated on the backing store medium for each record. In most computer systems, there must be an integral number of records on each physical block or sector on the backing store medium.

Individual data items occupy **fields** within a record. A field may be of fixed or variable width. The term **fieldwidth** refers to the number of characters in a field. Fields may be of different **type**: numeric, text, currency, date or codes where each character has a special significance.

The commonest way of identifying a record is by means of a chosen field within the record. This field is referred to as the **key** of the record. The only restriction on keys is that all the records in a file have distinct keys. For this and other reasons, more than one field is sometimes used as the key of a record. The fields are then called the **primary key**, **secondary key**, etc.

For example, consider the information in a telephone directory as a file. A record is the entry for one person. A record comprises four fields, namely surname, initials, address and telephone number. The primary key is the surname field, and the secondary key is the initials. The two keys together are sufficient, for practical purposes, to identify each person uniquely, whereas a surname on its own is not always enough.

26.2 File Structures

In the early days of computing, the structure of a file was largely determined by the storage medium available. Today the situation has been reversed. The nature of the computer application determines the structure of the files, which in turn determines the type of storage medium used. The commonest types of file structure are **serial** files, **sequential** files, **indexed sequential** files and **random** files. The following sections discuss these types of files.

Serial Files
A serial file is one in which the records are in no particular order. Serial files are mainly used for temporary storage of data, until a more highly structured file is created. Magnetic tapes and magnetic disks are equally suitable for storing serial files.

Sequential Files

A sequential file is one in which records are in order of one or more keys. The order may be numeric or alphabetic. For example, a file of examination results may be sorted in order of class of pass (primary key) and, within each class, alphabetic order of surnames (secondary key). Sequential files may be stored on magnetic tapes or magnetic disks, and are the backbone of the 'traditional' file processing systems mentioned in the previous chapter.

Indexed Sequential Files

Indexed sequential files are the commonest types of files in current use. As their name suggests, indexed sequential files are ordered files which also have an index. The **index** is a set of data which enables the key of a record to be associated with its physical disk address (Section 14.4). It is very similar to an index of a book, which relates words and phrases to page numbers. The index of a file is generally stored at the beginning or the end of the file, or, more commonly, as a separate file. If more than one level of index is used, as is often the case, different parts of the index may be stored throughout the file.

Since indexed sequential files require that data items be located by addresses, they must be stored on magnetic disks. A number of different indexing techniques are in use, but only one is discussed here. It is the simplest, and relates directly to the structure of a magnetic disk pack. It is called **cylinder-surface-sector** indexing.

For each disk pack of the file, there is a **cylinder index**, which relates each cylinder number to the highest key value stored in that cylinder. Once a cylinder has been selected, its **surface index** is used. This index relates each surface of the cylinder to the highest key value in that surface. Once a surface has been selected, its **sector index** is used. This relates each sector number to the highest key value within the sector. The required sector is then copied from the disk, and the required record located.

For example, consider a file which stores records of motor car parts. Each record concerns one part, with the part number being the key. Part numbers are in the range 00001 to 99999. The following table contains a portion of the cylinder index of the file, together with one surface and one sector index.

Cylinder Index		Surface Index for Cylinder 106		Sector Index for Surface 4	
Cylinder	Highest Key	Surface	Highest Key	Sector	Highest Key
1	00396	1	41177	1	41179
2	00785	2	41124	2	41186
...		3	41171	3	41194
105	41027	4	41223	4	41200
106	41421	5	41269	5	41207
107	41803	6	41318	6	41214
...		7	41368	7	41219
256	99999	8	41421	8	41223

Suppose it is required to access the record for part number 41192. Inspection of the cylinder index shows that this record is in cylinder 106. The surface index for this cylinder is then accessed. Inspection of this index shows that the record is on surface 4. The sector index for this surface is then accessed. This index shows that the required record is in sector 3. This sector is then copied from the disk, and searched for the required record.

It can be seen that locating this record required four accesses to the disk, once for each of the three indexes, and one for the data sector. After each disk access, the index or data sector is searched, in the memory of the computer.

One advantage of indexed sequential files is that it is easy to leave spaces in sectors, surfaces or cylinders for the insertion of new records. This allows a file to grow without having to be copied onto another disk, and re-indexed, too frequently.

Random Files

Random files are ones in which records are scattered at random on the storage medium. In order to access a record, there is a function which relates the key of the record to its address on the storage medium. This process is known as **address generation**. As in the case of indexed sequential files, this requires that magnetic disks be used to store the data.

It is occasionally possible to use the backing store address of a record as its key. In this case, accessing the record is extremely simple. More frequently, some calculation or manipulation must be carried out on the key of the record in order to produce its backing store address. One technique for this is called **hashing**, and the file structure is called a **hash table**. Problems arise when two different key values produce the same backing store address. Address generation techniques are investigated in more detail in the exercise at the end of the chapter.

Random files are most suited to applications where rapid access is required to individual records. If access to groups of records with consecutive keys is required, then indexed sequential files are much more useful. Random files are less common than indexed sequential files.

26.3   Blocking Strategy

The way in which the logical structure of a file - its records and fields - are arranged on the physical blocks of the backing store medium is the **blocking strategy** of the file management system. Blocking strategies vary according to the nature and structure of the file, and whether the backing store medium is disk or tape. The objectives are the same in all cases:

- To make the most efficient use of the backing store medium.
- To make access to files as quick as possible.
- To deal with enlargements and reductions in the file size in an orderly manner.

In almost all cases, an integral number of records is stored on a physical block. This usually leaves some blank space in each block, and many blocking strategies leave more than this minimum to allow for growth of the file. The term **packing density** refers to the ratio of backing store space used by a file at any time to the total space available. If files are expected to change in size very frequently, space is left in every block for new records. An alternative is to reserve overflow blocks at suitable positions on the medium for new records. If records are a variable length, then there are two possibilities: to allow the maximum possible record space for each actual record, or to reposition all the records on a block (and update the appropriate indexes) every time one changes in length. If space is short, the packing density is kept as high as possible, and new records are inserted wherever there is a large enough space. This leads to fragmentation of the file, and slows access to records.

26.4   Conclusion

This chapter has discussed some of the general principles of files and file structure. It prepares the way for the discussion of file processing, in the next chapter. The main points of the chapter are as follows:

- A file is a large collection of related data items, strictly organised as records and fields.
- The commonest types of file structure are serial files, sequential files, indexed sequential files and random files.
- In a serial file, records are stored one after another, with no ordering.
- In a sequential file, records are stored in order of one or more keys.

- An indexed sequential file has a separate index relating the physical disk address of each record to its key(s).
- A random file has its records stored in random order, with an address generation technique for locating each record from its key(s).
- The technique for allocating records to physical blocks of backing store is the blocking strategy of the file management system.

Exercise 26

1 Briefly define the following terms: file; subfile; record; field; fieldwidth; serial file; sequential file; indexed sequential file; random file; address generation; hashing; packing density; blocking strategy.

2 A word processing system includes a file of letters sent by the user of the system. There is a record for each letter, containing the name and address of the person to whom the letter was sent, the date and the text of the letter.
   a) Suggest one or more keys for a record, justify your choice.
   b) Suggest a suitable structure for organising the file. Consider likely uses of the file in making your choice. Include these uses in reasons for your choice of structure.
   c) State, with reasons, the storage medium you would use for the file.

3 A form of index sometimes used on indexed sequential files is called a **hierarchical index**. Like cylinder-surface-sector indexing, this has several levels of indexing. However, each level of index does not correspond to a physical aspect of the layout of the file on the disk.
   The top level index relates each index number of the next level of indexes to the highest key value contained in that index. Each of the next level of indexes has a similar structure, relating to a third level of indexes. Each of these indexes relates a set of block addresses to the highest keys within the block. For example:

Top level index		Second level index 11		Third level index 531	
Second level index number	Highest Key	Third level index number	Highest Key	Block Address	Highest Key
1	12509	501	125254	26501	132504
2	25038	502	125517	26502	132510
...	...	...	...	...	...
10	125250	530	132500	26543	132712
11	137503	531	132758	26544	132719
...	...	...	...	...	...
50	625341	550	137503	26550	132758

   a) Describe the steps in locating the record with key 132714, using these indexes.
   - b) Suggest why this method is slightly slower than cylinder-surface-sector indexing.

4 A technique for calculating the backing store address from the key, in random files, is called **folding**. For example, if the key is 9 digits long, then the three sets of three digits are added up to obtain the backing store address, as follows:

```
Key: 396 421 608          396
                          421
                      +   608
Backing store address:   1425
```

   a) Use this technique to calculate the backing store addresses of these keys: 492 117 503, 625 417 902.
   b) If the address thus calculated is already occupied, then the next available address is used instead. This principle is called **open hashing**. Assuming an initially empty file, use this principle to load records with the following keys: 462 803 906, 341 915 916, 638 702 831, 594 913 666.
   c) Load the records from part (b) in a different order. Comment on your findings.

5 a) Finger-prints can be classified in terms of less than ten characteristics such as the number of lines between two principal features. Discuss the use that could be made of a computer system to assist police with the identification of finger-prints. Explain what information would be stored, how a user of the system would make an enquiry and how the system could increase the effectiveness of retrieval of information.
   b) Describe a way in which files on finger-prints could be organised so as to facilitate the methods of retrieval.

27
File Processing

This chapter discusses the steps of some of the commonest file processing operations, namely data capture, validation, sorting (both in a computer memory and on backing store), merging, searching and updating files. To conclude the chapter, some techniques to ensure the security of data are introduced. The techniques are described in general terms, and implementation-dependent features are avoided. This helps to keep the descriptions as simple as possible. It must, however, be borne in mind that when these techniques are put into use, the software required can become extremely complicated.

27.1 Data Capture

The first step in any file processing operation is to get the data onto the computer. This is done either by direct reading from source documents, reading from bar codes, or by entering the data at a terminal. See Section 14.2 for details of the media and devices used.

In a number of data processing systems, a document which is the output from one process becomes the input to another. Such documents are known as **turnaround documents**. For example, most gas, electricity, water and telephone bills are printed by computer. They include a tearoff slip which is returned with the payment. The slip has a row of OCR characters printed along the bottom. When the slip is returned, some additional characters may be printed giving details of the payment. The slip then becomes the input source document for the program which records the payment of the bills.

27.2 Validation

Validation is the process of checking input data, before storing or processing it. A number of checks can be carried out; the ones used in each case depend on the application. Validation is one of the most important and time-consuming steps in many data processing systems.

The simplest checks are **type** and **range** checks. Type checks determine whether the data is of the correct type (alphabetic or numeric). Range checks determine whether numeric data is within an acceptable range. Various totals can be used to check input data. If batches of data are input, items in each batch can be added up, and the **batch total** (or **control total**) input. The total is re-calculated by the program, and compared with the one input. If the totals are different, an error has occurred. The same principle applies to **hash totals**, which are totals of data items within the same record.

Numeric data items of particular importance, such as the keys of records, often have **check digits** attached to them. The value of the check digit can be determined from the other digits in the number. The check digit is tested from time to time, to see if an error has arisen during copying of the data item. Examples of data items which include check digits are account numbers, credit card numbers, international standard book numbers and the numbers encoded by bar codes. There are several ways of calculating check digits in common use. Some of them are introduced in the exercise at the end of the chapter.

27.3 Sorting in Main Store

Sorting is a very common data processing technique. Some programming languages, notably Cobol, and most program generators have a single instruction to cause a file of data to be sorted. Much attention has been devoted to developing efficient ways of sorting, as it can be an extremely slow process.

For a set of data to be sorted, all the data must be in the main store of a computer. If the set of data is too large for this, it must be sorted in portions, each of which can be accommodated in the available main store. This section is concerned with the part of the process which takes place in the main store of a computer, using data which has already been loaded into the main store. A later section examines the problem of sorting larger sets of data.

An informal algorithm for a common sorting technique is now introduced. The technique is called **quicksort**, as it is one of the fastest sorting methods. Others include the insertion sort, tree sort, selection sort, Shell sort and bubble sort. Some of these are covered in the exercise at the end of the chapter.

Algorithm for Quicksort

If the set contains more than one record
then select the first record,
    partition the remaining records into two subsets:
        a **left subset**, with keys less than that of the first record
        a **right subset**, with keys greater than that of the first record,
    place the first record between the two subsets,
    quicksort the left subset,
    quicksort the right subset.
else the set is sorted.

Notice that the algorithm is recursive, in other words it calls itself repeatedly, for smaller and smaller subsets of the set of data. The example below shows the steps of quicksort applied to the keys of eight records in a file. The square brackets show which elements have not yet been sorted.

Original order of keys:
    [11 9 23 7 31 5 2 17]

Select first key (11) and partition the set:
    [9 7 5 2] 11 [23 31 17]

Quicksort left subset:
    Select first key (9) and partition the set:
    [7 5 2] 9 11 [23 31 17]

Quicksort right subset:
    Select first key (23) and partition the set:
    [7 5 2] 9 11 [17] 23 [31]

Quicksort the first remaining subset:
    Select first key (7) and partition the set:
    [5 2] 7 9 11 [17] 23 [31]

Quicksort the first remaining subset:
    Select first key (5) and partition the set:
    [2] 5 7 9 11 [17] 23 [31]

All remaining subsets are of length one element, and are therefore already sorted:

    2 5 7 9 11 17 23 31

Although this process appears anything but quick, it is in fact better than most of its rivals for larger sets of data. The reason for its speed is that data items are moved very quickly to positions close to their final ordering. The last few sort passes are to tidy up the final ordering.

27.4 Merging

Merging is the process of combining two ordered files of data to produce a single ordered file. The method is very simple, and is outlined in the algorithm below.

Algorithm for Merging

Records from ordered files A and B are to be merged to form ordered file C.

Repeat
    if all records from A have been removed
        then copy remaining records in file B to file C
    else if all records from B have been removed
        then copy remaining records in file A to file C
    else compare next records in files A and B
        copy the record with lower key to file C
Until all records from files A and B have been merged.

The important fact about this process is that it does not require that all the data be in the main store of the computer. One record from each input file is, in fact, sufficient. Thus files can be merged which are much larger than the capacity of the main store of the computer doing the merging.

Although merging is an important file processing operation in its own right, its most common application is to form part of a sorting process for files which are much larger than the capacity of the main store of the computer which is sorting them.

27.5 Sorting Large Files

A number of techniques are used to sort files which are too large for the main store of the computer. They are generally based on combinations of sorting and merging. The file which is to be sorted is divided into **strings**, each of which can be accommodated in the main store of the computer. Each string is sorted, and the sorted string copied to backing store. These strings are merged, creating successively larger strings, until the whole file has been merged into a single string.

The following sequence of merges illustrates this technique, though it is not actually used in practice. Consider a file which has been divided into eight strings. The strings have been sorted, and copied onto two magnetic tapes, as follows:

Tape A: String 1 String 3 String 5 String 7
Tape B: String 2 String 4 String 6 String 8

The strings are merged in pairs, the resulting strings being placed alternately on two further tapes.

Tape C: String 9 (String 1 + String 2) String 11 (String 5 + String 6)
Tape D: String 10 (String 3 + String 4) String 12 (String 7 + String 8)

These strings are again merged in pairs, and the resulting strings copied onto alternate tapes.

Tape A: String 13 (String 9 + String 10)
Tape B: String 14 (String 11 + String 12)

These two strings are merged to form a single string, which is the entire file, in order. The merging techniques used in practice are more complicated. They reduce the number of merges needed for a given number of strings. Nevertheless sorting a large file on a small computer is frequently the slowest step of the entire data processing operation.

27.6 Searching

Searching is the process of locating a record in a file, given the key of the record. If the file has an index, then the index is used to locate the record. If the file is randomly organised, then the process used to load a record is also used to access it. Otherwise, the file must be searched. Three common file searching techniques are discussed here, namely the **sequential search**, the **binary search** and the **tree search**.

Sequential Search

A sequential search involves examining every record in a file until the required one is found. It is only used if a small number of records are present, or if the file is not ordered. On average, half the records in the file have to be examined before the required record is located.

Binary Search

A binary search involves partitioning the file into smaller and smaller subsets, each of which is known to contain the required record, and each of which is half the size of the previous subset. An informal algorithm for a binary search is as follows:

Algorithm for Binary Search

If the set contains at least one record
then select the middle record
partition the remaining records into two subsets:
a **left subset**, with keys less than that of the middle record
a **right subset**, with keys greater than that of the middle record,
if the middle record is the required record
then **the required record has been found**
else if the key of the required record is
less than that of the middle record
then **binary search** the left subset
else **binary search** the right subset
else **the required record is not in the set**.

Notice that this algorithm is very similar in structure to that for a quicksort. Once again, it is recursive. The example below shows the steps of a binary search applied to the keys of eight records in a file. The required record has key value 7.

Initial situation:
2 5 7 9 11 17 23 31

Select middle record (key 9), partition set:
[2 5 7] 9 [11 17 23 31]

Required key is less than that of middle record, so binary search left subset:
2 5 7

Select middle record (key 5), partition set:
[2] 5 [7]

Required key is greater than that of middle record, so binary search left subset:
7

Select middle record (key 7), which is the required record.

It can be seen that the process of dividing the set into two subsets is carried out three times to locate the required record. In general, the maximum number of steps, for a file of N records, is $\log_2 N$. A binary search is much quicker than a sequential search. A binary search does not require that all the records of a file be in the main store of the computer. The backing store addresses of records can be used to locate the middle element of each set. This element must be copied into main store for examination. However, the requirement of backing store addresses does rule out the use of magnetic tapes.

Tree Search

A tree search is a systematic scan, or traversal, of a set of data stored in a tree structure. It is gaining importance because of its frequent use in artificial intelligence work. In some cases, the data to be searched exists before the search starts; in others the data is created before being tested, a process known as **generate-and-test**. For example, when a computer is playing chess, it generates a set of possible moves from the current state of the game, and tests each possibility to determine how advantageous it would be. The most favourable move generated is the one selected.

There are two types of tree search: the **depth-first** search where the search is carried out as far 'down' each branch of the tree before looking at another branch, and the **breadth-first** search which scans across all branches, one level at a time. See Figures 27.1 and 27.2. In practice, tree searches are often a combination of these two approaches. Tree searching can also be used as part of the process of sorting data, as investigated in the exercise at the end of this chapter.

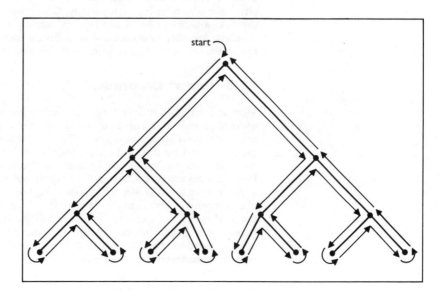

Figure 27.1
Depth-first tree search

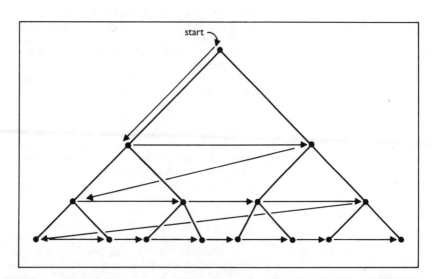

Figure 27.2
Breadth-first tree search

27.7 Updating

Updating a file involves amending, deleting and inserting records so as to bring the information in the file up to date. If the file to be updated is a sequential file, then the amendments data is sorted into the same order as the ordering of the sequential file. The systems flow diagram, Figure 26.4, in the previous chapter shows the process of updating a sequential file. A **transaction file** is used to update a **master file**, producing a new version of the master file. The process forms a cycle, since the up-to-date file produced on one occasion forms the file to be updated on the next occasion. In transaction processing systems, files are updated one record at a time: the new record overwrites the old one in its position on backing store, or is placed at the end of the file.

A common problem during file updating is **overflow**. This occurs when the updated version of the file is larger than the original, and too large for the backing store space allocated. The response to an overflow problem depends to a large extent on the operating system in use. Some will simply abort the updating process, while others will allow a file to be stored on more than one physical medium, at least temporarily. Others will suspend the operation so that the disk or tape can be 'cleaned up' by deleting redundant files or records from it. There are only two permanemt solutions to file overflow problems: either reduce the size of the file, or increase the amount of backing store allocated to it.

27.8 Report Generation

Most active files in a data processing system contain large volumes of data. In order to provide an accurate, up-to-date picture of the system, it is important to generate **reports** at regular intervals. These reports summarise the data on one or more files, and are intended for the information of managers at various levels of the organisation. One of the facilities of the fourth generation programming languages discussed in Chapter 23 is report generation.

As an example, consider a file containing records of all the sales by a particular company. A report might be generated from this file once a week, showing the total number of sales, the total value of the sales, and breakdowns of these figures by salesman, product group, area and method of payment. This report could be used by the sales manager. The total sales figures could be included in reports to managers at higher levels.

27.9 Data Security

The files used by most data processing systems are vital to the system. Any loss or corruption of data can lead to delays, loss of business or legal action being taken against the company. For these reasons it is essential that files be guarded against computer failures, program errors, human errors and malicious interference.

If files are stored on magnetic tapes, and updated regularly, it is common practice to keep the previous two versions of the file, together with the amendments used to update them. This is called the **grandfather-father-son** principle, each version being a **generation** of the file. If the current generation of the file is lost, it can be re-created from the previous generations.

If magnetic disks are used to store a file, then these are periodically copied, or **backed up** onto another magnetic disk or **dumped** onto a magnetic tape. All the data used to update the file since the last dump is kept. Dumping is often done as part of a **housekeeping** process, during which the file is 'tidied up', with out-of-date records being deleted and gaps closed up.

It is essential to keep a **log** of all operations carried out on a file. The log shows the dates on which various updates and backups took place, and includes identification numbers of the various disks and tapes used. Additional security precautions include keeping magnetic disks and tapes in fireproof safes, and storing copies at different sites, away from the computer.

Protection against deliberate data corruption is much more difficult, as it ultimately involves the trustworthiness of staff members. Some of the security precautions which are taken include restriction of access to computer and data preparation rooms, the use of passwords when logging on at terminals, and strict job segregation - programmers may not operate the computer, etc. The data in many secure files is **encrypted** - stored in a code which can only be deciphered by the software which handles the files. In some cases a special hardware 'key' must be attached to the computer before it can read encrypted files.

Good data security is achieved by constant vigilance, and strict adherence to specified procedures, in other words, 'working by the book'. Unfortunately, this tends to make some computing jobs rather tedious.

27.10 Conclusion

This chapter has covered the most common ways in which files of data are processed, and some of the problems which can arise during processing. The main points of the chapter are as follows:

- The main file processing operations are data capture, validation, sorting, merging, searching and updating.
- Validation techniques include type checks, range checks, hash totals, batch totals and the use of check digits.
- Problems which can occur during file processing are overflow, and the long time taken to sort files which are larger than the size of the computer memory.
- Steps must be taken to ensure the security of data against accidental or deliberate corruption. These include keeping up-to-date copies of the data, restricting access to the computer, passwords and data encryption.

Exercise 27

1 Briefly define the following terms: data capture; turnaround document; validation; batch total; hash total; check digit; sorting; merging; searching; sequential search; binary search; tree search; generate-and-test; depth-first search; breadth-first search; updating; file overflow; report generation; data security; grandfather-father-son principle; file dump; file processing log; data encryption.

2 A monthly payroll program requires the input of the following data for each employee: name, employee number, days worked, days on leave, days ill and days absent for any other reason.
   a) Suggest a suitable field layout for the input data, if it is to form one line on a VDU screen.
   b) Which data item is likely to include a check digit?
   c) What additional check(s) can be carried out on the data as it is input?

3 The batch total of a set of data is checked after the data has been input, and is found not to match the batch total which was input with the data. Later checks show that all data items are in fact correct.
   Explain where the error must be, and discuss the limitations on the usefulness of batch totals imposed by this situation.

4 A common method of calculating check digits is as follows: multiply each digit of the number, including the check digit, by a **weighting factor**, and add up the products. The check digit is chosen so that the total thus formed is exactly divisible by a suitable number, usually 11. For example:

number:	3	7	4	6	**5**	check digit
weighting factor:	9	5	3	7	1	
products:	27	+35	+12	+42	+5	= 121, exactly divisible by 11

Using the same set of weighting factors, calculate the check digits for the numbers 6297 and 5116. Use the symbol X if a check digit of 10 is required.

5 Carry out the steps of a quicksort on the following sets of numbers:
  a) 6 14 18 23   5   9 11 12,
  b) 5   9 11   3 14 19   2 27,
  c) 18 16 10 11   8   4   3   7,
  d) 8 15   9 16 10 17 11 18.
Comment on any effects of initial ordering, or partial ordering, on the steps of the process.

6 Assume that a computer memory can only contain four records of a particular file. Use the method outlined in Section 27.5 to sort a file with key values as follows:

17   4   9   21   8   5   20   2   7   11   15   6   3   1   19   13.

7 An informal algorithm for an **insertion sort** in ascending order is as follows:

Partition the file into two strings, the unsorted string followed by the sorted string.

For each record in the unsorted string, repeat

  Scan the sorted string until the first record is found with a key less than that of the record from the unsorted string.

  Move the record from the unsorted string to the position in front of the record located in the sorted string, moving the records in between forward by one position. (This also moves the boundary between the sorted and unsorted strings forward.)

For example, the steps to sort a string of four records are as follows. The boundary between the sorted and unsorted strings is marked |.

Initial situation: 35 11 47 18 |

Insert 35:   11 47 18 | 35

Insert 11:   47 18 | 11 35

Insert 47:   18 | 11 35 47

Insert 18: | 11 18 35 47

  a) Carry out the steps of an insertion sort in ascending order on each of the following sets of data:
     79 43 12 82 23 47
     45 34 56 23 18 14 12
     23 34 43 18 56 67 78
  b) Comment on the extent to which the data is 'shuffled' in each case, relative to the degree of ordering already present.

8 An informal algorithm for a **selection sort** in ascending order is as follows:

Partition the file into two strings, the unsorted string followed by the sorted string.

Repeat
  Select the record with the highest key in the unsorted string.
  Move this record to the front of the sorted string, moving the intervening records forward by one place. This moves the boundary of the sorted string forward by one place.

Until all records have been placed in the sorted string.

For example, the steps to sort a string of four records are as follows. The boundary between the sorted and unsorted strings is marked |.

Initial situation: 35 11 47 18 |

First pass: 35 11 18 | 47

Second pass: 11 18 | 35 47

Third pass: 11 | 18 35 47

Fourth pass: | 11 18 35 47

  a) Carry out the steps of a selection sort in ascending order on each of the following sets of data:
     79 43 12 82 23 47
     45 34 56 23 18 14 12
     23 34 43 18 56 67 78

b) Comment on the extent to which the data is 'shuffled' in each case, relative to the degree of ordering already present.

c) Compare the efficiency of the insertion and selection sort techniques.

9 Outline the steps of a binary search to locate the record with key 19 from a file with keys as follows:

4 7 8 10 11 19 23 31.

10 During the updating of a file, stored on magnetic tape, a power failure occurs. Both the source and the updated copies of the file are corrupted. Outline the steps involved in re-creating the up-to-date version of the file.

11 During the updating of a file stored on a magnetic disk, a **disk crash** occurs. The read-write head comes into contact with the surface of the disk, destroying the disk and damaging the disk drive. Outline the steps involved in re-creating the file.

12 Outline some of the measures taken to protect data from deliberate interference. Give your opinion on the effectiveness of these measures, and the wider implications of their use.

13 A suite of programs has been designed to maintain a file of credit accounts for a large number of bank customers. Each customer is allowed a specified amount of credit and the system keeps a record of his balance by processing transactions nightly.

Give a list of the programs required and their functions in the system.

Describe what procedures would be built into the programs to validate the input data.

Suggest how the file would be stored and justify your choice.

UL 78 II

14 a) Explain why the sorting of computer files of data is a process which may be frequently encountered in a data processing system.

b) Describe a procedure for the sorting of data on magnetic tape, assuming that two additional tape decks are available for the sort.

c) A generalised sort package has been written to sort data on magnetic tape. List the parameters which you would expect to supply in order to use such a package.

15 A gas board has about one million customers, each with a gas meter identified by a unique code of 8 digits; the code includes a check digit. The meter readings are of 6 figures, and readings are taken every 3 months. If a meter cannot be read an estimated reading is calculated. Describe how you would set about designing a computer system for the gas board, for the input of meter readings and the production of bills. Your description should contain:

a) a diagram showing the main activities within the system and their interrelationships;

b) a list of the files used with details of their structures, their expected sizes, the media on which they would be held and the arrangements for back-up copies;

c) the reasons for the choice of input medium;

d) details of the types of validation to which the input data is subjected;

e) a brief list of items to be covered in the documentation for the operators, for the management and for the programmers who are responsible for the maintenance of the system's software.

UCLES 81 Specimen I

28
Databases

This chapter introduces a relatively new, but rapidly developing area of computing, namely **databases**. The chapter explains the nature of a database, and discusses some of the advantages of using one. The topic is presented in broad outline only, as a detailed study requires some difficult concepts, and is beyond the scope of this course.

One example is used to illustrate several of the points raised in the chapter. This example concerns a potential user of a database, namely a mail order retailer, selling a wide variety of goods from a number of warehouses to customers throughout the country. Although this example is not a case study, it is nevertheless a very realistic application of a database.

28.1 What is a Database?

This question is first investigated in an informal way, before a precise definition of a database is given.

Most organisations which use a computer do so for more than one application. In the case of the mail order retailer, applications might include customer accounts, stock control and payroll systems. Each of these applications requires a large volume of stored data. The traditional approach to the storage of this data is to use files, as described in the two previous chapters. Each application has its own set of files, containing the data it needs, and structured according to its method of processing. In most cases, because all the applications are for the same organisation, there is a large degree of overlap of data between the files for the various applications.

If these files are replaced by a single, large, suitably organised collection of data, accessed by all the applications, then this collection of data is a **database**. In the case of the mail order retailer, the database is a single collection of data used for customer accounts, stock control and payroll applications.

A concise definition of a database is as follows:

A database is a collection of stored operational data used by all the application systems of an organisation.

The general idea of a database is illustrated in Figure 28.1.

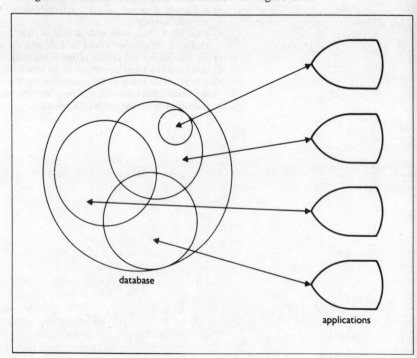

database

applications

Figure 28.1
A database: general concept

28.2 Advantages of Databases

Using a single, centralised store of data for all applications has a number of advantages. These include:

- Consistency of data: when a data item is updated, its up-to-date value is available to all users. This ensures that the data used by all the applications is consistent.
- Less data proliferation: because only one copy of each data item is kept, duplication of data is eliminated.
- Ease of setting up of new applications: when a new application is contemplated, much of the data it needs is probably already on the database. Extending the database and providing a new interface is generally quicker than starting the new application from scratch.
- Easier security monitoring: because all access to data is via a centralised system, a uniform system of security monitoring can be implemented. In most cases this is more effective than a number of separate security systems.

Databases do also have disadvantages. These are discussed in the assessment at the end of the chapter.

To get a more concrete idea of the advantages of using a database, consider again the example of the mail order retailer. Before the introduction of the database, every sale of goods to a customer required both stock control files and customer account files to be updated. This involved a duplication of effort, and any errors could lead to inconsistencies between the two files. With a database, only one update is required.

28.3 Database Concepts

There are two concepts essential to an understanding of databases: the ideas of data models and data independence.

Data Models

Although a database is a single collection of data, the data must appear to be different when viewed from different parts of the database system. Each user of the database must see a set of data suited to the particular application. Furthermore, the logical structure of the data might be different from the way it is physically represented on backing store media.

The way around these problems is the idea of a **data model**. A data model is the logical structure of the data as it appears at a particular level of the database system. Each user of the database has a different data model. For the example of the mail order retailer, consider the stock control and accounting applications.

The data model for the stock control application might be a set of **item records**, each containing an item number and a supplier. Associated with each item record is a set of stock movements, each comprising a date and a quantity supplied or dispatched. This data model is illustrated in Figure 28.2.

On the other hand, the data model for the customer accounting application might be a set of **customer records**, each containing a customer number and customer details. Associated with each customer record is a set of transactions. Each transaction includes a date, item number, quantity and price. This data model is illustrated in Figure 28.3.

In addition, there is the data model associated with the database as a whole. This model depicts the ideal, logical structure of the data, independent of the media on which the data is stored. All other data models are derived from this central model. It is the task of the various layers of the database system software to create and maintain these data models. The words **transformation** or **mapping** are used for the process of creating one data model from another.

	item number	supplier
item record	N 423 961 X	A. M. Jones

	date	quantity	
stack movements	03/08/80	4801	s
	03/08/80	5	d
	04/08/80	11	d
	05/08/80	7	d
	06/08/80	23	d

s = supplied
d = dispatched

Figure 28.2
Stock control data model

	customer number	customer details
customer record	C 491 267 4	P. Sharp 4 Elm Street Ashton

	date	item number	quantity	price
transactions	04/08/80	N 436 215 4	1	10.45
	04/08/80	N 391 204 9	1	23.16
	05/08/80	N 423 961 x	3	9.95
	10/08/80	N 104 723 5	2	38.47

Figure 28.3
Accounting data model

Data Independence

You will recall that a database is a large store of operational data. Because it is operational, it is changing all the time. Data items are constantly being updated, and new data is being added. In most cases, the total volume of data is increasing. On the other hand, new and improved data storage media are constantly becoming available. These are generally cheaper, more compact and quicker to access than before.

For these reasons, it is necessary from time to time to replace the media on which the data is stored. If applications referred directly to the storage media, this would require amendments to every applications program. These amendments would be slow, error-prone and costly.

Accordingly, the central data model of the database, and the user data models derived from it, are independent of the physical storage of the data. One level of the database system software is devoted to mapping the central data model onto the physical representation of the data. If the storage media are changed, only this layer of software needs to be altered.

This discussion gives rise to the idea of **data independence**. Data independence is when the logical structure of the data, i.e. the central data model, and associated user data models, are distinct from the arrangement of the data on any particular backing store medium. The data models are unaffected by any changes in techniques of storing the data.

28.4 A Database System

In common with most aspects of computing, a database is part of a system, namely a **database system**. A database system consists of the stored data, the various data models, a piece of software called a **database management system**, and a person called a **database administrator**. Figure 28.4 illustrates the overall structure of a database system.

The **database management system (DBMS)** is a large and complex piece of software, responsible for all aspects of the creation, accessing and updating of the database. Tasks it performs include transforming or mapping the data from one model to another, or between the central data model and the stored database. All interactions between users and the database are dealt with by the DBMS. This includes carrying out various security checks. A database management system is a real-time system, and has much in common with an operating system.

The **database administrator (DBM)** is the person in charge of the overall running of the database system. Duties of a database administrator include deciding on the information content of the database and the structure of the various data models, deciding how the data is to be stored, liaising with users, and defining a strategy for back-up storage and recovery from breakdown. This job requires a combination of software and managerial skills.

28.5 Structuring the Data Model

The central decision in the design of a database system is the structure of the data model. Almost every other aspect of a database system depends on this structure. Because the database is large, and there are many relationships existing between individual data items, a satisfactory structuring of the data is very difficult to achieve. Objectives of a well structured data model include efficiency of storage, ease of transformation to other models, speed of access to data and ease of modification of the model.

Three approaches to the structuring of data models are discussed. These are the **hierarchical**, **network** and **relational** approaches. Historically, these approaches have been developed in this order, with relational databases being the most recent, and rapidly becoming the most popular.

The Hierarchical Approach

The hierarchical approach involves creating a tree structure for the data. Different data items are stored at different levels, with some levels being 'below' others in the tree. The problem with the hierarchical approach is that not all databases fit naturally into a tree structure.

Figure 28.5 shows an attempt to create a hierarchical model of the data for the mail order retailer's database. Two levels of the hierarchy are shown, namely the customer/supplier record level, below which is a level of trading records. Each customer/supplier record has one or more trading records associated with it.

The Network Approach

In an attempt to overcome the rigidity of the hierarchical approach, the network approach to structuring a data model has been developed. In this approach, data items are linked to other data items by pointers, forming a network. Information is extracted by traversing the network in various ways.

Figure 28.6 shows a network data model for the mail order retailer's database. Notice how information is extracted by following various arrows through the network.

The Relational Approach

The relational approach is the newest and most promising method of structuring a data model. Using this approach, the data is presented as a set of tables, each

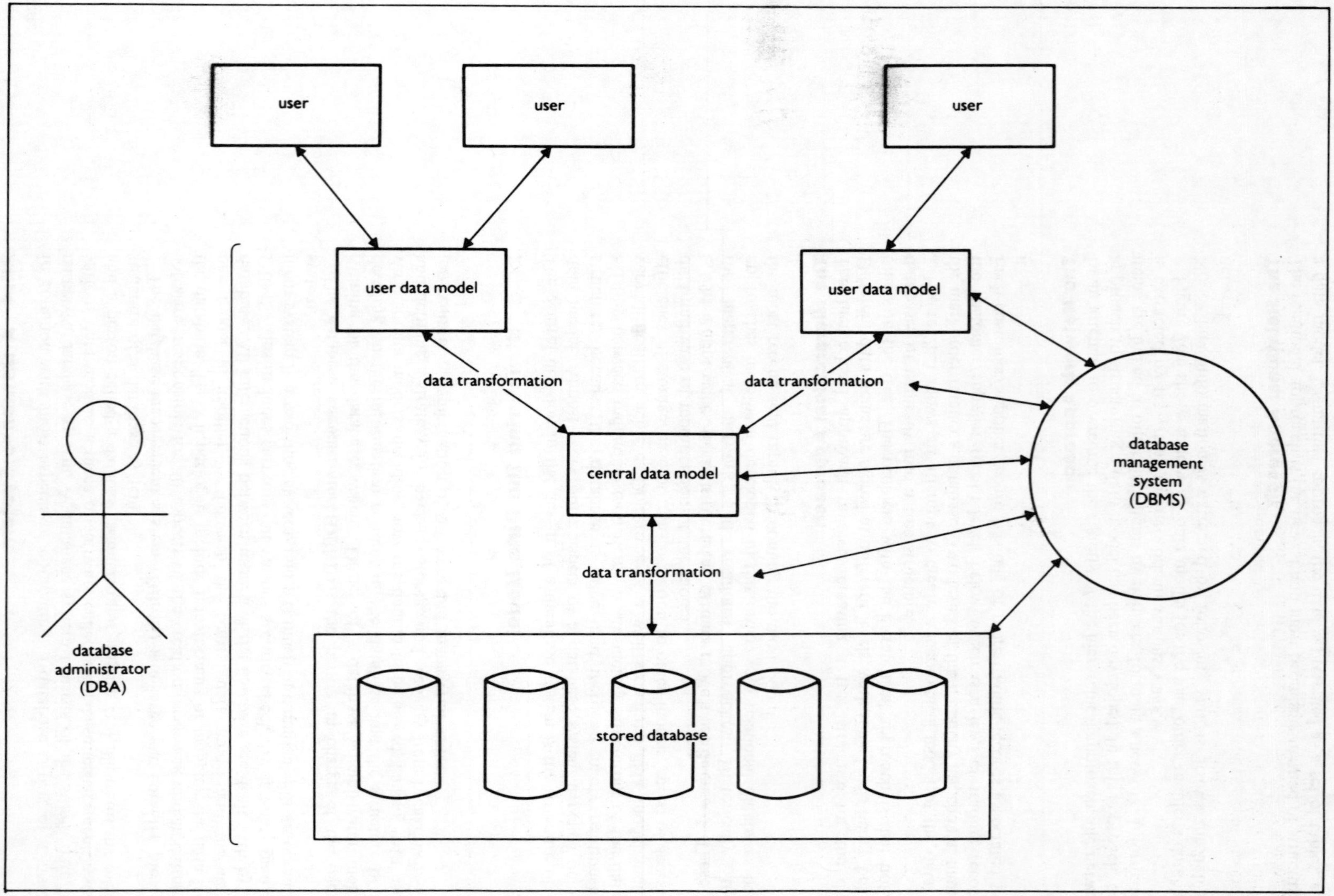

Figure 28.4
A database system

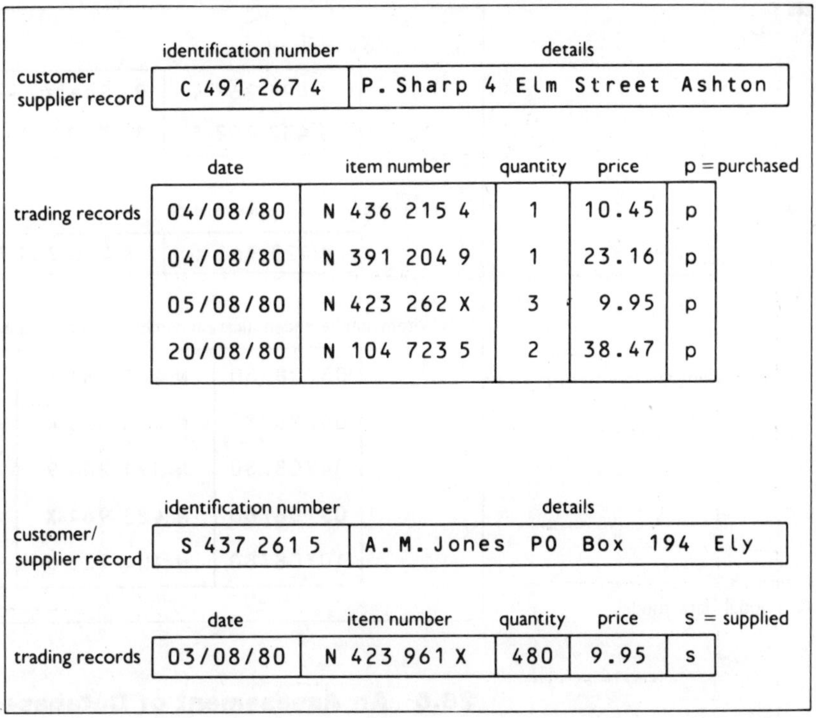

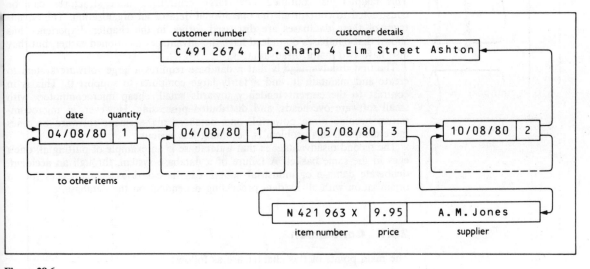

Figure 28.5
Hierarchical data model

Figure 28.6
Network data model

table representing a relationship existing between two or more data items. The model can be transformed by combining relationships via a common data item and deleting unwanted data items.

Figure 28.7 shows a relational data model for the mail order retailer's database. The tables can be joined to produce invoices and purchase orders. The item numbers and identification numbers are common columns.

The relational data model has the benefits of simplicity of concept, economy of storage, and a wide variety of applications which seem to fit naturally onto its structure. It is being used as the basis of fourth generation software development tools (Chapter 23) and is likely to be used extensively in fifth generation systems (Chapter 34).

identification/details relation

C 491 267 4	P. Sharp 4 Elm Street Ashton
S 437 262 5	A. M. Jones PO Box 194 Ely

item number/supplier/price relation

N 423 961 X	S 436 261 5	9.95

date/item numbers/identification number/quantity/transaction type relation

03/08/80	N 423 961 X	S 437 262 5	480	s
04/08/80	N 436 225 4	C 491 267 4	1	p
04/08/80	N 391 204 9	C 491 267 4	1	p
05/08/80	N 423 961 X	C 491 267 4	3	p
10/08/80	N 104 723 5	C 491 267 4	2	p

Figure 28.7
Relational data model

28.6 An Assessment of Databases

This chapter has outlined how large centralised data structures can be
constructed to contain all the operational data of an organisation. The advantages of these databases are discussed earlier in the chapter. Experience has
shown that databases do indeed have the advantages mentioned earlier, but they
also have two major disadvantages.

The first disadvantage is that a database requires a large software system to
create and maintain it, and a fairly large computer to support it. This is in
contrast to the current tendency towards small, cheap microcomputers with
small software overheads, and distributed processing. However, as microcomputers become more powerful, and database management software becomes
more compact, this problem is becoming less serious.

The second disadvantage is that a database is an example of putting all one's
eggs in the same basket. A failure of a database system, through an accident,
deliberate damage or industrial action, can have serious consequences for an
organisation with all its data processing dependent on the database.

28.7 Conclusion

The main points of this chapter are as follows:

- A database is a collection of stored operational data used by all the application systems in an organisation.
- A data model is the logical structure of a database as it appears at a particular layer of the database system.
- Data independence is when the logical structure of the data model is
independent of its physical structure on any particular backing store
medium.
- A database management system is the software which maintains the
database and supports all the applications which use the data.
- The three common approaches to data models are the hierarchical, network
and relational data models.

Exercise 28

1 Briefly define the following terms: database; data model; data independence; database system; DBMS; DBA; hierarchical data model; network data model; relational data model.

2 You will recall that a system is a collection of parts working together towards some common objectives. List the objectives of a database system.

3 Explain, in your own words, the significance of the concept of data independence.

4 Summarise the advantages and disadvantages of the use of databases.

●5 A news reporting agency uses a database system to store the text of all news items. News reports are supplied, by telex, by a number of correspondents, and then purchased by a number of newspapers and magazines.

The model of the data, from the correspondents' point of view, is as follows:

Correspondent record

Identity	Name
K 347 P	JOHN GREGGOROWSKI

News items supplied

Date	Text
05/11/80	TODAY RUSSIAN TANKS....
07/11/80	STRIKES IN POLAND....
08/11/80	URGENT DISCUSSIONS ARE....
11/11/80	THE SITUATION IS DETERIORATING....
12/11/80	NO SIGN OF AN END....

The model of the data, from the newspapers' point of view, is as follows:

Newspaper record

Identity	Name
N 417	WASHINGTON STAR

News items purchased

Date	Correspondent Identity	Text
04/11/80	K 007 L	LONDON EXPERIENCED....
07/11/80	K 347 P	STRIKES IN POLAND....
07/11/80	K 007 L	MISS WORLD....
09/11/80	K 291 A	ARGENTINA'S DICTATOR....
12/11/80	K 347 P	NO SIGN OF AN END....

a) Using *either* the relational or the hierarchical or the network approach, draw up a central data model for this system.

b) Explain how your data model can be used to determine which newspapers have bought any particular news item.

●6 Design in outline a suitable simple database system of your own. State the data model for each application, and also the central data model of the system.

7 RAPPORT is a relational database system first marketed by Logica Limited. It can be used on a wide variety of mini and mainframe computers. Find out about the system, specifically how concepts introduced in this chapter are implemented. (Alternatively use dBase II from Ashton-Tate as a case study.)

29
Data
Communication

Over the past century, a number of communications networks have been developed, to the stage where they now encircle the globe and reach into space. Radio, television and telephone links enable hundreds of millions of people to keep in contact with each other, often over distances of thousands of miles.

Although the earliest forms of communication systems used a digital code (the Morse code) for information transmission, the bulk of the development of these networks has been for voice and picture transmission (with the important exception of the telex system). With the advent of computers, the situation is changing again. Information is being sent, in digital form, in increasing quantities, as more and more computers are being linked to the local and global communications networks. The telecommunications networks in all industrial countries are in the process of changing from analogue to digital transmission. The combination of computers and communications systems is one of the major areas of technological development at present. It may yet have as profound an impact on the lifestyles of millions of people as the advent of computers, or of telephones, radio or television had in their time.

This chapter is a brief introduction to the field of data communication. The topic is discussed from several angles. The first part of the chapter concerns the way in which data is transmitted between two computers, or between a peripheral device and a computer. The second part of the chapter outlines some of the hardware configurations which can be built up around a data communication network. The use of computers as exchanges in digital telecommunications networks is also discussed. The chapter concludes with two case studies of data communications systems.

29.1 Concepts of Data Transmission

This section discusses some concepts relating to the transmission of data, in digital form, along a communications medium. These concepts are much the same whether the communication medium is a wire, a radio or a fibre optics link.

Bit Serial Transmission

Just as data is always stored and processed in a computer in binary form, so is it transmitted between computers in a binary form. Individual bits are grouped together to code characters, and characters are grouped together to form larger data structures.

If two digital devices are very close to each other, it is possible to connect them by a multi-strand cable which can transmit a number of bits simultaneously. This is **parallel** data transmission. In the majority of cases, where data is to be transmitted over any distance, a single carrier is used. In these circumstances, only one bit at a time is transmitted. This is called **bit serial** transmission.

Broadband and Baseband Communication

It is possible to transmit the binary values 0 and 1 over short distances using the presence or absence of a voltage, or a positive and a negative voltage to represent these values. When a fibre optics link of any distance is used, the situation is also very simple: a pulse of light signals a 1; no pulse signals a 0. Data transmission where the presence or the absence of a signal signifies a 0 or a 1 is known as **baseband** transmission.

For long distance communications by wire or by radio, a more sophisticated technique known as **broadband** transmission is required. There is a **carrier signal** of a high frequency, on top of which the data signals are sent. In most cases, variations in the carrier frequency are used, one type for a 0 and the other for a 1. Broadband communications systems allow a higher throughput of data than baseband systems, and are less prone to noise. The details of broadband and baseband techniques are beyond the scope of this course. It is sufficient to know that an **interfacing** device is placed at each end of the transmission line, to transmit and receive the appropriate signals for 0 and 1. Interfaces generally deal with the conversion of parallel data from the computer or peripheral device to serial data for the transmission line.

One of the commonest types of communications interfaces is called a **modem** (for **mod**ulator/**dem**odulator). Another device, which links with an ordinary telephone, is called an **acoustic coupler**. Both transmit and receive serial data along telephone lines.

The serial transmission of a set of characters is illustrated in Figure 29.1. Notice how the beginning and end of the bits for each character is marked.

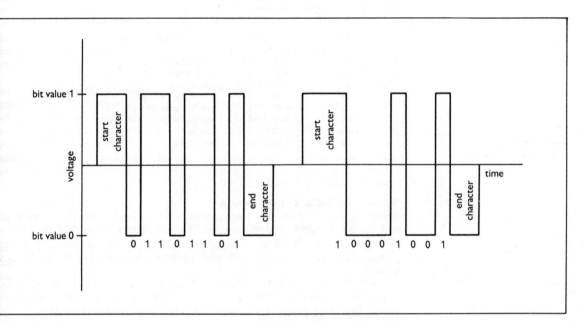

Figure 29.1
Bit serial data transmission

Simplex and Duplex

Verbal communication between people is not possible if both talk at once, or each waits for the other to speak. Similarly, in data communication, there must be ways of establishing in which direction transmission is taking place at any one time. There are three approaches to this problem, as outlined below.

Simplex communication is where transmission is in one direction only. This may be used, for example, for transmission of data from a remote input device to a processor.

Half duplex communication is where transmission may be in either direction, but not in both directions simultaneously. In other words, at any given instant, transmission is in one direction only. Ways of indicating that transmission is complete, and that the direction may therefore be reversed, are dealt with in the next section.

Full duplex communication is where transmission may proceed in both directions at the same time. This is the most sophisticated form of data communication.

Data Transmission Codes

Data transmission is an area where standardisation is very important. Any two items of equipment which adopt the same standards of data communication can be linked together.

One of the most essential standards in data communications is a code for the binary representation of characters. Fortunately there has been a very wide measure of agreement on this matter. Only a few character codes are used in data transmission, and one code, the **American Standard Code for Information Interchange (ASCII)**, is gaining prominence. An increasing proportion of data communication is in this code. (As mentioned in Chapter 3, this code is becoming increasingly popular for the internal representation of data in computers.)

Data transmission codes include representations of letters, digits and punctuation marks, as well as a number of **control characters**. These characters only have relevance to the transmission of data, and are not used for the storage or processing of data. For example, there are characters to signal the end of transmission, or the start of a block of data. The codes for some of the ASCII control characters are shown in Figure 29.2.

hexadecimal	binary	interpretation
01	00000001	start of header
02	00000010	start of text
03	00000011	end of text
04	00000100	end of transmission
05	00000101	enquire, who are you?
06	00000110	acknowledge
07	00000111	ring bell
08	00001000	backspace

Figure 29.2
ASCII control characters

Speeds of Data Transmission

Speeds of data transmission vary considerably, depending on the application, and the data communication medium. The unit of measurement of data transmission rates is the **baud**. The precise definition of the baud is rather complicated, but it may, for practical purposes, be regarded as one bit per second.

On an ordinary telephone line, a data transmission rate of 1200 or 2400 baud is generally used. On special lines, this rate may increase to 9600 baud (9.6K baud). Even higher rates are possible on other communication media.

Packets

When one writes a letter, the pages are placed in an envelope, which is generally of a standard size. A similar principle is used in many data communication systems. Data is transmitted, not in single characters, or groups of characters, but in packets.

A packet is a set of transmitted data, enclosed by strings of control characters. The control characters at the start and end of the packet follow a strict set of rules. The data within the packet is of a standard structure. A packet is the unit of transmission and reception within a particular data communication network. All devices connected to the network send and receive data in packets of the same type.

Communication Protocols

When one sends a letter, one must follow a number of rules imposed by the Post Office. For example, the address must be set out in a certain way, and the stamp must be in the top right hand corner of the envelope. Similar rules apply in the case of data transmission. These rules are called communication **protocols**.

Among other things, a protocol specifies the structure of a packet of data, what control characters are used and what procedures are followed for the transmission and reception of data. For half duplex transmission, the protocol specifies the procedure for changing the direction of transmission. Many communications protocols permit the data in packets to be **compressed**. Compression aims to reduce the number of characters which actually need to be transmitted, for example, by representing repeated characters as a counter followed by the character.

The advantage of a communication protocol is this: any two devices which use the same communication protocol can be linked together. For this reason, communication protocols are designed very carefully, in order to be as widely applicable as possible. At present, there are only a small number of protocols in widespread use.

Errors in Data Transmission

We all have experience of bad telephone lines, poor radio reception and erratic television pictures. These are all caused by interference, or **noise**, in the communications medium. Although careful design and higher quality (and more expensive) equipment can reduce the amount of noise, it can never be eliminated entirely.

Data communication is not immune to the problem of noise, although the situation benefits from the nature of digital transmission. As long as the signal for a 0 can be distinguished from that for a 1, a bit is correctly received. However, there is always a small probability that noise will cause the wrong bit value to be detected.

As it is impossible to prevent bits from being detected wrongly, the best that can be done is to try to detect when an error has occurred, and, in some cases, locate and correct the error. Most data transmission codes incorporate checks on the data transmitted. The commonest check is the inclusion of a **parity bit** in the code for each character. The question of parity is discussed in Section 3.12. Other checks include the insertion of **check characters**, or groups of check characters, as discussed in Section 14.7. One type of error correcting code, called the **Hamming code**, is discussed in the exercise at the end of this chapter.

29.2 Communications Networks

This section describes the commonest types of data communications networks. The different types of network introduced here are not to be regarded as rigid stereotypes, but merely as examples of common communications configurations.

Central Processor with Terminals

A large central processor linked to a number of remote-access terminals is the 'traditional' approach to data communication. This arrangement is illustrated in Figure 29.3. A refinement of this idea is to collect the lines to a number of terminals together at a suitable point, and connect this point to the processor by a single high volume data link. The device at the linking site is called a **multiplexer** or **cluster adaptor**. This technique is illustrated in Figure 29.4.

Intelligent Terminals

Instead of centralising all the processing in a computer network at one site, an increasingly common configuration makes use of **intelligent terminals**. The structure of the network is the same as that shown in Figures 29.3 and 29.4, but processing is shared between the CPU and the terminals. In many systems, the intelligent terminals are microcomputers which can be used on their own or as network workstations.

Computer Networks

Computer networks can include more than one processor, as shown in Figure 29.5. The processors can be long distances apart, connected by radio, telephone or satellite communication links, or they can be close together, often in the same building. The latter situation is known as a **local area network**. Local area networks are an increasingly popular computer configuration. They generally consist of a number of **workstations** and one or more **file servers**. The workstations are microcomputers with network interfaces, and the file servers have the disk drives which are shared by all the workstations.

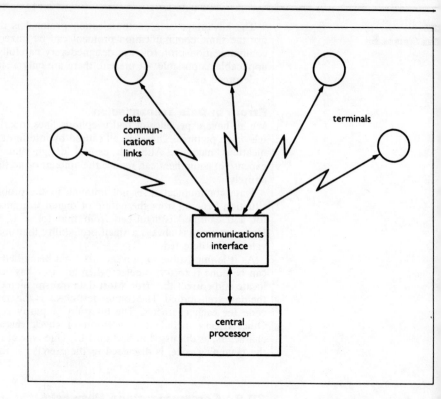

Figure 29.3
A terminal network

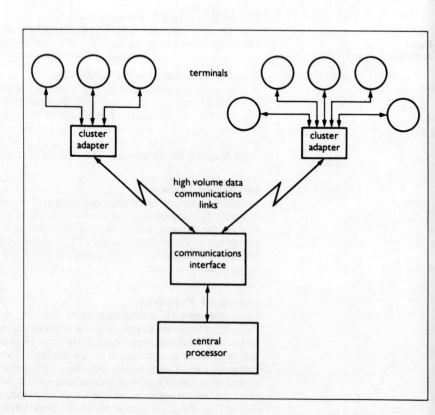

Figure 29.4
Multiplexing

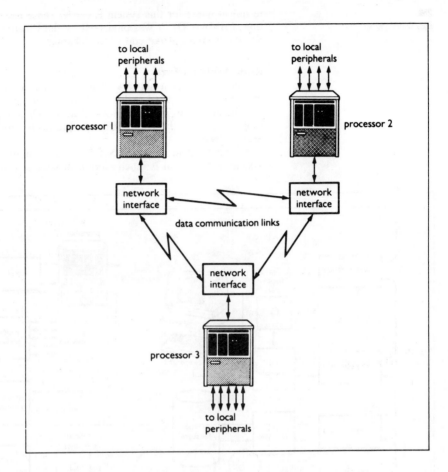

Figure 29.5
A computer network

There are several advantages of processors linked in this way. Resources such as disk drives and printers can be shared amongst the processors. The processing load is shared evenly between the processors. This is particularly significant if the processors are in different time zones, where off-peak times at one processor correspond to busy periods at others. The other major advantage is that a breakdown at one processor does not put the whole system out of action.

The major disadvantage of such a network is the size and complexity of the operating system required to control the network. A significant proportion of the time of each processor is spent doing 'housekeeping' tasks, in order to keep the network as a whole functioning smoothly.

29.3 Local Area Network Architecture

There are two approaches to local area network architecture: **common carrier cables**, and **ring architecture**.

Common Carrier Architecture

The majority of local area networks are connected by coaxial cable like that used for television aerials. The communications protocol is very simple: when a station has data to transmit, it waits until the carrier is quiet, and then sends its packets of data. The data is addressed to one or more destination stations. Every station receives the data, but only those to which it is addressed retain it. If two stations start transmitting at the same time, they detect a **collision** and stop sending. They wait for a short random interval of time before starting again. The technical name for this system is **carrier sense multi-access with collision detection (CSMA/CD)**. It was pioneered by the **Ethernet** local area network system. See the exercise at the end of this chapter.

Ring Architecture

A type of local area network currently under development is based on the idea of a **ring**. As illustated in Figure 29.6, the ring connects all the processors and peripheral devices in the network. Data travels in one direction only around the ring. Details of the communication protocols are given in the case study in Section 29.6.

A ring local area network is faster and more resilient than a CSMA/CD system. However, it is much more expensive to install.

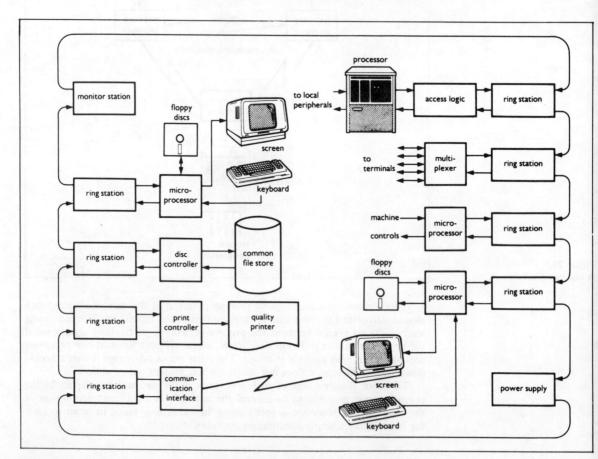

Figure 29.6
Ring architecture

29.4 Message and Packet Switching

Message switching is the work performed by a telephone exchange. It involves establishing a link between the originator of a call and the receiver of the call. The equipment interprets the digits of a dialled number by setting a series of switches. When all the switches have been set, the call is linked to its destination. The traditional mechanical apparatus still in use in many areas is slow, cumbersome and requires extensive maintenance to keep it in operation.

The modern technique of message switching involves the use of computers and digital telecommunications. Using specially designed hardware and software, these **electronic exchanges** can link lines extremely rapidly, keep records of which numbers have been connected, and supply the information necessary for the preparation of telephone bills. Digital electronic exchanges are software controlled, making them very flexible in use. Most circuits are duplicated, giving them a high level of **redundancy** to be able to cope with component failures. Digital electronic exchanges are being introduced into the telephone systems of most industrial countries. Examples include the **System X** developed by Plessey for British Telecom.

Similar to message switching, but used for computer data only, is **packet switching**. A packet switching network is a long-distance communications network between computers, using a combination of high-speed telephone lines, satellite links and microwave radio channels. See Figure 29.7. All data is sent in packets, as described in Section 29.1. The 'exchanges' on the system are **packet switching computers**. These receive incoming packets and route them according to their addresses. They may store the packets if the destination computer is not ready to accept them. They also act as an interface between communications links which may have different data transmission speeds. An example of a packet switching network is the **Swift** system for electronic funds transfer between banks.

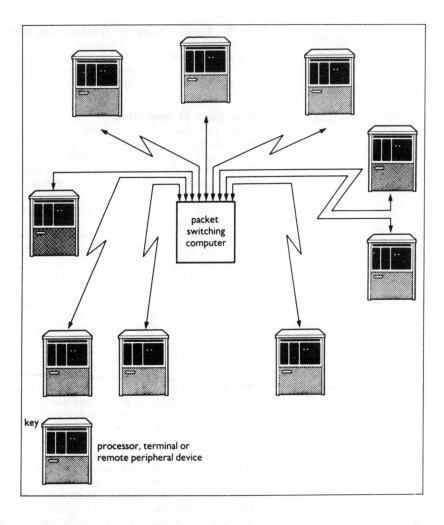

packet
switching
computer

key

processor, terminal or
remote peripheral device

Figure 29.7
A packet switching network

29.5 Case Study 1: Pixnet

A Pixnet data communication system consists of a set of units, each with associated software, which control all aspects of data communication within a network. The system is independent of any host computer, and works in such a way that all devices linked to the network appear to be local to each other. The Pixnet equipment handles such matters as data compression and re-routing of messages in the event of a line failure. Figure 29.8 shows a typical network configuration using these devices.

Network control units (NCU) are located at switching points in the network. These enable any device in the network to be linked to any other device. An NCU can also route data along alternative communication lines in the event of a line failure, or to minimise transmission costs. Attached to an NCU is the **network administrator's console** which provides overall network control, and supplies information on the current status of the network.

Local control units (LCU) provide the interface between processors and the data communications network. All data is presented by the LCU to the processor as if it originates from a local device. **Remote control units (RCU)** provide interfaces between remote peripheral devices and the data communication network. The actual communication links can be telephone lines, radio links, fibre optics connections, satellite links, or any combination of these.

29.6 Case Study 2: Cambridge Ring

The **Cambridge Ring** is the basic design for a local area network based on a data communication ring. It was first developed at Cambridge University in 1974, and versions of it are currently being marketed by several companies.

Principles of Operation

Figure 29.6 shows the arrangment of a typical ring. It consists of a number of **ring stations**, joined by a cable in a continuous loop. Each station has storage for a few bits of data, and the signal delay in the cable creates storage for additional bits in transit. The stations and the cable may be thought of as a circular shift register, around which bits circulate at high speed, generally 10 megabits per second.

The circulating bits are organised into one or more **slots**, and a gap. Slots generally comprise about 40 bits. Any station may insert a **mini-packet** of data into a free slot as it passes. The mini-packet contains the address of the sending station, the address of the receiving station, two bytes of data, some control bits and a parity bit.

The mini-packet circulates around the ring until it reaches the station to which it is addressed. If the station is ready to receive, it copies the mini-packet into its internal registers, and marks the packet as accepted. The mini-packet continues around the ring until it again reaches the station which transmitted it. The station notes whether or not the mini-packet has been accepted, and marks it as free. To prevent one station from dominating the ring, a station must skip a slot before it can use another slot.

The Monitor Station

The monitor station is responsible for starting up the ring, determining the number of slots in circulation and detecting and recovering from errors.

Each station checks the parity of all passing mini-packets. If a parity error is noted, an error mini-packet is sent to the monitor station. The monitor station fills all empty slots with random bits, and checks them if they return still empty. If the ring breaks, the first station 'downstream' of the break sends a continuous stream of fault packets to the monitor station. In these ways, a number of error checks are built into the ring. The monitor station plays an important part in the error detection process.

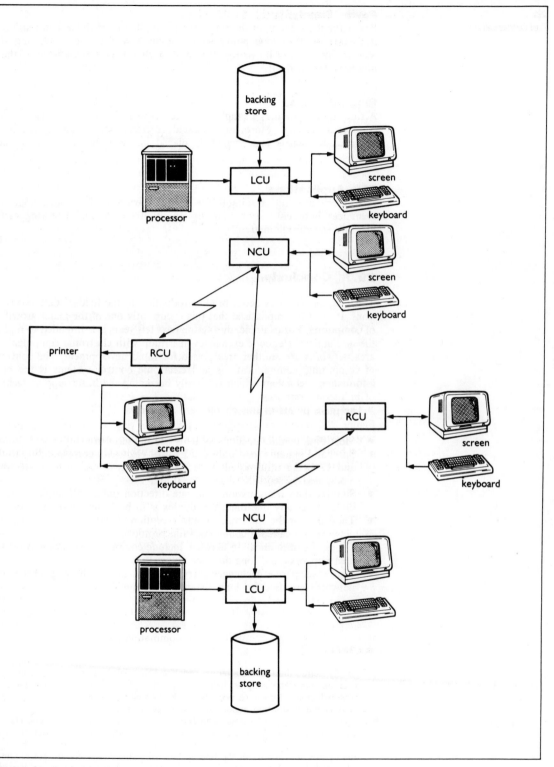

Figure 29.8
A Pixnet network

Power Supply

Power for the running of the ring itself is supplied from the monitor station and from one or more **ring power supply stations** in the ring. Each ring station requires local power for its registers, but the ring itself is not affected if the local power is switched off.

Ring Interfaces

A ring station provides a simple interface between the ring and a wide variety of connected devices. More sophisticated interfaces to certain processors are provided by **access logic**, which is placed between the ring station and the processor.

Ring Applications

A Cambridge Ring is suitable for a wide variety of local area applications. Distances between stations can be up to 100m. A complete ring can thus measure several kilometres.

29.7 Conclusion

This chapter has provided a brief introduction to the field of data communications. It must be emphasised that this is currently one of the major growth areas of computing. For example, during the next ten years it is intended to replace all the mechanical telephone exchanges in Britain with electronic equipment. Local area networks are another area poised for rapid development. The convergence of computing, communications and electronic control systems is the basis of **information technology** which is rapidly becoming the basic support technology of industrial countries.

The main points of this chapter are as follows:

- Most data communications systems use bit serial transmission.
- Baseband systems send pulses of light or electricity corresponding to the 0's and 1's being transmitted; broadband systems use a carrier wave which is modulated to send the signals for 0 and 1.
- Simplex data transmission is in one direction only; half duplex is in either direction at any one time; full duplex is in both directions simultaneously.
- The rules for the transmission and reception of data on a particular type of network are called a communication protocol.
- Types of communication network include computer terminal networks, local area networks and long-distance networks.
- Digital telephone exchanges carry out message switching; packet switching networks are used for long-distance computer links.

Exercise 29

1 Briefly define the following terms: serial and parallel data transmission; broadband; baseband; modem; simplex; half duplex; full duplex; control character; packet; protocol; noise; local area network; packet switching; interface.
2 Why is standardisation important in data communication?
- 3 The screen of a visual display unit shows 20 lines each of 40 characters. Data is transmitted to the VDU in packets, each packet containing the characters for one screen display, in order from the leftmost character of the top line, line by line, to the rightmost character of the bottom line. New-line characters are not required after each line. Data is compressed by representing repeated characters as a counter (occupying one byte, with most significant bit 1), followed by the character. For example, a blank line is represented as follows:

	first byte		second byte	
Binary	1010	1000	0110	0000
Hexadecimal	A	B	6	0
ASCII	Count = 40		space	

a) Write down, in binary, hexadecimal and ASCII, the string of characters needed to transmit a screen display containing the following characters:

A row of dots (Hexadecimal 2E) on the second and nineteenth lines.

The characters **MESSAGE ENDS** starting at the left side of the fourth line, the rest of which is blank.

All other lines blank.

b) Count the number of bytes transmitted, and comment on the effectiveness of the compression system. (Use Figure 3.1 for the ASCII codes of the characters.)

4 In addition to the Pixnet system, and networks based on the Cambridge Ring, there are a number of data communication systems currently available. Most large computer manufacturers market a system. Investigate one of these systems and compare it with the case study in this chapter.

5 A cluster adapter combines a number of 1200 baud lines into a single 9.6K baud line. If multiplexing information accounts for 10 per cent of the data on the high speed line, how many low speed lines can the cluster adaptor accept?

6 The Prestel **Viewdata** system, marketed by British Telecom in the UK and a number of other countries, is a system which is likely to have a considerable impact. The user interface of the system is a specially adapted television set which connects to an ordinary telephone line. The system is supported by a number of minicomputers, one in each major population centre. Having dialled into the system, users can access 'pages' of information on a wide variety of topics, using a simple hand-held keypad for control.

a) Find out more about the services provided by the Prestel system.

b) Draw a diagram showing the configuration of the Prestel network.

c) Find out how information is supplied to the system.

d) Write a report on your findings, and comment on likely development areas of the Prestel system.

7 A code which will detect and correct single-bit errors is the **Hamming code**. This code requires a number of even parity check bits in a data item. They are distributed in such a way that they do not check on each other.

Three check bits are required for a four bit data item, as shown in the table below:

			B1		B2	B3	B4
Data bits:			B1		B2	B3	B4
Check bits:	C1	C2		C3			
Digit numbers:	D1	D2	D3	D4	D5	D6	D7
Example	1	0	1	1	0	1	0
Check 1	*		*		*		*
Check 2		*	*			*	*
Check 3				*	*	*	*

In the example, the data bits are 1010 and the check bits are 101.

The digits are numbered from left to right, and the checks are determined by the binary equivalent of these digit numbers, expressed in the pattern of asterisks in the last three lines.

Each row of asterisks starts with a check bit. The remaining asterisks in the row indicate the data bits whose parity is indicated by the check bit. For example, the check bit C2 tests the parity of data bits B1, B3 and B4.

If a single bit error occurs, the three checks are sufficient to locate and thus correct the error.

For example, if the data is corrupted to 1011110, the checks are as follows:

Data: 1 0 1 1 1 1 0
Check 1: 1   1   1   0   fail (value 1)
Check 2:   0 1   1 0   pass (value 0)
Check 3:   1 1 1 0   fail (value 1)

If a check fails, it is given the value 1, and if it passes, the value 0. The binary number thus formed indicates the position of the digit which is wrong. In the above example, the number is 101, indicating that the fifth digit is in error, which is in fact the case.

a) Locate and correct the errors in each of the following data items, with Hamming check digits as above.

1 0 1 1 1 0 1
0 0 1 1 0 0 0
1 1 1 1 1 0 1

●b) An eight bit data item requires four Hamming check bits. Draw up a table, similar to the one above, showing the positions of the data and check bits, and the four checks to be carried out. (Hint: Start by drawing the binary pattern of asterisks.)

c) Write down some correctly encoded eight bit data items. In each case, introduce a single-bit error. Then perform the four checks, to ensure that they locate the error.

d) Repeat part (b) and (c) for 16 and 32 bit data items.

9 A local area data communication network which is arousing considerable interest is the **Ethernet** system, being developed jointly by Intel, Rank Xerox and Digital Equipment Corporation. The structure of a simple Ethernet is shown in Figure 29.9.

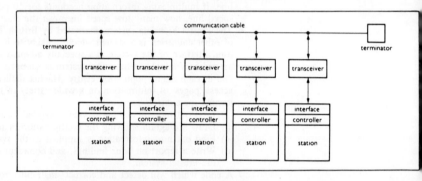

Figure 29.9
An Ethernet network

It consists of a single passive conductor, its 'ether', to which all communicating computers and peripheral devices are attached.

Any device may claim the 'ether' at any time, provided that it is not already in use. A simple mechanism exists for resolving contention between two devices which simultaneously try to transmit. Data is sent in packets of variable length, addressed to a receiving device. Transmission is bit serial, at a rate of up to 10 megabits per second.

a) Find out more about the design of Ethernet.

b) Compare and contrast its design principles with those of the Cambridge Ring.

10 a) Describe the structure of a network of computers which is such that a user at a console can gain access to and use any of the computers, however remote from him they may be.

b) What problems arise when large volumes of data need to be transferred from one computer to another in such a system?

c) Discuss one problem which you would expect to arise in using a terrestrial computer to control one in a space vehicle at a distance of several light-minutes.

OLE 80 II

30

Applications Case Studies

This chapter introduces a number of case studies of computer applications. The intention is to present a few applications, in a certain measure of detail, which reflect current trends in computing. In particular, the use of distributed processing and data communications is emphasised. All the case studies are real-time systems. An additional objective of this chapter is to give a more concrete form to many of the ideas introduced elsewhere in the book. These case studies show how many concepts of computing are being put into practice.

30.1 CBS European Manufacturing System

CBS is a worldwide organisation, dealing in a wide range of products and services. These include radio and television broadcasting, marketing records, cassette tapes, musical instruments and other leisure products, and publishing. CBS operates in a very large, but very competitive market, where demands change extremely rapidly. An efficient, flexible business approach, capable of rapid response to changing circumstances, is essential.

CBS UK carries on the operations of the company in Britain, and is closely linked to the company's European operation. One of the major aspects of its work is record production. In addition to producing records and tapes carrying their own labels, CBS UK does the production and packaging for a number of other record companies. Production takes place at a large factory in Aylesbury. Planning and overall management of the production is centred at the company's UK headquarters in London.

Computers in CBS

Computers play a vital part in the work of CBS. There is a large mainframe configuration in London, linked to two minicomputers, a microprocessor and other peripheral equipment at Aylesbury, and to a number of peripheral devices at the manufacturing plant in Haarlem, Holland. In addition, there are terminals at several of the other record companies for whom CBS produces records. The computer system is designed for continuous operation, and supports a number of real-time, transaction processing applications.

The application area chosen for this case stidy is the **European Manufacturing System**. This system monitors all aspects of record and cassette production in the UK and Holland, and will eventually be extended to Spain, to complete its coverage of CBS's European manufacturing plants.

The detailed study of the system, presented in the following sections, refers to the computer applications centred at the Aylesbury manufacturing plant.

Objectives of the System

The system has a number of objectives, many of which are inter-related. The most significant objectives are as follows:

1 To provide an up-to-the-minute picture of the manufacturing situation, at a number of levels of detail:
   in broad outline, for central management and marketing personnel;
   at an intermediate level of detail, for production plant managers;
   in great detail for plant operators.
2 To monitor the progress of each batch of records through the various stages of production.
3 To monitor the performance of a number of key items of equipment, notably record presses.
4 To provide a comprehensive information service for the parts warehouse, which stores labels, posters, bags, inserts and sleeves for the records. This information enables all the parts required for a particular batch of records to be collected together as efficiently as possible.

Manufacturing Overview

In order to understand the role of the computer in record production, it is necessary to gain some idea of the operation as a whole. Figure 30.1 shows the overall flow of events during the manufacture of a batch of records or cassette tapes. Notice that each product consists of a number of **parts** such as the sleeve, the record label and any special promotional material, etc. Figure 30.2 shows the stages of the production of a record. The unit of production is a **spindle** of records (60 seven-inch singles or 30 LP's). A batch consists of a number of spindles.

The role of the computerised monitoring system is shown in Figure 30.3. Corresponding to the three levels of information mentioned in the objectives of the system, there are three aspects of the operation of the system. These are referred to as the Management Reporting Systems, the Plant Operational System and the Plant Application Equipment System in the diagram.

Four aspects of this system are discussed in more detail. These are the printing of spindle tickets (part of the production control operation), press monitoring (the Dextralog system), warehousing, and collating and lane selection.

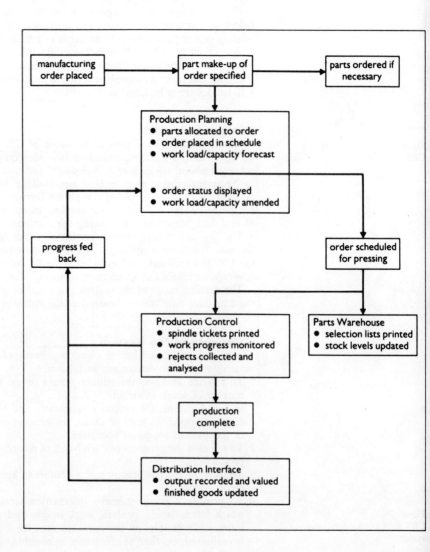

Figure 30.1
CBS manufacturing order flow

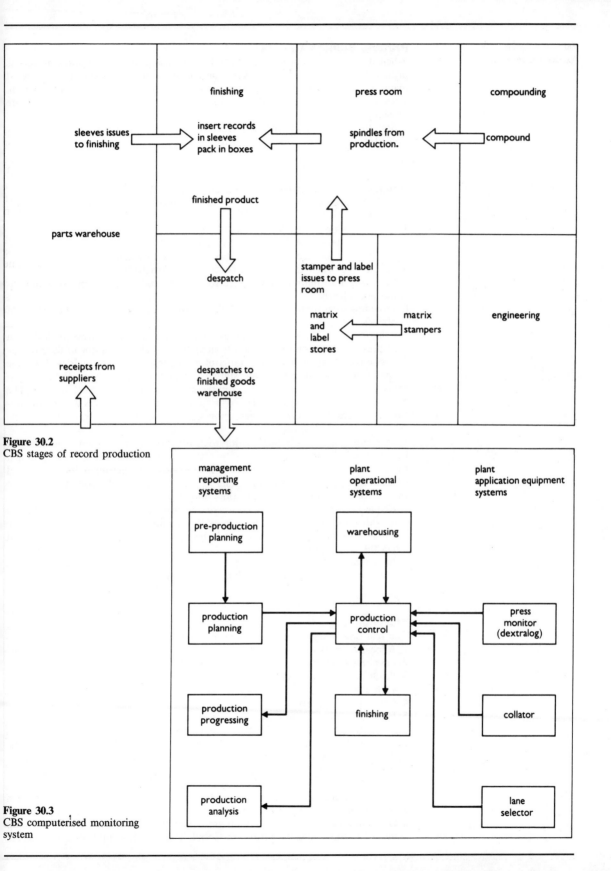

Figure 30.2
CBS stages of record production

Figure 30.3
CBS computerised monitoring
system

Printing Spindle Tickets

When a batch of records is scheduled for pressing, a set of spindle tickets is printed for the batch. These tickets contain items of information to be entered manually as the spindle progresses through the various stages of production. They also contain the bar code used in collating the spindles into batches before finishing.

Spindle tickets are the means of recording all the data relating to the production planning, monitoring and control.

Record Press Monitoring: The Dextralog System

The Dextralog press monitoring system provides a number of services, including:

1 The allocation of batches to record presses.
2 Counting the records produced by each press.
3 If a press is idle, recording the reasons for its stoppage.
4 Forecasting when the end of a batch will be reached.
5 Receiving information about rejected records, and updating pressing quantities accordingly.
6 Providing real-time statistics on the progress of batches and the status of presses.

The hardware of the system includes sensors in each record press, a device on each press for entering the reason for stoppages, a colour monitor in the production control room showing the status of each press, nine terminals with simple keypads for displaying real-time statistics, and two multiplexers. Processing is carried out on a dedicated Nova 3 minicomputer, with 32K of main store. The Nova 3 has a data link to a CTL 8040 minicomputer, which acts as a communications processor at the manufacturing site. The CTL is in turn linked to the central IBM mainframes.

Software consists of a module for each function of the system, synchronised by a simple transaction processing operating system. Each record press is polled by the operating system once every 20 seconds, to determine its status and whether it has pressed a record since it was last polled. Various modules are then invoked to process the data thus obtained.

Requests from the terminals are treated as interrupts. Modules are invoked to deal with these requests, and to display the required information on the screen. All nine terminals work together, in other words a request from any terminal alters the display on all of them.

In general, the Dextralog system works extremely well. Its only shortcoming is the lack of data validation built into the system.

Warehousing

The real-time warehousing system provides the following services:

1 Allocating rack positions to stocks.
2 Locating stock items.
3 Producing lists of stocks to be dispatched for a particular batch of records, in such a way as to minimise the movements of the unloading hoists.
4 Updating stock levels.
5 Reporting all stock movements to the mainframe computers.

The system is based on a CTL 8040 minicomputer, and includes terminals and a ticket printer as well as data communication links to the IBM mainframes. The software is built up around a CTL operating system called **TAD**, for transaction application driver. TAD allows a **foreground** of fully interactive transaction programs, and a **middleground** of 'batch' programs.

The foreground programs control data entry and validation. They produce a **logfile** of valid data, which is used by the batch programs. Foreground programs are specified by means of the program generating language which calls up standard routines, mostly written in Cobol. The middleground programs accept validation information from the logfile and process it. These programs are concerned with such matters as stock level updating. There are two such programs, both written in Cobol.

The warehousing system generally works very well, though if a failure occurs, processing must be started again from the beginning of the current logfile.

Collating and Lane Selection

When spindles of records have been pressed, they are loaded onto a ski-lift type conveyor belt to be transported to the finishing area. When the spindles arrive, they are **collated** (all the spindles of the same batch are collected together) and diverted to a lane for finishing.

Collating and lane selection is done on an automated racking system, together with controls on nearby conveyor belts. The control panel of this racking system is connected to a dedicated microprocessor, which controls the allocation of batches to racks, and the routing of incoming spindles accordingly, as well as the allocation of finishing lanes to batches, and the routing of outgoing spindles. Identifying data is read from the bar codes on the spindle tickets.

System Hardware

Figure 30.4 gives an overview of the hardware used by the CBS European manufacturing system, as well as by all the other CBS applications. The hardware is designed for uninterrupted 24-hour-per-day operation. Accordingly, several essential components, including the central processing units and many communications links, are duplicated. This spreads the processing load more evenly, and enables the system as a whole to continue to operate in the event of a failure of any single element.

As can be seen from the diagram, the hardware can be grouped into three functional elements. These are the central processing unit, mass backing storage and local peripherals in London, the data communications network linking the central configuration with a number of remote sites, and the equipment at remote sites such as Aylesbury.

Assessment

The computer system is an integral part of the workings of CBS. Should the system fail completely, there is no manual backup. In this event, record production and a number of other activities of the company are severely curtailed. The record of the computer system in this matter is very impressive. The sytem as a whole has been operational for more than 99 per cent of the time over the last few years.

The computer system enables CBS to maintain an extremely rapid, flexible and efficient record production process. The productivity per worker is very high. The computer system plays an essential part in maintaining CBS's leading position in a highly competitive field.

30.2 London Wide Area Traffic Control System

Moving people and goods around London is a major problem. With a sprawling city centre containing thousands of historic buildings, strict pollution laws and conflicting needs of business people, shoppers, workers and tourists, a completely satisfactory road system is impossible to achieve. In recent times the prohibitive cost of major roadworks has been an additional limiting factor.

The London Wide Area Traffic Control System is an attempt to make the best of the existing road network, by bringing the majority of the traffic lights in the inner part of the city under the control of a central computer system.

Development of the system started in 1968, when an experimental area in West London, containing some 70 sets of traffic lights, was brought under centralised control. As soon as it became obvious that the experiment was successful, Phase I of the scheme, encompassing the central area, commenced. In

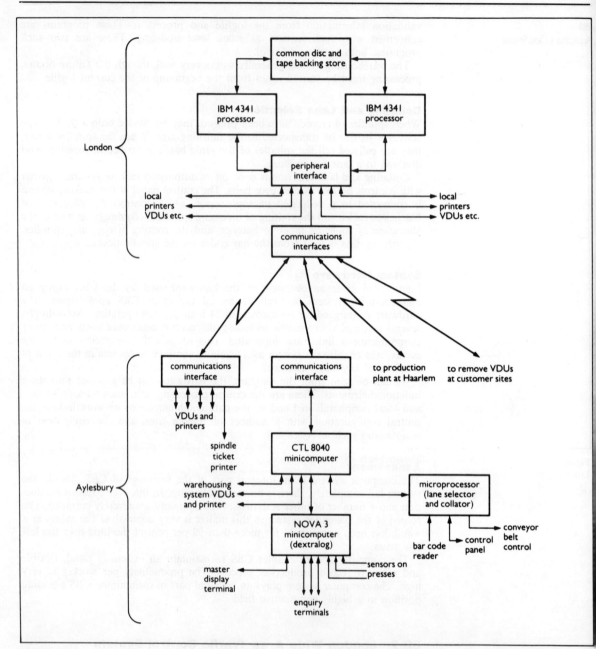

Figure 30.4
CBS hardware configuration

the period 1971 to 1975, approximatly 500 sets of signals, as well as 100 pedestrian crossing controls, were linked to the central network. From 1975 to 1980, an additional 450 sets of signals, and 400 pedestrian crossing controls (including the original 70 experimental signals) were incorporated as Phase II of the scheme. In 1980, it was decided to replace the computer hardware of the system, as well as changing to a new basis of traffic control. As this transition will take a number of years to complete, this account of the system describes both the old and the new versions.

See Figure 30.5 for a map of the areas covered by the various phases of the system.

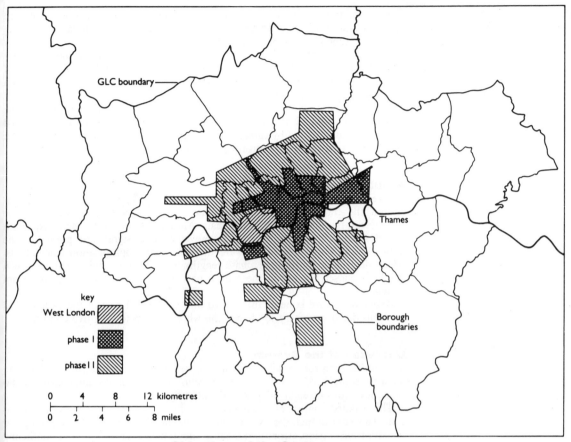

Figure 30.5
London traffic control area

Objectives of the System
Broadly speaking, the traffic control system has three objectives, namely:
1 Minimisation of the journey times of all vehicles in the controlled area.
2 Provision of real-time information on the state of the system to a central control room, staffed by police officers.
3 Continuously monitoring the performance of all the traffic lights in the network, and reporting any failures as soon as they occur.
From these objectives it can be seen that the system is not completely automated. Ultimate control of the traffic is in the hands of the staff of the control room. From here, computer control of each junction can be changed, or the junction released to local control.

Principles of Operation
As the principles on which the system operates are in the process of being changed, both the old and the new versions are described.

Fixed Timetable Control
The original principle of operation of the system is one of control by a number of **fixed timetables**. The junctions controlled by the system are divided into **groups**. Within each group, control of traffic is synchronised. Control is not always synchronised across group boundaries. The basic unit of control is the **subgroup**. A subgroup is a single isolated junction, or a number of adjacent junctions which must be controlled together.

A **timetable** specifies the duration of each phase of each traffic light in a subgroup. Timetables are computed from the configuration of each junction, the distances between junctions and traffic volumes in various directions. They are then adjusted manually on the basis of observation of traffic behaviour.

A set of timetables is produced for each subgroup of junctions, for each expected type of traffic conditions. For example, there are morning and evening peak hour timetables, a night timetable, and various timetables for emergency conditions and ceremonial occasions. Working on a weekly cycle, the computer automatically selects the timetable of each subgroup, depending on the time of day and the day of the week. Under normal circumstances, all the junctions in a group are on the same timetable.

However, the timetable for any particular subgroup can be changed from the control room, should the situation demand it. The control room has closed circuit TV monitors fed by cameras at all significant intersections. The lights can also be released to local control if necessary.

Adaptive Control

Unlike fixed timetable control, adaptive control is designed to take into consideration the traffic situation at the time. The control system adapts to the situation in its phasing of traffic signals. An adaptive control system requires a set of **detectors** to monitor vehicle movements at significant points in the network, and sophisticated software to perform the optimisation calculations, which determine traffic light phase lengths, in real time. The technique which has been chosen for use in the central part of the network is called the **Scoot** system.

Adaptive control is being introduced into the central part of the system. It is not considered necessary to change the whole system to adaptive control.

Operation of the System

The traffic control system consists of a central computer installation, an adjacent control room, a data communication network, and a number of **outstations** in control of each subgroup of traffic lights.

The detailed control of the lights in a subgroup is carried out by its outstation. This control includes interlocking of the individual lights. Thus a computer or data transmission error cannot cause simultaneous green lights in conflicting directions, for example. If communication with the computer is lost, the outstation provides local control of the lights.

The data transmission network carries control signals from the computers to the outstations, and sends monitoring information in the opposite direction. Lines leased from British Telecom are used for this purpose.

The computer installation is designed for continuous, 24-hour-a-day operation. Accordingly, there is a considerable amount of parellelism in the system, including standby processors. The hardware and software are described in later sections.

The traffic control room includes a number of **control stations**. At each station there is a visual display unit and several television monitors. A wide selection of information can be called up at a VDU. This includes information on the overall state of the network, as well as graphical displays of individual subgroups of junctions. The staff at the control room are in radio contact with all police cars and motor cyclists in the area. These can be called on to observe and report on the traffic situation where problems are occurring, or deal with a problem (such as a parked vehicle obstructing traffic) if necessary.

Hardware

As the hardware of the system is in the process of being replaced, both the old and the new configurations are described. The old hardware (Figure 30.6) is based on three Siemens central processing units. One controls the inner Phase I signals, another controls the outer Phase II signals, and the third is a 'hot standby' processor, ready to take over if either of the others should fail. A set of common peripherals can be switched to any one of the three processors. There is also a set of peripherals dedicated to each operational processor, including the interface equipment to the data communication links.

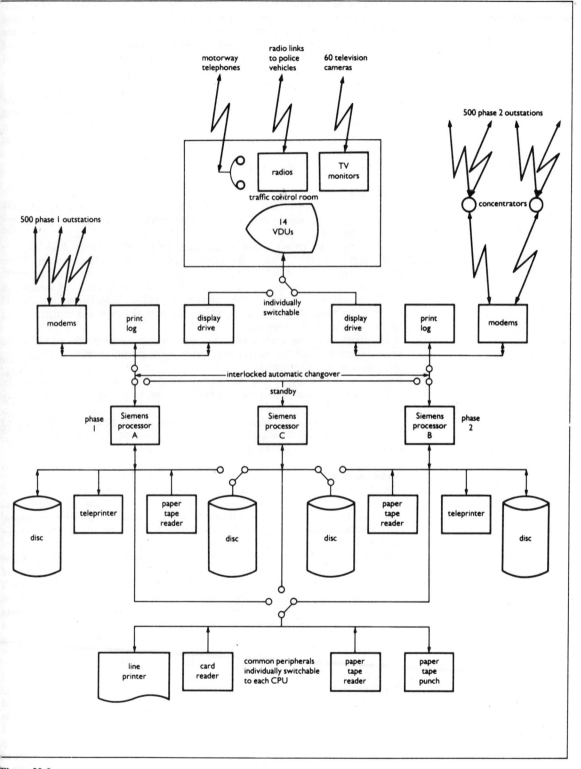

Figure 30.6
London traffic control: old hardware

The new hardware (Figure 30.7) consists of a network of distributed processors. One processor (Master Subsystem A) is in overall control of the fixed timetable area, while another (Master Subsystem B) is in overall control of the Scoot adaptive control area. Connected to these processors are a number of **cells**. Each cell contains a processor, which controls approximatly 50 subgroups of junctions. The outstations will eventually be replaced by solid-state microprocessor-based control units.

The master subsystems exercise overall control of the system, such as the selection of timetables. Cells exercise more detailed control, such as the timing of phases.

The new system is designed to take advantage of the latest developments in microprocessor and memory technology. The use of distributed processing gives the system a high degree of resilience in the event of component failures.

Software

Three different types of software are used by the system. There is the software for preparing the timetables, the fixed timetable control software and the adaptive control software.

Two programs, called COMPRESS and TRANSYT, are used to prepare traffic light timetables. This is done offline, using an IBM 370 computer. These programs are supplied with data specifying the layout of the road network, distances between junctions, expected (or desired) traffic speeds, and volumes of traffic in various directions. Some extremely complex calculations are carried out in order to produce timetables which minimise the expected transit time of all the vehicles in the network.

The fixed timetable control programs use the timetables produced offline to generate signals to all the outstations, and monitor the information coming from these outstations. Commands from the terminal in the control room are interpreted, and information is sent to these terminals in response to the commands. These commands can also cause a change in the timetable being used at any particular subgroup of junctions.

The adaptive control programs receive monitoring information on the current traffic situation. Optimising calculations are carried out in real time, and the phasing of the traffic signals is adjusted accordingly.

Assessment

The effectiveness of a traffic control system can be measured in a variety of ways. In addition to travel time, there are considerations of safety, fuel economy, pollution, ease of pedestrian movement, noise, adaptability to special circumstances, such as emergencies or ceremonial occasions, and the cost of the system. In a traffic network as large and complex as London's, only part of which is under central control, many of these yardsticks are very difficult to apply.

However, where measurements have been made, the results are extremely encouraging. On average, transit time is reduced by at least 28 per cent, compared with the same traffic signals under local control. Comparative figures of road accidents are not available, but the safety record with the controlled area is regarded as being good.

On the question of cost, the traffic control system scores extremely well. The most expensive element in the system is neither the hardware nor the software, but the lease of the data communication links. Furthermore, the cost of installing and maintaining the whole system is less than the construction and maintenance costs of half a mile of motorway.

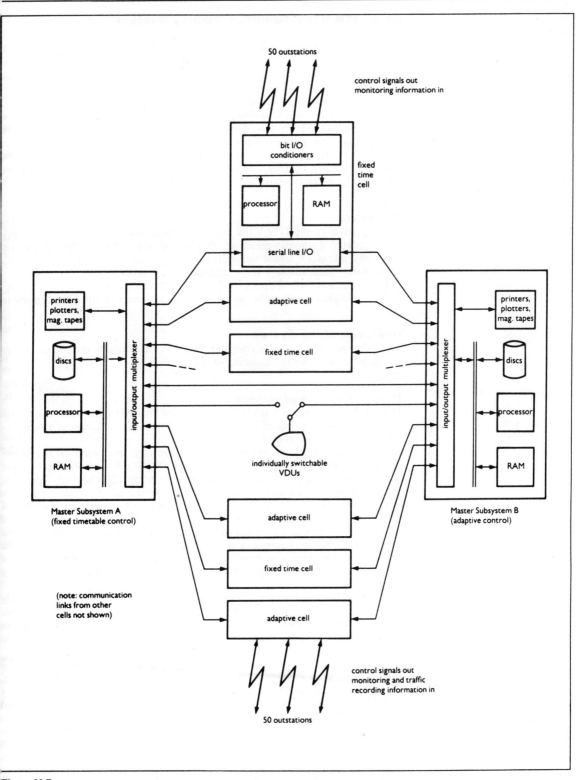

Figure 30.7
London traffic control: new hardware

30.3 ITN VT80 Graphics Display System

As television coverage of newsworthy events has become more sophisticated, there has been an increasing demand to be able to broadcast precise, up-to-the-minute information, in graphical form. This is particularly important in the coverage of elections and budgets, but is also very useful for news broadcasts.

Early attempts at graphical display required skilled signwriters, who would quickly write the required lettering before it was held up in front of TV cameras. Later, computerised character generators came into use, enabling captions to be superimposed on pictures. Currently, a number of television companies are turning to fully electronic means of generating graphics displays. The **VT80** system, developed by Independent Television News, is one of the first of these electronic graphics systems.

Objectives

The objectives of the ITN VT80 system are as follows:

1 To provide computer-generated graphics displays which can be injected directly into a TV signal transmitter.
2 To enable these displays to be updated in real time.
3 To permit a certain degree of animation in the displays.
4 To be simple enough to be operated by the presenter of the TV programme.

Operation of the System

There are two aspects of the operation of the system, namely the preparation of the displays, and the broadcasting of the displays.

Preparation of a programme

During the planning of a television programme, decisions are taken as to what displays are to be provided by the graphics system. Each display is a complete television picture, in colour.

The displays are then constructed from lines of text, columns of figures, graphs (particulary histograms) and other symbols. These symbols include maps, simple portraits of people and silhouettes of buildings. Symbols are input into the system by drawing them on special grids, and then specifying the contents of each area of the grid. A table of figures is then keyed in to define the symbol.

A certain amount of animation can be provided. For example, symbols can be coloured in after they have been displayed, histograms can 'grow' to their final size, and columns of figures can appear one line at a time. Displays can include variables whose value is updated while the programme is being broadcast. These variables include numeric quantities, or the colour to be assigned to a certain symbol.

When all the displays have been prepared, a list of them is prepared for the presenter of the programme. This list shows the number of each display together with a control key which calls it up, and in some cases one or two further control keys which initiate stages of animation of the display.

Broadcast of a Programme

During the broadcast of the programme, the presenter has the list of displays, a simple keypad and a monitor screen. The presenter calls up and animates the displays as they are required. Figure 30.8 shows the display guide used for the coverage of the 1980 USA presidential election. The producer of the programme sees the graphics display together with the pictures from the cameras. At any time, either the graphics display or one of the camera pictures can be selected for transmission.

While this is happening, information is arriving at the broadcast centre all the time, chiefly by telephone. Up-to-the-minute values of variables in the displays are entered at terminals.

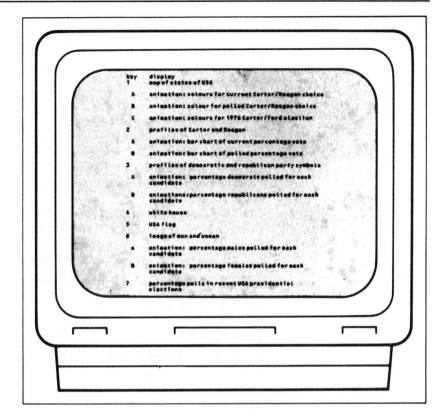

Figure 30.8
ITN VT80 presenter's guide

Hardware

Figure 30.9 shows the hardware used by the system. The processor is a PDP VAX minicomputer (Section 15.2). The most important device is the interface between the processor and the broadcasting system. This device is the VT80 which gives the system its name.

The VT80 links to the main store of the processor using direct memory access (DMA). It accesses the data for a display, in digital form, and creates the electronic form of this as a standard television signal. While the display is being broadcast, this signal is linked directly to the transmitter. The only other special hardware in the system is the simple keypad used by the presenter to select the display he or she requires.

Software

During the preparation of a display, a number of software routines are used. These create various parts of the display, such as characters of different sizes, outlines and shaded areas. These routines are written in Pascal or Macro, a PDP assembly language. Basic is also used for the preparation of 'rough' displays. These routines are then compiled or assembled to produce the machine code program for each display.

The data structure for each display is a **display file**. It consists of a set of data describing each portion of the screen, specifically the characters, position, colour and priority. There are eight levels of priority. Characters with higher priority will supersede characters with lower priority at the same screen position. Any position on the screen not defined in this way is assumed to be background. The background colour of various portions of the screen is also defined in the display file.

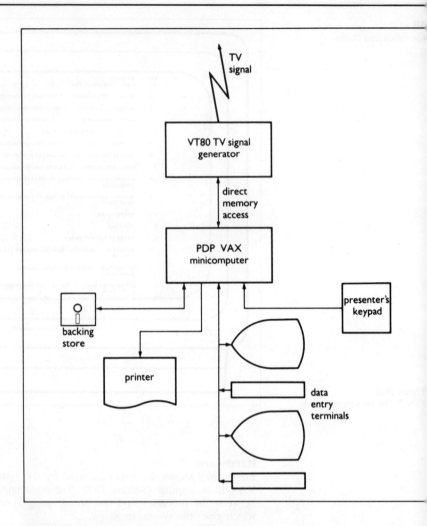

TV
signal

VT80 TV signal
generator

direct
memory
access

PDP VAX
minicomputer

presenter's
keypad

backing
store

printer

data
entry
terminals

Figure 30.9
ITN VT80 hardware

During a broadcast, all the display files are loaded into main store. When a particular display is selected, the VT80 is given the address of the start of its display file. The VT80 accesses the file and creates the TV signal for the display.

The operating system supporting these activities is the standard VMS system supplied with the VAX processor. Its most important feature is that it can be made to be **event driven**. In other words, once the operating system has initiated a particular routine, no interrupts are allowed until that routine is complete. This prevents the disruption of the animation of a display while it is being broadcast.

Assessment

The VT80 system is a 'home grown' product. All the software, as well as the special-purpose hardware (in particular the VT80 device itself), have been designed and implemented by ITN. The system is currently being marketed to other television companies.

In addition to fulfilling the objectives stated at the beginning of the case study, the VT80 system has some wider benefits. It enables a higher standard of television presentation to be maintained, and simplifies the production of a number of television programmes. The system is simple, fairly cheap, and easy to use. It is an example of a successful combination of computer and communications technology.

30.4   Meteorological Office Atmospheric Model

Computers are being used to an increasing extent to assist in weather forecasting. The computers receive and analyse weather reports from all over the world, and then run a simulation of the main trends in the atmosphere over a period of a few days ahead. The output from this simulation is used by the forecasters. In Britain, computer-assisted weather forecasting is done at two centres, the **Meteorological Office** at Bracknell and the **European Centre for Medium Range Weather Forecasts** at Reading. This case study is based on the work at the Meteorological Office, but the methods used at the medium range forecasting centre are very similar.

Objectives of Computer-Assisted Weather Forecasting
Computers are being used in weather forecasting in order to achieve the following aims:
1 To improve the accuracy and reliability of weather forecasts, and enable them to cover a longer period into the future.
2 To provide a wider range of weather forecasting services than was previously possible.
3 To reduce costs by taking over most of the routine work of logging incoming weather reports, producing maps and maintaining weather records.
In order to achieve these aims, the computers carry out the following tasks:

- Receiving all incoming weather reports on a global data communications network, and storing this information in a database.
- Validating incoming data and transforming it into a form which is compatible with the atmospheric model.
- Using a complex mathematical model to run a simulation of the main physical processes in the earth's atmosphere, in order to predict the overall behaviour of the atmosphere for some days ahead.
- Communicating the results of the simulation to forecasters, regional weather centre computers and other users of the data.
- Preparing maps of weather reports and forecasts.

These tasks require a combination of data communications, graphics for the maps, database management for the reports and numerical processing to carry out the actual simulation. The whole cycle of events must take place quickly, in order to meet the deadlines for the forecasts.

Mathematical Models of the Earth's Atmosphere
The behaviour of the earth's atmosphere may be described by a **mathematical model**. A mathematical model is a set of equations which describes, in a simplified way, the behaviour of a physical system. The equations in the atmospheric model enable the future state of the atmosphere to be calculated if its present state is known. They use the mathematical technique of **differential equations**. The basis of the model is as follows:

The earth's atmosphere is a continuous, approximately spherical layer of gas. It is bounded on one side by the earth's surface, which is of an irregular height and composition, and on the other side by space, with no definite edge. The most effective way to represent the atmosphere in a mathematical model is to regard it as a series of **layers**. The layers are not determined by altitude, but by the ratio of the atmospheric pressure in the layer to that at the ground. In this way the layers follow the contours of the ground. See Figure 30.10. The Met Office atmospheric models use fifteen layers, more closely spaced near the ground and at the commonest operating altitude of aircraft.

Within each layer, the atmosphere is regarded as a **grid** of points. The Met Office uses two models, the **global model**, which covers the whole world, and the

Figure 30.10
The Meteorological Office
atmospheric model

regional model, which covers Europe and the North Atlantic. In the regional model (Figure 30.11), the grid points are spaced at 3/4 of a degree of latitude and 15/16 of a degree of longitude. On average, the points are 75km apart. In the global model, the points are twice as far apart, covering the whole surface of the earth.

At each point, the computer stores values of the wind speed and direction, temperature and humidity for each of the 15 layers, as well as the atmospheric pressure at ground (or sea) level. When these values are known for all the points on the grid at a certain time, a complex set of mathematical equations is used to calculate new values a short time later. The equations calculate the movements of air and the flows of energy between the grid points. In this way the model steps forward in small time intervals from the present state of the atmosphere into the future. Because of the large number of grid points, and the complexity of the equations, millions of calculations are needed to advance by each time step. Sophisticated numerical techniques have been developed by meteorologists in order to solve the equations as efficiently and precisely as possible.

Weather Forecasting Hardware and Software
Figure 30.12 shows the network of computers used to assist in weather forecasting at the Met Office in Bracknell. There are three types of computer in the network: communications processors, front-end procesors and the main numerical processor.

Communications processors
A number of small **communications processors** are used to handle the huge volume of incoming weather reports received at the Met Office. These reports come from weather stations, lighthouses, weather balloons, ships, aircraft and satellites on the Global Telecommunication System run by the World Meteorological Office. The communications processors also re-transmit received data and forecasts to other computers on the network. The communications processors pass on received data to the front-end processors.

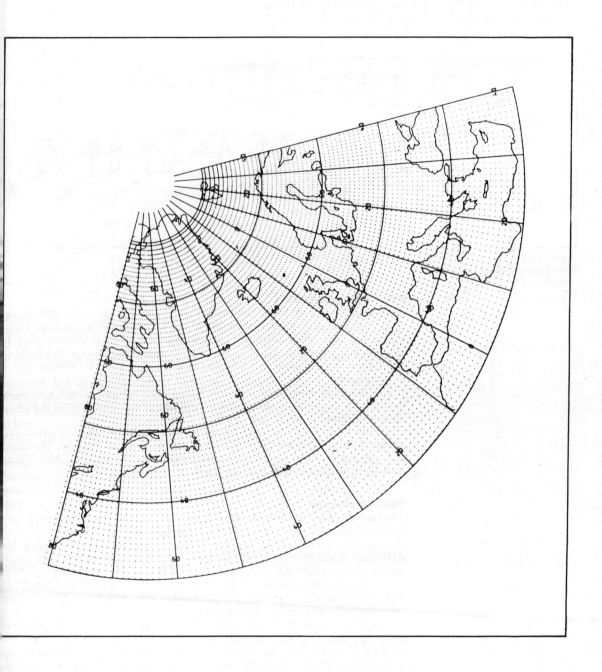

Figure 30.11
Grid points in the Met Office
regional model

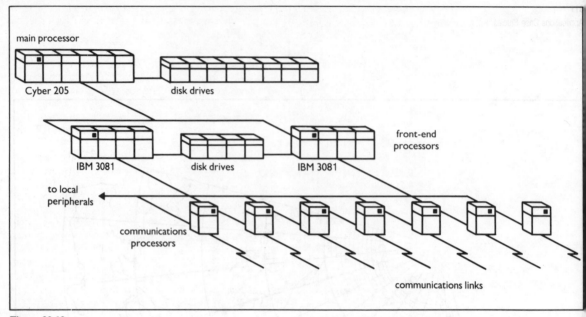

Figure 30.12
Meteorological Office computer
network

Front-end processors
The two IBM 3081 **front-end processors** receive the data from the communications processors, and validate it in several ways. In addition to the usual range checks, any data which differs too much from earlier values at the same place is rejected, as is any which differs by too much from adjacent reports. Any dubious reports are displayed on a screen for the meteorologists to decide whether or not to accept them.

The front-end processors then select data in order to prepare a **synoptic** database for use by the main processor. Synoptic data is all measured at or very close to a certain time.

Another task of the front-end processors is to produce maps of observed and predicted data. These are either printed or appear as screen displays. The front-end processors have direct communications links to regional Met Office computers, which can also produce maps.

Main processor
The **main processor** at the Met Office is a Cyber 205 supercomputer. It is a very large mainframe computer designed for scientific work. It has banks of registers to hold the numbers being processed at the time, and uses pipelining for multiplicaton and division. Pipelining means that large numbers of similar calculations can be carried out in a very short space of time. The main memory of the Cyber 205 can hold 2 million items of data, each item occupying 64 bits. (The European Centre for Medium Range Weather Forecasts has a Cray-1 main processor with very similar capabilities.)

The main processor has two functions. The first is to use the synoptic database prepared by the front-end processors to work out the initial data values at the grid points. The second task is to step through the calculations of the mathematical model, and calculate new data values at the grid points. The results are returned to the front-end processors for maps to be drawn.

Software
The software controlling the three types of computer has been developed by the staff of the Meteorological Office over the years. It is based on sophisticated

techniques for solving large numbers of complex equations as efficiently as possible. The computers must operate much faster than in real time, in order to project the calculations into the future.

Computer-Assisted Weather Forecasting in Operation

The Met Office in Bracknell follows a fixed 12-hourly cycle of events to receive and analyse incoming weather reports, run the atmospheric simulations and produce weather forecasts. The cycles start at noon and midnight GMT.

At midnight GMT, weather readings are taken by weather stations, high altitude balloons, aircraft, ships, lighthouses, buoys and satellites all over the world. The readings are relayed to the Met Office via the Global Telecommunications System. The data is received by the communications processors and passed on to the front-end processors. Here it is validated and added to the synoptic database.

At 0200 hours is the cut-off point for incoming data for the regional model. The main processor starts work on the synoptic database, analysing the data and working out the starting values for the grid points. None of the incoming reports are actually measured at the grid points. The first task of the main processor is to examine the available information near each grid point and obtain the values for each of the 15 layers at the point from it. The method of weighted averages is used. Some data (for example weather station or weather balloon data) is regarded as more accurate than other data (such as satellite data). When the analysis is complete, the results are returned to the front-end processors for maps of the reported weather to be drawn.

The main processor then starts work on the regional mathematical model. It moves forwards in steps of 7.5 minutes, and takes six minutes of real time to advance the simulation by 36 hours. The state of the model at every six hours from the start is returned to the front-end processor for further maps to be drawn. One of the maps produced in this way is shown in Figure 30.13. It shows the central area of the regional model.

The Senior Forecaster on duty uses these maps to produce the weather forecasts. He uses his knowledge and experience of meteorology to interpret the maps, and to decide to what extent to rely on the computer output. The first map (for 0600 hours) is checked against the latest weather reports and satellite photographs to see if the general trends predicted are actually occurring. When the overall weather situation has been decided by the forecaster, the details of the forecast are added to the computer results. For example, the computer does not at present take account of fog, and does not distinguish precipitation as rain, hail or snow. Thunderstorms are also not predicted by the computer. When this work has been done, the official Met Office forecast is issued.

In the meantime, at 0320 hours, the cutoff point for incoming reports for the global simulation model is reached. This data originates from all over the world, hence the longer collection time. The data is added to the synoptic database for midnight, and is checked and analysed as before. The main processor sets to work on the global model, this time advancing in time intervals of 15 minutes. The global model is run for a period of six days ahead, taking 24 minutes for the actual processing. At regular intervals, results are transferred to the front-end processors for maps to be drawn. These maps are used by the forecasters on duty in the preparation of longer term forecasts. They are compared with similar maps from the computers at the European Centre for Medium Range Weather Forecasts.

The output from the regional and global models is transmitted to regional Met Office computers. These centres have facilities for producing maps, and issue their own regional forecasts. The output is also transmitted directly to several computers belonging to airlines. The data is used in the preparation of flight plans by the airlines' computers. There are direct links with computers

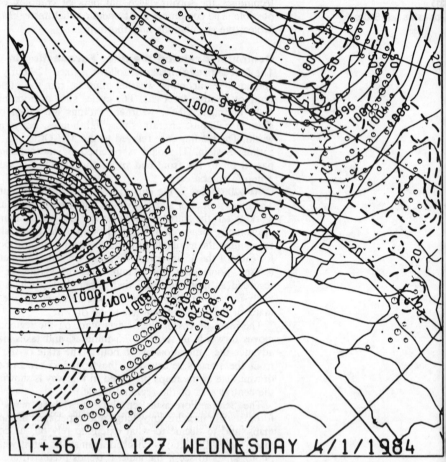

T+36 VT 12Z WEDNESDAY 4/1/1984

Figure 30.13
Output from the Met Office
atmospheric model

belonging to the BBC, which enable some of the weather maps seen on television to be produced from the Met Office computer output.

Assessment

At the current state of knowledge of meteorology and mathematics, completely accurate weather forecasts are impossible. In spite of the complexity of the mathematical models, they are a simplified description of the physical processes. The physics of the processes involved is not completely understood, and the weather reports on which the models are based are incomplete. The best that can be hoped for is an improvement in the reliability of forecasts with the introduction of computers.

The Met Office mathematical models in use at present, and the computers which run them, are not the first to be used. They replaced a simpler model and a less powerful computer in 1982. There is no doubt that the new computers are helping to produce more accurate and longer term forecasts. Most runs of the global model provide useful information up to four days ahead. The range of forecasting services which can be provided is also increasing. Detailed forecasts can now be requested for specific events where the weather is critical, such as the assembly of a North Sea oil platform.

Although the costs of the computers are very high, the savings brought about by improvements in weather forecasting are much higher. An increase of only a few percent in the value of a harvest is worth a very large sum of money. Aircraft flight paths are planned on the basis of weather forecasts, and the saving of fuel and time resulting from more accurate forecasts is significant.

Improvements in safety of motoring, shipping and aviation have undoubtedly saved many lives. Better weather forecasts have led to great savings in the costs of North Sea oil production.

30.5 Conclusion

The four case studies presented in this chapter give some idea of the ways in which computers are being put to use. In each case, the system has taken some time to implement, and is being modified all the time in the light of experience. Each application has brought great benefits, both to the computer users and to others affected by the system.

Exercise 30

1 Briefly describe the progress of a batch of records through the CBS manufacturing system. Mention each interaction of the batch of records with the computer system.
2 Describe the role played by data communications in:
  a) the CBS manufacturing system
  b) the London traffic control system
  c) the ITN VT80 system
  d) the Met Office weather forecasting system.
  In each case, discuss the consequences of a failure in the data communications network.
3 Briefly compare and contrast the techniques of fixed timetable and adaptive traffic control.
4 Using the new hardware configuration, control of each traffic light in the London network is exercised at three levels. Identify these levels, and state what degree of control is exercised at each.
5 Outline the steps taken to include in a display a variable item of information, which can be updated in real time, using the ITN VT80 graphics display system.
6 Suggest some additional uses for a television real-time graphics system.
7 The Met Office regional model covers the area from 30 degrees to 80 degrees North, with points at a spacing of 0.75 degrees, and from 80 degrees West to 40 Degrees East, with points at a spacing of 0.9375 degrees. See Figure 30.11.
  a) Calculate the number of grid points in the regional model.
  b) There are fifteen layers in the model. At each layer, there are four weather variables, as well as the surface pressure at the grid point. How many variables are there at one grid point?
  c) How many variables are there in the entire regional model? Comment on this result.
8 Discuss the benefits of a vector processing computer architecture when used for the processing of a complex mathematical model such as that used for weather forecasting.
9 Discuss the consequences of the availablility of reliable long-term weather forecasts for each of the following activities:
  a) agriculture
  b) civil aviation
  c) merchant shipping
  d) off-shore oil production
  e) gas and electricity supply systems
  f) tourism.
10 Assume that it is possible to link a home or school microcomputer to the Met Office computer network. State what information could usefully be transferred to the micro, how the information could be processed, and how it would be displayed or printed. Sketch some examples of the screen displays and printouts which would be produced.
11 Comment on the degree of dependence of the organisations mentioned in these case studies on their computer systems.
12 Using a computer application of your choice, conduct a study of the workings of the system. Use the same general approach as in this chapter, and write a report of your findings.

31
Expert
Systems

Expert systems are one of the first concrete results to emerge from the work in artificial intelligence. An expert system is one which provides a computer with a certain measure of intelligence in a particular field. In some areas of medicine, geology and engineering it has proved possible to transfer knowledge from expert practitioners to a computer. The computer can then be consulted, in most cases by other experts, to give advice in particular cases.

A definition of an expert system is as follows:

> **An expert system is a computer system which is able to draw reasoned conclusions from a body of knowledge in a particular field, and communicate to the user the line of reasoning by which it has reached a conclusion.**

The first expert system went into operation in 1965, but it is only in the mid-1980s that they have begun to be used on a significant scale. Expert systems are likely to be the main application area of fifth generation computers in the 1990s.

31.1 Objectives of Expert Systems

The purpose of an expert system is to provide reasoned advice at a comparable level to that provided by a human expert. This capability has two main aims: to enhance the abilities of leading experts in certain fields, and to make a high level of expertise available to less highly qualified practitioners.

The first aim takes note of the fact that some areas of human expertise, such as the diagnosis and treatment of cancer, are so complex that even the leading experts can benefit from the systematic, logical approach provided by a computer. A computer system will take into consideration all the knowledge at its disposal in the consideration of every case, and will follow known lines of reasoning exhaustively, no matter how complex they are. These capabilities complement the skills of a human expert, which are generally based on a mixture of knowledge, experience, insight and intuition.

The second aim attempts to raise the level of skill of professionals who are not themselves leading experts. A large number of medical practitioners fall into this category, particularly in developing countries. When expert systems become widely available, the skills of these practitioners should be significantly enhanced.

31.2 Techniques of Expert System Design

Expert systems draw reasoned conclusions from a knowledge base. When designing an expert system, the structure of the knowledge base, and how the knowledge is represented, is one of the main considerations. Factors taken into consideration are the size of the knowledge base, the completeness of the knowledge, and how precise it is. If the knowledge is in any way uncertain, a method of representation which includes some form of probability is used. One of the techniques of knowledge representation discussed in Section 7.3 is used in most cases.

In some expert systems, the expert knowledge is fixed into the system when it is constructed. In others, there is a built-in ability to learn from experience, including from mistakes made by the system. This latter approach is more complex, but generally leads to more useful systems. In many expert systems, the knowledge is completely separate from the rules for its manipulation. These are initially built as expert system **shells**. They are then supplied with the knowledge they require for their particular applications.

Most expert systems are programmed in Lisp (Section 19.7), but Prolog (Section 19.8) is being used to an increasing extent.

31.3 Applications of Expert Systems

A small number of expert systems are in use at present. These are mainly in the following fields:

- Medicine: Expert systems are in use for diagnosis and the planning of treatment in specialised fields. These include certain types of cancer, kidney diseases and some viral infections. Expert systems are also used to plan and monitor experiments, particularly in genetics. Expert systems for use by general practitioners in diagnosis and treatment are under investigation, but none are in widespread use at present.
- Geological Prospecting: Expert systems have already proved their worth in oil prospecting, and are now being used for other minerals.
- Designing Computer Configurations: Digital Equipment Corporation uses an expert system to design the computer configuration required when an order for a VAX minicomputer is placed. The expert system ensures that a compatible set of equipment is delivered, which meets the requirements of the customer.
- Chemistry: The analysis of chemical structures from mass spectrometer data is often done with the aid of an expert system.
- Legal Advice: Expert systems which give general legal advice, and assist in such matters as making Social Security claims, are at present under development.

When fifth generation computers become available, the range of applications of expert systems is likely to broaden. New areas could include education, and computer-aided design systems for products ranging from spacecraft to microchips.

31.4 Case Study 1: Mycin

The expert system **Mycin** was developed at Stanford University in the USA to assist doctors with advice on diagnosis and treatment of infectious diseases. The body of medical knowledge is stored in a form which includes a certainty value. This is a number in the range -1 to $+1$, where -1 means a negative association, and $+1$ means a definite positive association. A value near zero means that no correlation is known. For example:

Aids   HTLV 3   1.0

which means that the virus HTLV 3 is associated with the disease Aids, with a certainty factor of 1.0.

The knowledge is processed by a set of **production rules** of the form:

if <condition> then <action>

At the start of a diagnosis, many of the items of knowledge are incomplete, or the certainty factors in them are near zero. During a diagnosis, additional knowledge is accumulated, and certainty factors move towards -1 or $+1$. The process is interactive. The physician enters background information and symptoms, and is then asked to give further information by the computer, as it requires it. At the end of the diagnosis, the conclusions are displayed, together with their certainty factors. At any stage, the line of reasoning and intermediate conclusions may be examined by the physician.

The approach pioneered by Mycin has been extended and modified for use in other medical expert systems. Mycin is available as an expert system shell - **Emycin** - which may be used in other medical fields.

31.5 Case Study 2: Prospector

Prospector was developed by SRI International in association with the US Geological Survey. It performs three tasks: the evaluation of geological resources in a region, checking for certain deposits at a site, and selecting the best sites for drilling.

Prospector does not draw as clear a distinction between knowledge and the rules for its processing as Mycin does. Prospector uses a set of **models**, one for each investigation. Items of knowledge are stored as **spaces** in a model, with an associated probability. The spaces are connected by rules, which have two numerical factors which determine their strength.

An analysis starts with the construction of a model to suit the situation. At the outset, many of the probabilities are unknown or very low. As the analysis proceeds, the values of the probabilities are updated. An inference mechanism, consisting of a set of **production rules** is used. It refers to a **semantic network** of basic geological knowledge in order to decide the sequence of rules to apply. The user interface is interactive: either the user or the expert system can initiate steps, by asking questions or supplying information. At any stage the user can ask Prospector to explain its current line of reasoning or intermediate conclusions.

Prospector, and expert systems like it, have proved their worth many times over in exploration, notably for oil. The cost of the computer system is a very small fraction of the costs of drilling a test well, and improved siting of production wells brings in greatly increased revenue.

31.6 Conclusion

The main points of this chapter are as follows:

- An expert system is the application of artificial intelligence to a particular field of human expertise.
- Expert systems deal with vague and incomplete knowledge, and must be able to explain their line of reasoning to users.
- Some expert systems have their expert knowledge fixed in them when they are constructed; others have a self-learning capacity.
- Applications of expert systems include medicine, geological prospecting, chemical analysis, legal advice and computer-aided design.
- Expert systems are the main application area of fifth generation computers.

Exercise 31

1 Briefly define the following terms: expert system; expert system shell; production rule; semantic network.
2 Give reasons for the use of programming languages such as Lisp and Prolog for expert systems, rather than Pascal or Cobol.
3 Comment on the slow rate of acceptance of expert systems over the last twenty years.
4 Discuss the consequences of the widespread availability of medical expert systems for:
    a) industrial countries
    b) developing countries.
5 Discuss the consequences of the use of expert systems for the number of expert jobs available, and the nature of these jobs.
6 Significant expert systems in addition to those described in the text are:

Internist: general internal medicine
Dendral: analysis of chemical structures from mass spectrometer data
R1: configuration of minicomputer systems
Apes: general-purpose expert system shell.

Find out about one of these systems, and write a case study of it at the same level of detail as those in the chapter.

32
The Computing Industry

It has been widely predicted that by the year 2000, information technology - of which computing is the the major component - will have become the world's largest single industry. As a whole, the computing industry encompasses a wide range of activities. It provides employment for a large number of people, and is becoming an increasingly important element in the economy of all developed countries. In spite of upheavals from time to time, computing appears to be one of the few industries which is successfully weathering the storms of inflation and recession.

This chapter describes, in outline, the current state of the computing industry. As far as possible, a worldwide perspective is maintained. Various aspects of the manufacture and use of computers are covered, as well as some of the service industries which have grown up around computing. Mention is made of some of the professional associations in the computing field. The chapter concludes with a look at the activity which keeps the whole industry moving forwards so rapidly, namely research.

32.1   The World Computing Situation

From a world viewpoint, the computing industry is currently dominated by a struggle between the USA and Japan for the leading position. There are big readjustments taking place in Europe, as companies in the region attempt to keep their places in the world IT league, and to make a common market for IT goods and services.

The USA - the Centre of Gravity

The centre of gravity of the computing industry is undoubtedly the United States of America. Here, computers are designed, produced and used in the greatest numbers. The USA has the most highly developed user market for IT products in administration, commerce and industry. It is the home of a number of multinational computer manufacturing companies.

The USA is a world leader in one of the most important aspects of computer development, namely the design and production of VLSI chips. Most of this activity is centred in California, in an area known as Silicon Valley. However, during the last five years, the pace of innovation in Silicon Valley and elsewhere in the USA has slowed down. A number of companies have gone out of business, and others have merged or been taken over.

The UK and Europe - Software Expertise

Although a certain amount of computer design and manufacture takes place in the UK and Europe, the strength in this region is in the software area. Program language design, systems software development and applications programs are the subjects of intense activity at universities, software houses, computer manufacturers and user installations.

Concern has been expressed in recent years over the worsening balance of trade in IT goods and services in the UK, and the fact that an increasing proportion of the IT companies which are based there are subsidiaries of American or Japanese multinational corporations. In Europe there is increasing emphasis on collaborative projects involving academics and companies from more than one country. These are helping to strengthen the position of the European IT community against competition from the USA and Japan.

Japan - Significant Growth

Japan's proven capability to produce large volumes of high quality manufactured goods is extending into the computing field. A number of Japanese manufacturers are now producing a wide range of computing equipment. Production of electronic components for computers is an extension of the country's established electronics manufacturing capability.

Japan is now advancing from its traditional role as a perfector and mass producer of high-technology goods to that of an innovator. The country is playing a leading role in the research and development work aimed at bringing fifth generation computers into production by the mid-1990s. An increasing amount of new product development is taking place in Japan in all areas of information technology, and Japan's share of the world IT market is increasing. Japan's weakest area is software, but rapid progress is being made in that field.

OPEC Countries - Rapid Implementation

The massive shift of wealth to oil producing countries in recent years has led to many of these nations embarking on very ambitious development programmes. Many of these programmes include the importation of large, sophisticated computing systems, usually from the UK, Europe or the USA. Particularly strong application areas include defence, civil administration, hospitals and industrial production. The oil industry itself is a major user of computers. Many computer workers have been enticed to these areas by large, tax-free salaries and extremely attractive fringe benefits. However, the political and social instability in these regions is a major hindrance to their development, both in the computing field and in other areas.

The rate of growth of IT in this region is now slowing down, as the price of oil has dropped recently, and the political problems and frequent conflicts between countries in these areas have their effects.

Developing Countries - A Slow Start

Most developing countries have made an extremely slow start in the use of computers. The point has been made that computers are helping to widen the gap between industrial and developing nations.

There are a number of reasons for the lack of widespread use of computers in the Third World. The most significant reason is a lack of applications. Most work in developing countries is labour-intensive, and little would be gained by the use of computers. Other reasons include a lack of expertise, minimal service and support facilities, political and social factors which lead to a distrust of Western products, and a chronic shortage of finance. The poor quality of the basic infrastructure, particularly power supplies and telecommunications, is a particular problem.

How this situation will change in the near future is the subject of debate. It seems fairly likely that a number of factors will combine to keep the spread of computers in these countries to a very slow pace. However, should this pace increase, the Third World will become an enormous market for the whole range of computer products and services. The first major change is likely to be in telecommunications. A number of developing countries are in the process of planning or installing advanced digital telecommunications networks. These may help to create the infrastructure needed for further technological advances.

The USSR, Eastern Europe and China - Closed Doors

Although research and development in computing takes place in Communist countries on a large scale, there is very little cooperation between these countries and the West in the field of information technology.

The USSR and Eastern Europe have a policy of producing a unified range of computer equipment, with each country responsible for the development and production of certain units in the range. It appears that hardware development in these countries is several years behind that in the west. Microprocessors are just beginning to be produced, while such devices as floppy disk drives still have to be imported from the West. However, on the software side, particularly in scientific and mathematical programming, these countries are second to none.

Since the breakdown of relations between the USSR and China in 1961, China has pursued an independent course in computer development. For a variety of reasons, including political pressure, development has, until recently, been slow. Emphasis is on scientific, military and industrial applications. In recent years, pressure has been exerted within China to introduce new methods of working in all fields, including the use of new technology. This change of policy is taking some time to take effect, but it could lead to a very significant increase in the use of computers. The takeover of Hong Kong by China in 1997 will give China access to some of the most sophisticated computers in existence.

There are a number of reasons for the lack of co-operation between East and West in the field of computers. By far the most prominent is mutual distrust, as computers are a vital part of modern military systems, particulary nuclear weapons systems. Computer sales from most Western nations to Communist countries have to be approved by government agencies. The regulations which govern these transactions have been tightened over the years, to include software and even manuals. There is a desire in Communist countries to develop their own high technology products, and not to be dependent on imports from the West. There is also a lack of Western currency with which to pay for the computers.

32.2 The Computing Industry by Activities

One of the most significant activities within the computing industry is the manufacture of computer equipment. The next few sections examine various aspects of computer manufacture, and identify some of the most significant companies engaged in this work.

Original Equipment Manufacture

The raw materials of computers are integrated circuits and other electronic components, cathode ray tubes for VDU screens, keyboards, plugs, casings and a large number of other components. Companies which make these components are called **original equipment manufacturers (OEMs)**. There are many of these firms, but the most significant of them are the manufacturers of microprocessors and other large scale integrated circuits. Among the leading companies in this field are Motorola, Intel, Zilog, Rockwell and Texas Instruments in the USA, Fujitsu, Hitachi and NEC in Japan, and Ferranti, Mullard and Inmos in the UK.

Mainframes

Some of the largest corporations in the computing industry are those engaged in the design, development and manufacture of mainframe computers and associated software. A few computer manufacturers rank among the largest corporations of any kind in the world.

The leading company in this area, in terms of income, number of computers sold, number of employees and profit, is **International Business Machines (IBM)**. With branches all over the world, including agencies in Moscow and Peking, IBM has built up a sales and support network second to none. When electronic computers were first developed, during and after the Second World War, IBM was already an established manufacturer of office equipment. Although it was slow in moving into computers, once it entered the market, it soon reached a position of dominance which has never been challenged. It now dominates both the mainframe and the microcomputer markets. One of the most significant influences which IBM has on the computer market is its pricing policy. IBM keeps prices as low as possible, spreading the development cost of a product over its whole lifetime. Other manufacturers generally have little option but to follow IBM's lead.

Other prominent USA-based mainframe manufacturers are **Burroughs, Honeywell, Cray, NCR, Amdahl, Control Data Corporation** and **Univac** (Burroughs and Univac have recently merged). The leading British firm in this field is **International Computers Limited (ICL)**. **Olivetti** and **Philips** are the leading European IT corporations. In Japan there are **Fujitsu, Hitachi** and **Nippon Electric Company (NEC)**.

Although the strength of the companies mentioned in this section is in mainframe manufacture, many of them also supply minicomputers and microcomputers, as well as systems and applications software. The tendency is also increasing to sell a computer as part of a hardware-plus-software package.

Minicomputers

In spite of the pressure from microcomputers, the market for minicomputers does not appear to be declining at the present time. Minicomputers are also benefiting from the availability of cheap VLSI chips. They are now able to provide facilities which a few years ago were confined to mainframes.

As in the case of mainframes, the most significant manufacturers of minicomputers are based in the USA. **Digital Equipment Corporation (DEC)**, producer of VAX computers, is the most prominent. **Hewlett-Packard** and **Data General** are other important minicomputer manufacturers.

Microcomputers

Undoubtedly the fastest growing area in the field of computing is the microcomputers area. Performances are increasing and prices are tumbling, as a number of manufacturers compete in a potentially huge market. All the companies engaged in this area are far too numerous to mention, and a number have only stayed in business for a short time. A few of the significant ones are as follows: **Apple, Atari, Commodore** and **Radio Shack** in the USA; **Research Machines, Amstrad, Apricot, Acorn** and **Sinclair** in the UK; and **Sharp, Canon, Epson** and **Sony** in Japan.

Dedicated Microprocessors

In addition to being used in microcomputers, microprocessors are being incorporated into a growing number of other products. These products include calculators, watches, cameras, automatic production equipment, industrial robots, word processors, banking terminals, motor cars, aircraft, railway locomotives and juke boxes. Many of these products are produced by computer manufacturers. The rest are helping to keep a large number of other companies in business.

This is a very rapidly expanding field, with enormous potential for further development. However, it is also the field which is causing considerable concern in some areas. Particular problems are the possible increase in unemployment, and the lifestyle which would evolve in a world of chips with everything.

Peripherals

In the early days of computing, it was the usual practice for all the units of a computer system to be produced by the same manufacturer. These days it is becoming increasingly common for a computer installation to be assembled from units made by a number of different manufacturers. The peripherals used in these systems are **plug-compatible** with the processors. In other words, they can be connected directly to the processors, without any interfacing adjustments needing to be made.

The continued growth of computing, and the introduction of new types of peripherals, is creating a very large market for peripheral equipment. A number of manufacturers are currently engaged in this area. Among the most prominent are **Memorex**, the USA-based magnetic disk manufacturer, **Amdahl**, a producer of plug-compatible processors which link to IBM equipment, and **Epson**, a Japanese manufacturer of printers and other peripherals.

Computer Services

Computer services is the branch of the computing industry concerned with software. A large number of companies are engaged in some form of computer services. These companies are also known as **software houses**, **systems houses** and **computer bureaux**. Although the individual companies tend to be smaller than hardware manufacturers, together they form a substantial industry in their own right.

These companies provide a wide range of services, including standard software packages, consultancy, custom-built software, combined hardware and software packages and the hire of computing equipment. The phrase **turnkey contract** is used to describe the arrangement whereby a computer service company provides a complete, ready-to-use computer system, designed to the specifications of a customer. Consultancy is provided in such areas as computer systems design, management of projects, office automation, program design, purchase of computer equipment, marketing and the forecasting of future trends. Prominent UK software houses include **Logica**, **Data Logic**, **Scicon** and **CAP**.

Computer Media Suppliers

The computing industry supports a large number of suppliers of computer media. Traditional media such as printer paper are still in demand, though their market is beginning to dwindle. However, there is an increasing demand for magnetic disks and tapes, microfiches, OCR stationery, pre-printed stationery for computer output, and a large number of other products. As new devices come into use, a market is created for media to supply these devices. The majority of disk and tape suppliers are Japanese companies, such as **Maxell** and **Dysan**.

32.3　Users and User Groups

The majority of industrial and commercial organisations in the Western world are computer users. Most of these organisations are irrevocably committed to computers. In other words, they would be unable to continue to operate without their computer systems.

Many computer users are members of **user groups**. Each group generally represents the users of a particular type of computer. These groups enable users to discuss problems of mutual concern, and enable them to bring pressure on computer manufacturers to rectify faults which the users have found with their systems.

32.4　Professional Associations

As computing has spread to involve the work of more and more people, a number of associations have been formed to represent the interests of people who work with computers in various ways. Most prominent of these organisations are the **British Computer Society (BCS)** and **National Computing Centre (NCC)**, in the UK, the **Association for Computing Machinery (ACM)** in the USA and the **International Federation for Information Processing (IFIP)**.

Although each of these organisations has a unique character, their activities cover similar areas. Their most significant activities include the following:

1　Holding conferences, meetings and seminars on a variety of topics relating to computing. Some of these topics are very specialised, others are much broader issues, such as computers and privacy.
2　Publishing journals, weekly and monthly bulletins and newsletters, as well as books and pamphlets on matter relating to computers. Some of these publications are the accepted means of communicating new developments in computer research. Others contain news, editorial comments, product advertisements and advertisements of job vacancies in the computing field.
3　The creation and maintenance of standards and codes of practice for the computing industry.
4　Promoting debate on issues relating to the use of computers, such as privacy and unemployment, and giving evidence to Commissions of Enquiry into these issues.
5　Providing an informal meeting place for their members.

These organisations have helped to enhance the status of the computing industry, and provide an invaluable internal safeguard against abuses of the power of computers.

32.5 Research

It has been said that, in computing, yesterday's research is today's product is tomorrow's museum piece. Although this is somewhat of an overstatement, it does establish two points. Firstly, the pace of computer development is very fast, and, secondly, the leading edge of computing is research.

The importance of research to computing can be seen by the amount of money allocated to it, both by governments and by companies. All computer manufacturers, and many computer service companies, have research divisions. A large proportion of the income of these companies is allocated to these divisions. Some of the research is at the most fundamental level of semiconductor technology and computing theory, looking many years into the future.

Most universities, colleges and polytechnics have computing science departments. These departments have both a teaching and a research function. Unlike the situation in many other fields, there is generally very close co-operation between the academic world and the industrial and commerial world in the field of computer research. This has proved very fruitful in the past, and will no doubt continue to be so. Many of the new computing projects, aimed at the development of fifth generation computers, are collaborative ventures between academic and commercial organisations.

32.6 Conclusion

This chapter has provided a survey of the most significant aspects of the computing industry. It is an industry which includes a number of different activities. Indeed, much of its strength is in its diversity. Although it has reached the age of maturity, it retains its youthful optimism, and is still growing vigorously.

The main points of this chapter are as follows:

- The USA is the world leader in information technology, but its leading position is being increasingly challenged by Japan.
- Britain and the rest of Europe are struggling to maintain their position as a front-rank IT region.
- The rapid pace of IT implementation in OPEC countries is now slowing down.
- IT is gradually gaining acceptance in the Third World.
- The Eastern Bloc is striving to keep up with the West, but the level of contact between the two regions remains low.
- The IT industry can be divided into the following areas of activity: original equipment manufacture, user product manufacture (mainframes, minis, micros and peripherals), computer services and computer media supplies.
- Contact between IT professionals is maintained through professional associations.
- A significant proportion of IT revenue is spent on research.

Exercise 32

1 Briefly define the following terms: OEM; plug-compatible; turnkey contract.
2 Compare and contrast the computing situations in the USA and the USSR.
3 Suggest some reasons for the emergence of the USA as the world leader in computer manufacture.
4 Suggest some reasons for the rapid Japanese penetration into the computer market.
5 Give your views on the role of computers in Third World countries.
6 Summarise, in about 100 words, the most significant activities in the computing industry.
7 Give your own views on the importance of research to computing.
8 Investigate one or more of the profesional associations mentioned in Section 32.4. Write a report listing its activities, publications and areas of interest.
9 Select a major industrial activity such as motor car production, steel making or nuclear energy. Write an overview of the industry, using similar categories to the ones in this chapter. Then compare the industry with the computing industry, mentioning in particular relative rates of growth and future prospects.

33
Data
Processing
Personnel

This chapter concerns the people who work with computers. It covers the manufacture, programming and application of computers, as well as some of the services associated with computing. Descriptions are given of the commonest jobs done in the various fields. It must be remembered that job definitions in computing are not always very rigid. Working practices differ considerably from one organisation to another.

33.1 Computer Manufacture

As descibed in the previous chapter, there are two overall stages in the manufacture of computers, namely original equipment manufacture, and the design and assembly of complete computer systems.

Integrated Circuit Manufacture
Integrated circuits are designed and developed by **electronics engineers**, and fabricated by highly skilled workers using sophisticated equipment. Computers are used in the design, manufacture and testing of these circuits.

Computer System Manufacture
The complete process of designing and constructing a computer is extremely complex, and involves the work of a number of people. The stages are generally as described in the following sections.

Research
Most computer manufacturers have a research department, investigating new computer architectures, new hardware devices, new software techniques and new computer applications. **Scientists**, **research engineers** and **technicians**, as well as highly skilled **software engineers** are among the staff of these departments. A more detailed discussion of computing research is to be found in Section 32.5.

Design
The overall design of a new computer, or series of computers, is in the hands of **computer architects**. Modern computers are designed from both the hardware and the software point of view. Accordingly, **systems programmers**, who write the systems software for the computer, are also involved in the design process.

Construction
Highly skilled production workers are responsible for the various stages of construction and assembly of units. Production lines are not used. Generally, a team of workers is assigned to take a unit through all stages of construction and exhaustive testing.

Sales
One of the highest paid jobs in computing is that of **computer salesman**. Salesmen operate in an intensely competitive environment, where their level of pay depends to some extent on their sales figures. The process of selling a large computer system can take several months.

Installation and Maintenance
Field engineers are responsible for the installation and commissioning of new computer units, and the maintenance and repair of systems in operation. With many computers running 24 hours a day, this type of work often involves calls at unsocial hours.

33.2 A Data Processing Department

Traditionally, an organisation which uses a computer has a **data processing**

department, containing all the staff who work directly with the computer. A typical reporting structure for a large data procesing department is shown in Figure 33.1. Other departments and individuals in an organisation relate to the data processing department as **users** of the computing equipment. The description of a data processing department given here applies in particular to banks, insurance companies, airlines and many central and local government departments.

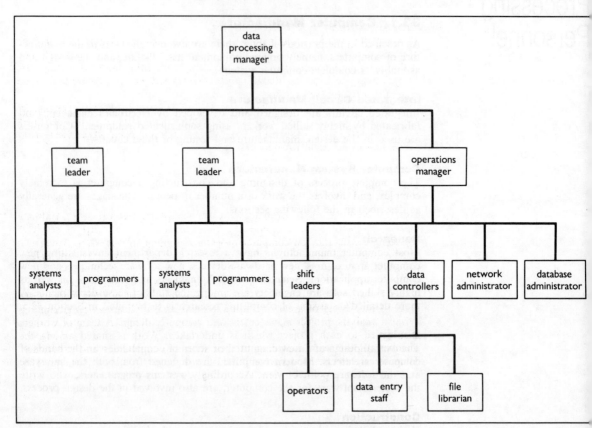

Figure 33.1
A data processing department

In overall charge of a data processing department is a **data processing manager.** Responsibilities of a data processing manager include formulation of policy, approval of projects, staff recruitment and maintaining the relationship of the department with the rest of the company.

The work of a data processing department has two aspects, namely the program development aspect, and the operations aspect. On the program development side, **systems analysts** are responsible for steering each project through the data processing cycle, as described in Chapter 25. **Programmers**, more properly called **applications programmers** in this context, are responsible for writing, correcting and maintaining programs, and producing various items of documentation, explaining how programs are used. However, the work of systems analysts and programmers is gradually merging into the profession of **software engineering**, as described in Chapter 24.

On the operation side, there is an **operations manager** in charge of scheduling the use of the computer, arranging for maintenance and ordering supplies. A team of **operators** man the computer room, often working in shifts under **shift leaders**. More about the work of a computer operator is to be found in Section 21.5.

The flow of data to and from the computer is sometimes supervised by **data controllers**, who ensure that the right data is available at the right time. Data

entry staff operate data entry terminals to keep up the supply of data to the computer. In many large computer systems, **file librarians** are responsible for the large numbers of magnetic tapes and magnetic disks used.

If the computer supports a database, then a **database administrator** is in charge of this aspect of the work. The responsibilities of a database administrator are discussed in Section 28.4. If a data communication network is used, this is often under the overall charge of a **network administrator**.

New Directions in Job Definitions

In many organisations, computers have become such an integral part of their operations that a separate data processing department is not required. The majority of the workers in such organisations make some use of the computer. Programming and systems design is often contracted out to software houses, or standard software packages are purchased.

An expanding computer application in this category is word processing. In many modern offices, all correspondence, contracts and similar work is done on word processing systems. Most of the people working in these offices use a word processing workstation to some extent.

33.3 Software Houses

Situated between computer manufacturers and computer users are **software houses**, or **computer service bureaux**. These provide a wide range of services, including consultancy on computer projects, designing software to a customer's specifications, selling software and supplying complete computer systems. These organisations are described in Section 32.2.

Many software houses have extremely flexible working arrangments, falling broadly under the heading of **software engineering**. Most of their workers are skilled in a variety of areas, including systems and applications programming, systems analysis, project management and computer design. A team of workers is assigned to each project which is undertaken. Work is shared among the members of the team according to their interests, capabilities and experience. There is no strict demarcation of jobs. When a project has been completed, the team is disbanded. Workers are assigned to other projects.

33.4 Conclusion

This chapter has given a survey of the commonest jobs created by the use of computers. It must be emphasised that, in spite of rising unemployment in many areas of work, there is generally a shortage of workers in the computing industry. Salaries in the computing field are, in the majority of cases, extremely attractive.

Exercise 33

1 Outline the work done by each of the following: electronics engineer; systems programmer; computer architect; field engineer; data processing manager; systems analyst; applications programmer; operations manager; data controller; file librarian; database administrator; software engineer; network administrator.

2 A small number of computer architects are responsible for the majority of the computer designs in use today. These include Gene Amdahl (IBM 360 and 370 series), Seymour Cray (Cray-1 and Cray-2) and Stephen Jobs (Apple II and Apple Macintosh). Find out more about the work of one or more of these computer architects.

3 Suggest one or more possible career paths for someone who starts working in the computing field as an applications programmer.

4 Compare working arrangements in a software house with those in a car assembly plant.

5 The list of data processing jobs mentioned in this chapter is not exhaustive. By studying the computer press, or some other suitable source, identify some jobs not described here. Write brief accounts of the nature of these jobs.

6 Comment on the fact that there are virtually no unskilled jobs in the computing industry.

7 One of the prime requirements for a job in the computing field is experience. This makes it difficult for new graduates, or people transferring from other areas of work, to obtain their first job in computing. Investigate this situation and comment on it.

8 The computing industry has the lowest membership of Trade Unions of any industrial sector in the UK. Find out more about this situation, and comment on it.

34
Fifth Generation Computers

In October 1981 the computing world was shaken by an announcement, made in Japan, of a research and development initiative aimed at producing an entirely new generation of computers by the early 1990s. The new computers - given the name **Fifth Generation Computers** - are to incorporate a much higher level of artificial intelligence than contemporary computers. They are aimed at a very wide range of applications, many including voice recognition.

Japan offered to join other leading IT nations in an international collaborative effort to bring these computers into existence. This offer was declined in favour of a number of regional and national development programmes, which are discussed below. These programmes are now under way, and the race is on to develop computers with enhanced intelligence - which will make even the most powerful contemporary computer obsolete.

34.1 The Nature and Objectives of Fifth Generation Computers

Fifth generation computers aim to be able to solve highly complex problems, ones which require reasoning, intelligence and expertise when solved by people. They are intended to be able to cope with large subsets of natural languages, and draw on very large knowledge bases. In spite of their complexity, fifth generation computers are being designed to be used by people who are not necessarily computer experts.

In order to achieve these very ambitious aims, fifth generation computers will not have a single processor, or a small number of tightly coupled processors as computers do today. They are being designed to contain a large number of processors, grouped into three major subsystems: a **knowledge base system**, an **inference mechanism** and an **intelligent user interface**. See Figure 34.1.

The knowledge base system has a very large store of knowledge, structured in one of the ways described in Section 7.2, with a set of processors which access and update the knowledge. It is likely that knowledge bases will evolve from current work in relational databases (Section 28.3). Operations on knowledge bases require the manipulation of large numbers of individual elements: this manipulaton will be done in parallel by the arrays of knowledge processing elements.

The inference mechanism draws reasoned conclusions from the knowledge base. Much of its processing will be drawing logical inferences of the:

if <condition> then <action>

variety. Accordingly, the processing power of a fifth generation computer is expressed in **logical inferences per second (lips)**. The target is in the range 50 to 1000 million lips (compared with a current performance of 10 to 100 thousand lips). Most of this improved performance is planned to be achieved via highly parallel architectures, such as the **dataflow** and **graph reduction** architectures discussed below.

The intelligent user interface is the point of contact between a fifth generation computer and its user. Many of these will be based on communication in a large subset of a natural language. Others will make extensive use of advanced graphics, including **image processing**. The intention is to build a user interface which is close to the natural way of thinking of the user, rather than close to the way of working of the computer, as is the case with contemporary user interfaces. See Figure 34.2. The intelligent interface will contain its own set of processing elements - image processing systems may have an array of processors, one per pixel of the display.

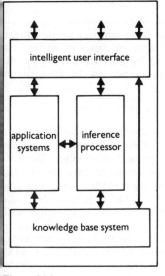

Figure 34.1
A fifth generation computer

34.2 The Fifth Generation Development Programmes

There are five major programmes under way to develop fifth generation computers: the Japanese **Icot** programme, the **MCC** and **Darpa** projects in the

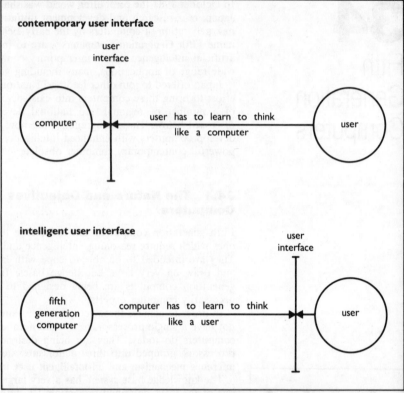

Figure 34.2
User interfaces

USA, the **Esprit** initiative in the EEC and the **Alvey** programme in Britain. There is a certain measure of collaboration between the programmes, but the research results in each project are intended to be implemented within the region. Most research and development is being carried out by consortia of corporations and universities.

Japan: the Icot Programme
The Japanese **Icot** project is regarded as a critical element in Japan's industrial performance, and continuing prosperity, in the 1990s and beyond. A central institute (Icot) has been set up, where the basic research takes place. Development work is done under contract by Japanese computer corporations and universities. A number of main research streams are being followed, including advanced computer architecture, systems software, VLSI chip technology and applications for the new computers. A cyclic progression is intended, with advances in each area being used to assist in the next stages of all the others. For example, the first series of workstations for the researchers are sequential inference computers, programmed in a derivative of Prolog (Section 19.8). Advances in architecture are intended to lead to the development of parallel inference computers for the next phase of the research.

The USA: Darpa and the MCC
Much of the USA fifth generation research and development is being co-ordinated by the **Defense Advanced Research Project Agency (Darpa)**. Darpa allocates US government funds to IT projects with actual or potential military applications. Many such projects are in the field of fifth generation computers. The work is carried out by IT corporations to Darpa specifications.

In order to keep up with the Japanese programme, a group of IT corporations in the USA have set up the **Microelectronic and Computer Technology Corporation (MCC)**. The MCC carries out research and advanced product development, and makes the results available to sponsor corporations for implementation. The sponsors include Digital Equipment, National Cash Register (NCR) and chip manufacturers Motorola and National Semiconductor. IBM is not a member of the MCC.

The EEC: Esprit

The **Esprit** programme is the EEC's response to the Japanese fifth generation initiative. It has a small central directorate, which sponsors projects carried out by consortia of corporations and universities in EEC countries. Up to 50% of the cost of a project is paid for from EEC funds. The range of projects is somewhat wider than those undertaken by the other groups, including such areas as office automation. The Esprit programme is likely to merge into the wider Eureka initiative which aims to co-ordinate research and development in a number of high-technology fields.

The UK: The Alvey Programme

The advanced information technology programme in the UK, the **Alvey** programme, has a central directorate which allocates state funds covering up to 50% of the cost of approved projects. The programme is centred around four key **enabling technologies**: **software engineering** (Chapter 24), **VLSI chip architecture** (Chapter 11), **intelligent knowledge based systems** (Section 34.5) and **intelligent user interfaces** (Section 34.6). These technologies are regarded as the keys to the new generation of computers. Alvey funds are granted on condition that the research is developed into products by British companies.

34.3 Fifth Generation Hardware

Fifth generation computers will be made of silicon or gallium arsenide chips using very large scale integration. They will be based on parallel archtectures very different from today's sequential processors.

Very Large Scale Integration

Fifth generation computers are to be constructed from large numbers of densely packed VLSI chips. At present, the largest chips contain hundreds of thousands of elements; for the fifth generation, millions of elements per chip are required. The narrowest conducting paths on a present-day chip are half a micron wide (a micron is a millionth of a metre): this width is likely to reduce to a quarter of a micron. The ultimate limit on the performance of a chip is the speed of light, which is the speed at which electrical signals travel along a conductor. In order to achieve nanosecond performance (thousands of millions of operations per second), all the components of a computer have to be contained within a 30 cm cube (light travels approximately 30 cm in a nanosecond).

The chips are unlikely to be processing and memory chips as we have them at present, but arrays of identical elements, each carrying out such operations as image processing and searching. Local memories are likely to be incorporated into these special-purpose chips. An early example of a chip of this nature is the **transputer** from Inmos. The transputer combines a high-speed processor, local memory and communication channels on a single chip. Arrays of transputers are built up to form the parallel architecture of a fifth generation computer system.

These requirements mean that the methods of designing chips and the structures which support, connect and cool them will be much more sophisticated than those used today. Extensive use will be made of computer-aided design systems for all stages of chip and processor design.

Parallel Processing

The central requirement of fifth generation computer architectures is for parallel processing. At present two types of parallelism are used: processing arrays and pipelining (see Section 15.4 for an example). These are known as **regular parallelism**, since the degree of parallel processing is under central control at all

332
Fifth Generation Computers

times. Fifth generation computers will require **irregular parallelism**, where control is decentralised, or **data driven**. The two most promising forms of irregular parallelism are **dataflow architecture** and **graph reduction** architectures.

Dataflow Architecture

Dataflow architecture is based on a network of processors, where the output from one is connected to the input of another. The connections are made in such a way that they reflect the parallelism of the program which is running. For example, if a program contains the statement:

if <condition 1> and <condition 2> and <condition 3>

then <action>

the corresponding dataflow network is as shown in Figure 34.3. The three conditions are evaluated in parallel, their results are fed into another processor configured as an AND gate, and the result goes to the processor which performs the action if required. In this way, data flows through the network of processors. Some operations are performed in parallel, and some in sequence.

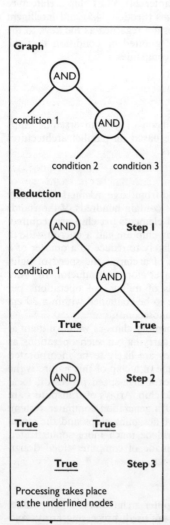

Figure 34.4
Graph reduction

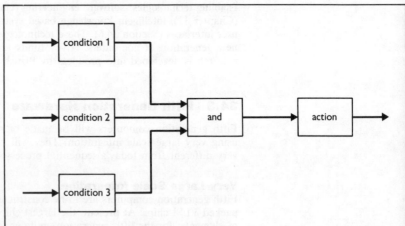

Figure 34.3
A dataflow netword

Graph Reduction Architecture

Graph reduction architecture is also based on a network of processors. A computation is transformed into a graph, which has a tree structure. Nodes are evaluated as soon as all the information they require is available, and the intermediate results are passed back up the tree. Evaluation takes place in parallel wherever possible. See Figure 34.4 for an example. Graph reduction architecture is particularly suited to running programs written in applicative languages (Section 18.3).

The Alvey **Flagship** project aims to develop a complete computer system based on graph reduction architecture.

Intelligent CAD Systems for Chip and Computer Design

It will be quite impossible to develop the chips and carrier structures required for fifth generation processors using even the most advanced computer-aided design (CAD) systems in use at present. Work is under way, particularly in Japan, to develop integrated CAD systems with a certain measure of design intelligence built into them, in order to manage the complexity of fifth generation hardware. The Japanese aim is to incorporate advances in fifth generation hardware and software into the CAD systems used to design the next stages. The ultimate aim is to produce and test designs automatically from specification and connect the design equipment directly to the fabrication systems, forming a

silicon foundry. In this way, it is hoped that chips will be brought into production in weeks or months, instead of years as at present.

34.4 Fifth Generation Software

Fifth generation software is likely to be at least an order of magnitude bigger than the largest programs in use at present. Much of it will be based on techniques of artificial intelligence. Many of the processing circuits in fifth generation computers will be special-purpose elements, requiring special types of instructions to control them. In most cases it will not be possible to develop software on the hardware which will eventually run the application. In many applications, notably military applications, the correctness and reliability of the software under all possible conditions is critical.

Meeting these requirements is extremely difficult. Fifth generation software will be developed using programming languages such as Lisp, Prolog, Occam and the applicative language, Hope (Chapter 19). Integrated software development environments, and the latest techniques of software engineering (Chapter 24) are needed to develop software to the required standards of performance and correctness.

34.5 Intelligent Knowledge Based Systems

Intelligent knowledge based systems (IKBS) are the central elements of fifth generation computers. They use inference to apply knowledge to perform a task. They require at least the following capabilities: classification, concept formation, summarising, selection, searching, reasoning, planning, modelling, the use of 'common sense' rules, and the ability to learn. Most of these are beyond the capabilities of present-day computers.

Research and development work is under way on various aspects of these problems, the most important - and the most difficult - being an adequate method of knowledge representation. See Section 7.2. A number of techniques of knowledge processing are being tried out. These include **evidential reasoning**, based on the way people draw conclusions from bodies of evidence, such as that presented at a trial, and **procedural learning**, based on the way experts learn to solve difficult problems. Efficient methods of searching large databases are also being investigated.

34.6 Intelligent User Interfaces

Intelligent user interfaces aim to make fifth generation computers usable by far more people than use computers at present. This is in spite of the complexity of the systems, and the fact that many users will not be computer experts. The technique is to make the computer behave much more as a person would expect. Two main channels of communication are being emphasised: the use of natural language (Section 7.7), and image processing (Section 7.8).

Although a complete natural language will be beyond the capabilities of even a fifth generation computer, the intention is to enable them to use a large enough subset to make a number of voice-driven applications possible. Image processing requires the computer to be able to accept video pictures as input, and generate output of the same quality. Some approximation to three-dimensional vision is required. Intelligent interfaces will be supported by a complete hardware and software subsystem of the computer, as described above.

34.7 Applications of Fifth Generation Computers

A very wide range of applications are planned for fifth generation computers, although their precise capabilities will not become clear until more development work has been done. Many applications will be expert systems (Chapter 31) of some sort.

The main industrial application is likely to be intelligent robots, with some degree of visual perception, and the ability to be instructed to attain certain goals, rather than to perform a sequence of steps, as at present. The robot will work out the sequence of steps to be performed, according to the goals, and external conditions of which it is aware.

Military applications include strategic and tactical planning and decision support systems, and automated weapons systems. The latter include intelligent guidance systems for missiles, and missile defence systems for aircraft and ships. Digital communications systems which are secure against electronic counter-measures are a likely by-product of VLSI chip design.

In commerce, corporate knowledge bases are likely to be constructed on top of corporate databases. Decision support systems for managers will use these knowledge bases to assist with planning and evaluation. The voice-activated word processor is the ultimate aim of a number of fifth generation projects, with a very large potential market awaiting the first team to achieve it. Automatic, or (more realistically) semi-automatic language translation systems are a similar application.

34.8 Conclusion

The fifth generation development projects are the main thrust of computer development for the next five to ten years. Large sums of money, and the time and energy of some of the leading IT experts in the world are being devoted to the work. The risks are very high, since many of the principles on which fifth generation computers are to be built did not exist five years before the start of the projects. However, the risks of withdrawing from the work are even higher. It is quite clear that if any national or regional group achieves a significant lead in the development of fifth generation computers, that group will be the dominant force in information technology at least until the turn of the century.

The main points of this chapter are as follows:

- The aim of a fifth generation computer is to apply reasoning to knowledge, in order to solve highly complex problems.
- Fifth generation computers comprise a knowledge base processor, an inference mechanism and an intelligent user interface.
- The processing power of a fifth generation computer is measured in logical inferences per second.
- The five fifth generation development programmes are the Japanese Icot programme, the Darpa and MCC projects in the USA, the Esprit project in the EEC and the Alvey programme in the UK.
- Fifth generation computers will use parallel architectures such as dataflow or graph reduction architecture, based on VLSI chips.
- Fifth generation hardware will be developed on integrated CAD systems with direct links to fabrication equipment.
- Fifth generation software will be written in declarative or applicative programming languages, and developed using software engineering techniques on integrated software development environments.
- The central elements of fifth generation computers are intelligent knowledge based systems.
- Intelligent user interfaces are designed to suit the way of thinking of the user, rather than that of the computer. Natural languages and image processing are the main techniques.
- A wide range of applications is planned for fifth generation computers, including expert systems, intelligent robots, voice-driven word processors and intelligent missile guidance systems.

Exercise 34

1 Briefly define the following terms: fifth generation computer; knowledge base processor; inference mechanism; intelligent user interface; enabling technology; intelligent knowledge based system; data driven control; dataflow architecture; graph reduction architecture; evidential reasoning; procedural learning.

2 Draw dataflow networks for each of the following program segments, incorporating as much parallel processing as possible.

   a) if <condition 1> or <condition 2> then
       begin
          <action 1>;
          <action 2>;
       end;

   b) if <condition> then <action 1>
                  else <action 2>;

   ●c) begin
       read(a, b, c, d);
       e: = a + b;
       f: = c + d;
       g: = a / c;
       h: = b / d;
       i: = (e / f) * (g / h);
       write(e, f, g, h, i);
     end;

3 a) How many processing elements are required to support a graphics display with a resolution of 1024 by 1024 pixels, and one processor per pixel?
   b) If each processing element is connected to its eight nearest neighbours, as shown in Figure 34.5, how many interconnections are there in the whole array?
   c) If 256 processing elements for a square of adjacent pixels are fabricated on a single chip, how many chips are required?
   d) How many external connections does each chip require? Each processor has a connection to its pixel in the screen, as well as those to its neighbours.
   e) Comment on the above results.

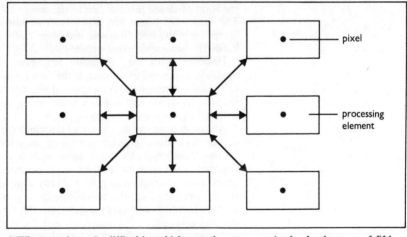

Figure 34.5
Image processing array elements

4 What are the main difficulties which must be overcome in the development of fifth generation computers?

5 Discuss the differences between the ways in which research is carried out by the five fifth generation programmes.

6 Suggest some further applications of fifth generation computers, in addition to those mentioned in the text.

7 Comment on the implications of the availability of computers with enhanced intelligence.

35
Computing in Perspective

This chapter views the subject of computing in a broader perspective than that of the rest of the book. To be able to do this, some of the ideas introduced in previous chapters are restated in more general terms. In addition, the social, economic and political background of computing is investigated. Where possible, a worldwide point of view is maintained, though the situation in Britain is often used as an example.

Some of the material introduced here is contentious, and will become increasingly so in the near future. It is impossible to be completely unbiased in presenting such material. The best that can be done is, wherever possible, to present both sides of the argument. Several questions in the exercise at the end of the chapter invite you to form and clarify your own opinions on some of the topics presented.

35.1 A Second Look at the Question 'What is a Computer?'

Much of the early part of this book is devoted to the question, 'What is a computer?'. Having studied the workings and applications of computers, and the moves towards fifth generation computers, it is appropriate at this point to return to the original question.

A computer is a tool. Like a hammer, washing machine or car assembly plant, it is an extension of a person's capability to carry out a task. Although a computer is a very general-purpose tool, all the tasks it can help to perform are in one field of activity, namely information processing.

A computer has two major aspects, namely its hardware and its software. The hardware, increasingly comprising very large scale integrated circuits, gives a computer its general-purpose information processing capability. Hardware is small, very reliable, uses very little electrical power, and is very cheap. The software of a computer dedicates it to performing specific tasks. The software, in the form of stored instructions to the computer, is generally structured in layers. The innermost layers are closest to the hardware of the computer; the outer layers form the interface with the user. Software is expensive, and, relative to hardware, somewhat error-prone.

However, with the increasing tendencies to store software on read-only memory, to control computers at the very lowest level by micro-instructions, and to include circuits in computers dedicated to specific tasks, the boundary between hardware and software is becoming blurred. This tendency will increase with fifth generation computers.

Although a very wide variety of computers is now available, the designs of all digital electronic computers are based on a few principles set out just after the Second World War. These principles include the storage of data and instructions together in the main store of a computer, and the idea of an instruction cycle to process one instruction at a time. Many contemporary computers have modified these principles, but the modifications are still variations on the same basic theme. The fifth generation represents the first significant move beyond these original principles.

A computer is a system, a set of components working together to achieve some common objectives. In use, computers are components of larger systems including the social, economic and political systems of modern society.

Finally, computers have been called 'intelligent'. This description must be treated with caution. A computer is more intelligent than a hammer, but less intelligent than a person. Computers can draw reasoned conclusions, but they cannot take initiatives, respond to unforeseen circumstances or make moral judgements.

35.2 Computers at Work

Whenever there is a need to process information, computers can be put to work

Information processing includes storing and accessing information, creating and updating data structures, sorting and selecting information, performing calculations and drawing conclusions. Computers can accept input from their environment, and in turn supply output to their environment. They can control machinery. Computers are being linked to data communications networks to an increasing extent.

But the work done by computers can also be seen in a wider context. Computers create jobs for a large number of people who work with them, but put others out of work by taking over their jobs. The information processed by computers is sometimes sensitive personal information. Computer applications include such contentious areas as the guidance of nuclear weapons and the filing systems of secret police forces.

The next few sections of this chapter are a very brief exploration of the wider implications of the use of computers.

35.3 Implications of Computing

Computers have already had a profound impact on the economic and social fabric of the societies in which they are used. With the increasing availability of cheap microprocessors, an even wider impact is predicted. Some alarming prophecies have been made in this connection. However, computers cannot be judged in isolation. Together with inflation, recession, war, famine, pollution, prejudice, and the effects of other technologies, computers are just one of the factors influencing the nature and direction of contemporary societies. To further complicate the situation, computers interact with these other factors.

The social implications of the use of computers is a very large, complex and controversial subject. All that can be done within the confines of this book is to outline the specific issues where concern has already been expressed, and give a broad overview of the pressures which are affecting the course of modern societies, showing the place of computers among these pressures.

35.4 The Areas of Concern

There has been unease about the effects of computers ever since they were first introduced. Misleading and exaggerated accounts in books, films and newspapers, and in television and radio reports have made the situation worse. But the biggest problem is the ignorance, on the part of the majority of people, of the nature, capabilities and limitations of computers.

This general unease has gradually focused on three major areas of concern about the implications of computers. These issues are employment and unemployment, privacy of personal information, and the use of computers in establishing and maintaining political control. Each of these issues is now briefly discussed.

Employment and Unemployment

It is an inescapable fact that computers and microprocessors in other devices put people out of work. But on the other hand, computers create jobs, both directly and indirectly. Jobs created directly include all the people who design, construct, program and operate computers. This is an enormous, prosperous and growing industry. By their contribution to efficiency and productivity, computers create and preserve jobs in an indirect way.

The net effect of all this is that computers are changing the nature of employment. Jobs are lost in manual and semi-skilled areas, and created in skilled and professional areas. Jobs are being lost in traditional manufacturing industries, and being created in service industries. This implies that a shift in training patterns, and considerable retraining of displaced workers is necessary, as one attempt to cope with the problem.

In the present economic climate, computers are not the only cause of unemployment. The recession which has recently affected many Western nations, and the consequent drop in demand for such products as steel, motor cars and chemicals, are far bigger causes. For these reasons, studies of the unemployment that has been caused by computers, and projections of the unemployment that computers will cause, are contradictory. Very few firm conclusions can be drawn from them. This is not, however, a cause for complacency.

It seems that each application of computers must be judged on its merits, from the point of view of employment and unemployment. In all cases, it is necessary to take a broad view of the situation, in an attempt to see the long term effects, and wider implications, of the introduction of computers at a particular place.

Privacy
The issue relating to the use of computers which affects the greatest number of people is the privacy of personal information stored by computers. Who should have access to this information? How safe is this information against unauthorised disclosure? Although manual methods of storing personal information have been in operation for a long time, the widespread use of computers for this purpose makes the problem potentially far worse. In theory, it is now possible to obtain millions of items of information in a few seconds.

There are in fact two aspects to this problem: the deliberate disclosure of information by the people or organisations which store it, and the 'theft' of this information by outsiders.

With regard to the first aspect of the problem, a number of countries now have legislation regulating the storage and dissemination of personal information. These countries include the USA, France, Sweden and Canada. EEC countries are obliged to pass legislation in accordance with a set of guidelines on the subject. In Britain, the Data Protection Act of 1984 is in the process of being implemented. It creates a register of all users of computerised personal information. In terms of the Act, users must declare all the purposes for which they intend to use the data, and data subjects have access to their records. Certain police and national security systems are exempt from the Act.

Concerning the second part of the problem, various attempts have been made to provide adequate security for stored confidential data. These include 'scrambling' the data into a code, limiting access to computers and terminals, and systems of passwords for people 'logging on' to the system. Just how effective these measures are, remains to be seen.

Computers and Political Control
One of the most sinister applications of computers is their use by security forces in a number of states, to store and process information about terrorists, spies, subversives and other 'persons of interest' to these forces. Indirect evidence suggests that this is a very widespread computer application, though official confirmation of the existence of these computers is rare.

The problem is that there are no public safeguards on the use of such computers. Most people would agree that every available resource needs to be used against spies and terrorists, but where does one draw the line? There is also evidence that so much information is gathered by some of these systems that it is impossible to sort out the vital from the trivial.

35.5 Computers in a World of Change
It has been pointed out since the days of ancient China that the only constant fact about civilisation is that it is changing. This section is an attempt to give a very brief assessment of the forces of change which are currently in operation, and identify the place of computers among these forces.

It seems that the pressures for change currently at work fall into five very broad categories. These are political and religious pressure, resource pressure, population pressure, pollution pressure and technological pressure. Each of these is briefly discussed below.

Political and Religious Pressure

Both religious and political views incline people to have visions of the kind of society in which they want to live. In some countries, these pressures have their outlet in the political institutions of the state. Changes occur from time to time, but without too much dislocation or upheaval.

However, there are also numerous instances where political and/or religious motivation has led to terrorism, civil wars, forcible changes of government and conflicts of all types between and within states. Many such conflicts remain unresolved today, and in many parts of the world, no stable solutions are in sight. The ever-increasing power of available weapons, including nuclear weapons, is an additional factor which compounds the seriousness of these problems.

Political and religious pressure is the oldest and most visible force for change at present in operation. But it must now take its place among other pressures, and be affected by them.

Resource Pressure

Over the last two decades it has become apparent that a number of the earth's natural resources are becoming seriously depleted, and will be completely used up in the foreseeable future if present trends in the consumption of these resources continue.

The most obvious resource in this category is oil. Oil producing countries have realised the degree of dependence of industrialised nations on their output, and the fact that their reserves are limited. Accordingly, the price of oil is being pushed steadily higher, with a number of consequences for both producers and consumers.

Other minerals, including a number of metals, are being depleted at an alarming rate. Renewable resources like timber and fish stocks are used up faster than they can replenish themselves. Species of plants and animals are becoming extinct, depleting once and for all the 'pool' of genetic material available on earth.

Resource pressure is forcing a change in the way of life of many people. Its worst effects are being felt by poor and underprivileged individuals and nations at the present time, but it will begin to affect everyone in the near future.

Population Pressure

In spite of a number of efforts to control it, the global population is increasing at a disturbing rate. The largest increases are occurring in the poorest countries. It is almost impossible for food production to keep pace with population growth. The result is that North America and Europe have grain surpluses, wine lakes and butter mountains, while much of the rest of the world has malnutrition and famine.

Population pressure is a factor in the miserable way of life of a significant proportion of the people of the world. It may yet demand a change in the way of life of the rest before a more satisfactory state of affairs is reached.

Pollution Pressure

It is becoming increasingly clear that harmful substances are being released, by a number of industrial processes, into the air, water and ground which are beyond the capacity of the environment to dispose of. In spite of considerable success in some areas, notably the control of air pollution in certain cities, the problem of pollution is becoming worse. Certain enclosed seas such as the Baltic and the Mediterranean are in danger of losing their capacity to support marine life. A number of European forests are in danger of destruction by acid rain. An increasing number of poisons are present in air, water and food supplies. The percentage of carbon dioxide in the atmosphere is slowly but steadily increasing.

Most pollution is being caused by industrial nations. Pollution pressure is forcing these countries to change in a number of ways. Industrial, agricultural and domestic practices are having to adjust to increasingly stringent regulations. If pollution is not brought under control in the fairly near future, the consequences could be extremely serious.

Technological Pressure

Ever since the industrial revolution, technology has been the driving force in the evolution of Western societies. Each major breakthrough has had profound social repercussions. Furthermore, it appears that the pace of technological innovation is quickening.

Since the Second World War, we have seen jet engines revolutionise long distance transport, transistors lead to a multiplicity of cheap, high quality electronic devices, television create a global village, nuclear energy provide a significant proportion of electric power, nuclear weapons transform war into a potential global catastrophe, and computers become an essential aspect of industrial and commercial activity. Genetic engineering is poised to become a significant technology in medicine and chemical production. Each of these changes has had beneficial and detrimental effects. One of the disadvantages is the upheaval caused by constant change, a phenomenon becoming known as future shock.

Computers must take their place amongst the technological innovations which are propelling societies forward. Although computers are a major influence, they are not the only influence in this field. Technological pressures must, in turn, take their place amongst the other pressures mentioned in previous sections. It very seldom happens that all these pressures are acting in the same direction. One reason for the complexity and lack of cohesion of contemporary societies is that they are at the mercy of a number of different forces, none of which is very clearly understood, pushing the societies in different directions.

35.6 Conclusion

This chapter has presented, in a very condensed form, a retrospective overview of the nature of computers, the work they do, and some of the effects they are having on the societies in which they are used. The place of computers among the many pressures determining the course of these societies has also been discussed.

This chapter has skirted round the question 'Are computers a good thing?' Occasionally, rather extreme answers, in one direction or the other, are given to this question. This chapter makes the case that the answer to this question must lie between the two extremes.

On the one hand, consider the situation where computers are used to the maximum extent which is technically possible. The result would be an economic and social disaster, with massive unemployment, widespread discontent and disorder amongst large sections of the population, a highly regimented way of life and repressive governments.

On the other hand, consider the situation where computers are phased out completely. This would result in the collapse of the financial systems, and of most industrial and commercial organisations in all developed countries. Supplies of food, gas, electricity and water would be adversely affected. Standards of local and national administration, policing and medical service would suffer. The high standard of life which we have come to expect would no longer be possible.

The sane alternative is to steer a middle course, judging each computer application on its merits, and taking into account both the immediate and the wider implications of the situation. In the foreseeable future, the further spread of computers will probably become a political issue. The more people there are who know something about computers, the better are the chances of reaching a satisfactory consensus on these issues.

Exercise 35

1 Put the question 'What is a computer?' to a number of people not concerned with computing. Make a note of the answers you receive.

In the light of your findings, discuss any common misconceptions about the nature of computers you observe. Discuss the significance of these misconceptions in relation to the further acceptance of computers, and suggest ways in which these misconceptions might be reduced.

2 Identify the design principles of computers which have remained the same since the Second World War.

●3 Identify the most significant aspects of computing which may be described as systems. State briefly the objectives and significant interfaces of each system, and mention any major subsystems.

4 In the light of your knowledge of computers, identify one or more accounts of the impact of computers in a book, film, newspaper, television or radio programme which may be described as 'exaggerated and misleading'. Justify your choice(s).

5 Give your views on the issue of computers and unemployment. Include your comments on the following topics:

Whether computers are in any way related to other major causes of unemployment, such as declining industries like steelmaking, shipbuilding and motor car manufacture.

Whether you think that the increased job opportunities created by computers offsets the unemployment they cause.

What the effect of computers on unemployment will be in the future.

6 Name some areas in which you think computers should not be introduced because of the unemployment which would be caused.

7 Find out the attitude of some Trade Unions towards the introduction of computers.

8 Give your views on the issue of computers and privacy. Include your comments on the following topics:

The extent to which privacy is already being abused by various computer applications.

The potential for abuse of privacy in the future, by computer applications.

Whether further legislation should be introduced in this area, and, if so, what form the legislation should take.

9 Find out about the privacy laws existing in some countries. Briefly describe each situation you investigate, and identify similarities and differences between them.

10 Give your views on the issue of computers and political control. Mention what (if any) safeguards you think should be placed on the use of computers in this area.

●11 Outline some of the most significant changes which, in your view, have been brought about by the introduction of the following technologies: telephone; radio; television; motor cars; jet passenger aeroplanes; nuclear weapons.

12 Give your own views on the most significant factors causing change in societies today. Identify the relative importance of computers among these factors.

36

Revision Exercises

All the questions in this exercise are taken from past examination papers in Computing Science. In most cases, questions cover material in more than one chapter of the book.

1 a) Explain the difference between an **operand** and an **operand address** as used with reference to an assembly language. State four ways in which the address part of a machine level instruction may be used and give an example of each.

b) Describe one method of representing alphanumeric characters for storage in a fixed word length of 24 bits. State two machine code operations which are desirable for the internal manipulation of such characters.

c) Describe, with the aid of a diagram, one method of storing data items based on the principle of **last-in-first-out**. Draw flow diagrams to show how an item of data can be removed from the store you have described and how an item of data can be input, incorporating tests to examine whether the store is full or empty as necessary.

AEB 79

2 a) Explain, with the aid of a block diagram, how the major functional units of a simple computer are interrelated with respect to the flow of information (i.e. instructions and data) and the flow of control commands.

Note: Use firm lines to show information flow and dotted lines to show flow of control commands.

b) Draw a flow diagram to represent the basic process of the **fetch-execute** cycle in the control unit of a typical computer, naming and stating the functions of any special register involved. Your diagram should show how the cycle takes account of jumps, address modification and indirect addressing.

Note: You are not required to discuss or represent the electronic circuitry of the control unit.

AEB 79

3 a) Explain how multiprogramming assists in maximising the use of the central processor.

b) Discuss the term **interrupt** making particular reference to **peripheral interrupts** and **error interrupts**.

AEB 79

4 a) What is meant by the term **operating system**? State four of the functions of an operating system.

b) Describe what is involved when an assembly language program is translated into machine instructions including in your discussion reference to **labelled instructions**, **jump instructions** and **directives**.

AEB 79

5 An engineering company manufactures components using numerically controlled machine tools. The main computer users in the company are:

a) Accounts and Finance Section who are responsible for administrative tasks such as invoicing, orders and payroll.

b) Operational Research Section who investigate how processes may be made more efficient.

c) Development Section who produce programs for machine tools.

   i) For each of the above sections, name a high level language that would be suitable for their applications, describing the features that make appropriate.

   ii) All programs submitted to the Computer Section are run under an operating system. Give a brief description of a control language for an operating system and explain how it assists the user.

AEB 79 B

6 In relationship to computer systems, explain the meaning and purpose of the following:
   i) feasibility study;
   ii) system flowchart;
   iii) source document and turnaround document;
   iv) system maintenance.

AEB 79 II

7 Variables declared in a routine which is called recursively cannot be allocated fixed storage space.
   a) Explain why this is so.
   b) Describe briefly, by means of diagrams or otherwise, how storage could be allocated and released as required.

UCLES 81 Specimen I

8 a) Explain with the aid of diagrams how data records can be deleted from and inserted into a linked list. Describe from a programmer's point of view how to set up a linked list and how to manage the free storage.
   A list of identifiers is stored as follows:
   i) the character codes of the first and the last characters of the identifier are added to the length of the identifier and the result is divided by 16, the remainder providing a hash value;
   ii) the entry in a hash table corresponding to the hash value contains either zero, indicating no identifier with this hash value, or a pointer to an identifier;
   iii) associated with the identifier is a value of either zero, indicating no further identifiers with this hash value, or a pointer to another identifier with this hash value.
   b) Show this structure in a diagram, and describe how a new item may be added to the list.
   c) What is the purpose of the type of calculation described above in (i)?

UCLES 81 Specimen II

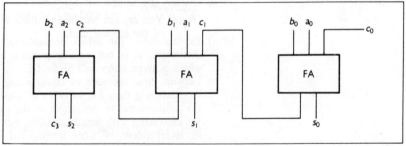

9 Figure 36.1 is a block diagram of a parallel adder that can add 3-bit binary 2s complement numbers $a_2 a_1 a_0$ and $b_2 b_1 b_0$. (Each block marked FA in the figure is a full adder.)
   a) i) Write a truth table for c_2 as a function of a_1, b_1 and c_1.
      ii) Minimise this function and draw a minimal logic circuit that has as inputs a_1, b_1, c_1 and output c_2.
   b) Draw the figure again but now with extra gates needed for computing

   $$b_2 b_1 b_0 - a_2 a_1 a_0$$

   using three full adders. State the value that should be applied to c_0 when subtraction is required, but do not show internal details of any full adder.
   c) Draw a circuit that has as inputs a control signal d and two binary numbers $b_2 b_1 b_0$ and $a_2 a_1 a_0$.
   If $d = 1$ the output of the circuit is to be $b_2 b_1 b_0 - a_2 a_1 a_0$. If $d = 0$ the output of the circuit is to be $b_2 b_1 b_0 + a_2 a_1 a_0$. Subtraction must be achieved by using three full adders. Your diagram should show how c_0 is determined by d. Do not show internal details of any full adder, but represent each full adder by a block marked FA, as in the figure.

JMB 79 I

10 Order processing is implemented in both batch and real-time mode. Describe briefly two applications to illustrate respectively each mode of implementation.

For each application give details of the method of data collection and conversion to machine readable form. Explain why the data collection methods are appropriate.

In both cases there will be a need for data validation. Suggest ways in which this validation can be done.

UL 79 I

11 a) What is an **interrupt**? Give three examples of situations which can lead to interrupts.

b) Why do different interrupts have different priorities? Illustrate your answer by discussing a situation in which two interrupts of different priority have to be dealt with together.

c) Describe how input and output can be carried out under system (rather than program) control and indicate the advantages of this.

OLE 78 I

12 a) Define the terms **pointer**, **linked list**, **tree**, **first-in-first-out list**.

b) Explain how pointers can be used (i) to add a new item to a linked list, (ii) to remove an item in the middle of such a list, (iii) to join two such lists to form a single list.

c) Show how storage in terms of linked lists could be used to hold information about distances between towns.

OLE 78 I

13 a) Describe the structure of the files which would be needed by a regional health authority to contain a computer record of the medical history of patients living in its area.

b) What computing equipment would be necessary if such files were to be used by hospital staff and general practitioners?

c) What benefits might be secured by such a system?

d) Discuss the safeguards for confidentiality which would be desirable in such a system, and explain how they could be provided.

OLE 78 II

14 a) Explain why, for tables of information held alphabetically, as in a dictionary, it is not usually possible to compute the exact address at which a given entry will be found.

b) Explain three methods of constructing and using such a table in which the searching time for an entry is respectively:
  i) proportional to the length of the table;
  ii) increasing with length of table, but less than proportionally;
  iii) independent of table length, but dependent on the proportion of storage filled by the table.

c) Give one example in each case to illustrate situations in which each of these methods would be appropriate.

OLE 80 I

15 Draw a diagram to represent a linked list held in immediate access storage, where it is required to hold both forward and backward links.

Draw a similar diagram to show how the list is represented when it is empty of data items.

Give an algorithm, diagrammatically or otherwise, for the insertion of a new item at the end (tail) of the list.

Would this linked list structure be suitable for the storage of a **stack**? Give reasons for your answer.

UL 80 I

16 Describe how the following data structures may be organised when used by a program in an assembly language, indicating how data is placed in and retrieved from each structure:
a) an array,
b) a stack,
c) a tree.

UL 80 II

17 Explain how a multiprogramming system functions.
   A time-sharing system with many terminal users is using a multiprogramming operating system. Describe the way in which the file system can be arranged so that users can share files. What is meant by security and reliability in the context of file processing?

UL 80 II

18 A particular index-sequentially organised file has only one level of indexing and only one index, which has already been read into immediate access memory. The file is subdivided into blocks and the index has one entry per block. There is no overflow. Omitting low-level details, give an alogorithm either in words or with the help of a flowchart, for efficiently retrieving one record from this file, given the key.

JMB 80 I

19 a) Simplify the logic circuit in Figure 36.2.
   b) The arithmetic and logic unit (ALU) of a particular computer has eight functions such as **ADD, SUBTRACT, NEGATE, ADD COMPLEMENT**, and so on. The ALU function is selected by a three-bit function code. One of the control inputs to the ALU should be set equal to zero for functions **ADD, AND, SUBTRACT**, and **ADD COMPLEMENT**, and should be set equal to one for the other four functions. Design a minimal logic circuit whose output is this control input to the ALU and whose input is the three-bit function code. The function codes for **ADD, AND, SUBTRACT** and **ADD COMPLEMENT** are respectively 001, 010, 101 and 110.
   c) A simple multiplexer circuit has six binary inputs a, b, c, d, x, y and one output p. Inputs a, b, c, d are data bits and x and y are control inputs. Draw a logic design for this circuit such that:

   if x = 0 and y = 0 then p = a;
   if x = 0 and y = 1 then p = b;
   if x = 1 and y = 1 then p = c;
   if x = 1 and y = 0 then p = d.

JMB 80 I

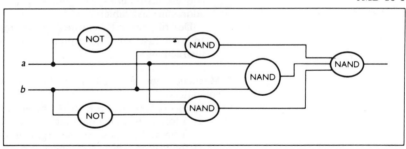

Figure 36.2

20 a) Using either address modification or indirect addressing, write an assembler language program to read thirty characters and output them in the reverse order. Beside each instruction write an explanatory comment to say what that instruction does.
   b) Write an assembler language program to read one character into an accumulator, and either print letter E, if the parity of the character code now in the accumulator is even, or print letter O, if it is odd. Use shifting and counting to determine parity. Beside each instruction write an explanatory comment to say what that instruction does.

JMB 80 II

21 Various systems are available that enable a user at home to receive computer data via a television set.
   Assuming that such systems were developed to enable home users to receive and transmit information and to create and use data files, suggest, with reasons,
   a) the facilities which such a service should provide for the user;

b) how this service could be used to manage household and personal affairs;

c) how this service could change the nature of the data processing industry.

JMB 80 II

22 A large retail organisation, having department stores in a number of large towns, wishes to install a central computer at the head office, with on-line terminals at each store and at a central warehouse in order to control stock.

a) Suggest, with reasons, a configuration for the computer system and indicate clearly the use of the terminal devices.

b) Construct systems flowcharts that show both the functions of the system as well as the use of files.

c) Explain what benefits the organisation might reasonably expect from the installation of the system.

JMB 80 II

23 Explain the functions of the following personnel in a computer installation, clearly identifying any inter-relationships between them.

   i) Systems Analyst
   ii) Programmer
   iii) Computer Operations staff
   iv) Job Control clerk

JMB 80 II

24 a) Many computers use a status register to hold condition codes which communicate the outcome of previous actions to conditional jump instructions.

   i) Describe **three** different condition codes.
   ii) What types of instruction affect condition codes?
   iii) Illustrate the action of a conditional jump in the execute phase of the fetch-execute cycle describing the function of any registers you mention.

b) It is required to write a section of program that transfers control to one of 18 different locations dependent upon an integer in the range 0 to 17. This integer is held in a location labelled SELECT.

   The machine upon which this is to be programmed supports one address instructions with indexing (address modification) and indirect addressing available.

   Describe **two** different methods of implementing the required function. In each case your description should consist of a set of one address instructions.

AEB 84 I

25 Magnetic tape is used as a backing storage medium on mainframe computers.

a) In this context describe, with the aid of diagrams,
   i) a format in which data may be stored on magnetic tape, including the form and purpose of the begining and end of tape markers,
   ii) the way in which a magnetic tape drive operates, including the effect of the write permit ring.

b) A particular magnetic tape drive records data at 1600 bytes per inch, the read/write speed of the tape is 75 inches per second and the inter block gaps are 0.5 inch.
   i) Calculate the transfer rate of this tape drive.
   ii) Calculate the **effective** transfer rates in reading a file of 1 megabyte held in
      (1) 512 byte blocks
      (2) 1024 byte blocks
      (3) 2048 byte blocks
      (4) 4096 byte blocks
   You may assume the tape continues to travel at read/write speed over the inter block gaps.
   iii) What practical limitations might there be in increasing the block size?

AEB 84 I

26 Figure 36.3 represents a canal lock. A and C are lock gates which when open allow boats to pass from one part of the lock to another. B and D are sluices which when open allow water either side of the respective lock gate to find its own level. Lock gates should only be opened when the water on either side of them is at the same level.

A sensor is attached to each lock gate and to each sluice. These sensors send a 0 for open and a 1 for closed.

a) Derive a Boolean function which takes the value 1 in the dangerous situation when water is allowed to pass from the UPPER part of the lock to the LOWER part of the lock in an unrestricted way.

b) Simplify this function and represent this in NAND logic only.

c) Show the sequence of Boolean functions (7 in all) for a boat to pass from the LOWER part of the lock to the UPPER part of the lock in a safe way. You should start and end with the water levels as shown above and all the lock gates and sluices closed.

d) Suggest a method whereby the level of the water in the INNER part of the lock can be sensed by a digital computer.

AEB 84 I

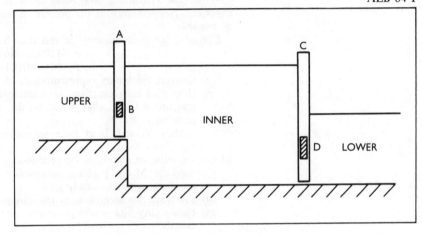

Figure 36.3

27 The numeric values 23, 1, 19, 3, 8, 27 are held in the order given and are to be organized as
   i) a linked list,
   ii) a binary tree.
a) Describe, with the aid of diagrams, each of these two data structures.
b) The above values are held in a one-dimensional array A. By using an additional array NEXT and a variable FIRST show how these values may be represented in ascending numeric order using a linked list. Show clearly the value of FIRST and the elements of NEXT.
c) Construct a flowchart or a pseudo code algorithm to show how an additional value may be inserted into a linked list of this form. Assume that a variable FREE gives the subscript of the first free location in A.
d) Construct a diagram showing how the above values would be held in a binary tree which facilitates sorting, assuming the value 23 to be the root.
e) Comment on the number of comparisons required to locate a particular value in a binary tree as compared with a linked list.

AEB 84 II

28 In the context of a data processing system write brief notes on the following:
a) feasibility study,
b) validation procedures,
c) security,
d) application system maintenance.

AEB 84 II

29 a) Describe the principles of operation of a stack. Assuming the existence, within the central processing unit of a special stack pointer register, SP,

state and describe the machine code instructions that are required to implement the stack.

What is the criterion which determines the size of the SP register?

b) Describe how the contents of two memory locations, A and B, could be added together and the result placed in a third memory location C, using:
   i) two address instructions,
   ii) one address instructions, and,
   iii) zero address instruction(s) and a stack facility.

c) Describe how the linkage to and from a closed subroutine can be supported by
   i) a machine without a stack facility
   ii) a machine with a stack facility.

In each case state and describe the instructions that are required to effect entry to and exit from a closed subroutine.

AEB 85 I

30 A machine M holds normalised floating point numbers in 12-bit registers. The mantissa occupies the leftmost 8 bits and is held as a two's complement fraction, the remaining bits being used as a two's complement integer exponent. Normalisation is the process of retaining as many significant bits as possible.

Consider two such numbers A and B as follows

A 011001010101
B 100111010011

a) i) Convert the binary representations of A and B into denary.
   ii) If instead each mantissa were interpreted as a fraction in sign and magnitude form, what would be the denary values of the above bit patterns A and B.

     Show A and B in their normalised form using this alternative representation.

b) i) Describe an algorithm (in pseudocode or otherwise) that will run on machine M, to perform subtraction of normalised floating point numbers, without rounding off.
   ii) Illustrate this algorithm by showing its action in calculating A-B.
   iii) How many bits would the mantissa require to store this difference exactly?

c) Discuss the problems of representing zero in normalised floating point numbers.

AEB 85 I

31 a) Write brief notes on each of the following processes which are carried out when developing a program:
   i) program design,
   ii) program writing,
   iii) program documentation.

b) Describe how you would **test** a program which is designed to read from a keyboard, in a random order, a number of transaction records each with several fields, to update a master file with these records causing several master file records to be modified and also to print an analysis of the transaction records.

AEB 85 II

32 A certain hospital has a large computer system providing many interactive VDU's which are used in the wards, consulting rooms and by the hospital administration.

a) Discuss, with reasons, the advantages and disadvantages of such a system when compared with a manual system.

b) From time to time parts of the computer system will fail. On one such occasion the disk controller fails causing a master file to be corrupted and the loss of the morning's transactions. Discuss the steps that could have been taken beforehand to minimise the possibility of vital information being lost.

c) Discuss the steps that may be taken to maintain the confidentiality of information in such a system.

AEB 85 II

33 Each morning in the post a holiday company receives the following documents:

    i) bookings for holidays from travel agents,

    ii) payments from travel agents for holidays.

    Every week each travel agent receives a statement of confirmation of bookings, together with a financial statement showing how much has been paid and how much is still owed by each of his customers against a particular holiday.

a) For this batch application construct a system flowchart which shows how the outputs can be produced from the given inputs. Describe the files which you propose for this system.

b) Briefly identify the problems and advantages which are inherent in this batch mode of operation and discuss how the system could be improved by the introduction of on-line terminals in the travel agents' offices connected to the holiday company's computer.

JMB 84 I

34 a) Explain how the following pieces of software are used in the translation of a high-level language program:

    i) compiler,

    ii) linkage editor,

    iii) loader.

b) Why might it be necessary to use an assembler in such a compilation process?

c) A program is written in one high-level language and has subroutines written in another high-level language. The program also accesses graphics routines which are stored in a graphics library. Describe how the compilers, linkage editor and loader are used. What information is passed between **each** of the compilation phases?

JMB 84 I

35 An agency concerned with letting flats to students keeps a record for each flat in its system. Flat owners can ask the agency to put a record for a newly available flat on the agency's files. Students can request information about flats and, on payment of a fixed fee, can inspect a flat of their choice. They may then decide not to take the flat in which case their transaction is complete or they may decide to take the flat. If a flat is taken, the rent is paid monthly in advance to the agency. The agency deducts a percentage handling fee and forwards the remainder of the rent to the owner. Students give one month's notice to terminate their tenancy at which point the agency asks the owner whether he or she wishes to remove the flat from the system or to keep it available for a further let.

Using a systems flowchart, or otherwise, describe the operation of the agency.

The agency is thinking of using a computer to help in the operation of this system. What additional information would you request from the agency before giving advice on whether a computer would be a suitable purchase for this task? If it was decided to buy a small two-user computer system, what files should be kept? How would these files be accessed and maintained?

JMB 84 II

36 A newsagent wishes to computerise his paper delivery system. Each household informs the newsagent of the papers, magazines, periodicals and comics they wish to take, together with their name and address. A household's order can be changed at any time. Each day the newsagent marks up and collects, into bundles, the papers, etc. to be delivered by the newspaper boy or girl.

A householder can inform the newsagent when he will be away on holiday so that deliveries can be stopped during absence. The newsagent also wishes to inform his wholesaler of his requirements for papers, etc. for the following order period.

The system also maintains accounts for each household.

a) Suggest suitable file, record and data structures for this system, giving reasons.

b) Explain how the newsagent could use the system when marking up and putting papers into order for subsequent delivery.

JMB 85 II

37 a) Describe the content and structure of computer files to hold the information which would be needed to run a credit-card system.

b) Explain how organisations accepting credit-card transactions could be linked to the system to enquire about credit-worthiness of purchasers. What safeguards would be desirable for such enquiries?

c) Explain, with the help of a flow diagram, what processes would need to be carried out by the central computer of such a system.

OLE 82 II

38 An item can be identified by means of a bar code. When this is read by a light pen the following four bit sequences are placed in a 32-bit word:
   i) the binary representation of 13 (1101);
   ii) the binary representations of each of six decimal digits;
   iii) the binary representation of 13 again.

   The bar code may be read forwards, or backwards, in which case the 32-bit pattern is completely reversed.

a) With the help of a flow diagram, or otherwise, describe an algorithm for deducing the six digit number and converting it to binary.

b) Why is 13 a suitable value for the first and last four-bit sequences?

OLE 83 II

39 a) Explain the terms **main store, paged store, virtual store**.
   Describe one advantage and one drawback of a virtual store system.

b) What is an **autonomous transfer** to a peripheral device? How can **double-buffering** allow transfers to take place in parallel with computing?

c) What is an **interrupt signal**? Give two reasons why an interrupt signal might occur.

OLE 84 II

40 For a computerised national telephone directory-enquiry system for Great Britain:

a) What should be stored on file for each individual subscriber?

b) What keys should be made available to the operator for locating the entry for a subscriber? Why is this choice of suitable?

c) Should other people be allowed access to the system?

d) How should the files be stored to enable fast retrieval for each type of key?

OLE 84 II

41 A company is engaged in the manufacture and marketing of buttons of various designs. Included among its activities are the following:
   i) ordering and maintaining a stock of raw materials;
   ii) scheduling production according to known requirements and forecasts for orders, existing stock of buttons, and the availability of materials, labour and machinery;
   iii) marketing the company's products, receiving orders, and making sales forecasts;
   iv) maintaining a stock of buttons and fulfilling orders for them;
   v) handling all of the company's financial transactions;
   vi) providing overall management of the company and planning for the future.

   These six fields of activity are broadly the responsibility of six departments in the company, respectively known as Raw materials (R), Production scheduling (P), Sales and marketing (S), Button dispatch (B), Accounts (A) and Management (M).

   Describe, by means of an outline flow diagram with notes, the flow of data between these departments within the company. Identify the activities in which a computer system might be involved, and in each case explain how it would be used.

UCLES 83 I

42 A fully indexed file which has a large number of records of variable length, and which is subject to very frequent insertions and deletions, is held on a disk. The structure of the file is illustrated in Figure 36.4 and described below.

The file occupies a number of blocks, some of which contain records, some of which contain the index, and the rest of which are free. The records in the file are not stored in any particular order, but each has a key field by which it is referenced. After the last record in each record block there is an end marker.

The index consists of two parts, a primary index which occupies a single block, and a secondary index occupying several blocks. The secondary index contains an entry for each record in the file, consisting of a copy of the record key field and the number of the block in which it is stored. Each block of the secondary index contains a count of the number of entries in it followed by the entries, and all the entries in the secondary index are held in ascending order of key. The primary index block contains the block number of the first free block (or -1 if there are none) , and a count of the number of secondary index blocks followed by an entry for each block in the secondary index. These entries consist of the highest key referred to in that secondary block, together with its block number, and they are held in ascending order of key.

Each free block contains a single entry, the block number of the next free block, or -1 if there is none, to form a chain starting with the first free block referred to in the primary index.

Describe briefly the actions which may need to be taken when a record with a given key is to be deleted from the file. Your description should include consideration of the special cases that may arise.

UCLES 83 II

43 The following production rules attempt to define a fairly wide class of 'ordinary' decimal numbers.

$<$number$>$ ::= $<$sign$><$unsigned integer$><$point$><$unsigned integer$>$
$<$sign$>$ ::= $+$ | $-$
$<$unsigned integer$>$ ::= $<$digit$>$ | $<$digit$><$unsigned integer$>$
$<$digit$>$ ::= 0 | 1 | 2 | 3 | 4 | 5 | 6 | 7 | 8 | 9
$<$point$>$ ::= .

The rules do not allow
a) numbers without a sign (e.g. 27.32),
b) integers, with or without a sign (e.g. 4, -6),
c) numbers without an integer part or without a fractional part (e.g. $-40.$, .72).

Rewrite the rules so that the numbers in (a) to (c) are allowed.

UCLES Dec 83 I

44 An area water authority wishes to introduce a computerised billing and accounting system for its customers. The authority issues bills annually based on the size of a property. Customers may elect to pay their bills monthly, half-yearly or yearly. Customers who do not pay their bills at the required time are sent a reminder at the end of each month, and if bills still remain unpaid after three months customers may have their water supply disconnected.

a) Suggest an efficient method of producing bills and inputting customer payments into the system.
b) Describe the content, structure and organisation of the files used within the system.
c) Draw an annotated system diagram which shows how customer accounts could be maintained. Your diagram should indicate clearly the programs that are used and when they are run, as well as the files that are accessed.

UCLES Dec 83 I

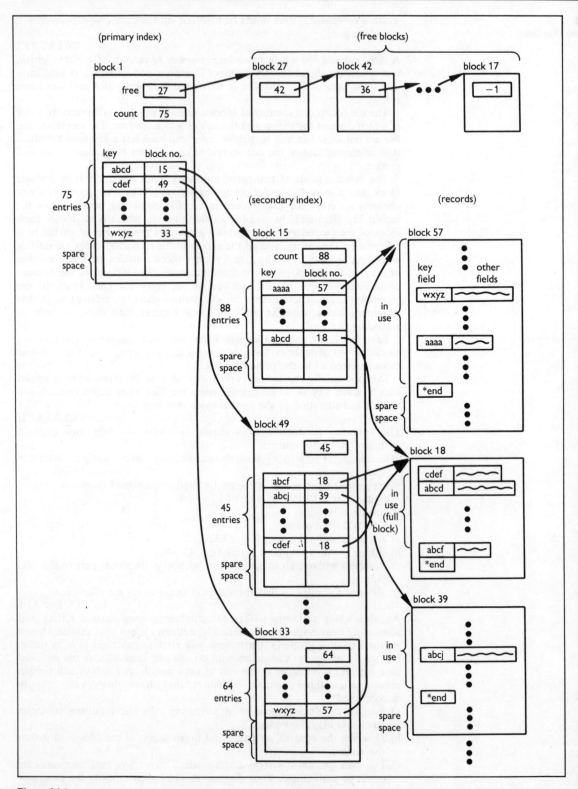

Figure 36.4

45 A computer system is to be installed in the intensive care unit of a hospital to monitor continuously each patient's temperature, heart rate and blood pressure, and to report any significant changes in a patient's condition to the nursing staff. Describe the hardware and software features that you would expect such a system to have, and explain how they would be used.

Explain how it may be possible to use the same computer system to carry out other tasks within the hospital such as routine hospital administration, while still performing the same patient monitoring task as before.

UCLES Dec 83 II

46 A tumble dryer is a machine which dries clothes after they have been washed. It consists of a rotating drum in which the clothes are tumbled, a fan which blows air through the drum, and a heater which heats the air as it enters the drum. The user of the tumble dryer may switch it on or off, and may set a dial which indicates a maximum temperature for the air entering the drum. Apart from this the machine is controlled by a microprocessor.

The machine has two sensors which provide data to the microprocessor. There is a temperature sensor where the air enters the drum and there is a humidity (or 'wetness') sensor where the air leaves the drum. When the machine is switched on the drum rotates, the fan blows, and the heater is adjusted so that the air entering the drum is maintained at about the temperature indicated by the setting of the dial (TMAX). This continues until the humidity of the air leaving the drum is below a preset level (HMIN). At this point the heater is switched off, but the drum and fan continue to run for another ten minutes.

a) The signals from the two sensors need to be converted for use by the microprocessor. Explain what this means.

b) Illustrate the control process for the tumble dryer, by means of a flow diagram or otherwise, and describe the algorithm followed by the microprocessor, making clear any assumptions you consider appropriate.

UCLES 84 I

47 A program that processes the weekly payroll for a company requires the following data for each employee.

> Name
> Employee number
> Number of hours worked on Monday
>
> .
> .
>
> .
>
> Number of hours worked on Saturday
> Number of days absent due to illness
> Number of days absent due to holiday

a) Which data item is most likely to include a check digit? Why?

b) What additional checks can be carried out on the data as it is entered into the computer?

c) Suggest and justify an appropriate method for entering the data into the computer for subsequent processing.

d) State one advantage of storing this data on a computer file in fixed length records and one advantage of using variable length records.

e) Draw a system diagram of the weekly payroll run. Comment on the content of any additional files that are required and the backing store used.

UCLES Dec 84 I

48 What is meant by an **application package**? In addition to programs, what would you expect to be provided within such a package?

What are the advantages and disadvantages of implementing an application package compared with the development of a set of programs within a user's own data processing department? Explain how verification and validation might occur at the various stages of using an applicaiton package to process a given batch of data.

UL 84

49 A multi-access computer system, which is intended mainly for program development and execution, contains the following items of system software
  i) an operating system with a monitor, a scheduler, a file manager and interrupt service routines,
  ii) a loader,
  iii) an editor,
  iv) an assembler,
  v) a compiler.
a) Describe the purpose of each item of software mentioned above.
b) Discuss how these items of system software are used together in the development of a program.

UL 84

50 Discuss, in an **essay**, the reasoning behind and the implications of setting up a computer network within one building. Consideration should be given to the advantages and disadvantages of a network compared with stand-alone microcomputers; include reference to security, reliability and system management aspects.

UL 85

37
Glossary of Terms

This glossary contains definitions of the technical terms introduced and used in the book. In a few cases, a word or phrase has more than one meaning depending on the context. When this occurs, the alternative meanings are marked.

absolute address an address which identifies a memory location without any modification being required.

abstract data type a data type defined in terms of its abstract properties, without regard to its representation on any particular medium.

acceptance testing testing of a computer, item of software or data processing system by its intending users.

access privileges an indication, on a file or memory segment, of the extent to which the information in the file or segemnt may be shared.

accumulator a register storing a data item during processing.

acoustic coupler a device used for data transmission and reception which interfaces with a telephone handset.

address a number which locates a particular storage space in main store or on certain types of backing store.

address generation the process of obtaining the address of a record in a random file from the key of the record.

address modification indexed, indirect or relative addressing.

address space the set of all addressable locations in a computer memory.

addressing mode the method of addressing used in a particular machine instruction.

algorithm a description of the steps needed to carry out a task.

alphanumeric character a character which may be a letter or a digit.

American Standard Code for Information Interchange (ASCII) a code very commonly used for data transmission, and becoming increasingly popular for data representation in memory and on storage media.

analogue data data in the form of physical signals where the strength of the signal is proportional to the magnitude of the data.

analogue-to-digital converter an interface which converts between analogue and digital data representation.

application generator a software tool which generates certain types of application programs automatically from specification.

applications programmer a programmer whose work is concerned with developing applications software.

arithmetic and logic unit (ALU) the part of a processor where arithmetic and logical operations are performed.

array a fixed number of data items of identical type, stored together, with each element accessible via an array index.

artificial intelligence the ability of a computer to behave in a way which, if it were the behaviour of a person, would be regarded as intelligent.

artwork the diagrams showing the layouts of the layers of an integrated circuit or printed circuit board.

assembler a program which translates from the assembly language to the machine language of a particular computer.

assembly language a programming language whose data structures correspond to the physical structure of the registers and main store of its host computer, and whose instructions are closely related to the machine instructions of the computer.

assignment the process whereby a variable takes on a value.

associative store a cache store which, when supplied with the value of a data item, returns the address of the item.

attribute a property of a data item in a file on a database system.

background processor a processor in a multiprocessor configuration which runs applications.

backing store storage for large quantities of data, accessible to a processor.

backing store control unit a unit which controls the flow of data to and from a set of backing store devices.

bar code a character code in terms of patterns of thick and thin stripes.

base language the language in which a compiler is written.

base register a register which holds the start (lowest) address of the area of memory which a process is permitted to use.

baseband a technique of data transmission where the encoded data is sent directly along the communications medium, without a carrier signal.

batch processing the running of a number of programs in succession, in a batch.

batch total the total of various numeric items in a batch of input data.

baud a rate of data transmission which is approximately equal to one bit per second.

beat the time interval for one stage of a pipelined operation.

beta test the second stage of testing a hardware or software product, by prospective users.

biased exponent a method of writing the exponent of a floating point number where a fixed number, the bias, is subtracted from the exponent in order to determine the power of two.

binary base two.

binary coded decimal (BCD) a numeric code in which each decimal digit is coded separately in binary.

binary search a method of searching a file involving partitioning it into successively smaller subsets, each of which is known to contain the required record.

binary tree a tree in which each node may have at most two subtrees.

bistable see **flip-flop.**

bit a binary digit, a 0 or a 1.

bit serial data transmission the transmission of data one bit at a time.

block (1) the unit of data transferred to or from a magnetic tape or disk in one operation, and stored as a physically separate entity.

block (2) a structural element in programs in certain high level languages.

blocking factor the number of records per block for a file stored on a magnetic tape or disk.

blocking strategy the method of allocating records to physical blocks of a backing store medium.

block-structured language a high level programming language which allows programs to be structured in blocks.

BNF a notation for writing syntax rules.

Boolean algebra a system of notation for Boolean logic.

Boolean logic the theory of mathematical logic, first investigated by Boole.

Boolean operation an operation which transforms one or more Boolean variables, producing a Boolean variable as a result.

Boolean variable a variable which can have either of two values only.

bootstrap loader a program which, with minimal assistance, loads itself onto a computer and then enables other programs to be loaded.

branch a transfer of control from one part of a program to another.

breadth-first search a search technique in which all the alternatives are considered before the detailed consequences of any one are examined; compare with **depth-first search**.

breakpoint an instruction which causes the running of a program to be suspended.

broadband a technique of data transmission in which the data is sent along the communications medium 'on top of' a carrier signal.

buffer a storage area for data in transit to or from main store or a peripheral device.

build to construct a program from its constituent modules.

bus a passage for the transmission of data, address and control signals within a computer.

byte a set of bits containing the code for one character, generally eight bits.

cache store a small, fast memory between a processor and a large main store.

call to transfer control to a procedure, function or subprogram.

carry bit a bit which is set if there is a carry out of the most significant place during addition.

carry prediction circuits logic circuits used in fast parallel adders to determine the value of each carry directly from the inputs.

cell a storage space in a computer memory.

central processing unit (CPU) the unit of a computer system in which processing takes place.

character code a code in which each character is coded separately as a set of binary digits.

character printer a printer which prints one character at a time.

character set (1) the set of characters which can be represented in a particular character code; (2) the set of all characters which may be used by a particular computer or programming language.

check digit a character appended to a data item (generally numeric) which enables the validity of the item to be checked.

check sum a data item appended to a transmitted block of data, containing the sum of the codes of other bytes or words in the block.

chip a common word for integrated circuit.

circular buffer a fixed area of store containing a queue, in which the rear of the queue 'wraps around' to the top of the area whenever it reaches the bottom.

circular list a list in which items are linked in a closed loop.

clock cycle the basic timing interval of a processor.

clock pulse generator a device which generates timing pulses for a processor.

cluster adaptor see **multiplexer**.

Codasyl the official committee which administers the standards and upgrades of Cobol.

code generation the production of object code during the compilation process.

commissioning starting up and testing a new computer.

communications processor a processor handling the communications traffic between a main processor and a communications network.

common block a block of data which is common to more than one segment of a program.

compiler a program which accepts a source program in a high level language and translates it into an object program in a machine language.

compression a technique for the reduction of the number of characters transmitted in a data communication system.

computer a collection of resources, including digital electronic processing devices, stored programs and sets of data, which, under the control of the stored programs, automatically inputs, processes, stores, retrieves and outputs data, and may also transmit and receive data.

computer architect a person responsible for the overall design of a computer.

computer operator a person who operates a computer.

computer output on microfilm (COM) reducing displayed output onto microfilm.

condition code a bit which indicates the current status of a processor.

Conference on Data Systems Languages (CODASYL) the overall steering committee for the maintenance and development of Cobol.

console log a record of all the commands to an operating system, and messages from the system, in chronological order.

constant a data item which retains the same value throughout the running of a program.

content-addressable store see **associative store**.

control character a character used in data transmission to perform some control function.

control memory memory (generally a special portion of ROM) in which microcode is stored.

control switch a solid-state switch regulating the passage of data on a bus.

control total see **batch total**.

control unit the unit which controls the step-by-step operation of a processor.

co-processor a processor which acts in parallel with another processor.

cross assembler an assembler which runs on a different computer from the one for which it is assembling programs.

cylinder a set of tracks, vertically above each other on a magnetic disk pack, which can be accessed with the read-write head in the same position.

data information in a coded form, acceptable for input to, and processing by, a computer system.

data capture the process of obtaining data for a computer system.

data channel a pathway for the passage of data inside a computer.

data communications system a computer system based on a data communications network.

data controller a person who controls the flow of data to a computer.

data dictionary a table giving the properties of the data files in a database system.

data driven control the control of a parallel computer architecture by the requirements of the data flowing through the system.

data encryption the representation of data in a secret code.

data entry staff people who operate data entry terminals.

data highway see **data channel**.

data independence the separation of the (logical) data model of a database from the (physical) structure of the stored data.

data model the logical structure of the data as it appears at a particular level of a database system.

data processing a general term describing the work done by a computer.

data processing cycle the sequence of steps of the development and maintenance of a data processing application.

data processing department the division or section of a company with direct responsibility for data processing.

data processing manager (DPM) the person in charge of a data processing department.

data security the application of safeguards to protect data from accidental or deliberate misuse.

data structure a set of data in which individual items are related in a particular way, and on which certain precisely specified operations can be performed.

data type a data item or data structure having certain properties.

database a collection of stored operational data used by all the application systems of an organisation.

database administrator (DBA) the person in charge of the overall running of a database system.

database management system (DBMS) the software responsible for all aspects of the creation, accessing and updating of a database.

database system a computer system centred on a database.

dataflow architecture a type of parallel computer architecture in which a network of processors reflects the structure of the processing operations, and items of data flow through the network.

deadlock the situation arising when two programs prevent each other from continuing because each holds a resource needed by the other.

declaration a statement of the name and type of a variable in a program.

declarative language a programming language which expresses programs as a set of logical relationships between items of data.

decoder a logic circuit which selects one of a number of outputs according to the code of an input signal.

dedicated computer a computer designed for a specific task or narrow range of tasks.

dedicated register a register with one specific function.

default value the value assigned to a data item unless explicitly overwritten by a user.

depth-first search a search technique in which all the consequences of one particular alternative are considered before another alternative is examined compare with **breadth-first search**.

descriptor file a file in a database system which describes the data in another file.

descriptor register a register which contains information about a data structure currently being accessed.

device a physical unit which carries out some operation.

device driver a software module which controls the operation of a particular device, such as a disk drive.

diagnostic error message a message output by a compiler, indicating the location and cause of an error in a program.

diagnostics the process of locating an error and determining its cause, carried out by a compiler.

diagnostic program a program which examines the current state of a computer, displaying the contents of various registers and store locations.

dictionary a set of information created and accessed during the compilation process.

diffusion a technique for placing a precisely controlled amount of impurities on the surface of a chip wafer.

digital the representation of data in discrete quantities.

digital plotter an output device which draws maps, plans, engineering drawings, etc.

dimension the number of indices associated with an array.

direct data entry (DDE) data entry directly onto backing store.

direct memory access (DMA) direct access by peripheral devices to main store, bypassing processor registers.

directive an assembly language instruction which does not have a counterpart in machine language.

directory a table of the files or records to be found on a particular magnetic disk or disk sector.

disable interrupts to make a processor unreceptive to interrupts.

disk buffer a portion of memory which holds segments of data during transfer to or from magnetic disk.

disk cartridge an enclosure containing a single exchangeable disk.

disk crash a read-write head coming into contact with the surface of a magnetic disk, and damaging both the disk and the read-write head.

disk drive a device which reads from and writes to a magnetic disk.

disk pack a set of magnetic disks on a common shaft.

distributed array processor (DAP) a processor with parallel elements which can carry out an operation on all the elements of an array simultaneously.

DMA controller a device which controls the direct memory access mechanism in a computer.

documentation a written description of how a program works, how it is to be used, or how it is to be run on a computer.

doping the process of implanting a chip wafer with carefully controlled amounts of impurities.

dump to copy an entire file onto another storage medium, generally from a magnetic disk onto a magnetic tape.

dynamic data structure a data structure which changes in size while in use.

dynamic memory solid-state storage in which data 'leaks away' and must be refreshed periodically.

editor a utility program which allows other programs or data files to be typed and edited.

electronics engineer an engineer who specialises in the design and construction of electronic systems.

emitter coupled logic a technique for manufacturing integrated circuits.

emulate to simulate the behaviour of one computer, at machine language level, on another computer.

enable to activate a logic circuit or component.

enable interrupts to make a processor receptive to interrupts.

enabling technology a fundamental technology which paves the way for subsequent developments.

encryption key a number which enables encrypted data to be decoded.

erasable programmable read-only memory (EPROM) programmable read-only memory which can be erased and re-programmed.

etching dissolving away the unwanted areas in a layer of a chip wafer.

even parity see **parity bit**

evidential reasoning a technique of knowledge processing based on the way in which bodies of evidence are evaluated in order to draw conclusions.

exception call a call to an operating system from a user program when an error condition arises.

exchangeable disk pack a set of magnetic disks which can be removed from a disk drive.

execute to carry out a machine instruction or a program.

expert system a computer system which automates a measure of human expertise in a particular field.

expert system shell a software package containing the deductive aspects of an expert system without any particular knowledge base.

exponent the power of two of a floating point number.

feasibility study a preliminary study of a proposed data processing application which indicates whether or not further investigation and development should take place.

fetch the phase of an instruction cycle in which a machine instruction is fetched from store.

field the place allocated for a particular data item, on a data storage medium or in a data structure such as a record.

field engineer an engineer who commissions, maintains and upgrades computers at user sites.

fieldwidth the number of characters in a field of a file.

FIFO first-in-first-out, describing a queue.

fifth generation computer a computer which applies reasoning to a knowledge base in order to solve highly complex problems.

file a collection of data, structured in a particular way, and used for a particular purpose.

file dump a copy of a file on a backup medium such as magentic tape.

file librarian a person responsible for the magnetic tape and magnetic disk files at a computer installation.

file overflow the situation which arises when the storage space allocated to hold a file, or a portion of a file, becomes insufficient for the data in the file.

file processing log a record of all the processing steps carried out on a file.

file processing system a type of data processing application where the emphasis is on the periodic updating of files.

firmware software permanently stored on read-only memory.

fixed point number a number in which the binary point occupies a fixed position.

flag a single bit register used in the control and synchronisation of peripheral devices.

flip-flop a logic circuit which has two stable output states. An input signal can cause it to 'flip' from one state to the other.

floating point number a number expressed as the product of a fraction of magnitude between 1/2 and 1 and an integral power of two.

floppy disk a small flexible magnetic disk.

flow soldering machine a machine which solders all the chips on a printed circuit board in one operation.

foreground processor the processor in a multiprocessor configuration which is in overall control, and provides external links to the background processors.

format the layout of input or output data.

fourth generation language a programming language which generates code from certain types of specifications.

frame the coding area for one character on magnetic tape, being a row of bit coding positions across the width of the tape.

front panel the front surface of a unit, generally containing switches and indicator lights.

front-end processor a processor which controls flow of data into and out of a main processor.

full adder a logic circuit which adds two bits, together with a previous carry, to produce a sum and a carry.

full duplex describes data transmission in both directions simultaneously.

function a portion of a program which evaluates a function, and which is invoked from any point in the program at which the function is used.

functional decomposition a technique of program design by expressing the operation of the program as a mathematical function, and then specifying the detailed steps as subsidiary functions.

functional specification a document which states how an item of hardware or software, or a computer system, is intended to operate.

gate a functional element which carries out a Boolean operation in a logic circuit.

gate delay the time interval between a change in the input signals at a gate and the stabilisation of its output signal in its new state.

general-purpose computer a computer capable of a wide range of applications.

general-purpose language a programming language, in most cases a high level language, suitable for a wide variety of applications.

general-purpose register a register which can fulfil a number of functions.

generate-and-test a process often used in artificial intelligence software, to investigate all the possible consequences of some action, and evaluate them in some way.

global variable a variable whose scope is an entire program.

grandfather-father-son principle a method of ensuring the security of data by keeping three generations of a file, as well as the information needed to update the generations.

graph reduction architecture a type of parallel computer architecture in which the task to be performed is represented as a graph, and processing operations are carried out in order to reduce the graph to obtain a single result.

graphics terminal a VDU capable of graphics displays.

Gray code a data code in which the code for each character differs in one bit position only from that for the previous character.

half adder a logic circuit which adds two bits, producing a sum bit and a carry bit.

half duplex describes data transmission in alternate directions, but not in both directions simultaneously.

Hamming code a data code with sufficient built-in checking for a single bit error to be corrected and a multiple bit error to be detected.

hardware the physical components, solid-state and otherwise, which make up a computer.

hard-wired control the execution of machine instructions directly by hardware.

hash total the total of various numeric items within a record.

hashing an address generation technique, where the address of the first possible location of a file is generated.

hexadecimal base sixteen.

hierarchical data model a database structure based on a tree configuration.

high level language an application-oriented programming language, one which is a convenient and simple means of describing the information structures and sequences of actions required to perform a particular task.

high order digits a group of digits in a number with the highest place values.

high resolution graphics graphics displays with a fine level of detail.

immediate access store storage in which each location can be written to or read from immediately.

immediate operand a data item located in a machine or assembly language instruction.

implementation the putting into practice of a design or concept, under a particular set of circumstances.

implementation language the version of a programming langauge as implemented on a particular type of computer.

index a variable which indicates the position of an element in an array.

indexed address an address to which the contents of an index register must be added in order to obtain an absolute address.

indexed sequential file a sequential file which includes an index relating the key of each record to its address.

indirect address an address which locates the address of a data item.

inference processor the central element of a fifth generation computer system, which performs logical inferences on items of knowledge.

information the meaning given to data by the way it is interpreted.

information processing a general term used to describe the work done by a computer.

information storage/retrieval a type of data processing application where one or more large stores of information are continuously kept up to date, and may be accessed at any time.

input data supplied to a computer from its environment.

input device a device which supplies input to a processor.

instruction cycle the sequence of actions required to carry out one machine instruction.

instruction decoder a set of logic circuits which interpret an instruction as a sequence of control signals.

instruction register (IR) a register which contains the current program instruction.

instruction set the set of machine language instructions for a particular type of computer.

integrated circuit a single solid-state unit, containing a number of transistors and other components, which performs one or more logic operations.

intelligent knowledge based system (IKBS) a computer system which applies techniques of artificial intelligence to sets of knowledge in order to solve problems.

intelligent terminal a terminal which incorporates a certain amount of processing capability.

intelligent user interface a user interface which is designed in accordance with the requirements and way of thinking of the user, possibly using a natural language.

interface a point of contact between one module and another, or between a module and its environment.

interpreter a program which enables a computer to run programs in a high level language, statement by statement.

interrupt an external signal causing the execution of a program to be suspended.

interrupt line a signal line used to generate an interrupt.

interrupt service routine a program module which provides the initial response of a processor to an interrupt.

inter-block gap a gap left between successive blocks on a magnetic tape.

ion implantation a technique for doping a layer of an integrated circuit, during construction.

job control language (JCL) the language in which instructions to an operating system are written.

Josephson junction a solid-state switch, working at a temperature close to absolute zero, which forms the basis of a logic circuit.

K a unit of stored data, $1K = 2^{10} = 1024$.

Karnaugh map a table used for the simplification of logic expressions.

kernel the most privileged layer of an operating system, which contains the protection mechanism and certain direct hardware interfaces.

key a data field which identifies a record.

knowledge base procesor a functional element of a fifth generation computer, which accesses and updates the knowledge base of the computer system.

label a sequence of characters which identifies a program line.

large scale integration (LSI) the inclusion of thousands of transistors and other components on a single integrated circuit.

leaf a terminal node of a tree.

level of privilege a figure which determines the degree of access to system resources of a program.

lexical analysis the first stage in the analysis of a source program by a compiler.

LIFO last-in-first out, describing a stack.

limit register a register which holds the end (highest) address of the area of memory which a process is permitted to use.

line printer a printer which prints all the characters in an entire line in one operation.

linkage editor a portion of systems software which links separate modules of a program into single executable module.

linked list see **list**.

list a set of data items, stored in some order, where data items may be inserted or deleted at any point within the set.

load-and-go compiler a compiler which translates, links, loads and runs applications programs in a single sequence of operations.

loader a portion of systems software which copies a machine language program into the store it will occupy during execution, and adjusts any relative addresses contained in the program.

local area network a data communication system connecting a number of computers and other devices in the same vicinity.

local variable a variable whose scope is limited to one block of a program.

location the storage space for one data item.

logic circuit a circuit, resembling an electrical circuit, connecting a number of logic elements.

loop a portion of a program which is repeated.

low level language a machine or assembly language.

M a unit of stored data, $1M = 2^{20} = 1\,048\,576$.

machine language a programming language which controls the hardware of a particular type of computer directly.

macro-instruction a single instruction in an assembly language or a system command language, which represents a group of instructions.

magnetic bubble memory a random access store made up of a substance in which small zones of magnetism move, each zone storing a 0 or a 1.

magnetic disk a data storage medium comprising a metal or plastic disk coated with a magnetisable substance.

magnetic ink character recognition (MICR) recognition of characters printed in a magnetic ink.

magnetic tape unit a device which reads from and writes to magnetic tape.

main store solid-state storage directly accessible to a processor.

mainframe a large computer, consisting of a number of free-standing units.

mantissa the fraction part of a floating point number.

mark sensing detection of shaded areas in a document.

mask a logic circuit which selects certain bits of a data item.

masking using a template to mark the areas of a layer on a chip wafer which are to be etched away.

medium a physical substance on which data is stored.

medium scale integration (MSI) the inclusion of hundreds of transistors and other components on a single integrated circuit.

megabyte one million bytes.

memory address register a register, connected to a main store via a decoder, which holds the address currently being accessed within the store.

memory cycle the sequence of steps to read a data item from, or write a data item to main store.

memory data register a register which holds a data item during transfer to or from a main store.

memory map a diagram showing the allocation of regions of the address space of a computer for particular purposes.

merging the process of combining two ordered sets of data to produce a single ordered set.

message switching the routing of a message from its origin to its destination in a data communications network.

metal oxide silicon (MOS) a method of manufacturing integrated circuits.

metallisation evaporating a thin layer of a metal onto the surface of a chip wafer.

microcode instructions which carry out the steps of a machine instruction at the level of opening and closing gates.

microprocessor a single chip containing most of the processing circuits of a computer.

microsecond millionth of a second.

microcomputer a computer based on a microprocessor.

mnemonic a group of letters, generally representing an operation code in an assembly language.

modem a modulator/demodulator, a device which forms the interface between a computer and a telephone line used for data transmission.

module an interchangeable unit, performing a specific function, and having a specific interface to its environment.

module library a library of procedures and functions in object code, which can be linked to other object code modules to form an executable program.

most significant digit the digit in a number with the highest place value.

multiplexer a device which interleaves communication from a number of data channels onto a single data channel.

multiprogramming a method of computer operation where a number of programs are in various stages of running at any time.

multi-access the simultaneous access of a number of users, via terminals, to a computer.

multi-port memory a memory which has a number of input/output ports.

nanosecond one thousand millionth of a second.

network administrator the person in charge of the running of a computer network.

network architecture a computer configuration containing a number of communicating processors and other devices.

network data model a database structure based on a series of links between data items, forming a network.

node a data item in a tree.

noise interference in a data communication channel.

normalisation adjusting the binary point in a floating point number so that the magnitude of the fraction part is between 1/2 and 1.

n-type semiconductor a semiconductor which has been doped to contain an excess of electrons.

nucleus the lowest software level of an operating system, providing a small number of essential services to higher levels.

null pointer a pointer which does not point to anything.

object language the language into which programs are translated by a compiler or assembler.

object program a program in the object language of a compiler or assembler.

octal base eight.

odd parity see **parity bit**.

offset the address count from the start of a data structure to a particular element in the structure.

ones complements a binary code in which the most significant bit represents one less (in magnitude) than the corresponding twos complement value.

operand a data item used in a machine instruction.

operating system a program, or set of programs, driving the raw hardware of a computer, which manages the resources of the computer in accordance with certain objectives, presenting higher levels of software with a simplified virtual machine.

operation code the part of a machine instruction which determines the type of operation to be carried out.

operation table a table which shows, for a particular logic operation, the values of the output variable resulting from all possible combinations of the input variable.

operations manager the person in charge of the running of a computer installation.

operator documentation an account of the operator procedures needed to run a program.

operator's console the device which enables the person operating a computer to interact with it.

optical character recognition (OCR) recognition of printed characters by a light scanning process.

optimisation producing of the most efficient object code by a compiler or assembler.

ordered list a list in which items are in numerical or alphabetical order.

original equipment manufacture (OEM) the manufacture of components such as integrated circuits, switches, casings, etc. for computers and associated devices.

output data supplied to its enviroment by a computer.

output device a device which supplies data from a computer to its environment.

overflow the occurrence of a numerical result which is outside the limits imposed by the number representation used.

overflow bit a status bit which is set when overflow occurs.

overlay a portion of the code of a program which is held on backing store and copied into main store when needed.

oxidation the process which forms an insulating layer of silicon dioxide on a chip wafer.

packed decimal a BCD code using four bits per decimal digit.

packet a unit of transmitted data, enclosed by strings of control characters.

packet switching the routing of data packets from their origin to their destination across a data communications network.

packing density the ratio of the amount of backing store space used by a file to the total amount available.

page a set of consecutive memory cells, the contents of which are swapped to and from backing store in order to create a virtual memory.

page table a table which associates virtual page numbers with the addresses of the corresponding pages in memory.

parallel adder a logic circuit which adds all the bits of two numbers at the same time.

parallel data transmission the transmission of a number of data bits simultaneously, generally by means of multi-strand cable.

parallelism the performance of several actions simultaneously inside a processor.

parity a method of self-checking involving the use of a parity bit.

parity bit a bit in the code for a data item which is set to a 0 or a 1 so that the total number of 1s in the data item is even, for even parity, or odd, for odd parity.

parity check a check to determine whether the parity of a data item is correct.

parsing (1) the application of a set of rules of syntax to a source program by a compiler; (2) the application of the rules of syntax to a passage in a natural language in order to analyse its structure.

peripheral a device, linked to a processor, which performs an input, output, storage or data communication function.

photoresist a light-sensitive substance used in the process of masking and etching chip wafers.

pipelining a processing technique using an independent unit for each stage of an operation, the units being connected in sequence via buffers.

place value the weighting assigned to a digit in a number, depending on its position.

plug compatible describes items of computer equipment which can be connected together directly.

p-n junction a junction between a p-type semiconductor and an n-type semiconductor.

polling checking peripheral devices at regular intervals to see if they have data to transmit, or are ready to receive data.

pointer a data item which contains the address of another data item.

pop to remove a data item from the top of a stack.

portable describes programs which can be run on more than one type of computer.

precedence the order in which operations in an expression are carried out.

precision a measure of how closely a number can approximate its exact value

predicate a logical relationship between two or more items.

predicate calculus the formal techniques for applying the rules of inference to predicates.

procedure see **subprogram**.

procedural language a programming language which expresses programs a sequences of operations to be carried out by a computer.

procedural learning a technique of knowledge processing based on the way in which experts acquire specialised knowledge.

process control the continuous monitoring and/or controlling of an operational process by a computer.

processor a unit, printed circuit board or single chip in which processing takes place.

production rule a rule which specifies how a syntactic structure or element of a knowledge base is derived from another syntactic structure or element of a knowledge base.

program a set of instructions which control the operation of a computer.

program counter (PC) a register which stores the address of the current program instruction.

program design a method of carrying out the sequence of steps from the initial concept of a program to the final tested and accepted code.

program documentation an account of the structure and workings of a program.

program specification a document which states the objectives and main functional steps of a computer program.

program status bit see **condition code**.

program structure the way in which a program is built up from its constituent modules.

program testing a series of tests carried out by the developers of a program or program module before passing it for system testing.

programmable read-only memory (PROM) read-only memory which can be loaded under program control.

programmer a person responsible for designing, writing, testing, correcting maintaining and documenting computer programs.

proof of correctness a sequence of logical assertions by which the correctness of a program module is proved under stated conditions.

proposition an association between two or more items, linked by a logical relationship.

protection the prevention of unauthorised access to programs, data or areas in memory.

protocol a set of rules, used in data communication systems, which specify the packet structure and the procedures to be followed for transmission and reception.

prototype a demonstration version of a proposed computer program, in order to check that the initial specifications are correct.

pseudo-operation see **directive**.

publication language the version of a programming language used for the publication of algorithms.

push to insert a data item on the top of a stack.

push-down list see **stack**.

push-down stack see **stack**.

p-type semiconductor a semiconductor which has been doped to contain a shortage of electrons.

queue a data structure in which items are added at the rear and removed from the front.

quicksort a particulary efficient method of sorting data.

random access describes a data storage medium or file structure where the time taken to access a data item is independent of its position on the medium or in the file.

random access memory (RAM) solid-state storage, in which data can be accessed from any location.

random file a file in which records are not in any order, but are located by an address generation technique.

read-only memory (ROM) solid-state storage which can be read from but not written to.

read-write head a device which detects or creates magnetised areas on a disk or tape.

real-time processing processing which must keep pace with some operation which is external to the computer.

record a set of data items which are related in some way, generally forming the unit of data in a larger structure such as a file.

recursion the capability of a procedure or function to call itself.

reference language the definitive version of a programmng language, independent of any implementation constraints.

register a storage element for one data item, for a particular purpose such as control, processing or data transmission.

relational data model a database structure based on a set of tables which define relationships between data items.

relative address the offset of a data item from the machine instruction containing the address.

relocatable code instructions and data which can be moved in main store without the need to change any addresses within the code.

remote job entry (RJE) the submission of programs for processing at sites remote from the computer.

report generation the process of summarising the information in a file and generating a report containing this summary information.

reserved word a word which has a defined meaning in the context of a programming language.

reset (1) the input to a flip-flop, a signal on which causes the flip-flop to change to its 0 state; (2) the updating of a program counter so that it contains the address of the next machine instruction.

resource a functional unit, portion of memory, program or set of data within a computer.

result register temporary storage for the output from logic circuits.

ring a local area network based on a closed loop of cable.

root the node at the 'top' of a tree.

root directory the top level directory in a hierarchical directory structure.

rounding error the error introduced in a number when it is rounded to a certain number of binary or decimal places.

rule of inference a general logical rule which is used in predicate calculus.

rule of precedence a rule which establishes in what order other rules are applied to data items.

run-time diagnostics a set of procedures provided by a software development system in order to check a program while it is running.

sampling frequency the frequency at which an analogue signal is sampled by an analogue-to-digital converter.

scalar processor a processor based on single registers and sets of processing circuits; compare with **vector processor**.

scheduler part of an operating system which determines the sequence in which programs are run.

scope the part of a program in which a particular variable can be used.

searching the process of locating a record in a file or data structure, given the key of the record.

second source an alternative source of supply for a component of a computer.

sector a unit of stored data on a magnetic disk.

segment a portion of memory used for a particular purpose.

self-checking code a code which contains enough information within the coded form of the data item to determine whether the data item has been coded or transmitted correctly.

semantic network a network structure for the representation of knowledge on a computer.

semantics the meaning of a passage in a natural language.

semiconductor a material such as silicon which conducts more electricity than an insulator such as porcelain but less than a conductor such as copper.

sequencing the flow of control from one program instruction to the next.

sequential file a file in which the records are in order of one or more keys.

sequential search a method of searching a file by accessing each record in turn until the required record is found.

serial access describes a data storage medium where the time taken to access a data item depends on its position in the medium.

serial adder a logic circuit which adds the bits of two input numbers one pair at a time.

serial data transmission the transmission of data, using a single communications medium, one bit at a time.

serial file a file in which the records are in no particular order.

set the input to a flip-flop, a signal on which causes the flip-flop to change to its 1 state.

shell the layer of an operating system closest to the hardware of the computer.

shift register a register which enables bits of a data item to be shifted from one position to the next.

side effect the inadvertent alteration of the value of a variable by a step of a program.

sign-and-magnitude code a code in which the sign of a number and its magnitude are represented separately.

sign extension copying the sign of a low order byte into all the bits of the high order byte of a word.

simplex describes data transmission in one direction only.

single program operation a type of computer operation where only one program is run at a time.

slave store see **cache store**

soak test running a computer, component, chip or program for a long time in order to detect any malfunctions.

software the programs which direct the operation of a computer.

software development environment an integrated set of cross-compilers, program generators and other software development tools, used in the development of applications software.

software development tool a set of programs which assists in the development of certain types of applications software.

software engineer a person who designs and writes computer programs in accordance with the principles of software engineering.

software engineering the development of software which satisfies strict conditions of correctness and performance, in a scheduled, budgeted and cost-effective way.

software front panel software which displays the contents of processor registers on the screen of an operator's console.

software house a company whose activities are centred on the production of computer software.

software lifecycle the cycle of design, development, installation and maintenance of a software item.

software package a complete, self-contained computer program which is designed to be purchased and used by a large number of users for a particular task.

sorting the process of arranging the data items in a structure, particularly the records in a file, in some order.

source document an original document containing data for input into a computer system.

source language the programming language which is accepted for translation by a compiler or assembler.

source program a program, in a high level language, which forms the input for a compiler.

special character a character such as a punctuation mark which is not an alphanumeric character.

specification language a programming language, above the level of high level languages, for stating the specifications of a task.

spooling maintaining a queue, on backing store, of data for output, generally by a printer.

stack a collection of data items which may only be accessed at one end.

stack base the fixed end of a stack.

stack pointer (SP) (1) a pointer which indicates the current address of the top of a stack; (2) a register which contains the current address of the top of the stack in a computer memory.

standard form a way of writing decimal numbers as the product of a fraction between 0 and 1 and an integral power of ten.

statement an instruction in a high level programming language.

static data structure a data structure which stays the same size once it has been created.

static memory solid-state storage which retains data as long as power is switched on.

status bits see **condition codes**.

stepwise refinement a top-down technique of program design, starting with an initial statement of the overall steps of a program, and expanding each step as a set of more detailed steps until enough detail has been added to form the basis of the code of the program.

store and forward a type of packet switching where data is stored at intermediate points while in transit.

string (1) a set of characters stored together; (2) a subset of a file which is small enough to be accommodated in a computer main store.

subfile a file containing a subset of the records of another file.

subprogram a portion of a program, which carries out a specific task, to which control can be transferred from any point in the program, and from which control returns to the point from which it was called.

subroutine see **subprogram**.

subsystem a part of a system which accomplishes a part of the goals of the system.

subtree a portion of a tree, itself having a tree structure.

sum of products a form of a logic expression comprising a number of product terms (linked by the AND operation) which are connected by the OR operation.

supercomputer a large mainframe computer.

symbolic address a group of characters which represent the address of a data item or instruction.

syntax (1) the rules which govern the structure of a program in a particular language; (2) the rules which govern the makeup of sentences in a natural language.

syntax analysis the determination of the structure of a source program by a compiler.

syntax error a violation of a syntax rule of a programming language by a program written in the language.

system a collection of parts working together towards some common goals.

system development the sequence of steps from the completion of the design of a system until it has been accepted for operational use.

system design the sequence of steps from the initial specification of a data processing system to the stage where the system is ready to be programmed.

system implementation the process of putting a computer system to work in a particular environment.

system investigation an initial feasibility study to determine whether or not work should proceed on the design and development of a computer system.

system maintenance the periodic alteration of some aspect of a data processing system in the light of experience or changing requirements.

system specification an outline of a proposed data processing application including a statement of the objectives of the system, and a summary of the overall working of the system.

system testing the testing of a data processing system as a whole.

systems analyst a person responsible for the analysis and overall design of a data processing system.

systems diagram see **systems flowchart**.

systems flowchart a diagram showing the overall structure of and flow of data through a system.

systems programmer a programmer whose work is concerned with systems software.

systems software the layers of software, generally comprising operating systems, assemblers and compilers which transform the hardware of a computer into an application-oriented machine.

target language the language into which programs are translated by a compiler.

teletype a terminal comprising a keyboard and a character printer.

terminal a general-purpose input/output device.

terminal node a node at the 'bottom' of a tree.

test data data which is specifically designed to test the working of a program

three level memory a computer memory consisting of cache store, main store and backing store.

time sharing a method of computer operation which allows computing time to be shared among a number of users.

time slicing a scheduling policy in which each program is in turn allowed a short interval of processor time.

token a set of characters representing a syntactic object during compilation or assembly.

top-down method a technique of program design which starts with a statement of the overall steps of a program and adds detail in a systematic way.

top of stack the point at which data items may be added to or removed from a stack.

track (1) a circular path on the surface of a magnetic disk, on which consecutive bits of data are recorded.

track (2) a row of bit coding positions along the length of magnetic tape.

track (3) a thin metal conducting strip on a printed circuit board.

transaction processing (1) a type of data processing application where transactions are processed in real time.

transaction processing (2) a type of operating system which controls the running of programs so that transactions are processed in real time.

transistor an electronic component, one or more of which can be made to carry out a logic operation.

transistor-transistor logic (TTL) a method of manufacturing integrated circuits.

transputer a single-chip processor with on-board memory designed as the processing element in a parallel computer architecture.

tree a hierarchical data structure, in which each element is linked to one element above it, and zero, one or more elements below it.

tree sort a sorting technique based on the use of a tree.

tree traversal a systematic scan of all the nodes of a tree.

truncation error an error which occurs when bits of a number are discarded without any rounding taking place.

truth table see **operation table**.

turnaround document a document which is output by one stage of a computer system, and, with additional information entered on it, forms the input for another stage.

Turing Machine an abstract computer, designed by Alan Turing, having the theoretical properties of an actual computer.

turnkey contract a contract for the supply of a complete, ready-to-use computer system, including hardware and software.

two-pass assembler an assembler which scans the source code of programs twice during assembly.

twos complements a binary code, using the usual place values, except that the most significant bit represents a negative quantity.

underflow the occurrence of a numerical result which is less than the lower limit imposed by the number representation used.

uncommitted logic array (ULA) an array of identical logic gates on a chip, which are customised by suitable interconnections to dedicate the chip to a particular purpose.

uninterrupted power supply a unit which ensures a constant power supply to a computer.

updating the processs of bringing a file or other collection of information up to date.

upgrade to enhance or extend the hardware or software of a computer system.

user a person who uses a computer system.

user documentation an account of how a program is to be used.

user group a group of people or organisations which are users of the same make of computer equipment.

user interface the means of communication between a computer system and the person using it.

utility programs programs for various 'housekeeping' tasks such as file creation, copying files, routing messages and providing mathematical facilities.

validation the process of checking input data before storing or processing it.

variable a data item which can change its value during the running of a program.

variable wordlength the use of words of different lengths in a computer system for the representation of data.

vector processor a processor with a parallel architecture based on vector registers and banks of processing circuits.

vector register a bank of identical registers treated as a single unit in machine instructions, and where processing operations are carried out on all elements in the registers in parallel.

very large scale integration (VLSI) the inclusion of tens of thousands of transistors and other components on a single integrated circuit.

virtual machine the image of the hardware of a computer created by various layers of software, especially an operating system.

virtual memory the image of a computer memory presented by an operating system to higher levels of software.

visual display unit (VDU) a terminal comprising a keyboard and display screen.

volatile memory see **dynamic memory**.

wafer a circular slice cut from a silicon crystal on which chips are formed.

Winchester disk a small high-capacity hard disk.

word a set of bits which can be manipulated by a computer in one operation.

wordlength the number of bits in one word.

work station a terminal, intelligent terminal or microcomputer at which certain tasks are carried out.

wrap-around carry a carry from the most significant to the least significant bit of a number.

yield the proportion of usable chips on a wafer.

38

Teachers' Notes

These Notes are intended for the guidance of a teacher of Computing Science at Advanced level or equivalent. They indicate some of the ways in which this book can be used. It must be emphasised that the best preparation for the use of this book as course material is a familiarity with its contents: one of the intended uses of the book is as a 'briefing text' for teachers about to start a course in Computing Science at Advanced level or equivalent.

Use of the Book

Computing is a broad, many-faceted subject, with complex inter-relationships between its constituent topics. Accordingly, the structure of this book has been chosen with great care, in order to provide a logical path through the topics, and a cumulative flow of information. However, not every chapter in the book depends on all its predecessors, as shown in Figure 38.1. There is scope for selection of material, and variation in order of presentation, depending on circumstances.

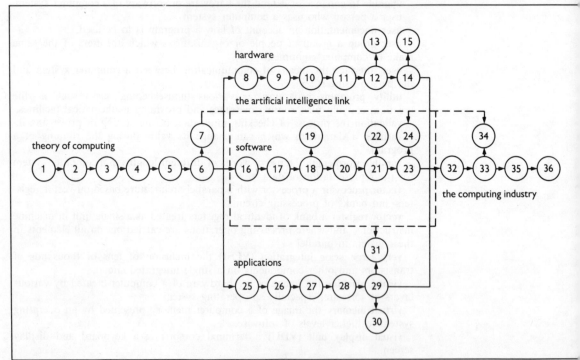

Figure 38.1
Chapter dependencies of
Computing Science

For a Computing Science course, it is recommended that the chapters be followed more or less in sequence. If pressure of time is great, then the case study chapters, Chapters 15, 19, 22 and 30, can be glossed over lightly, or left for pupils to peruse in their own time. It is certainly not recommended that all the high level language case studies in Chapter 19 be 'ploughed through'. A selection must be made according to circumstances. Similarly, chapters on artificial intelligence (Chapter 7), software development tools (Chapter 23), software engineering (Chapter 24), expert systems (Chapter 30), fifth generation computers (Chapter 34) and social effects of computers (Chapter 25), can be treated fairly lightly, as they contain material which is not (yet) in many Advanced Level Computing Science syllabuses. Nevertheless, the material they contain is vital for any pupil who intends to further his or her studies in computing, or plans a career in the computing industry.

If this book is intended for a Computer Appreciation course, then the essential material is the principles of computing (in particular Chapters 1 to 3 and Chapter 9) and the applications and implications of computers (Chapters 25 to 33). The more technical chapters on hardware and software can be treated lightly or omitted.

39
Answers to Exercises

Answers to exercises have been selected for inclusion here on the basis of the following criteria:

- If a question requires a brief, specific answer then it is included. The only exceptions are 'comprehension' questions and ones which require definitions of terms; answers to the latter are to be found in the Glossary of Terms.
- Where questions require discussion, in selected cases a few relevant points are included. In most cases, conclusions are not drawn, as the merit of answer lies in the logic of its argument, and not in the 'correctness' of its conclusion.
- Answers to questions from past examination papers in Computing Science are not included.

Exercise 2

2 Systems: central and local governments, automatic pilot, any organ of the body, solar system.
Non-systems: crowd of looters, shuffled pack of cards, components of a computer before assembly.

3 Slide rule: no, not automatic or programmable.
Automatic washing machine: no, does not process information.
Programmable pocket calculator, television game: no, only performs part of the work of a computer, or yes, but only a dedicated computer.
Motor car electronic ignition system: no, does not contain a stored program.

4 In many cases, the distinction between the device and a computer is fine, based on the nature of the processing done. Examples include robots, electronically controlled cameras, multi-function digital watches.

7 Examples include many modern buildings, most electrical apparatus, plumbing systems, telephone systems, camera lens systems.

8 Advantages include:
- Ease of replacement of faulty modules
- Ease of expansion by adding more modules
- Ease of understanding of design principles
- Ease of planning for future enhancements.

Exercise 3

2 The electronic components of computers are all bistable devices. Advantages are simplicity and wide tolerances.

3 Roman numerals.

4 Each character is coded separately as a set of binary digits.

5 a) Add the binary codes of the two digits, and the carry bit

If the sum exceeds nine (1001)
then Subtract ten (1010) from the sum
Set the carry bit to 1
else Set the carry bit to 0

b) Assuming that one of the numbers has been 'padded' with leading zeros if necessary, so that both numbers are of the same length:

Set carry bit to zero
Repeat, for each digit of the numbers from the right
Add a pair of digits and the carry bit as in part a)
Create an additional digit for the sum, containing the carry bit

6

	four bits	six bits	eight bits
3	0 0 1 1	0 0 0 0 1 1	0 0 0 0 0 0 1 1
−3	1 1 0 1	1 1 1 1 0 1	1 1 1 1 1 1 0 1

Duplicate the leftmost bit of the number to fill the new positions. The process is called **sign extensions**.

7

	four bits	six bits	eight bits
3	0011	000011	00000011
−3	1100	111100	11111100

Same process as with twos complements.

8

	bits	twos complements range	ones complements range
a)	4	−8 to 7	−7 to 7
b)	6	−32 to 31	−31 to 31
c)	8	−128 to 127	−127 to 127
d)	16	−32768 to 32767	−32767 to 32767
e)	n	-2^{n-1} to $2^{n-1}-1$	$-(2^{n-1}-1)$ to $2^{n-1}-$

9

	−1	$\frac{1}{2}$	$\frac{1}{4}$	$\frac{1}{8}$	$\frac{1}{16}$	$\frac{1}{32}$
$\frac{3}{8}$ =	0	0	1	1	0	0
$-\frac{7}{16}$ =	1	1	0	1	1	0
$-\frac{17}{32}$ =	1	0	1	1	1	1
$\frac{3}{8}$ =	0	0	0	1	1	0

10

		mantissa sign	$\frac{1}{2}$	$\frac{1}{4}$	$\frac{1}{8}$	$\frac{1}{16}$	...	exponent sign	8	4	2	1
a)	10 =	0	1	0	1	0		0	0	1	0	0
	15630 =	0	1	1	1	1		0	1	1	1	0
	$\frac{-1}{128}$ =	1	1	0	0	0		0	0	0	0	1
	$\frac{7}{128}$ =	0	1	1	1	0		1	0	1	0	0
	$\frac{-5}{1024}$ =	1	1	0	1	0		1	0	1	1	1
b)	80 =	0	1	0	1	0		0	0	1	1	1
	−3072 =	1	1	1	0	0		0	1	1	0	0
	$\frac{5}{512}$ =	0	1	0	1	0		1	0	1	1	0
	$-\frac{1}{2}$ =	1	1	0	0	0		0	0	0	0	0
	1.5 =	0	1	1	0	0		0	0	0	0	1

c) From $\frac{1}{2} \times 2^{-15}$ ($=\frac{1}{65536}$) to 2^{15} ($=32736$).

11 b) First two bits must be 0 1 or 1 0 unless the number is zero.

12 a) 8

b) 16

c) Suggestions in the region of mantissa: 56 bits, exponent: 8 bits.

13

decimal	binary	octal	hexadecimal
45	101101	55	2D
21	10101	25	15
32	100000	40	20
4097	1000000000001	10001	1001

14 a) Parity error in 5th byte.

b) Parity error in 7th column.

c) 7th bit in 5th byte (should be 0).

15 a) No, the parity bit might have been copied incorrectly.

b) No, two bits might be in error.

c) Parity will detect that a single bit error most probably has occurred.

16 Computers monitoring/controlling machines, computers analysing scientific experiments.

Exercise 4

2 Data structures enable large, potentially unwieldy collections of data to be managed by relatively simple operations. Concepts associated with data structures have led to advances in computer architecture. Data structures have improved the design of programs.

3 a) Indexes in books, filing systems, maps.

b) Casual conversations, clues in a crime.

5 a) Array, stack, tree.

b) Each is easy to implement in a computer memory, using pointers. Each is important for a wide range of computer applications.

6 To mark an empty stack, the end of a list and a terminal node of a tree.

7 Split the string at the point of insertion, obtaining <leftstring> and <rightstring>. Form a new string by joining <leftstring>, <newstring> and <rightstring>.

8 a) Let index $I = 1$
While $I <= 10$ repeat
    Let $Z(I) = X(I) + Y(I)$
    Increase I by 1
  b) Let total $T = 0$
Let index $I = 1$
While $I <= 10$ repeat
    Let $T = T + X(I)$
    Increase I by 1
  ●c) Let product $P = 0$
Let index $I = 1$
While $I <= 10$ repeat
    Let $P = P + X(I) \cdot Y(I)$
    Increase I by 1

● **9** b) If $A(I,J)$ goes into $B(K)$ then $K = 3(I-1) + J$
  ●c) If $A(I,J)$ goes into $B(K)$ then $K = 3I + J$

10 a) $21 - 10 \div 5$:

stack 21		21
stack 10		10 21
stack 5		5 10 21
divide 10 by 5, stack result		2 21
subtract 2 from 21		19

  b) $6 \times (4 + 5) \times 3$:

stack 6		6
stack 4		4 6
stack 5		5 4 6
add 4 and 5, stack result		9 6
multiply, stack result		54
stack 3		3 54
multiply, stack result		162

11 c) Disadvantage: the queue 'moves' in the memory of the computer.

12 a) See Figure 39.1.
  b) See Figure 39.1.
  c) Pointers A2 and C1 point to the new data item B.
    Pointer B1 points to data item A.
    Pointer B2 points to data item C.

13 See Figure 39.2.

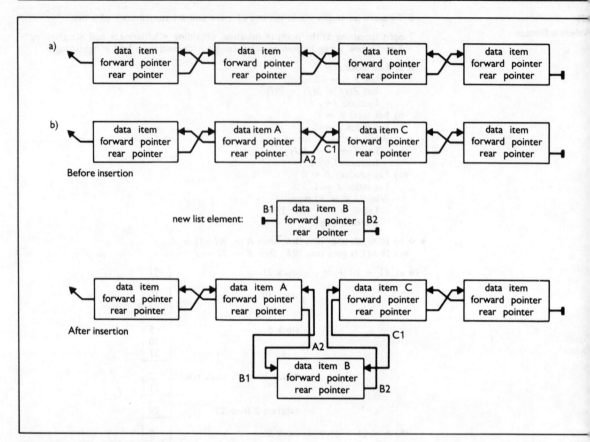

Figure 39.1 Exercise 4 Question 10

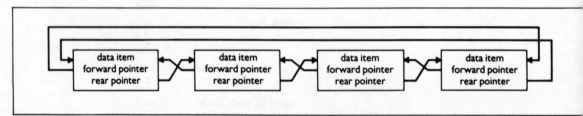

Figure 39.2
Exercise 4 Question 13

14 Insertion

If there is at least one free element in the array
    then Repeat, from the front of the array
            Compare element to be inserted with current array element
    Until element to be inserted is earlier in alphabetical order than current array element
    Mark current array element
    Repeat, from rear of array to marked element
        Move element one place down in array
    Insert new element in front of marked element.

Deletion follows a similar pattern, to locate the element to be deleted, and move remaining elements up one place. A free space is inserted at the end.

Comment: Storing ordered data in an array involves a lot of movement of array elements during insertion and deletion.

15 See Figure 39.3.

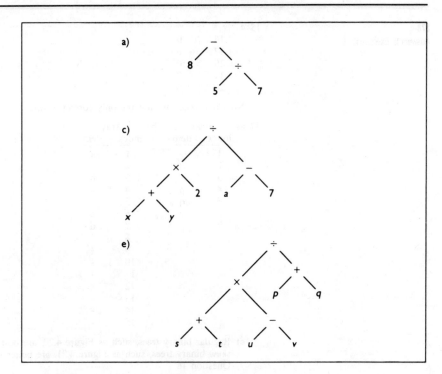

Figure 39.3
Exercise 4 Question 15

16 a)

pointers array		data array	
index	item	index	item
1	1	1	control module
2	6	2	input module
3	8	3	processing module
4	12	4	output module
5	0	5	calculation module
6	2	6	backing store transfer module
7	0		
8	3		
9	14		
10	16		
11	0		
12	4		
13	0		
14	5		
15	0		
16	6		
17	0		

b)

pointers array		data array	
index	item	index	item
1	1	1	+
2	5	2	x
3	9	3	p
4	0	4	q
5	2	5	−
6	13	6	r
7	15	7	s
8	0		
9	5		
10	17		
11	19		
12	0		
13	3		
14	0		

15   4
16   0
17   6
18   0
19   7
20   0

Note that these are not the only correct answers.

17 a)

array	
index	item
1	+
2	×
3	−
4	p
5	q
6	r
7	s

b)

array	
index	item
1	a
2	-
3	b
4	-
5	-
6	c
7	d
8	-
9	-
10	-
11	-
12	e
13	-
14	-
15	-

c) Regular binary trees, such as Figure 4.20, are best stored by this method, but skew binary trees, such as Figure 4.21, are better stored by the method of Question 16.

18 a) Figure 4.20: $p \times q + r - s$
Figure 4.22: a e c b d
b) Interchange lines 'output node' and 'traverse right subtree'.
c) Figure 4.17: 7 4 9 × +
Figure 4.20: $p\ q \times r\ s - +$
Figure 4.22: e c d b a

Exercise 5

3

			−8	4	2	1
2 + 5:	2	= 0	0	1	0	
	+ 5	= 0	1	0	1	
	7	= 0	1	1	1	

Carry in = 0, carry out = 0, answer correct.

6 + 3:	6	= 0	1	1	0
	+ 3	= 0	0	1	1
	− 7	= 1	0	0	1

Carry in = 1, carry out = 0, answer incorrect.

4 − 5:	4	= 0	1	0	0
	− 5	= 1	0	1	1
	− 1	= 1	1	1	1

Carry in = 0, carry out = 0, answer correct.

−2 −7:	− 2	= 1	1	1	0
	− 7	= 1	0	0	1
	7	= 0	1	1	1

Carry in = 0, carry out = 1, answer incorrect.

4 Same overflow rule as for twos complements.

5 Product = 1 0 1 1 0 1 1 0

6 Use a working area layout as in Figure 5.1, except that area B is not used. The algorithm is:

Initially, B contains zeros, A the divisor and D the dividend
Repeat, for each bit of the numbers
   Shift the bits in C and D together one place to the right
   If the contents of C is greater than the divisor in A
     then Subtract A from C, placing the result in C
         Place a 1 in the least significant bit position of D
     else Place a 0 in the least significant bit position of D
When the process is complete, the quotient is in D and the remainder is in C.

7

	mantissa					exponent		
	sign	$\frac{1}{2}$	$\frac{1}{4}$	$\frac{1}{8}$	$\frac{1}{16}$	sign	2	1
A + B =	0	1	0	0	1	0	1	1
B + C =	0	1	0	0	1	0	1	0
A × B =	0	1	0	1	0	0	1	1
A × C =	0	1	1	1	1	0	0	1

8 Range of positive numbers: 2^{-32} (= 2.829 × 10^{-10}) to 2^{31} (= 2 147 483 648).

9 a) 0 1 1 1
    1 0 0 0
    1 0 0 1 1 0

b)

	mantissa					exponent			
	sign	$\frac{1}{2}$	$\frac{1}{4}$	$\frac{1}{8}$	$\frac{1}{16}$	sign	2	1	
A + B =	0	1	0	0	1	0	1	1	no change
B + C =	0	1	0	0	1	0	1	0	no change
A × B =	0	1	0	1	0	0	1	1	more accurate
A × C =	0	1	1	1	1	0	0	1	no change

Exercise 6

2

Inputs			Outputs			
A	B	C	AND	OR	NAND	NOR
0	0	0	0	0	1	1
0	0	1	0	1	1	0
0	1	0	0	1	1	0
0	1	1	0	1	1	0
1	0	0	0	1	1	0
1	0	1	0	1	1	0
1	1	0	0	1	1	0
1	1	1	1	1	0	0

4 $D = A + (B \cdot \overline{C})$
$H = (\overline{E + F}) \oplus (\overline{F \cdot G})$
$L = (\overline{I} \cdot J \cdot K) + (\overline{I} \cdot J \cdot \overline{K})$

5 See Figure 39.4, page 381.

● **6** $A \oplus B = (A + B) \cdot (\overline{A \cdot B})$

7 b) $K = \overline{\overline{A} + \overline{B}}$ simplifies to $K = A \cdot B$.
    $L = (C + \overline{D}) \cdot (C + \overline{E})$ simplifies to $L = C + \overline{D + E}$.
    $M = (P \cdot (\overline{Q \cdot R})) + (P \cdot (Q \cdot R))$ simplifies to $M = P \cdot (\overline{Q + R} + Q \cdot R)$.

● **8** $D = \overline{A} \cdot B \cdot C + A \cdot \overline{B} \cdot \overline{C}$

9 $A \cdot B = \overline{\overline{A} + \overline{B}}$

10 a) See Figure 39.5.
   b) See Figure 39.5.
   c) Any combination of logic operations can be expressed in terms of the NAND operation only.

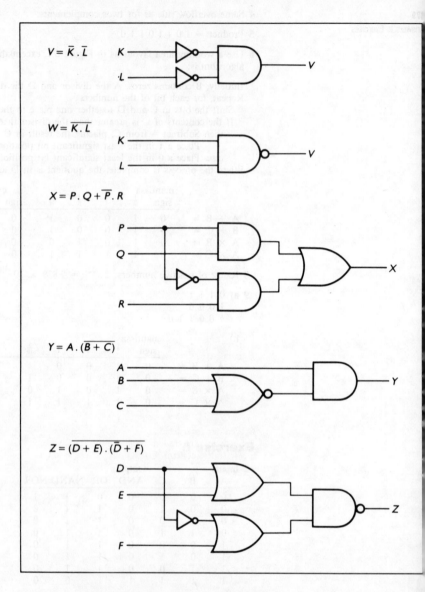

$V = \overline{K} . \overline{L}$

$W = \overline{K . L}$

$X = P . Q + \overline{P} . R$

$Y = A . (\overline{B + C})$

$Z = \overline{(D + E) . (\overline{D} + F)}$

Figure 39.4
Exercise 6 Question 5

11 a) D = $\overline{A} \cdot \overline{B} \cdot \overline{C}$ + $\overline{A} \cdot B \cdot \overline{C}$ + A·$\overline{B}$·C + A·B·C
  = $\overline{A} \cdot \overline{C}$ + A·C
 b) E = $\overline{A} \cdot B \cdot \overline{C} \cdot \overline{D}$ + $\overline{A} \cdot B \cdot \overline{C} \cdot D$ + $\overline{A} \cdot B \cdot C \cdot \overline{D}$ + $\overline{A} \cdot B \cdot C \cdot D$ + A·$\overline{B}$·$\overline{C}$·D + A·$\overline{B}$·C·D
  = $\overline{A} \cdot B$ + A·$\overline{B}$·D
 c) E = $\overline{A} \cdot \overline{B} \cdot \overline{C} \cdot \overline{D}$ + $\overline{A} \cdot \overline{B} \cdot C \cdot \overline{D}$ + $\overline{A} \cdot B \cdot \overline{C} \cdot D$ + $\overline{A} \cdot B \cdot C \cdot D$ + A·$\overline{B}$·C·$\overline{D}$ + A·B·C·D
  = $\overline{A} \cdot \overline{B} \cdot \overline{D}$ + $\overline{A} \cdot B \cdot D$ + A·$\overline{B}$·C·$\overline{D}$ + A·B·C·D
  = $\overline{A} \cdot (\overline{B} \cdot \overline{D}$ + B·D) + A·C·($\overline{B} \cdot \overline{D}$ + B·D)
  = ($\overline{A}$ + A·C)·($\overline{B} \cdot \overline{D}$ + B·D)

Exercise 7

2 a) and b) Most orderings can be supported by a suitable argument.
  c) Only the first task.
  d) The second and fourth tasks.
  e) Some computer involvement in all the tasks is possible during the next ten years.

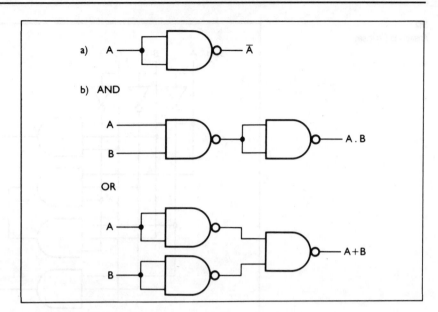

Figure 39.5
Exercise 6 Question 6 a) and b)

3 likes(Susan, Fred)
likes(Susan, Helen)
likes(John, Jean)
likes(Susan, Jean)

4 a) saw = (1) perceived visually
            (2) realised
c) Alternative interpretations of a single word can change the meaning of an entire passage.

6 Weather forecasts
Stock market traders' dialogue
Air traffic control instructions
Operating theatre dialogue.

Exercise 8

2 a) 1 0 1 0 1 0 0 0   b) 1 0 0 0 1 0 0 0

3 a) 8   b) 2^n

●**4** a)

Inputs			Outputs	
A	B	C	S	T
0	0	0	0	0
0	0	1	1	0
0	1	0	1	0
0	1	1	0	1
1	0	0	1	0
1	0	1	0	1
1	1	0	0	1
1	1	1	1	1

c) See Figure 39.6.

●**5** See Figure 39.7.

●**6** Relevant points:
   • A logic circuit can be thought of as a module, connected to other logic circuits by inputs and outputs.
   • Many logic circuit modules are constructed as integrated circuits.
   • A logic circuit module can be replaced by another, with a different but equivalent arrangement of logic gates.

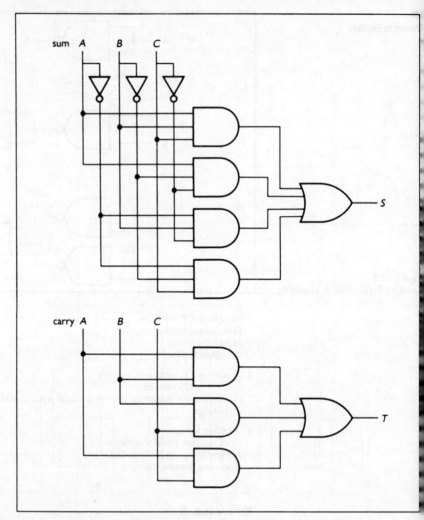

Figure 39.6
Exercise 7 Question 4 c)

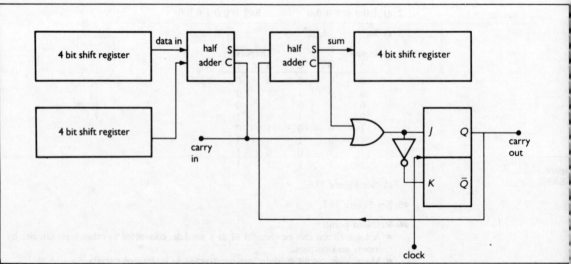

Figure 39.7
Exercise 7 Question 5

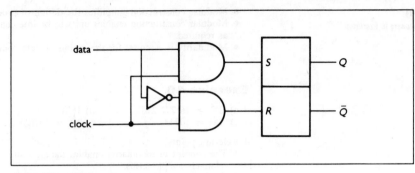

Figure 39.8
D type flip-flop

8 See Figure 39.8.

●**9** See Figure 39.9.

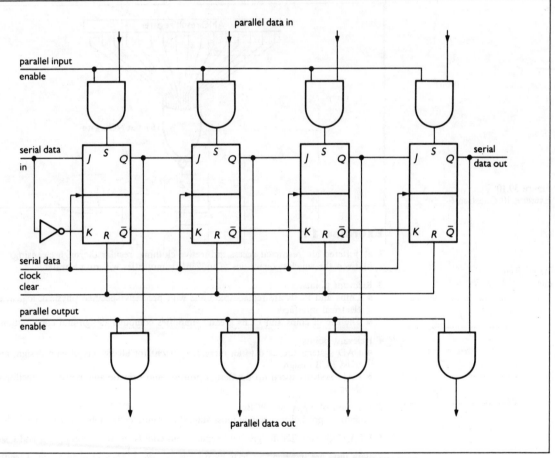

Figure 39.9
USART

Exercise 9

2 Relevant points:
- The concept of modularity enables the structure of a computer system to be expressed at a number of different levels of detail.
- Most computers are constructed as separate modules.

- Modular construction simplifies the design of processors and peripherals.
- Modular construction enables units to be interchanged, allowing systems to grow as required.
- Modularity is essential for the design of data communications equipment.

Exercise 10

3 a) 2^{24} = 16 777 216   b) 16M
c) 1M = 1024K   d) 2^{32} = 4096M

4 Relevant points:
- The concept of modularity enables the structure of a processor to be explained in relatively simple terms.
- Each module of a processor may be implemented as a single chip.
- The same processor design may be implemented by different but equivalent chips.

6 a) See Figure 39.10.

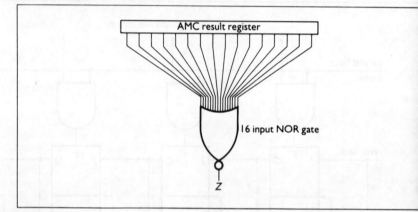

Figure 39.10
Exercise 10 Question 6

Exercise 11

2 a) Filtered air, restricted access, protective clothing, regular thorough cleansing.
b) Even the smallest quantities of unwanted impurities will ruin a wafer.

3 Relevant points:
- Chips and PCBs are replaceable units with precisely specified physical, logical and electrical interfaces.
- The use of chips and PCBs greatly simplifies computer design and construction.

4 Relevant points:
- CAD systems are used to an increasing extent for all aspects of chip design, and most PCB design.
- CAD systems speed up the design process, and provide automated test facilities for designs.

5 Insertion of chips into PCBs.
Potential applications include most stages of computer assembly and testing.

6 ULA chips simplify designs, and reduce chip counts, power consumption and cost.

7 Beta tests are independent tests by prospective users. They provide essential feedback and lead to the rectification of most faults before volume production commences.

Exercise 12

2 Absolute address: to access individual data items at known locations.
Indexed address: to access the elements of an array.
Indirect address: to access data items from a structure such as a list or tree.
Relative address: to access relocatable data or code.
Immediate operand: to store a constant.

3 The data item whose address is located at address **49B6** is loaded into the accumulator. Since the address at location **49B6** is **3521**, the data item at this address, **AB02**, is loaded.

4 a) For positive and negative numbers:
Arithmetic shift left has the effect of multiplication by 2.
Arithmetic shift right has the effect of division by 2.

5 0046, 0116

6 Stack: **CCDD** Stack pointer: **01FC**
AABB

7 As an eight bit twos complement number, **80** = −128. As a sixteen bit twos complement number, **FF80** = −128. The process of sign extension preserves the value of both negative and positive numbers.

8 a)

Address	Instruction	Comments
0000	08	Length of arrays, 8 bytes or 4 words.
0001		Array 1, already loaded.
to 0008		
0009		Array 2, already loaded.
to 0010		
0011		Array 3.
to 0018		

Start of program

0019	2122 0000	Load byte at address **0000** to index register.

Start of loop to add each pair of numbers

001D	0320	Decrease index register by 1.
001F	0320	Decrease index register by 1.
0021	670E	Branch to address **0031** if negative.
0023	1114 0001	Load first array element.
0027	1314 0009	Add second array element.
002B	1214 0011	Store total in third array.
002F	61EC	Branch to address **0010**.

End of loop

0031	8500	End of program.

b) FFFE (= −2)

c) The array length in location **0000** and the start addresses of the arrays will change, as will the location of the program. Branching instructions, being relative, are not affected.

d) The instruction at address **0027** becomes **1514 0009.**

9

Address	Instruction	Comments
0000	001F	Address of first character, later of current character.

Start of program loop

0002	2113 0000	Load character at address in location **0000** to accumulator.
0006	2A11 7E	Compare with end marker **7E**.
0009	6212	Branch if equal, to address **001D**.
000B	7410	Signal output device to unload output register.
000F	6DFE	Branch back to this instruction if output not complete.
0011	1112 0000	Load address of current character to accumulator.
0015	0210	Increase contents of accumulator by 1.
0017	1212 0000	Store address of next character in location **0000**.
001B	61E5	Branch to address **0002**, to output next character.

End of program loop

001D	8500	Halt.
001F		First character.

Exercise 13

2 The functional units and buffers for the pipeline are shown in Figure 39.11. During each 'beat', data passes from a buffer, through a functional unit, to the next buffer. The hardware used by each buffer is physically separate from that used by the other buffers. Problems include:
  - The duration of each 'beat' is the same. Several stages take a variable amount of time, depending on the instruction.
  - Branch or jump instructions can result in the wrong instructions being loaded into the pipeline.

3 All the instructions in the loop are loaded into the cache while the loop is being executed. This increases the processing speed of the computer.

4 a) 320 microseconds.
  b) 630 microseconds.
  c) 320 + 10(n − 1) microseconds.

5 They emphasise the shortcomings of the 'elementary' view of a computer, as an 'automatic, electronic information processing machine' (Section 1.4) and give credence to the view of a computer as a 'collection of resources' (Section 2.3). Advanced processor features do not, however, contradict either of these views.

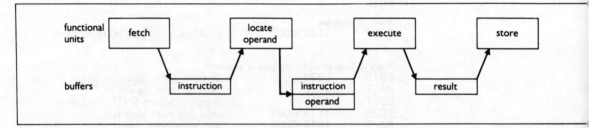

Figure 39.11
AMC instruction pipeline

Exercise 14

2 1200 characters per second.

3 a) 20 000 blocks.
  b) 2 microseconds.
  c) 50 microseconds.
  d) 1340 seconds, approximately 22 minutes.
  e) 40 seconds.

4 a) Flag A goes from 1 to 0
    Flag B goes from 1 to 0
    Character loaded into buffer
    Flag B goes from 0 to 1
    Flag C goes from 0 to 1
    Then
    Flag C goes from 1 to 0
    Flag B goes from 1 to 0
    Character copied from buffer
    Flag B goes from 0 to 1
    Flag A goes from 0 to 1
  b) Flag A indicates that the peripheral is ready for the transfer of another data item. Flag C indicates that the processor has completed a transfer of data.
  c) Most of the delay will occur waiting for flag A to be set to 1 by the peripheral.

●6 The program uses the index register to 'count in' the characters, and assign them to successive store locations. The characters are added to a running total as they are input. This total is then compared with the checksum characters.

Address	Instruction	Comments
0000	0000	Running total of characters, initially zero.
0002		Space for input characters.
to 0009		
000A		Space for checksum
000B		

Start of program

Address	Instruction	Comments
000C	0210	Clear index register.

Start of loop to input characters

Address	Instruction	Comments
000E	7110	Signal peripheral device to load input register.
0010	6CFE	Branch back to here if input not complete.
0012	7210	Copy character to accumulator.
0014	2214 0002	Store character at address (0002 + index).
0018	1312 0000	Add running total into accumulator.
001C	1212 0000	Store new value of total.
0020	0220	Increase index register by 1.
0022	1A21 0007	Compare index with 0007.
0026	66EG	Branch if less than or equal, to 000E.

Start of loop to input checksum

Address	Instruction	Comments
0028	7110	Signal peripheral device to load input register.
002A	6CFE	Branch back to here if input not complete.
002C	7210	Copy character to accumulator.
002E	2214 0002	Store character at address (0002 + index).
0032	0220	Increase index register by 1.
0034	1A21 0009	Compare index register with 0009.
0038	66EE	Branch if less than or equal, to 0028.

End of input loop

Address	Instruction	Comments
003A	1112 000A	Load checksum to accumulator.
003E	1A22 0000	Compare with running total.
0042	6204	Branch if equal, to 0048.
0044	0110	Clear accumulator (check fails).
0046	6104	Branch to 004C.
0048	1111 0001	Set accumulator to 1 (check succeeds).
004C	7410	Copy to output register.
004E	7310	Signal peripheral device to output character.
0050	60FE	Branch back to here if output is not complete.
0052	8500	Halt.

Exercise 15

1 A general-purpose register may be used for a number of functions, such as accumulator, index register, stack pointer, program counter. The VAX uses general-purpose registers.
A special-purpose register is used for one function only. The RM Nimbus, ICL 2900 series and the Cray-2 use special-purpose registers.

2 One-address: RM Nimbus, ICL 2900 series, Cray-2. Two-address: VAX.

4 ICL 2900, Cray-2.

5 a) 7.
b) AMC: 80 clock periods per loop cycle, 2560 for entire process.
Cray-2: 35 clock periods.
Comment: the AMC takes about 7000 times as long as the Cray-2.

6 ICL 2900 series. It is designed as a 'high level language processor', which makes extensive use of a stack.

Exercise 16

2 a) CLR A
   STO A   DT1

```
          b) LOA  A  N  +16291
             STO  A     CS1
          c) LOB  A     CTR
             INC  A
             STB  A     CTR
          d) LOA  A     AB1
             CMP  A     AB2
             BZE        EQU
          e) LOA  A  N  /EF/
             PSH  A
             LOA  A  N  /CD/
             PSH  A
             LOA  A  N  /AB/
             PSH  A

        3 RTA  WRD
          NM1  WRD
```

Start of subprogram

```
          SBP  POP  A
               STO  A     RTA
               POP  A
               STO  A     NM1
               POP  A
               CMP  A     NM1
               BGE        LT2
               LOA  A     NM1
          LT2  PSH  A
               LOA  A     TRA
               PSH  A
               RTS
```

End of subprogram, start of main program

```
          STR  LOA  S  N  +127
               LOA  A  N  +16693
               PSH  A
               LOA  A  N  +25252
               PSH  A
               JSR        SPB
               POP  A
               HLT
```

5 a)	HI1	WRD	+10000	High-order word of integer 1.
and b)	LI1	WRD	+8763	Low-order word of integer 1.
	HI2	WRD	+20000	High-order word of integer 2.
	LI2	WRD	+14261	Low-order word of integer 2.
	HSM	WRD		High-order word of sum.
	LSM	WRD		Low-order word of sum.

Start of program

LOA	A	LI1	Load low-order word of integer 1.
ADD	A	LI2	Add low-order word of integer 2.
STO	A	LSM	Store in low-order word of sum.
LOA	A	HI1	Load high-order word of integer 2.
ADC	A	HI2	Add high-order word of integer 2 plus previous carry.
STO	A	HSM	Store in high-order word of sum.
HLT			Halt.
END			End of program.

c) Unless a loop is used, the program is as above, with the addition of **LOA**, **ADC** and **STO** instructions.

•d) Twos complement subtraction always results in the correct bit pattern for the low-order word, even if the low-order word of the second number is larger than that of the first. In the latter case, the high-order word of the difference is too large by 1, since this has been 'borrowed' for the low order subtraction. This situation is indicated by the overflow bit being set during low order subtraction. Using data areas as for part a), the program is as follows:

```
            LOA A   LI1     Load low-order word of integer 1.
            SUB A   LI2     Subtract low order word of integer 2.
            STO A   LSM     Store in low-order word of difference.
            STC             Set carry bit.
            BVS     NXT     Branch if overflow set by subtraction.
            CLC             Clear carry bit.
        NXT LOA A   HI1     Load high-order word of integer 1.
            SBC A   HI2     Subtract (high-order word of integer 2 + carry).
            STO A   HSM     Store in high-order word of difference.
            HLT             Halt
            END             End of program.
```

6 The program uses a subset of the instructions in Example Program 16.2.

```
    PTR WRD     LE1     Address of first item, later of current list item.
```

Start of program loop

```
    NXT LOA A   PTR     Load address of current list item to accumulator.
        INC A           Increment accumulator, to become address of pointer
                        part of list item.
        STO A   PTR     Store address of pointer part of list item.
        LOA A I PTR     Load pointer part of list item to accumulator.
        BZE     OUT     Branch out of loop if it is zero.
        STO A   PTR     Store address of next list item.
        BRN     NXT     Branch to instruction labelled NXT to continue loop.
```

End of program loop

```
        LOA A   PTR     Load address of pointer part of last list item.
        DEC A           Decrement accumulator, to contain address of last list
                        item.
        HLT             Halt.
    LE1 BTE     /A/     First list item.
        WRD     +0      Pointer part of first list item.
        END             End of program.
```

9 The version of the program written below uses a third working area, **WAO**, to allow for a possible double length product.

```
    IN1 WRD     +2647   Integer 1.
    IN2 WRD     +3159   Integer 2.
    WAO WRD     +0      High-order word of product.
    WA1 WRD     +0      Low-order word of product.
    WA2 WRD     +0      Working area.
```

Start of program

```
        LOA A   IN2     Load integer 2 to accumulator.
        STO A   WA2     Store integer 2 in working area.
```

Start of multiplication loop

```
    NXT BZE     OUT     Branch to end of program if number in accumulator
                        is zero.
        LOA A   WA1     Load low-order word of product.
        ADD A   IN1     Add integer 1.
        STO A   WA1     Store new value of low-order word of product.
        LOA A   WAO     Load high-order word of product.
        ADC A N +0      Add carry from previous addition.
        STO A   WAO     Store new value of high-order word of product.
        LOA A   WA2     Load working area to accumulator.
        DEC A           Decrease accumulator by 1.
        STO A   WA2     Store new value of working area.
        BRN     NXT     Branch to continue loop.
```

End of multiplication loop

```
    OUT HLT             Halt
        END             End of program.
```

11 A store instruction with an immediate operand makes no sense.

Exercise 17

3 Checking the assembly language program for errors, and reporting the nature and position of any encountered.

4 A label can only be associated with one absolute address in the symbolic address table of an assembler.

5 An additional entry in the table of mnemonic and machine operation codes, and routines to carry out any special assembly operations required by the new instruction.

6 AMC machine language

Address	Instruction
0000	1121 <u>0001</u>
0004	1A21 <u>001B</u>
0008	650C
000A	11TT <u>0064</u>
000E	2214 <u>0018</u>
0012	0220
0014	61<u>EE</u>
0016	8500

Exercise 18

2 Machine independence and problem orientation.

3 The inefficiency of software development using low level languages.

5 Similarities: use of character symbols, words and constructions based on rules of syntax. Differences: natural languages are not precisely defined. A valid program in high level language has only one interpretation, whereas natural languages can be vague or ambiguous, or have several levels of meaning.

6 a) x: lines 2 to 19
   count: lines 3 to 19
   v: lines 10 to 14.
   b) Yes.
   c) No.
   d) local variables: w, v, y, z
   global variables: x, count.
   e) line 17.

7 a) Y = 3, X = 3
   b) LET T = X
      LET X = Y
      LET Y = T

8 a)   READ (1, 200) I, J, K, L, M, N
          200 FORMAT (I2, 1X, I2, 1X, I2, 1X, I4, 1X, I4, 1X, I4
   b) 3614 2915 23 79 63725489
   c) Advantages: precision, ability to check data as it is input. Disadvantages: tedious, error-prone, difficult to program.

9 a) y = 5   b) y = 10   c) y = 10
   d) y = 9   e) y = 0
   f) Using 'elementary' Basic:
      100 IF X<0 THEN 120
      105 IF X>9 THEN 120
      110 LET Y=9-X
      115 GOTO 125
      120 LET Y=10
      125 REM CONTINUE
   The logic of this program is not nearly as easy to follow as the Pascal statement.

Exercise 19

2 The three strongest reasons are the theoretical emphasis of Algol, its poor input/output facilities and the increasing popularity of Pascal.

4 Algol's aim of being a 'universal programming language' is very lofty, and rather idealistic. Pascal's aim to be a simple, well-structured teaching language which is easy to implement on a wide range of computers, is much more realistic.

5 Reasoned cases can be made for Pascal, Basic and C.

6 Possible reasons (for both languages) include their suitability for the type of work for which they are designed, and their ease of use by people working in the particular fields to which they apply.

9 Fortran, Algol: strong
Cobol, Basic, Pascal, C: moderate
Lisp, Prolog: weak

Exercise 20

3 Interpretation is simpler than compilation, and requires only one copy of the program being interpreted.

4 b) 469.31   valid   .734   valid
   4325   invalid   45.6.7   invalid
   846.   invalid

  c) <decimal number>::={<number>}{<decimal point>}{<number>}
  d) <signed decimal number>::={<sign>}{<number>}
                                    {<decimal point>}{<number>}
     <sign>::= + | −
     All example numbers are valid.

6 The application program is compiled, with calls to the utilities regarded as unresolved external references. The utilities are copied from backing store, and the linkage editor deals with the call and return addresses. The loader places all the modules in their final positions for running, and transforms relative addresses as required.

7 a) Valid   b) Invalid   c) Invalid   d) Valid
  e) <condition>::=<variable><relation><constant> |
                     <variable><relation><variable>

8 a) Valid.
  b) Valid.
  c) Valid.
  d) Invalid - error 2.
  e) Invalid - error 2.
  f) Invalid - error 3.
  g) Error 1: No number present.
     Error 2: Duplicate sign in number.
     Error 3: No digits in number.
     Error 4: Duplicate decimal point.

●h)

State	\+	−	Next character digit		E	*
1	2	2	3	4	error 5	error 1
2	error 2	error 2	3	4	error 5	error 3
3	error 2	error 2	3	4	5	exit
4	error 2	error 2	4	error 4	5	exit
5	6	6	7	error 6	error 7	error 8
6	error 2	error 2	7	error 6	error 7	error 8
7	error 2	error 2	7	error 6	error 7	exit

Error 5: Invalid number before exponent.
Error 6: Decimal point in exponent.
Error 7: Duplicate exponent symbol.
Error 8: Incomplete exponent.

9	**Basic**	**AMC Assembly Language**		
a)	`100 LET L=J+K`	`LOA`	`A`	`J`
		`ADD`	`A`	`K`
		`STO`	`A`	`L`
b)	`50 IF C>10 THEN 200`	`LOA`	`A`	`C`
		`CMP`	`A N`	`+10`
		`BGT`		`XX0`
c)	`100 FOR K=1 TO 20`	`LOA`	`X N`	`+1`
		`NXT CMP`	`X N`	`+20`
		`BGT`		`OUT`
	`110 LET J(K)=J(K)+1`	`LOB`	`A D`	`J`
		`INC`	`A`	
		`STB`	`A D`	`J`
	`120 NEXT K`	`INC`	`X`	
		`BRN`		`NXT`
		`OUT`		

10 One instruction is placed outside the loop, which is repeated 9 times, with three operations per repetition.

```
    LOA X N +1
    LOA A N +100
NXT CMP X N +27
    BGT     OUT
    STB A D W
    INC X
    STB A D W
    INC X
    STB A D W
    INC X
    BRN     NXT
OUT
```

12 See Figure 39.12.

Exercise 21

2 The program is written for the virtual machine produced by the operating system, and not for the raw hardware of the computer.

4 Single program operation.

6 The control and resource management of a large computer system, comprising more than one processor, large numbers of peripherals and several data communications channels is an extremely complex task.

8 It is the only part which has direct access to most of the 'real' resources of the computer. All requests for these resources must be channelled through it.

9 The programmer is freed from the problems of store allocation, and does not have to resort to such techniques as overlay programming.

10 Objectives: efficient management of the resources (chiefly main store) of the computer, and simplifying the use of peripherals.
features: a simple main store manager, controllers for each peripheral and a mechanism to allow the user to interrupt an applications program.

11 No software is infallible, and only an operator can respond to unforeseen circumstances.

12 a) Address GO.
b) Address GO + 1.
c) *
d) Control is transferred to the start of the program, at address GO.
e) A machine code program is loaded, as a set of characters, from a paper tape to main store, starting at address GO. When the end of the program is reached, control passes to the first program instruction.

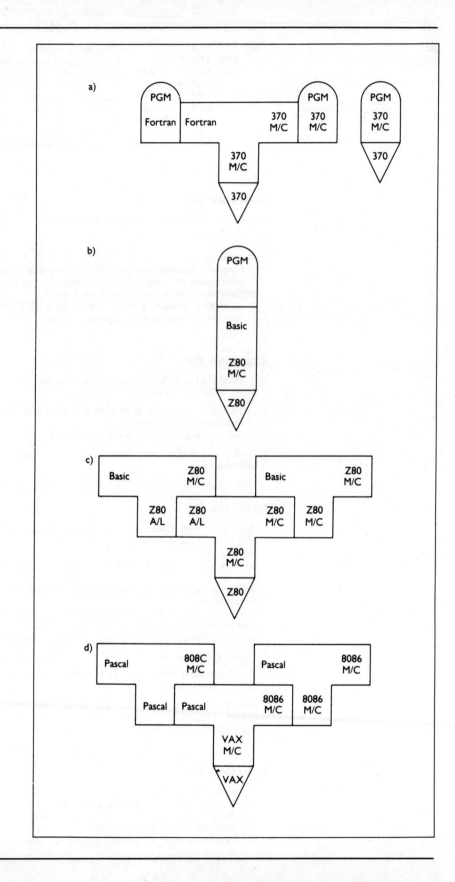

Figure 39.12
Exercise 20 Question 12

```
●f)     CLA              Clear index register.
   STR  IRQ P            Request paper tape reader to input a character.
   HRE  BIN      HRE     Branch to this instruction if input not complete.
        INP A            Copy character from input register to accumulator.
        CPB A N /*/      Compare character in accumulator with *.
        BEQ       GO     Branch to instruction labelled GO if equal.
        STB A D GO       Store accumulator contents at (GO + index).
        INC X            Increase index by 1.
        BRN       STR    Branch to instruction labelled STR.
   GO
```

Exercise 22

1 a) Unix, VME/B. b) Unix, VME/B. c) VME/B.

2 Unix, VME/B.

6 Relevant points:
   a) Computer manufacturers are obliged to develop computers which are similar to others using the same operating system.
   b) Developing portable software is much easier.
   c) Users have access to a wider range of software. Communication between different computers using the same operating system is easy.

Exercise 23

2 a) suitable b) suitable c) suitable d) not suitable
   e) not suitable f) suitable.

3 a) The rapid production of prototypes enables users to test the consequences of their specifications at an early stage.
   b) Software more suited to the needs of users.

4 Further development of software, less revision during development, simpler maintenance.

Exercise 24

2 Similarities: both based on data dictionaries, both include application generators, both lead to cost-effective, high-quality software.
Differences:
Software development tools are limited to commercial applications, environments are not.
Software development environments give assistance with proofs of the correctness of programs, tools do not.
Software development tools use a single specification language, environments use multiple programming and specification languages.
Software development environments include the program design phase, tools do not.

3 Formal proofs are the only way of ensuring the correct operation of software.

4 To an increasing extent, software is being developed on computers different from the ultimate host machines.

6 Basic has no facilities for block structuring, local variables, parameter passing or linkage of separately compiled modules. It is not consistent with the philosophy of strict program structure.

Exercise 25

3 a) Periodic processing.
   b) Real-time system, transaction processing.
   c) Periodic processing.
   d) Real-time system, process control.
   e) Database system, or real-time system, information storage/retrieval.

5 At almost every stage, but most common are after feasibility study, system investigation or acceptance testing.

6 Feasibility study, system investigation, system specification, evaluation of possible packages against the system specification, choice of package, acceptance testing.

7 They are not an adequate test of the robustness of the system.

8 Increased costs, particcularly wage costs, delays and loss of business, and the computer acquiring a bad reputation.

9 At system specification time, or when parallel running is commenced. Possibilities include: guarantee of no redundancies, inducements of free re-training for higher-paid jobs, undertakings to improve working conditions and, above all, keeping employees adequately informed about what is going on.

10 The system outlined below is one possibility:
   a) See Figure 39.13.
   b) One each for sale recording, updating of stock sales file, updating of cash takings file and transmission of stock sales file.
   c) Algorithm for sale recording program:

   Set sale total to zero
   Repeat, for each item sold
     Input stock number and quantity
     Access price from stock file
     Display stock number, quantity, price and amount
     Print stock number, quantity, price and amount on sales slip
     Add amount to total
   Display and print total
   Input amount of cash, cheque and gift voucher tendered. Calculate change.
   Display and print amount tendered and change.

   d) Training of data entry terminal operators. Ensuring that the prices displayed on goods are always the same as those in the price file.

Exercise 26

2 a) Possible keys are name and date, or reference allocated to each letter.
   b) One possibility is: fields for name, address, date and each line of text of the letter, each field starting with the tab position of the first character in the line.
   c) Any medium other than disks will make editing very difficult.
4 a) Search top level index or first key greater than 132714. This corresponds to second level index 11. Search second level index 11 for first key greater than 132714. This corresponds to third level index 531. Search third level index 531 for first key greater than 132714. This corresponds to block 26544. Copy block 26544 to main store, and search it sequentially for key 132714.
   b) During cylinder-surface-sector indexing, the disk drive head is 'homing in' on the required sector. During hierarchical indexing, the location of the required block is only determined at the last step.

5 a) 412 117 503 has address 1112.
      625 417 902 has address 1944.
   b) 462 803 906 has address 2171.
      341 915 916 has address 2172.
      638 702 831 has address 2173.
      594 113 666 has address 2174.
   c) Loading in a different order will result in different addresses for the records.

Exercise 27

2 b) Employee number.
   c) A check on the total of the various categories of days. A check of the name against employee number on a reference file.

3 The batch total calculated before the data was input is wrong.

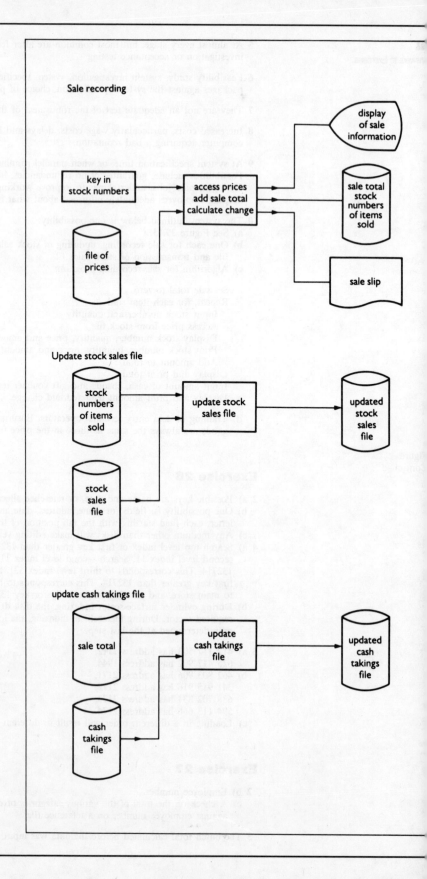

Figure 39.13
Exercise 25 Question 10
(continued on next page)

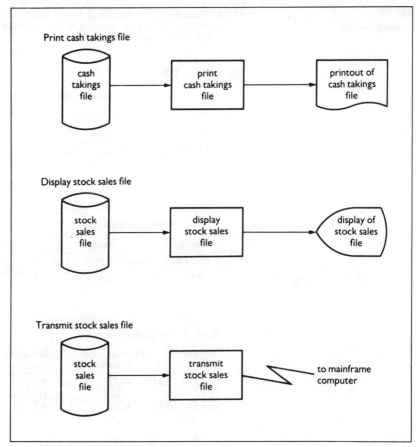

Print cash takings file

cash takings file → print cash takings file → printout of cash takings file

Display stock sales file

stock sales file → display stock sales file → display of stock sales file

Transmit stock sales file

stock sales file → transmit stock sales file → to mainframe computer

Figure 39.13
Continued

4 6297<u>3</u>
5116<u>4</u>

6 String 1: 17 4 9 21, sorted: 4 9 17 21
String 2: 8 5 20 2, sorted: 2 5 8 20
String 3: 7 11 15 6, sorted: 6 7 11 15
String 4: 3 1 19 13, sorted: 1 3 13 19

Tape A: String 1 String 3
Tape B: String 2 String 4

Merge in pairs:
Tape C: String 1 + String 2: 2 4 5 8 9 17 20 21
Tape D: String 3 + String 4: 1 3 6 7 11 13 15 19

Merge to a single string:
Tape A: 1 2 3 4 5 6 7 8 9 11 13 15 17 19 20 21

9 Initial situation:

   4 7 8 10 11 19 23 31

Select middle record (key 10) and partition set:

   [4 7 8] 10 [11 19 23 31]

Required key is greater than that of middle record, so search right subset:

   11 19 23 31

Select middle record (key 19) which is the required record.

10 Re-run the backup (grandfather) copy of the tape with the previous transactions to re-create the current version of the tape. Then update the current version with the current transactions, to re-create the new version.

11 The backup copy of the disk is re-run against all the transactions since it was backed up. The current updating is then repeated. Another backup copy of the disk is made before and after updating.

Exercise 28

5 Specimen answer using a relational model:

a) Table 1: Correspondent Identies

Identity	Name
K347P	John Greggorowski
...	

Table 2: Newspaper Identities

Identity	Name
N417W	Washington Star
...	

Table 3: News Items

Date	Correspondent Identity	Newspaper Identity	Text
04/11/80	KOO7L	N417W	London experienced..
07/11/80	K347P	N417W	Strikes in Poland...
07/11/80	K347P	N327T	Strikes in Poland...
...			

Note that if an item is bought by more than one paper, then multiple entries are inserted in Table 3. A more efficient relational approach is to introduce a news item identity, and have a fourth table of this together with the text of the item. The third table would then contain the news item identity instead of the text.

b) Table 3 is used to locate the newspaper identities of all newspapers buying a news item with a given date and correspondent entry. Table 2 is then used to locate the names of the newspapers.

Exercise 29

● 3 a) First row:

	binary	1010	1000	0110	0000
	hex	A	8	6	0
	ASCII	Count = 40		space	

Second row:

	binary	1010	1000	0010	1110
	hex	A	8	2	E
	ASCII	Count = 40		.	

Third row:

	binary	1010	1000	0110	0000
	hex	A	8	6	0
	ASCII	Count = 40		space	

Fourth row:

	binary	0100	1101	0100	0101
	hex	4	B	4	5
	ASCII		M		E

... 8 characters ...

	binary	0100	0100	0101	0011
	hex	4	4	5	3
	ASCII		D		S

Rest of	binary	1111	1111	0110	0000
fourth to	hex	F	F	6	0
to eighteenth	ASCII	Count = 127		space	
rows		... repeated a total of 4 times ...			
	binary	1101	0000	0110	0000
	hex	D	0	6	0
	ASCII	Count = 80		space	

Nineteenth row: see Second row.

Twentieth row: see First row.

b) Total characters transmitted: 28.
Total characters (including blanks) displayed: 800.

5 78 lines.

●**7** a) Data: 1 0 1 1 1 0 1

Check 1: 1   1   1   1 pass (value 0)
Check 2:   0 1   0 1 pass (value 0)
Check 3:   1 1 0 1 fail (value 1)
Error code 100: error in 4th digit.

Data: 0 1 1 1 0 0 0

Check 1: 0   1   0   0 fail (value 1)
Check 2: 0 1   0 0 fail (value 1)
Check 3:   1 0 0 0 fail (value 1)
Error code 111: error in 7th digit.

Data: 1 1 1 1 1 0 1

Check 1: 1   1   1   1 pass (value 0)
Check 2: 1 1   0 1 fail (value 1)
Check 3:   1 1 0 1 fail (value 1)
Error code 110: error in 6th digit.

b)

			B1		B2	B3	B4		B5	B6	B7	B8
Data bits:			B1		B2	B3	B4		B5	B6	B7	B8
Check bits:	C1	C2		C3				C4				
Digit numbers:	D1	D2	D3	D4	D5	D6	D7	D8	D9	D10	D11	D12
Check 1:	*		*		*		*		*		*	
Check 2:		*	*			*	*			*	*	
Check 3:				*	*	*	*					*
Check 4:								*	*	*	*	*

Exercise 30

4 Local control: interlocking lights, detailed light changes. Subgroup control: in cell of central computer, implementation of timetable.
Top-level control: in master subsystem, allocation of timetable.

7 a) Latitude: no of points = 50/0.75 = 67
Longitude: no of points = 120/0.9375 = 128
Total points = 8576
b) 61
c) 523 136

Exercise 31

2 The main processing operation of an expert system is drawing inferences: Prolog and Lisp are designed for processing of this sort.

Exercise 33

2 The usual stages are: applications programmer, team leader, project manager, data processing manager; or applications programmer, systems analyst, system designer, project manager, data processing manager.

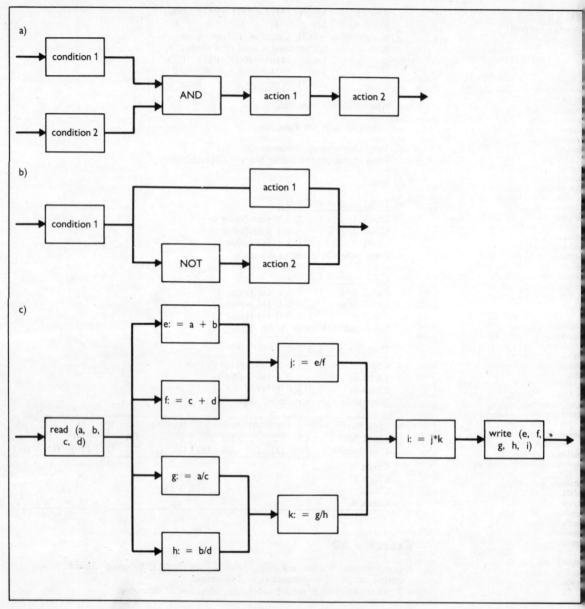

a)

b)

c)

Figure 39.14
Exercise 34 Question 2

5 Other jobs include: components purchasers, technical authors, consultants, recruitment officers, database analysts.

6 The main implication is the amount of training and re-training that is necessary if the computing industry is to absorb a significant number of those currently unemployed.

Exercise 34

2 See Figure 39.14.

3 a) 1M (1 048 576)   b) 4M   c) 4096   d) 44

4 Knowledge representation, VLSI design and fabrication, parallel architecture, software engineering, intelligent interface design, natural language recognition, applications design

Index